András TÖRÖK's

BUDA*PEST*

A Critical Guide

For the memory of Peter Doherty (1943–2009),
an adopted son of Budapest, whom we miss a lot.

András TÖRÖK's

BUDA*PEST*

A Critical Guide

Illustrated by
ANDRÁS FELVIDÉKI

PARK KÖNYVKIADÓ
BUDAPEST

The 7th completely revised edition

Edited by Vera Tönkő, Marianne Szalay
Interior design and typesetting by Péter Budai
Ground Plans by Andrea Réti
Cover design by Gábor Gerhes
Cover photo by Manuele Zunelli
Cover photo of the author by Zsolt Szigetváry
First english version translated by
Peter Doherty† and Ágnes Enyedi, edited by Zsuzsa Gáspár
Consultants to the first edition:
Dr. Zoltán Szentkirályi† and Dr. Balázs Vargha†,
András Barabás
Sixth edition revised with the assistance of
Flóra Török and Alexander Fyjis-Walker

*When this edition had already been sent to press,
Budapest City Council changed the name of Roosevelt tér – the Pest
end of Lánchíd (Chain Bridge). The new name is Széchenyi tér.*

Published in Hungary by Park Publishing Ltd.
1024 Budapest, Keleti Károly utca 29., Hungary
www.parkkiado.hu

CONTENTS

The Grand Dame of antique studies is making another pencil mark in her dictionary of Homerian vocabulary by Elisher and Frölich: to correct another hasty and improbable phrasing. She is going to have one too many classes tomorrow. The Wild-Looking Professor is desperately looking for the letter "i" with a long accent, commonly called "long i" on the keyboard of his laptop still not perfectly adapted to the accented letters of his mother tongue. The Smollett and Joyce scholar is undoing his ponytail on leaving the television studio, wondering why he is never invited into a live show and what unusual thing he would do to baffle the public on such an occasion. The Enfant Terrible Renaissance Philologist is putting on another LP on his antiquated analogous turntable, one of those Beethoven renderings from the Berlin of the late thirties he keeps on praising so much. The emerging Papessa of Philosophy is completing in her pretty head the soft copy of an essay on an obscure idea of a trend-setting French thinker, while trying to put her adolescent son in bed, in vain – the essay is ready for printing and print. The poet of smooth, evocative rhymes and scholar of iconoclastic notions on auxiliary verbs is badly expecting a call. Not necessarily that of his steady.

There are vibrant, frustrated expectations all over town.

(From the Simplicissimus Reader:
"Egghead Budapest, Nine Thirty Two in the Evening")

"Peasant Girl at Eastern Railway Station" is the title of
this snaphot taken in 1930, by Gyula Eötvös. Every day
dozens of them arrived here, in the hope of a better life.
If you are a first-time visitor here, Gentle Reader, you may
have a similar disposition. I hope you have a nice hotel
room, and unlike this young lady, no misunderstanding
has spoiled your very first day. She must have missed
the other maid from the same village who promised to
come pick her up.

ON BEING THE INVISIBLE HOST: A PREFACE

BUDAPEST, my birthplace, was once compared to Vienna by visitors. "With the Danube, the ring boulevards, the eclectic and revival buildings, the city is a second Vienna, but in a more modest edition", they would say. Others might remark, "true, Mother Nature has been more generous here, but regarding historic buildings, it cannot even hold a candle to Vienna. On top of that, the Hungarian language does not resemble any other European language."

Budapest has now earned a higher reputation than this among stag party visitors, city hoppers and other independent-minded tourists and travellers, who come from Paris, Amsterdam, Warsaw or St. Petersburg. My friends, mostly my age, whom I have been showing around over the last thirty years usually sing the city's praises beyond the point of politeness.

They have said they found Budapest to be truly cultured and truly European. They have said that from certain points of view the city has preserved the old, humane qualities of the past better than many other cities, where development has swept the past away. They have remembered staircases badly needing renovation, locksmiths' workshops with wooden floors and the smell of oil, and small suburban family-run restaurants. They have been fascinated by the grand riverbank architecture, and the beauty of the three bridges in the middle of the Danube. They have also said that the historic buildings seemed familiar to them – perhaps because quite a few of them are copies – and that they were pleasantly accessible.

It was not so much the grandeur as the beauty of the buildings that captivated them. My friends have even remarked that the city was like a sleeping beauty still hidden from the eyes of Europe. Those who have returned after the return to democracy in 1989–1990 have said that Budapest is now even better. It is more accessible than ever before, and it has become an interesting mix of a slow-paced, eccentric European city and a hectic, cosmopolitan beehive. It's a sort of "sandwich city" – one slice in one street, and the other in the next street.

"We would not have gotten as far as we did without you", my friends told me. And that was more than a simple compliment. The spirit of the city had revealed itself to them, a spirit which can get close to you only with the help of a native. I wrote this book to provide an invisible host for visitors to Budapest, in the same way that I was a real host to my satisfied friends.

THIS BOOK's goal is to combine the advantages of three types of travel guides: the Baedeker-type (full of dry facts on old buildings, kings and battles) the critical guidebook and the alternative guidebook. Obviously it will not be exhaustive in all three modes.

THERE IS a Hungarian saying for things that seem impossible: "an iron ring made out of wood". Even if this book cannot overcome the language difficulties travellers may have – which are decreasing as more Budapesters speak English these days – it will put them at ease to make their own plans to discover the city. After all, it is easier to get help with the language from friends, business partners, interpreters or hotel receptionists, than it is to get ideas for spending your time.

The above lines were originally written in 1988 for the first edition. Since then at least three things have changed:
– the city,
– the author,
– the technology for gathering information.

So, pretty much everything has changed, and that has forced the author to adapt the present book – almost in the way that websites work. My aim still remains: to share my feelings and knowledge on everything about the city – to hop from information to information – on paper.

I have two dreams. The first one means the end of the paper version of my book. I dream of a single sheet you can carry around, with the actual page you need available. Technologically, this is imminent.

But somewhat simultaneously, I have another dream, equally strong and recurrent. I want to produce a book that is readable, something that you can't put down, even after you have returned to your hotel. I want to produce a book that people want to read in their beds in Budapest. The problem is that the two dreams cannot be really reconciled. But, I will keep on trying!

Please share your opinions, feedback, and suggestions. I would love to know how you think I have succeeded with my dreams. *(See the card and the website on the last page).*

"Villagers Following St. Stephen's Day in the Castle" was the title of this photograph given to me by the archivists of the Kiscelli Museum. It was taken in 1920 by István Kerny (1879–1963), who was a post office executive all of his adult life. He considered himself an amateur fine art photographer. Photo journalism apparently defies the famous maxim: In case of a good picture, the onlooker is not intrigued by what is beyond the image's frame.

THE COW AND THE SOCIAL SAFARI

An Introductory Metaphor for Serious Travellers

Budapest has changed a lot in the eyes of serious travellers since this book was first published in 1989. For me it has changed almost beyond recognition. By this I don't mean the growing number of luxury restaurants, the ever nicer shops, and the Viennese prices in some places.

The society of scarcity has changed to a society of affluence and squalor. Respect for the traditional cityscape has returned, but there is also unbelievable visual pollution. There are billboards by the thousand; the brand names of the two biggest, ever-warring soft drinks manufacturers are on shop signs everywhere; and façades are littered with fluorescent-lit cigarette packets.

Even I don't really remember that meek and mellow dictatorship, which melted away in front of our very eyes around 1989. To refresh your memory, Gentle, Serious Reader, since the good old days are still here, in every cupboard and under every carpet – let me give you a short explanation of how things were.

You should know that this ancien régime was different than the others in Eastern Europe. Most Hungarians did not cry out against it every morning after getting up. On the contrary, they had to remind themselves what kind of a régime they were living in on the weekends. They laughed at the ignorant "politicians", and – at least my friends, the egghead dissident folk – detested money.

We wore ragged blue jeans from twenty to thirty and our hair was reluctant to follow the spirit of the times, into a shorter and shorter style. We read a lot of books, but very few newspapers, and then always between the lines. We didn't expect this world to disappear in our lifetimes. We were conditioned to irreverence and to having absolutely no responsibility outside the family. Then one day some of us found ourselves in the government, responsible for budgets of billions of forints.

Being born in 1954, I didn't have any memories of the revolution in 1956. My best friend, a poet and scholar, did. His "story of the Cow" beautifully explains this era.

In the dark 1950s, his story went, his family didn't think the régime would last. They felt as if a big dark Cow that was grazing over the beautiful meadow of Hungary had suddenly sat down. But that darkness, they thought, was not going to last forever: it is the very nature of cows that one day they get up. And the Cow did get up for the thirteen short, but glorious days of the 1956 revolution. After that nobody thought that she would ever leave. Some people – including me – thought it was not a Cow, just a cow-shaped piece of rock. And it is possible to live under a rock – if you are some species of fungus.

Around 1982 the government decided to introduce some "reforms": after inventing lukewarm water they opted for inventing hot water. They began letting small businesses open and flourish, which would eventually erode the remaining ideological features of the system. Previously, a district hall official could refuse permission for a shoemaker's shop to open just by saying that there were already enough shoemakers in a given neighbourhood.

That made a slow but dramatic impact on Budapest. Better and better shops began appearing. The gentrification of the Inner City began, first making the then isolated "tourist reservation" (like those of the Indians) just a bit bigger, later spreading throughout the area within the Grand Boulevard, which is affectionaltely known as the Nagykörút. These changes slowly began to effect my generation. Some of us now felt that it was worth earning money so as to spend it in an intelligent way. Some of us were not interested in money at all – we continued publishing the half-dozen underground papers read by a few thousand people. Some were interested in both. Some in nothing. But everyone thought that the régime could not become more liberal than it had already become. Common sense was increasingly infiltrating everyday life. But not enough to abolish one of the stupidest laws (and my own favourite): until late-1989 if you had a car less than three-years-old, you could only sell it to the state at a depressed price. Thus, a three-year-and-one-day-old car was much more expensive than a three-year-old car.

But who remembers those days? Suddenly, to our astonishment, the Cow began to fidget, and slowly, very slowly began to get up. It was a slower and less dramatic event than it was in some of the other countries around Hungary. Nobody was killed, there were hardly any demonstrations, and the international press showed little interest.

In a couple of years, Hungary might become one of those smaller, prosperous, boring countries. Not yet though.

When the Cow left, we hoped the grass would recover overnight. Alas, it didn't. New Cows came from our very own barns. Some swore that they spotted some new Cows coming in from the West. Some patches of grass have recovered wonderfully by now. Some others are in worse shape than ever before. On May 1, 2004 we joined a major grass recovery programme called the European Union. It might accelerate the grass recovery process.

Come check Budapest out from time to time. It can easily amount to a Social Safari for the Discerning Traveller.

(October 1997 – February 2011)

For recent developments since this edition went to press, see:

www.budapest-criticalguide.hu

A CITY

FOR THOSE
WHO WANT TO COME SOON

György Lőrinczy's photo was taken in Café Muskátli in 1967 and was a sort of symbol of the thaw after the 1956 revolution. In the center of the picture there is a typical golden youth of the times. On the wall there is an old photograph which is noteworthy because, it shows that the first wave of nostalgia had already reached Budapest. The Good Old Days were already becoming trendy.

A CRASH COURSE IN BUDAPEST

An Exercise in Civic Boosterism

(The Absolute Minimum You Should Know if you Aim to Be Called Well-Informed by Locals on Your First Day)

Budapest is the overgrown capital of the Republic of Hungary, inhabited by about 1.7 million restless people. One in every six citizens of this country live here and almost 60 percent of the country's GDP is produced here. Budapest's population has steadily diminished since the fall of the Wall, mainly because of suburbanisation. Most Budapesters are readers, and not only of the telephone numbers in the television commercials. This chapter is a crash course in the practical information you'll need to explore Budapest. It includes information on transportation, getting around and communicating. It also reveals the places where Budapest eggheads gather, meet, and take foreign egghead friends whom they desperately try to impress. Most of the places mentioned here are found later in the book in more depth.

First, I should explain what I mean by "egghead". I borrowed this term from the United States of the early 1960s. This was, as far as I know, a highly ironic term for those intellectuals who were brought to state administration by President Kennedy, persons who did not even have a minimum of practical knowledge. I intend to revive the term in this book. But in this book, "egghead" means people who were born, typically in Budapest, between the late 1940s and the early 1970s and were fully social-ized in the dictatorship which they detested. They were hyper-critical of the existing régime and the establishment, and they knew that "the only thing that cannot be ever taken from you is what you have read". They loved music, literature, the arts and parties, and not only on the weekends. They did not care for money, power or a second home. Rather, they wanted to under-stand what Goethe and John Lennon wrote, in the original lan-guage. In normal societies these people are so few that they are negligible in the social sense of the word. The late totalitarian

Budapest was a strange place, where they were visible – especially for the growing number of expats. I especially remember how a young literary teacher, Ferenc Takács, quipped in the mid 1980s, paraphrasing typically, Voltaire: *"Those who did not live during the late Kádár era, knew nothing of the sweetness of life."*

The Basic Setup of the City Budapest covers an area of 525 square kilometers and consists of 23 municipal districts. It is rare that a city has two parts so distinct from one another: hilly Buda on the western side of the Danube and Pest, twice the size and totally flat, on the other side. In the Middle Ages the two were independent and were only joined in 1873, along with Óbuda, to form the modern city. In the 15th century, when Buda was in its heyday, it was considerably larger and more important than Pest. Its population is estimated to have been about 24,000, whereas Pest had only 4,000 residents. To put Budapest's population in perspective: after the Turks were driven out at the end of the 17th century, Buda had about 600 residents and Pest had just 300.

Strictly speaking, the Danube is the main thoroughfare that divides the capital in two as it flows southwards. At the northern limit of the city, the river is almost a kilometre wide and further down it encircles two islands. Downriver from Margaret Island (Margitsziget), which lies between Margit and Árpád híd ("híd" is "bridge" in Hungarian), the Danube narrows considerably. It is at its narrowest at the foot of Gellérthegy where it's only 230 metres across. Its average water-level here is 96 metres above sea level.

The hills of Buda are between 150 and 500 metres high and, with the exception of Gellérthegy, they rise gently. The higher peaks form a semicircle some eight or so kilometres from the city centre. Even Pest is not as flat as it seems to be, since it rises steadily. The tenth district, Kőbánya, is at the same height as Castle Hill, which is more than evident if you go there by bike. All of this explains why we get such magnificent views of Pest from the vantage points in Buda. Since the rise on the Pest side also forms a semicircle, Budapest could (with some poetic exaggeration) be said to compete with Naples or Rio de Janeiro, which are considered to be some of the world's best-located towns. It is also rare that a city reflects so many of the different landscapes found in the rest of the country. To the west, beyond Buda, there are the hills and valleys typical of Transdanubia. To the east, behind some small hills not so far from Pest, the Great Plain stretches out perfectly flat. To the north there are hills, though with the highest peak at 1,015 metres, they are not very high.

BRIDGES AND BOULEVARDS

The historic centre of Buda can still be seen today on Castle Hill, but almost nothing has survived of Pest's historic centre, which was between Deák Ferenc utca and Szabadság híd (roughly between the first and third bridges south of Margit híd). This area, which is officially part of the fifth district, is what we still call the city centre (or downtown). The edge of this district is flanked by the Kiskörút (the "small boulevard"), which con-

Making Sounds in a Winter Morning

The duty officer at Déli pályaudvar (Southern Railway Station) is pushing a button: the electronically recorded railway signal is reverberating on the barren slopes of Martinovics-hegy. The train to Kaposvár is leaving in two minutes.

A short-haired, reasonably dirty young man is dragging a wheeled plastic bin past a pair of swinging doors deep in Elizabeth Town. A large collection of front door keys is twinkling around his neck.

The high-end Japanese audio equipment in the modest home of a freelance sociologist duly begins to play the Rákóczi March at exactly 5:57 a.m., as programmed weeks before. Radio Bartók, the egghead channel, begins broadcasting in three minutes.

The divorced lady math teacher is carefully pulling up the wooden shutters, loudly enough to wake up her aspiring athlete daughter. While doing this her husband used to wake up all the street.

A busy and youthful grandfather is trying to start the unbecoming engine of one of the last Trabant cars in (formerly) upwardly mobile Újlipótváros – for the ninth and last time. He has to go by bus to take care of a grandchild with the flu.

Small, bearded King of Dubbing is overturning a half empty plate for the cats, while returning from an all night session. They completed roll three of a new Greenaway movie. He has to leave for a rehearsal in four and a half hours.

Meanwhile: the bleakest of the bleak winter winds of Budapest, heard all along. No tune, just pitch. Not worth getting up as early as that. Not for that sound.

sists of Bajcsy-Zsilinszky út, Károly körút, Múzeum körút and Vámház körút.

From the Pest end of Margit híd runs a semicircular avenue, built in the Parisian style, called the Nagykörút (the "Grand Boulevard"). It reaches the Danube at both ends, joining Margit híd in the north and Petőfi híd in the south. The nagykörút is the name for Szent István körút, Teréz körút, Erzsébet körút, József körút and Ferenc körút, taken together. Both the Nagykörút and the Kiskörút are just commonly used nicknames, however, street signs will not have those names written on them.

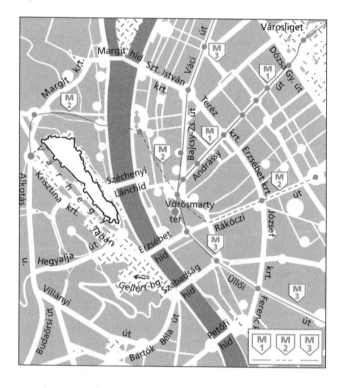

The semicircle continues on the Buda side, although not quite as regularly as in Pest. Thus the circle is completed by Irinyi József utca, Karinthy Frigyes út, Villányi út, Alkotás utca and Margit körút, and there we are again at Margit híd (most of this can be travelled by trams 4 and 6).

Budapest was more or less built within this circle by the early 20th century, with some additional building along the main roads running out of town such as Andrássy út, which ends in

Városliget (City Park) in the east. Árpád híd, which is the bridge north of Margit híd, is the beginning of an outer semicircular ring which includes Róbert Károly körút, Hungária körút and Könyves Kálmán körút. The latter had just reached the Danube again in the south when Lágymányosi híd was built besides the rail bridge, Déli vasúti híd. Pest had spread more or less this far by the beginning of World War Two.

The outer ring roads join five major roads that carry traffic from the city towards the suburbs: Váci út, Andrássy út, Rákóczi út (which continues on Kerepesi út), Üllői út and Soroksári út, respectively. Metro lines run along all of these except the last. With the exception of Andrássy út, the history of these main roads goes back to the middle ages. Their names indicate the cities which they lead to.

The somewhat lackluster Váci utca is a former main street of Pest. Halfway along this street is the Pest end of Erzsébet híd, the first of the two modern bridges in the city. On the Buda side, the road from the bridge turns sharply to the right and starts climbing steeply, leading to the motorway to Vienna and Lake Balaton.

Weather is far from boring in Budapest, but it is pretty predictable. It can be very hot in the summer when temperatures of 30 degrees Celsius (86 degrees Fahrenheit) are common. It can theoretically be very cold in the winter, but that only happens every five or six years. A really heavy snowfall is somewhat rare, but is usually followed by slush and filthy piles of frozen snow pushed to the curb. Dusk falls early in the winter, between 3:30 and 4:30 p.m. and the sun is rarely seen. However, the other three seasons make up for this. In Hungary we celebrate name days which are usually the feast days of saints. The name days of Sándor, József and Benedek fall between March 18 and 21 and, the saying goes, they bring the warm weather in their bags. Indeed, this is usually the time when spring allows us to shed our winter topcoats – and it's a good time to visit. Stormy days total about 30. If it rains on Medárd Day (June 8), however, tradition has it that the next forty days will also bring rain.

PHONES

Wired and wireless Budapesters can hardly remember the pre-cell-phone days when waiting for telephone installation before 1989 lasted years, sometimes a dozen or more. In the early 1980s a member of parliament in the Communist government made a suggestion that telephone applications should be made inheritable.

Budapesters hardly ever use the big, coin-operated tele-phones and few use telephone cards any more. Everyone now uses cell phones. The card-operated phones speak in Hungarian and English and accept the phone cards that are sold at newsa-gents around town. The proper way to ask for one is "Kérek egy telefonkártyát" (Keeh-rek edy telefon-kaahr-tyaaht). Then comes the inevitable question about the type, since they come in differ-ent denominations. Find your way out of this by writing down the value of the type of card you want.

GSM providers all have roaming partners abroad. If your phone does not automatically shift to your own provider, it is worth trying to adjust it manually to keep your bill down.

INTERNET, WIFI

If you don't have a laptop or an Internet-ready phone, Café Vakvarjú (*VI. Paulay Ede utca 7.*) is a huge café and restaurant with some desktops for Internet access. (See Walk Four.) Another option is Café Gerlóczy (*V. Gerlóczy utca 1.*) or Farger (*V. Zoltán utca 18.*, corner of Szabadság tér). In most of the Libri Bookshops there is Internet (not free), notably at I. Batthyány tér, on the upper level of the Market Hall. There are dozens of smaller places, and new ones are always appearing. WIFI is free in many places.

Some nicer place include:

A38 SHIP, *Danube, Buda end of Petőfi híd*
CAFÉ DUMAS, *I. Fő utca 17.* (Institut Francais)
CAFÉ EKLEKTIKA, *VI. Nagymező 30.*
CALIFORNIA COFFEE COMPANY, *VI. Teréz körút 38.*
DISCOVER HUNGARY, *VI. Lázár utca 16.*
CAFÉ DUNAPARK, *XIII. Pozsonyi út 38. (See Walk Five)*
SPINOZA HÁZ, *VII. Dob utca 15.*
CAFÉ STEX HÁZ, *VIII. József körút 55-57. (See Walk Five)*
SARK, *VII. Klauzál tér 14.*

ADDRESSES & LETTERS

Everyone thinks that bigger post offices are quicker because they have more staff. They do, but they are also busier and queues are longer than at the smaller post offices. Since our walks begin at Vörösmarty tér, note the side street (Dorottya utca) at the northern end of the square where Post Office No. 51 is located.

(*V. Dorottya utca 9.*, T: 318-6441, open Monday to Friday 8 a.m. to 4 p.m., closed noon to 12:30)

You will notice that some addresses are given with the district number in Roman numerals first, and some with a four-digit postcode in Arabic numerals. For speedier delivery, the latter should be used. The correct way to address an envelope in Hungary is:

```
                    KOVÁCS JÁNOS
                    BUDAPEST
                    King Kong utca 6.
                    1054
```

The logic of the postcode is that "1" indicates that the address is in Budapest, the next two digits indicate the Budapest district, and the final digit indicates the sorting number. This address would translate as 6 King Kong street, in the fifth district.

DISTRICTS AND NEIGHBOURHOOD NAMES

Budapest has 23 districts, which are traditionally signified using Roman numbers before the street name. On street signs you will also notice that neighbourhood names are written. Smaller districts have one or two neighbourhoods, while some bigger ones have dozens. Some are very poetic, especially in Buda. District II consists of 31 neighbourhoods, which include names like "Hermit Garden Town" (Remetekertváros) and Pashas' Field (Pasarét). To use these neighbourhood names is increasingly fashionable among younger intellectuals. Some use them on their business cards in a hyphenated form: Budapest-Pasarét, or Budapest-Lipótváros.

MONEY

The forint (Ft or HUF) became the Hungarian currency in August 1946 after a period of extremely high inflation was brought to an end. January 1997 was a historic date in the modernisation of Hungary: the forint became freely convertible, making life much easier for Hungarians going abroad and for everyone visiting us. Most Hungarian people seriously think that Hungarian paper money is one of the nicest in the world. Opinion makers, on the other hand, hate it but find it fitting for a visually backward country. By issuing the 20,000 forint note, Hungary completed a 10-year banknote and coin reform in 2001. It will be the last in Hungarian monetary history before we merge into the Euro zone, probably the late 2010s.

The essence of the reform was to issue long overdue smaller format banknotes and to leave behind our artists and poets who were portrayed on the old ones. The new ones portray medieval kings with false dignity on their faces (sometimes resembling heavy drinkers) which are more difficult to forge.

Those artistic failures are the direct consequence of a lack of competition. Believe it or not, all of these "beautiful" images were designed by the resident graphic artist of the Banknote Printers, a state-owned operation. The dislike for competition in matters like this was further strengthened after an unsuccessful design contest in the course of the coin reform. Though paying with credit cards is possible in many shops, it is wise to ask in advance at restaurants, especially in the smaller ones.

THE SINGLE MOST IMPORTANT EGGHEAD BOOKSHOP

The Írók Boltja (Writers' Bookshop) is at Liszt Ferenc tér where Japán, a famous coffee-house known for its fine Oriental décor, was located. Nothing survived of the original. You can sit here and have tea, watch the crowd leafing through the new publications and literary reviews from all over Hungary and from the Hungarian-speaking regions of the countries nearby. Hungarian literature is the shop's forte (and it also carries translated Hungarian literature), and there is a book launch almost every afternoon at 4 p.m. Check out the innovative window displays of new titles. After a great deal of toing and froing, the shop was sold to its enthusiastic staff in the mid-1990s, who naturally had to borrow a huge amount of money for the purchase. (*VI. Andrássy út 45.*, www.irokboltja.hu)

THE SINGLE MOST IMPORTANT FOREIGN LANGUAGE BOOKSHOP

The shop with the deceptive name "Bestsellers" is operated by an immigrant from Britain, Tony Lang, who had some Hungarian blood, but no prior command of the language when he arrived. He moved to Hungary to buy a shop, which happened to be a food shop with permission to sell other goods. For a year there were some bottles of Heinz sauce to demonstrate that it was a food shop after all. These days it is a centre for the expatriate community and sells all kinds of fiction, non-fiction, reference books, newspapers, magazines and fine stationery. There is also a nice selection of books in French. (*V. Október 6. utca 11.*, www.bestsellers.hu, open Monday to Friday 9 a.m. to 6:30 p.m., Saturday 10 a.m. to 5 p.m., Sunday 10 a.m. to 4 p.m.)

EXPAT MEDIA

Professional expats nowadays only seem to click, they only read the English version of *Time Out*, a monthly publication here. They more and more appreciate the bi-weekly *Funzine* – a free general interest publication, what really emanates fun and often wanders to new paths, edited by young Budapest insiders (and also looks great). The *Budapest Sun* was established by an American professional couple not long after the Changes of 1990, but has changed hands a couple of times since then. It only survides online. The weekly *Budapest Times* is the *Sun's* younger competitor, and has slightly better coverage of Hungarian politics and business. The *Budapest Business Journal* is a more serious weekly, published for the busy kind of expats who run Hungarian branches of multinational companies. *Budapest in Your Pocket* is a useful quarterly publication. *Where Budapest* is a low-key, reliable magazine that is available in most hotel rooms.

Budapest egghead expats tend to read *The Hungarian Quarterly*, a prestigious journal that is notable for its translations of modern short stories and poetry. It has a lively review section, and articles on the country and its history. It is written in impeccable English by senior Hungarian opinion-makers. *Pilvax* is a newer literary journal that features short stories, poems and literature from Hungary and Central Europe. Did it survive, Gentle Reader, for you to read it? – I am not sure... The website Caboodle.hu is a comprehensive portal that features news, original features, tourism information, directories and forums. Xpatloop.com gathers news that was previously published elsewhere. Pestiside.hu is a popular irreverent blog and Chew.hu is Hungary's biggest English language food site.

www.budapestsun.hu
www.budapesttimes.hu
www.bbj.hu
www.hungarianquarterly.com

www.inyourpocket.com/hungary/budapest
www.caboodle.hu
www.xpatloop.com
www.pestiside.hu
www.chew.hu

PAPERS THAT HUNGARIAN EGGHEADS READ

For want of a better newspaper, Hungarian eggheads tend to read the formerly Communist, now (foreign-owned) independent *Népszabadság* ("People's Liberty") the largest circulation daily. In 1990 Péter Esterházy, the influential writer, wrote about this paper: "Now it is only its name I hate," which the paper used the following week as an advertisement. Others include *Heti Világgazdaság* (the *Economist*-like weekly, which was established ahead of its time in 1979), *Élet és Irodalom*, a literary weekly, and *Magyar Narancs* ("Hungarian Orange", which is a sort of cross between the *Village Voice* and *Libération*). It is named for the Communist government's silly one-time attempt at growing oranges. See the film *The Witness (page 334)* for more on the name.

THE LISZT MUSIC ACADEMY

The most important venue of the prodigiously lively classical music scene is the Liszt Music Academy. Its landmark art nouveau building and big concert hall are worth visiting, even for a minor musical event. The smaller room opens from the first floor, where there is a huge painting, The Spring of Arts. There was musical graffiti in the gents' restroom downstairs in the late 1980s that read "Viva Brüggen!", but it disappeared during a redecoration. Béla Bartók and Zoltán Kodály used to teach upstairs. It is being renovated, for the time being. (*VI. Liszt Ferenc tér 8.*, at Király utca, www.lfze.hu). See Walk Five.

KATONA JÓZSEF THEATRE

One of Europe's best companies, this theatre is a member of the European Theatre Union (which includes the British National Theatre and the Royal Shakespeare Company), and it has staged more than a hundred performances abroad. The theatre was established in 1982 by innovative, though mainstream, actors and directors who were forced out of the National Theatre. It has a large repertoire, including well-known classics. It plays in a small house, in an even smaller studio nearby called Kamra ("Larder"), and in a third, tiny space, for super-experimental and poetry events. In the bigger place there are only about 250 seats, so it's not easy to get in, and there are no performances in English. (*V. Petőfi Sándor utca 6.*, www.katonajozsefszinhaz.hu)

CINEMAS

The ever-growing number of multiplexes has killed most of the traditional one-screen cinemas in Budapest. But the rich art movie supply – almost on a level on par with Paris and New York – is still here. One, the Corvin Film Palace, is the flagship of a company called Budapest Film, owned by the city of Budapest. (See Walk Five.) General conversion pains (due to the free market) somewhat delayed the Hungarian movie scene's attempt to follow international trends. But by the end of 1998, the number of movie seats in Hungary had doubled with several new multiplex cinemas opening. The biggest complex, called Arena Plaza, opened in early 2008 with 22 screens, including a 3D IMAX theatre. It is located near Keleti pályaudvar (Eastern Railway Station), in the site of a former racetrack.

If you are a cinema buff and you care about the general atmosphere of the place, then you should visit the Uránia National Motion Picture House *(See Walk Three, page 197.)* or the Puskin Cinema (*V. Kossuth Lajos utca 18.*), which was originally built in 1926 and was called Forum cinema. It has been called Puskin since 1952 and its name was not changed in 1990, when the names of the other Communist-era cinemas (Red Star, May 1, Bastion, and the like) were changed back to the original. Beware of the abbreviation "mb." (Hungarian speaking) in the listings. MOM Park multiplex in Buda is the specialist of subtitled versions of blockbusters.

STAIRS

The most famous and best known stairs in Budapest – and the most romantic place to meet a wife, girlfriend or girl friend – are those of the National Museum near Kálvin tér (See Walk Three). That is where people think Sándor Petőfi, the youthful leader of the 1848 Revolution, recited his freshly written poem National Song on the afternoon of March 15 (although research has proved this wrong). Another staircase that is ideal for the first or second date, or the first kiss in daylight, is on the Pest riverbank – off the embankment, halfway between the Lánchíd and the Erzsébet híd (somewhat closer to the latter). The more passionate the relationship is, the closer to the water you'll have to sit, in order not to be disturbed.

The most stylish stairs these days are indoors: not in a staircase, but in the foyer of the French Institute. If you have a look at them on the occasion of an opening, you will see how well they serve their purpose: to see better and to be seen better, the two reasons for which one goes to an opening.

A nice way to go up to the Royal Castle is on one of the dozen stone staircases. The nicest of them lead from Water Town (Víziváros). When you look behind you, you will see a changing landscape of Pest.

The gaudiest and by far the most ridiculous stairs are at the corner of Váci út and Dózsa György út in the 13th district at the base of the "skyscraper" of the Municipal Waterworks. It is a stretch of staircase about twenty metres wide that never got to be used. There are dozens of pre-cast concrete flowerbeds placed across the stairs, very near the bottom of what must be the world's ugliest and least used staircase.

STARING AT OTHERS AND GETTING AWAY WITH IT

Riding up and down the metro station escalators is perfect for people watching, especially at Kossuth Lajos tér (lower middle class), Lehel tér (working class, no escalator, though) and Blaha Lujza tér (a perfect mix). Or ride Bus 15 and look outwards at the changing social scene, from terminus to terminus at sunset. (You can board at either end: Boráros tér or Gogol utca.) In Budapest people tend to switch on their lights, but not draw their curtains right away. But to take advantage is not nice, not even in Hungary. You could be scholarly, however, and call it "applied people-watching".

AN UNMISTAKABLY OLD / NEW CAFÉ

Café Centrál which was a legend between 1887 and 1949, reopened in January 2000. It is authentic and credible, with modern food and no hint that it's a modern recreation of the original. Thankfully, it does not feel like a museum piece either.

When it was reopened, the Mayor and the Minister for Culture were happily present, and there was a surprise flying visit from the Prime Minister himself. As guests started to leave

there were some who accompanied the proprietor bent on following a hallowed tradition of throwing the key into the Danube,
signifying that this coffee house should never close (*V. Károlyi
Mihály utca 16.*, open daily 8 a.m. to midnight). See Walk Three
for details.

BUDAPEST'S KERTS, COURTYARD PUBS AND ROOFTOPS

Since 2000, a series of temporary May to September garden and
courtyard pubs/cafés began to appear around Budapest in abandoned buildings and in green areas like Margaret Island. In 2011
the following places are the most popular: Pótkulcs, Szimpla kert
and Kuplung. Ask around, some of them will not exist when you
come and other new ones will have surely popped up. These
bars also go by the name "romkocsma" (rom-kotsh-ma), which
means "pub in a ruin".

Since 2007 another related summer trend has emerged: "roof
pubs". The first of its kind opened on the roof of the Corvin
Department Store, on Blaha Lujza tér, called Corvintető (Corvin
Roof). Fecske (literally "swallow", but it hints at an old fashioned
men's bathing suit), opened soon after on the roof of Komjádi
Swimming Pool. As these places don't have temporary permits,
they may become more permanent favourites.

Check out www.pestiside.hu for a listing of the latest kerts
and roofs.

LEGENDA CRUISE SHIPS

This book recommends travellers to discover Budapest on their
own... But not even the readers of this book can walk on water.
In 1990 a company called "Legenda" first challenged the state-
owned cruise service. They still want to be ahead of the others
– they emanate a quasi insane endeavour to please theirguests.
They have special "all-window" boats, they offer the recorded
text in 30(!) languages. Their website explains the routes via ani-
mation, and needless to say that you can reserve a ticket via the
internet. They even explain sites on a map... It is the next best
thing to have a local friend with a motorboat and with a practice
in guiding picky travellers... (Departure from Vigadó tér, www.
legenda.hu)

THREE BATHS NOT TO MISS

Budapest is known for its fantastic bath houses. The three most spectacular are: A Turkish, an art nouveau and a pseudo-Roman one. The Rudas Baths is in Buda, to the left of Erzsébet híd. Part of it is a wonderfully preserved Turkish bath. The bath inside the Gellért Hotel was completed in 1918 *(See Walk Three, page 181–183.)*, and the Széchenyi Baths is the largest year-round one. Located in Városliget, it was named after a 19th century statesman. See Walk Four for details. Visit www.spas.budapest.travel to learn more.

TWELVE PLACES TO MEET A BUDAPEST FRIEND

One should not set up an appointment with a Budapester in the open-air, especially not during the winter. They tend not to be on time, or not on the dot, at any rate. So try to agree to an appointment indoors, preferably in a place which does not cost you anything. Here are some suggestions:

7 a.m.	At the Széchenyi Baths, either in the open-air pool where you can swim (you'll need a swim cap there), or inside in the middle "common thermal bath", which is the one with windows in a semi-circle. (*XIV. Állatkerti körút 11.*) See Walk Four.
9 a.m.	At Café Gerbeaud, in the middle, flat-ceilinged room, under the oil painting, The Altar Boy and the Apprentice Confectioner. It opens at 9 a.m., so try to be there before the other tourists, whom Budapest eggheads try to avoid. (*V. Vörösmarty tér 7.*) *See page 88–89.*
11 a.m.	At the big oak table in the main hall of the Museum of Ethnography, which is the former Supreme Court. (*V. Kossuth Lajos tér 12.*, closed on Monday) See Walk Two.

1 p.m.	In the ground floor covered courtyard of the Budapest Central Library's main branch. The former stables are now a café. (*VIII. Szabó Ervin tér*, closed on Sunday, unfortunately, and usually in the month of July) See Walk Three.
3 p.m.	At Burger King on Oktogon "Square", on the second floor by the rail, where you'll have a view of the Nagykörút. It is outdated, post-modern popular taste – too many colours and objects. (*VI. Oktogon tér 3.*)
5 p.m.	In The gallery of the New York Coffee House, which was the birthplace of modern Hungarian literature, and has been beautifully restored. (*VII. Erzsébet körút 9–11.*) See Walk Five.
7 p.m.	By the fancy indoor fountain in the WestEnd City Center mall, which is in a rectangular floor to rooftop space called Millennium Square. (*XIII. Váci út 1–3.*, at the entrance across from Radnóti Miklós utca.)
9 p.m.	At the Corvin Cinema in the chairs upstairs on the right, which are just above the Café Casablanca. (*VIII. Corvin köz 1.*) See Walk Five.
11 p.m.	At Café Művész, in the inner room with its traditional splendour. The clientele is generally elderly, but not at that hour. (*VI. Andrássy út 29.*) See Walk Four.
1 a.m.	At the Stage Pub, which is so-called because it is adjacent to the Pesti Színház (the Pest Theatre). Opened in 1995, it's likely to be a constant in Budapest's rather quickly changing nightlife scene. It operates a course for wannabe bartenders and attracts theatre folks. (*V. Aranykéz utca 8.*, closed on Sunday)

3 a.m.	At Nagyi Palacsintázója ("Granny's pancakery"), a round-the-clock Hungarian style pancake bar which offers pancakes stuffed with every conceivable kind of filling, sweet and savory, with meat or without. (*I. Batthyány tér 5.*) See Walk Two.
5 a.m.	At the Copy General headquarters, where you are likely to bump into an architecture student desperately trying to meet his latest deadline or an eccentric composer with fresh music to be given to a string quartet in the morning. (*V. Kálmán Imre utca 22.*)

The hundred-year-old elegant art nouveau bath on Dohány utca became a cinema, and then was neglected for many decades. The adjacent wing was a hotel that closed in 1970. It is one of the success stories since a new hotel saved a landmark space. The 150-square-meter roof terrace added a nice new view of the Great Synagogue and the Buda hills. About a dozen boutique hotels were added to the Budapest scene since 2000, and they are still coming. Hopefully they can find their regulars.

CHOOSING A PLACE TO STAY

By now, most people reading this book will have already reserved a place to stay in Budapest. If not, visit my web site, www.budapest-criticalguide.hu, where you will find hotel recommendations for various types of travellers, such as:

For a Conference-hopper who Wants to Avoid Fellow Conference-hoppers

For Affluent Newly-weds Who Want to Rejuvenate themselves After Eventful Nights

For a Tennis-freak Junior Manager of a Multinational Company

For a Man Wanting to Impress His High school Sweetheart, After 50 Years

For the Affluent Expatriate, Who Loves Downtown, and Is On the Verge of Buying a Flat of His/Her Own

"I Hate Big Hotels"

"I Love the Opera and Classical Music"

"I Want Fin-de-siècle Splendour and Want to Have a Pool Indoors"

"I Don't Want to See the Marriott from the Outside"

"I Like Traditional Splendour, but I Don't Mind Minor Glitches in Decoration and Service if I Can Pay Accordingly"

"I Insist on Hundreds of Shops and a Movie Theatre In-House"

"I Love the Urban Jungle"

"I Want to Stay in a Historical Area, but Don't Want to Pay for it"

"I Want a Small, Old-fashioned, Family-run, Five Star Hotel

Renaming streets was a terrible habit of totalitarian régimes in Hungary. That's why there is now the possibly too-strict-rule which forbids naming a street after a person until he/she has been dead for more than 25 years. The great poet János Pilinszky (1921–1981) lived not far from this minuscule street, which was earlier named "Rainbow Way". The law requires the old name to remain in place, crossed out in red, for at least two years – a tourist-friendy rule. (Photo by the author.)

FINDING YOUR WAY AROUND

TOURIST INFORMATION

The Tourinform office is just half a minute's walk from the junction of the three underground lines, and a minute's walk from Vörösmarty tér, where our walks begin.

TOURINFORM:
438-8080 (Round the clock.)
V. Sütő utca 2.
www.tourinform.hu
open daily 8 a.m. to 8 p.m.

There is information here in German, English, Russian, French, and sometimes Italian. The office has up-to-date information on transport, accommodation, activities, sights, and events. They will help you arrange accommodation only in certain special cases, but they will assist with the necessary addresses and telephone numbers. There are about twenty people on the changing, but remarkably experienced staff, who are always happy to pass on their own knowledge of the city. For automated phone information from Hungary call (06-80) 630-800, from abroad call +36 (30) 303-0600.

VISTA TRAVEL CENTER

World tourism has developed a lot during the last decades, but the Vista Travel Center must be one of the most innovative travel agencies in the world. Located in a beautiful space with interesting Australian aboriginal décor, the place offers an abundance of travel-related services and the community spirit projected by the staff is hardly found elsewhere. There are a series of unexpected discounts if you stand and sit at certain places. The chairs in front of the airfare department range from first class plane seats to office chairs to wooden stools (the person who happens to sit on the latter is entitled to a discount). I hope it still works like that. The interior was said to have appeared in a dream to co-founder János Kurucz, a journalist and travel freak. The other founder, Ferenc Pogány, is a biologist who also had never worked in the tourism business before. They simply wanted to provide better services than the ones they had received on their travels. Discover the basement as well, complete with a video lounge and a café. Vista also has other smaller locations throughout the city. (Travel agency: *VI. Andrássy út 1.*, at the corner of Paulay Ede utca, Café: *VI. Paulay Ede utca 9.*, www.vista.hu) See Walk Four.

THE BUDAPEST CARD

This two or three-day pass offers unlimited travel on public transportation, entry to many museums, and substantial discounts on sightseeing, baths, restaurants and a plethora of other things that make Budapest special. The date of purchase is stamped when the card is issued, and you have to sign it the way you do a credit card. Having it makes life more comfortable and getting around easier. You can buy it at travel agencies, metro stations, museums and other places.

FOUR KINDS OF MAPS

In hotels and travel agencies you are given a miniature one-page map, which is highly unsatisfactory for the serious traveller. The Budapest Citymap for Tourists, which is published by Budapest Transport Ltd. (BKV), is useful and is available from ticket vendors in the larger metro stations. But the ideal map depends on why you are here and what you need.

The Best Map for the One-Weekend Conference Tourist Who Wants to Get Away for a Short While
• *Budapest: the inner part (Budapest belső területe)* Inside the unattractive, ever changing cover, there is a very practical, easy-to-use map. The back shows the inner city areas in such detail that even the numbers of the buildings are indicated at corners of the streets. There is a comprehensive street index for both sides of the map (Cartographia Publishers, 1:7500).

• *Streetwise Budapest* This is a quite ingenious, folded, laminated map which gives a telltale overview of the inner parts of the city. You can order it online for a little less than 8 dollars (*28 Church Street, Harvard Square, MA 02138*, T: +1 (617) 497-6277).

Map for a Young Couple from Ukraine on Honeymoon, Who are Staying with Relatives in the Outskirts

• *The Map of Budapest* A Hungarian-made map showing the whole city with the districts in different colours, which is sometimes helpful even to a foreign visitor. All tram and bus routes are indicated. There is a full index. It includes a very well-designed inset map of the centre (Cartographia Publishers, 1: 20000 and 1: 35 000).

Map for the Business Traveller Who Wants to Find New Premises for His/Her Central European Headquarters

• *The Atlas of Budapest* A large-format, spiral-bound book, covering 96 settlements in the immediate vicinity of Budapest. The scale is 1:20 000, and 1:10 000 for the inner city parts. It has street numbers and it indicates one-way streets. There is a comprehensive portrayal of cemeteries and pre-fab housing estates and an easy to use, quite large print, full index. It weighs 730 grams and is almost A4 format (Cartographia Publishers).

Map for an Architecture Freak Who Wants to Visit Every Single Address in the "For Serious Addicts" Part of This Book

• *Cartographia's Budapest* Sold in a transparent plastic folder, this is basically a locally edited version of the Falk map, simply printed as a traditional flat map (i.e. you cannot leaf through it). A separate section details the metro system. There is a full index on the back. Landmark buildings are in primitive, but useful, 3-D drawings.

SOME GREAT MAP SHOPS

Földgömb- és Térképbolt (Globe and Map Shop) Near the Arany János utca metro stop, don't expect a vast, London or New York style selection here. This small, but recently enlarged shop has a helpful staff and interesting awkwardly-coloured wall maps for schools. (*VI. Bajcsy-Zsilinszky út 37.*, T: 312-6001, open Monday to Friday 8 a.m. to 6 p.m.)

Térképkirály (Map King) 200 metres from the above shop, this place is its competition. (*VI. Bajcsy-Zsilinszky út 23.*, T: 472-0505, open Monday to Friday 9 a.m. to 6 p.m.)

Óbuda Térképszalon (Map Saloon) This small, intimate shop is in a quarter called Újlak, which overlooks the amphitheatre for Roman soldiers. The quarter is being rehabilitated with great care with respect to the original scale, and it's attracting many successful businesses. (*III. Bécsi út 85.*, T: 388-8188, open Monday to Friday 8 a.m. to 6 p.m.)

Antique Maps The name of the Központi Antikvárium means Central Used and Rare Book Shop. The owners kept the well-known name from the times of state ownership, since it was a known brand. (*V. Múzeum körút 13–15.*, T: 317-3514, open Monday to Friday 10 a.m. to 6.30 p.m., Saturday 10 a.m. to 2 p.m.)

VIEWPOINTS

The most famous viewpoints, Castle Hill and Gellérthegy, are included in our first and third walks. Here are some other view-points worth visiting:

The dome of the Basilica In the fifth district on Szent István tér, the lower observation deck around the dome opened in the mid-1990s and is still largely unknown to Budapesters. There are 302 steps and a lift that takes the weaklings to the top. After some 200 steps the scene changes: you climb out of a specially built tube into the inside of the dome in a wrought iron con-struction. Then you'll see the space between the inside and the outside of the dome, which is quite a thrilling experience. The panorama outside will keep you enthralled for at least fifteen minutes. Take your time and discover the hidden sights that are invisible to ordinary mortals. Notice the drop on top of Andrássy út 9, the former ING building, and other delicacies. The dome is only open from April 1st to October 30th. See Walk Two.

The "elbow" of Margit híd Where the bridge bends, opposite the island, stand as close to the river as possible for a breathtak-ing, unusual view. It's a kind of third panorama of the river, although anglers might obstruct your view in every season. See Walk Two.

The look-out tower on János-hegy The tower is situated at the highest point in the city, on top of the 529-metre-high János-hegy (John Hill). Four platforms, one above the other, encircle the wall of the tower. On an average day, visitors can see places 75 kilometres away in all directions. On especially clear days some have even seen the High Tatra Mountains, 215 kilometres away. The best way to get there is by Bus 190 or by using the Chairlift *(see page 53)*.

The look-out tower on József-hegy This small look-out tower in district two on Józsefhegyi út is made of brown stone. It's neither well-known nor in good shape, but there is a full view of the city, the bridges, the Danube bend and the Buda hills. The easiest way to get there is by bus 91 or 191. With luck, the neo-Nazi graffiti will be gone by the time you get there.

Martinovics-hegy On the top of Gaál József út in district 12, this 259-metre-high hill has another unusual view of the city, especially of Castle Hill. In fact, the top of the hill is a nature reserve almost directly above the busy Moszkva tér. It is also a favourite rendezvous for dog owners and their dogs. At dusk, when street-lamps are being lit, is an especially pleasant time to walk up here. It's a fifteen minute walk from Moszkva tér.

Árpád tower Take bus 11 here and then walk up Látó hegyi út from the terminus. The tower itself has echoes of the rural folk architecture of Transdanubia. This charming spot is practically unknown to non-Hungarian travellers.

TAXIS

As with everything in Budapest, there have also been far-reaching changes on the taxi front. As opposed to the grim situation of the early 1990s, nowadays you can get a taxi at any time and in almost every part of the city within minutes. A number of taxi companies are just a telephone call away.

But chaos on the taxi front still prevails. Obviously, it doesn't matter how serious an offence they commit, nobody can really be stripped of his taxi permit. Recently city hall managed to maximise fares and simplify the fare system. Enforcement is still not great in Budapest, but I can sense a slow change.

Taxis can be hailed in the street, but they are only for hire if the "TAXI" sign is lit up. If you are ordering one by phone, give the address, then your full name and telephone number. English is almost always understood. Try to avoid the "hyenas" queuing at hotels and at the railway stations. The worst are those working at the airport. Insist on the meter being turned on – and on paying in forints.

At the airport the situation is still bad, though the taxis now belong to the airport. You are better off taking the Airport Shuttle (T: 296-8555), which is a minibus service that takes you to any Budapest address. It can also pick you up for your return flight. This is a fair, reliable and affordable service. At hotels, insist on the receptionist ordering a taxi for you. Otherwise, you can be sure of going on a zigzag route and of being overcharged.

Fötaxi (T: 222-2222) is the official taxi partner of Budapest Airport. It operates on a fixed price, depending on the part of town to which you are going. You are informed of the price in advance by the dispatcher.

I may be biased, and I don't very often resort to taxis, but there are four companies who do seem straightforward. You can usually ask for a non-smoking car, and in the summer you can insist on an air-conditioned car. Most companies can send you a "category A" car, which is always air-conditioned and is usually a Mercedes. They charge the same, but you are expected to give a higher tip. You can also ask for an English-speaking driver. The following companies all monitor problems and record orders (which means there is progress on the taxi scene). Fötaxi, established in 1913, is the oldest company.

Fötaxi:	222-2222
City Taxi:	2-111-111
Buda Taxi:	2-333-333
Tele5 Taxi:	555-5555
6x6 Taxi	266-6666

Taxi drivers in Budapest are generally talkative people who circulate the latest news and know about everything. Look for the taxi driver's badge of honour on the dashboard: plaques given for a quarter of a million, half a million, and one million accident-free kilometres.

One of the oldest taxi driver jokes may also be known elsewhere: A driver drives straight through all the red lights without hesitation. When he arrives at a crossing where the traffic lights are green, he stops immediately. "Can't we go now?" asks the customer, who is shaken up from the ride. "No way", the driver says, "this is when my colleagues are coming from the right".

INTRODUCTION TO PUBLIC TRANSPORT

Budapest has proverbially good public transport, which has become increasingly foreigner-friendly. Maps can be found at more and more tram stops and ticket vending machines "speak" several languages. I recommend walking as much as possible before using the metro and tram lines. Cars have multiplied insanely lately (which means that it's better to take the metro or trams because traffic doesn't effect them). If you remember – apart from the three metro lines – Tram 2 (on the Pest riverfront) and Trams 4 and 6 (on Nagykörút) you will be able to get pretty much everywhere in the city centre where you are unwilling to walk. Bus routes are more difficult to find out about.

As most Budapest residents travel with a monthly card, they do not really understand the public transportation fare structure. There are uniform tickets which can be used on the trams, buses, trolleys and the metro. Tickets must be validated by punching them in a machine or sliding them into the electronic readers at the metro entrances. If the trams and buses are packed, pass your ticket to someone beside the puncher to punch it for you. Tickets can also be bought in quantities of ten or twenty and must be kept together in the packet in order to remain valid. There are also day tickets; three day "tourist" tickets; weekly tickets; and monthly tickets. For the monthly ticket you need a photo, for the weekly card just an ID. People over the age of 65 travel for free. Also, citizens of the European Union. You cannot buy tickets on trams, buses or trolleys. They must be bought at the pénztár (cashier) at metro stations (until about 8 p.m.), newsagents or vending machines.

Your tickets are likely to be checked by inspectors while you're traveling, entering the metro or riding the trams, buses and trolleys. Inspectors either wear a uniform or disguise themselves as housewives carrying large shopping bags. In either case the inspector will state: "Kérem a jegyeket ellenőrzésre" ("show me your tickets for checking"). Inspectors are not often tolerant of confused foreigners, so be sure that you have a valid ticket. After 8 p.m. you can only enter buses and trolleys through the front door where you'll need to produce your pass or ticket to the driver. Some tram routes begin as early as 3 a.m. Every bus, tram and trolley stop has a sign showing when the last vehicle leaves the terminus, which is usually between 11 p.m. and midnight. "Utolsó kocsi indul …" means "the last car leaves at …". There are also signs posting information about night trams and buses. The metro runs between 4:30 a.m. and 11:10 p.m. daily and in rush hour trains run at intervals of about every two minutes.

Check www.bkv.hu for detailed information about transportation routes, schedules and prices.

THE METRO

The yellow metro line (M1) runs between Vörösmarty tér in the city centre (where our walks begin) and Mexikói út, a journey that takes just over 10 minutes. The entrances to most stations and the notices on the walls are copies of the originals. The train carriages date to the 1970s when the old trains from the end of the 1890s were, unfortunately, replaced by more modern ones.

The red line (M2) takes passengers from a large housing estate in the east of Pest, to Keleti pályaudvar (Eastern Railway Station), to the centre of Buda, to Moszkva tér, and finally to the Déli pályaudvar (Southern Railway Station). The line crosses under the river between the Parliament and the Lánchíd (Chain Bridge) and the entire journey takes about 20 minutes. In all red line stations there is a rubber strip on the edge of the platform which you may not step on until the train has stopped. If you do, a voice will, with increasing hysteria, shout over the loudspeakers: "A biztonsági sávot kérem elhagyni". ("Leave the Security Strip, Will You?!") Naturally, most foreign visitors do not understand the warning, which will be repeated until a Hungarian passenger taps them on the shoulder and gestures to them to step back. The night bus 78 serves most of the M2 route.

The blue line (M3) takes passengers from an industrial district in southeast Pest, through the downtown area, to the northern part of Pest in 28 minutes. The night bus 182 follows the M3 route. All three lines meet at Deák tér.

The green line (M4) is currently being built which will connect Keleti pályaudvar (Eastern Railway Station) with southern Buda. It's scheduled to open in 2013.

BUSES

Most people in Budapest, some 40 percent of all mass transit passengers, travel by bus. There are more than 200 bus routes, all of which are served by the blue Hungarian and Swedish-made buses. Perhaps half of them are articulated buses with accordion-like connecting sections to make turning corners easy. They are as characteristic of Budapest as double-deckers are of London.

On busy routes, buses with the numbers in red are express buses (the route is the same, but with fewer stops). Buses with red numbers followed by a red letter "E" (e.g. 173E) are express non-stop buses, which stop only at the two termini. You can board the bus through any door. After boarding, validate your ticket in the punch or electronic machines. The bus stops only if there is someone waiting to get on or off. If you wish to get off, you signal to the driver by pushing the button above the doors. People do not queue at bus stops, they just board the nearest door.

TRAMS

There have been trams in Budapest for more than a century. The tracks were laid by competing companies which kept their trams in their own colours, which originally were not yellow. Until the late-1970s there were still various types of trams and Budapesters had preferences for certain ones. Some trams had open platforms and more adventurous passengers, or those who could not find any room inside the tram, stayed outside. Children naturally preferred the platform, which gave them the sense of being master of a ship as the tram swayed along.

A few years ago many of the yellow trams were replaced by buses, but this trend has now stopped and there has even been a new tram line laid (Tram 1 on the Outer Boulevard), still to be built to the end. In 2000 the city of Budapest bought dozens of used trams from Hanover. The matter became a political controversy and the city government nearly collapsed over it. Another controversy followed the introduction of the new Nagykörút trams. They are the longest single space trams anywhere in the world, manufactured in the Vienna factory of Siemens. They allegedly began full service without the required test period – the local elections were too near, the political opposition said. They have been in operation since 2006.

TROLLEY BUSES

There have been trolleys in Budapest since 1949 (though there was a short-lived single line in the 1930s in Óbuda). There are 13 routes at present and they are numbered starting from 70 because it was Stalin's 70th birthday when the first line appeared. The pantographs of trolleys frequently come loose providing a favourite piece of street theatre when the driver jumps out, assembles a long pole, catches the loose current collector with it, and reconnects it with the overhead wire.

A Bus Ride at Twilight, Budapest, 7:11 p.m.

An exercise in applied people-watching: balancing on that thin borderline between the lands of genuine inquisitiveness and sheer voyeurism.

The number is 15, the terminus you need is in the south, at Boráros tér in Ferencváros. Take a seat on the right at the window. You will capitalise on the hitherto unexplained phenomenon: Budapest people who live in ground floor flats switch the light on exactly when they sense twilight, and close the shutters 22 minutes later on the average. It is that gap that offers you a chance.

You will see nineteen homes with antlers on the wall (two shot in person), innumerable homes with a television on (watched in not more than two dozen), five oversize posters on back walls showing the same corner of Tahiti islands, old Mrs. Kovács, weeping over a letter from Transylvania, one upright piano with camp operetta scores on, a cross on the wall in nine homes, complete with Christ in five, ninety-two flats with some bulbs blown and not replaced for financial reasons, four wall-to-wall bookshelves, overcrowded with fresh, unread acquisitions, two antique sets of hi-fi equipment, with turntables, young Miss Szabó shouting over the phone to a girlfriend, in a bitter case of a dress unreturned on time, one mother of a student architect, finishing the graduation design of her son, who is taking his first short nap after three days.

The other terminus is at the poorer end of Újlipótváros in the north. Do not stay on the bus – it is not worth taking the journey back. The shutters are down. Think and process instead.

OTHER PUBLIC TRANSPORT

The cog-wheel railway (Fogaskerekű or Tram No. 60) began running in 1874 and has since been electrified. It climbs into the Buda hills, beginning at Városmajor (near Moszkva tér) and reaching Széchenyi-hegy station in around twenty minutes. The distance between the two termini is 3.7 kilometres and the difference in height is 327 metres. The trains run daily from 4:25 a.m. to midnight.

The Children's Railway (Gyermekvasút) begins near the last stop on the cog-wheel train line. The trains run on an eleven kilometre narrow-gauge track and make an enchanting trip through the woods. It is actually run by children, naturally with adult helpers for some of the tasks.

The Chairlift (Libegő) runs eight metres above the hillside from a valley called Zugliget to the highest peak in the city, the lookout tower on János-hegy. There is a 262 metre difference in height between the two termini and it takes twelve minutes to make the journey. It operates between 9:30 a.m. and 4 p.m. and in summer between 9 a.m. and 5 p.m. It is closed every odd Monday.

The Cable Car (Sikló) was reopened in 1986, having been entirely reconstructed from the damage it suffered during the war. It takes visitors from the Buda end of the Lánchíd up to Castle Hill in one minute. It also can carry prams and wheelchairs.

DRIVING

I wouldn't recommend driving to anyone who doesn't know the town very well, not even the emigré who comes back for an occasional visit. It is hell to drive in Budapest for several reasons. Cars are more than seven years old on average. Pollution is not as bad as it once was (since more cars now run with catalytic converters), but the air can still be bad. There was a small parking enforcement revolution in Budapest in the 1990s. Hundreds of meters were installed with notices in three languages. Meters are regularly checked and wheel clamps are given if the car does not obstruct traffic (if it does obstruct traffic, the car is towed). The area covered by the system increases every year. Fines should be paid the same day, as they are substantially more painful the following day (and even more on the third day). Paying from mobile phones is also possible. There are entrance gates to the Castle District, which will keep you entirely out of certain areas (unless you are staying in a hotel there). So you should park before you reach the plateau and use one of the dozen staircases to get to the top. There are other problems with the car situation in Budapest as well. Vans still load in daylight (often at high noon), causing bottlenecks at every corner. Traffic manners are slowly improving. The bigger the car, it seems, the more aggressive the driver. So take a taxi. Or take a tram. Best of all, walk.

BIKING IN BUDAPEST

Getting around by bike is nice from early spring to late autumn, but only on the weekends. There are a growing number of bike routes, even along fancy Andrássy út. When it was rebuilt in the early 1990s a cycle lane was added between the sidewalk and the parking lane. Drivers, however, are traditionally hostile to cyclists, so beware of them. Renting a bike is not easy in Budapest. One reliable source is Zebra Bikes, which has been in operation for a significant amount of time. (*V. Sütő utca 2.*, in the courtyard behind McDonald's.) A Paris style network of ultra cheap rentable bikes is to be launched in 2011 or 12.

WEEKENDS

Budapest empties every Friday evening between spring and autumn for the weekend. Families rush off to "Balcsi" (the affectionate name for Lake Balaton) or to their "plots" elsewhere in the countryside. Many people have summer places somewhere along the 180 kilometres of Balaton's shoreline. The more desirable ones are on the hills of the northern shore, which shelves more steeply than the other side. Family "plots" are usually somewhere around Budapest and are, quite simply, a small piece of land with a small house built of stone or wood, usually with a lovingly tended lawn and a vegetable garden. The high number of summer houses is due to the restrictions that were placed for many years on the housing market. People simply were not able to afford their own home in the green belt around Budapest, but wanted to have a sense of space and a garden of their own. Significantly, the first motorway built in Hungary linked Budapest not with Austria or Yugoslavia, but with Lake Balaton. During the Sunday evening cavalry charge back to Budapest the number of lanes could be doubled without having any noticeable effect. The other popular weekend destination is Dunakanyar (the Danube bend) to the north of Budapest. Szentendre, Leányfalu and Visegrád are the fashionable places and there are some lovely old villas in their centres, which are surrounded by thousands of uncool "little boxes" (as Pete Seeger once ironically sang.) On weekends then, the tempo of Budapest becomes more relaxing. Buses and trams run less frequently and far fewer cars take to the streets.

"The Walk of Iván Mándy, the author". This photo was taken in 1969 by János Reismann (1905–1976), a man who was an illegal Communist who spent many years in the prison of his comrades. Iván Mándy (1918–1995) was a soft-spoken writer of short stories with a strong dream-like atmosphere, a chronicler of the life of the funny underdogs. Some of his stories were converted into very successful films. Do the hairdressers recognize him? Or do they just laugh at him, the one listening to inner voices?

THAT AWFUL HUNGARIAN LANGUAGE

Enzensberger, the globetrotting German poet, once complained that Hungary was the only country with Latin script that he had ever visited where he couldn't make out even a pharmacy sign. He was right: pharmacy is *gyógyszertár* in Hungarian. This monster of a word was coined, together with hundreds of others, to save the country from permanently becoming German-speaking, as it almost did during the first two decades of the 19th century. And miraculously, Hungary did manage not to become another Ireland – a small country with old lively arts and litera-ture, but without its own language. By the way, the official lan-guage of Hungary until 1844 was not German, but Latin. Literacy in Latin was widespread in the educated classes and lingered on for another hundred years until the otherwise beautiful Russian language was forced on Hungarian schools.

One can learn how to read Hungarian in half an hour (its spelling is logical), but a lifetime is too short to understand it, let alone speak it. It is not an Indo-European tongue: it belongs to the Finno-Ugric family of languages. Finnish is a distant relative, but is totally incomprehensible to us.

If you look at a Hungarian book you will see lots of diacritical marks, two of which, "ő" and "ű" was, for many years missing from the IBM standard character set, which made life hell for Hungarian computer users. On average, every sixth Hungarian letter is accented in some way or other – though only the vowels (which can be long or short). Consequently it is still possible to write metric poetry, or hexameters, in Hungarian. In English, or Modern Greek, for instance, it is not. Hungarian poets are well aware of this.

Though there are only three tenses – present, past and future – Hungarian conjugation is incredibly tricky. There are two sepa-rate sets in each of the three tenses: the "transitive set" and the "intransitive set". So when I want to say "I read a lot" or "I am reading", I use one set. I use the other set when I read something

György Tibor Szántó,
historian, publisher, translator, "godfather"

When you tire of the constant traffic noise and the window shopping which is inevitable on Erzsébet körút, you might want to find some peaceful island nearby with benches for tired walkers. Rescue is at hand! Please turn to the right at either Barcsay or Wesselényi utca (with your back to Blaha Lujza tér) and go one or two blocks. You cannot miss Almássy tér, a triangular "square" that serves as a playground for the young and the youthful, and as a green park for the elderly. The park-goers must all live in the picturesque surrounding late-19th/early-20th century apartment blocks that were built in styles ranging from mock-Gothic to art deco. The man who gave his name to this surprisingly colourful and well-proportioned, small-town-like square is Pál Almássy (1818–1882), who was a hero typical of the 19th-century landed gentry. The statue in the middle of the square, however, is of Antal Csengery (János Csiszér, 1822–1880), another hero of that same ardent period. He is regarded as the father of public schooling in Hungary. He brought education to the lower-middle-class, that is, the young people who had to start work at the age of 18. Take your time looking around Almássy tér. Note the houses once designed for petty bourgeois families in this definitely working-class neighbourhood. If you happen to find an open gateway, take a peek at the pretty, hundred-year-old staircases with wrought iron railings and amazingly shaped floor tiles (even on the circular foyers popularly referred to as "gangs"). Each house is subtly different from the next. The smell that comes from the kitchens, though, is identical throughout and must also be a hundred years old. The southern part of the square is, in fact, a short pedestrian street (Almássy utca) with wooden benches and some thirsty-looking greenery in graffiti-covered containers. The pavement here is for children to draw on.

in particular. Students with an English background will find it strange that the imperative is the most complicated business to put together. For most foreigners, Hungarian is intriguing, if not barbaric in sound. Eva Hoffmann, an American author, talks about the "utterly perplexing sounds of the Hungarian language, with its Bartókian syncopations and sensuousness." She continues: "Even when they speak English, Hungarians manage to transport some of the off-rhythms and softness of their own language into that flatter tongue, English, and give it strange, lunar resonances". Do we?

The only good news for the very obstinate is that there is no gender for nouns and that word order is quite free (or, as experts say, "fluid"). A word will carry slightly different meanings in different positions, however. This freedom, needless to say, is due to the unusually rich morphology of the language. If you take a closer look at any Hungarian book you will see very long words, most of them divided at the end of lines.

Believe me, Hungarian is not an ugly language. Here is the list a great Hungarian poet, Dezső Kosztolányi (1885–1936), made of what he thought are the most beautiful words in our language: *láng* (flame), *gyöngy* (pearl), *anya* (mother), *ősz* (autumn), *szűz* (maiden), *kard* (sword), *csók* (kiss), *vér* (blood), *szív* (heart), *sír* (grave). Interestingly his favourite words were the short ones in this language where words tend to be three syllables long.

THE MOST IMPORTANT HUNGARIAN WORDS

Yes	Igen
No	Nem
Thanks	Köszönöm
Hungarian	Magyar
Nice (*in most sentences*)	Szép
Can I Have a Glass of Water?	Kérek egy pohár vizet
Red Wine	Vörösbor
White Wine	Fehérbor
Naff	Ciki

TWELVE COMMONPLACE SENTENCES YOU CAN MAKE US HAPPY WITH

A mai napig jól emlékszem arra, amikor az önök aranycsapata 6:3-ra legyőzte az angolokat a Wembley-stadionban...

I clearly remember when your Golden Team beat England 6–3 at Wembley. *(This only applies to senior citizens, since it happened in 1953.)*

Szeretnék Szentendrére elmenni, hogy megnézzem a világhírű Kovács Margit Múzeumot.

I want to get to Szentendre, to visit the "world famous" museum devoted to the art of the late Margit Kovács. *(Kovács was a ceramist practically unknown abroad.)*

BUDAPEST BESTS

Mihály Ráday, former television anchorman, landmark preservationist, crusader.

"At Least Adopt a Horse!" – that was our slogan in 1995. We were trying to raise funds to give a facelift to the Városligeti körhinta with a four-page colour brochure. We managed to find some old pictures, so a remake of the almost entirely stripped façade and the dome (which had been pulled down after World War Two) was well underway. We also had plans to reproduce the carved gates which had been replaced by hideous aluminum ones: an act worthy of a prison sentence for the perpetrator. It was the British ambassador at the time, Sir John Birch, who gave the campaign its first push. "My mission in Hungary will be over in six months. Before I leave I would gladly contribute five or six hundred pounds to the restoration of something of value in Budapest," he had once told me. "If you have an idea, don't hesitate to tell me." Not much later I called him and asked if we could meet in the Amusement Park. The ambassador climbed on the körhinta. We had a great ride. I told him that the old name of our amusement park had been the "English Park" until the Communist coup in the late 1940s. Then I made my pitch. With the help of his one million forints, we could

Maga sokkal jobban tud angolul, mint én magyarul.

Your English is far better than my Hungarian.

Úgy hallottam, hogy a magyar diákok szokták megnyerni a matematikai diákolimpiát.

I've heard that Hungarian students tend to win the Mathematical Olympics. *(It used to happen, but recently education experts have been rather preoccupied with declining average standards.)*

A magyar nők nagyon csinosak.

Hungarian women are very pretty.

Budapest rengeteget fejlődött, mióta itt jártam.

Budapest has developed a lot since I was here.

---

start planning the real work, I told him. Thanks to Sir John Birch and all the other generous donors, today the old körhinta is just as beautiful as in 1906. It was he who taught me the charming British word "merry-go-round". Hungarian anglophiles tend to use the word "carousel", since that was the title of the American musical version of the celebrated play by Ferenc Molnár. Originally entitled Liliom, it's a sentimental comedy about the love of a merry-go-round operator and a servant girl. Have you inspected the comely frescos of the körhinta? Have you noticed the hand-carved and hand-painted torch-bearing angels, the chariots, the ships and the "magic steeds"? Have you noticed that every single horse has a distinctive face and features and that their leather saddles were made by craftsmen 100 years ago? You haven't? It's high time you went to look. Otherwise, if I'm asked what to see in Budapest, I tend to suggest two things not available to the west of us: Turkish baths and Hungarian art nouveau. Visit the Király Baths, Rác Baths or the Rudas. Then off you should go to Pest, where you can admire Ödön Lechner's yellow ceramic bees heading for their hives on the walls of the former Post Office Savings Bank (which is today's State Tresury, see Walk Two).

Nagyon szép ország Magyarország.

Hungary is a very pretty country.

Hogyan tudott a kis Magyarország ennyi Nobel-díjast és nagy tudóst adni a világnak?

How could little Hungary have given so many Nobel Prize winners and other great scientists to the world? *(Most of them were Jewish Hungarians who emigrated to America because of the anti-Semitic and anti-intellectual climate in the 1920s.)*

A magyar boroknak alig van párja a világon.

Hungarian wines have hardly any rivals anywhere in the world. *(Unfortunately they do however. Wines from Chile and Australia are the most obvious ones.)*

Az 1920-as trianoni békeszerződés tényleg nagyon igazságtalan volt, de most, hogy bent vannak az Európai unióban, egész Európa az önöké lett, az összes tengerekkel.

The Versailles Peace Treaty of 1920, which made Hungary much smaller, was really very unjust. But now you are in the Union, and all of Europe has become your own, with all of her seas. *(Hungary in the Middle Ages was even bigger than it was in 1920. It is difficult for Hungarians to accept the small country status – even if her neighbours are getting smaller and smaller.)*

Fantasztikus, hogy Budapest megint a kávéházak városa lett!

It is great that Budapest has become a city of cafés, again! *(True, no doubt.)*

Szépek a magyar bankjegyek!

How nice Hungarian banknotes are! *(This is a downright lie. They are to disappear in the mid 2010s.)*

Budapest is a great and remarkable city, with many uniquely and singularly naff things. However, the author is well aware of the fact that over-using the word "naff" is naff in itself. A Budapest guest of his, a great Australian professor advised to drop the word "naff" altogether. Unfortunately, the author could not. A serious description of early 21st century Budapest needs that term.

The revolution of 1956 lasted only 13 days. Its ingenious symbol was "the flag with a Hole" – people hated the Communist hammer and sickle in the middle of the Hungarian flag, so they simply cut it out. This photo by Ferenc Berendi emanates the atmosphere of an autumn streetscape, a remarkably car-free one.

SOME HISTORY

A Brief History of Hungary

The collective memory of the Hungarians also includes Roman times, though Hungarian tribes lived happily in the east around the Ural mountains when the Roman legions settled in the 1st century, and when they left at the beginning of the 5th century. The Hungarians (who are relatives of the Finns and the Estonians) arrived in the Carpathian Basin at the end of the 9th century. There were seven tribes, led by Álmos, Előd, Ond, Kond, Tas, Huba and Töhötöm. Árpád was the overall commander. For a time, Hungarians raided Western Europe, but in 955 they were fatally defeated. Hungarians had to decide whether to settle and convert to Christianity, or to disappear as dozens of other peoples had. They opted for the latter, and in 1000 King Stephen (later St. Stephen) accepted the crown from pope Silvester II. Thus, Hungary chose Western Christianity, which was a significant move at the time. During the reign of the first king, the strong administrative structure of counties was formed – one that managed to survive for many centuries. Christian faith slowly took the upper hand. Still, paganism remained strong for many decades, resulting in revolts. Medieval Hungary was much larger than the present one: what is now Slovakia and part of Romania, the Principality of Transylvania, and part of Croatia were included. National feelings did not really exist at that time. Documents were written in the official language, Latin, until 1844.

In 1241–1242 a Mongolian invasion devastated Hungary and forced king Béla IV to build fortified castles on hilltops, thus Buda Castle was built. In 1301 the "Árpád House" was discontinued, András III had no male offspring, and the Anjou Charles Robert was invited to the throne. He and his son, Louis the Great, consolidated the country and integrated it to the Europe of the day. It was during his reign (1340–1380) when the Turkish threat first appeared, and he defeated them in 1374. The Turks attacked Hungary many times after that, but the great commander, the low-born János Hunyadi kept them at bay. His greatest victory took place at the battle of Belgrade in 1456. Two years later his son, Matthias Hunyadi, was elected king, and that proved to be the zenith of medieval Hungary. Fast development, Renaissance influence, a strong army, and European politics are all synonymous with his reign, which is still one of the historical epochs that most Hungarians feel nostalgia for. Matthias realized that his country in itself was too weak to withhold the Turks – his goal was to become the Holy Roman Emperor. He even managed to conquer Vienna, and he died there suddenly and unexpectedly. After his death, Hungary quickly slid downhill. In 1526 the Turks miserably defeated the weak Hungarian army. Even the king, the young Louis II, drowned in a spring while running away. In 1541 the Turks captured Buda, and then for a century and a half stagnation followed (though this was also combined with religious tolerance and the construction of many bath houses). Hungary, as a matter of fact, was cut into three parts: the middle part and the south were under Turkish occupation, the north and the west belonged to the Habsburg Empire, and the semi-independent Principality of Transylvania was balancing between his two Big Brothers. Mind you, Transylvania, considered the cradle of Hungarian civilization, is a sort of Kosovo for most Hungarians, even today. The fact that it belongs to Romania is very difficult to accept.

After several attempts, a united European army finally liberated Buda in 1686, and soon all of Hungary was freed from the Turks. To the amazement of the Hungarian nobility, Hungary was not given back its independence, in any form. It was simply incorporated into the Habsburg Empire. This led to a series of riots calling for secession from the Empire. The most important was led by Prince Ferenc Rákóczi II (1703–1711). During the 18th century, Hungary also benefited from lots of general development, especially during the reign of Maria Theresa (1740–1780). For instance, the formerly Turkish-occupied territories were re-populated. Meanwhile, Hungarians almost lost their language to German (a blessing and a curse at the same time, if one thinks of the Irish). Thanks to some dozens of writers, poets and scholars, who launched the language renewal movement in the first decades of the 19th century, the language survived. Partly thanks to the innovators who invented hundreds of brand new words – from oxygen and hydrogen to medical and philosophical terms. Then came the so called Reform Age when an abundance of new institutions were established, from the Hungarian Academy of Sciences and Letters to the Stock Exchange and from the National Museum to facilities for horse racing. Many of these initiatives were taken by Count István Széchenyi, who was called the "greatest Hungarian".

On March 15, 1848 a revolution broke out, and it gradually evolved into a War of Independence. After a promising military

András Váradi, biochemist,
watch collector, flea market fanatic

*For more than 30 years now I have been going to the Ecseri
flea market every Saturday morning. I get up brutally early
and I prefer to get there before 7 a.m. During the last few years
my interest has mostly been focused on old mechanical wrist-
watches. Since then, I have become an advanced flea-market
addict: I can be happy now even if I leave the market empty-
handed. "How much of a discount would you give from half
your price?" is an old Ecseri flea market witticism, still often
overheard. Here are some rules of thumb, for your use:*

- *Don't ask for a price unless you really want to buy the item.*
- *Always decide in advance the maximum you are willing to
pay for it.*
- *Be a man (even if you are a woman), and stick to this
maximum.*
- *Don't let yourself be tricked: if you are asked about the
price, hand the object straight back. Or offer half of your
maximum. Then try one third.*
- *It is forbidden to interfere. If the piece is in somebody else's
hands, wait until he puts it down.*

*Practically everybody is a character in the flea market, except
for the noisy tourists with too much money. A man in his
fifties comes here every Saturday and sells old Hungarian
peasant glasses – wine and brandy bottles from the 18th and
19th centuries. During the week he is a homicide squad detective. Another character is the remarkable high-school physics
teacher who sells old telephones and vintage radios. Certainly
the most prominent obsessive flea market-goer is a somewhat
small, bearded man, with a small golden earring in his left ear
and ponytails, almost always in boots. He is Vladimir ("Jani")
Péter, a professor at MoME University and a silversmith who
is the designer of the Wladis range of jewelry. He is generally
an attentive listener. But not here – he hardly notices friends
because he is so immersed in scanning "the stuff" (mere piles
of junk to the uninitiated). Eating at the market is no gourmet
occasion. At the small buffets people enjoy the traditional ultra-
high cholesterol diet: juicy sausages, grilled pork ribs, smoked
knuckles with the skin on, blood pudding and tripe stew. It is
like a real-time educational video explaining why Hungarians
die so early. I only eat the sweets there.*

situation and many victorious battles, the Russian tsar was asked to send troops and the situation quickly turned around.

After a bloody revenge – the execution of thirteen generals and the peace-seeking, compromising Prime Minister Lajos Batthyány – un-parliamentary dictatorship only gave way to a quasi-democracy when (one year after the defeat of Koniggrätz by the Germans) the Austrian Empire was converted to the Austro-Hungarian Empire. (The so-called *Compromise – Kiegyezés* in Hungarian; *Ausgleich* in German – was signed in 1867.) This meant that there was now almost equal partnership and faster development. It was a veritable Golden Age for Hungary which lasted until 1914. Modern school systems were established, and there were equal rights for all religious denominations, including Judaism. A massive immigration of Jews from the Ukraine lasted for decades. Hungary benefited because the super-fast development of the financial system and of industry was partly because of the endless energy of the new capitalists and industrialists. Fresh immigrants chose to become Hungarians – they dreamed of total assimilation. During that time, Budapest, which was established by connecting three smaller towns in 1873, became a metropolis. Hundreds of cafés, an opera house (with Gustav Mahler as director for some years), museums, elegant public buildings, bath houses, and grand bridges attracted more and more visitors. The peak year of the era was 1896, when a grand exhibition was held to celebrate the 1000th anniversary of the Hungarian tribes coming to the Carpathian Basin.

Unfortunately, the Hungarian ruling elite blocked the further federalisation of the Monarchy, refusing to share power with the Croatians and the Czechs, which had tragic consequences in the years to come. Hungary not only lost many citizens in World War One, but it also lost the war, two thirds of its territory, and much of its mineral resources. It gained tens of thousands of highly educated refugees who had to live in railway carriages for many months since the country was unable to give them any housing.

After the war, Hungary became a bleak and uninspiring country. First there was a short-lived Communist dictatorship (the "red terror"), followed by the "white terror". Rear-admiral Miklós Horthy became regent in a "kingdom without a king". The peace treaty of Versailles (referred to as the Treaty of Trianon in Hungarian, as it was signed in the small Trianon palace) was signed in 1920, and inter-war politics was dictated by the hope of getting back the lost Hungarian territories. Hungarian Jews were blamed for Hungary's defeat in the war, for Trianon, and for everything. In 1920 the first European anti-Semitic law was passed, the infamous "numerus clauses" law, which prescribed that the student body universities could only be six percent Jewish, since that was the proportion in the population. Though the law was lifted in 1927, the poison was there in Hungarian society. Needless to say, Hungary joined the axis, Italy and Germany, in the hope of re-gaining some territory. It was not entirely in vain.

In 1938 some territories were returned, later even more. But Hungary was on the wrong side again, and the Soviet Union did not respect these territorial changes after the war. Germany insisted that Hungary accept tough anti-Jewish legislation, three laws, one after the other. The last even criminalised sexual intercourse between Jewish Hungarians and non-Jewish Hungarians (except for decorated Jewish-Hungarian soldiers, who were considered real Hungarians).

The war was a disaster for Hungary, in every respect. It lost hundreds of thousands of troops, its territory was devastated, and its towns bombarded. In the spring of 1944 Germany invaded the country, and forced the deportation of Jews beginning in the provinces. Then the process was stopped. Even though in October Hungarian fascists took power and about 70,000 Jewish Hungarians died of ill health and random killings, one can say that Budapest Jewry (though it was decimated) more or less survived. More than 500,000 Hungarian Jews from the provinces were deported and murdered, which was nearly all of them.

The rest is more or less well-known. The Red Army did not give up Hungary, on the contrary. After tolerating democracy until 1947, in 1948 it orchestrated a coup d'état, and the Hungarian Communist Party took power. Nationalisation followed in 1949. Scarcity, cruelty, fabricated trials, closed borders, stagnation, and nationalist rhetoric were typical of the Dark 1950s, under the dictatorship of Mátyás Rákosi, a bald, small, chubby, singularly unattractive-looking person. On October 23, 1956 a student demonstration began and it ended as a revolution. It only lasted thirteen days, but it was a sort of redemption for many Hungarians. Two hundred thousand mostly educated young people left the country. Then terror came: hundreds were hung, (including Prime Minister Imre Nagy, the Communist with a human face), and thousands were imprisoned. Nothing was the same after that. From the mid-1960s a snobby, more or less human-faced Communist society came into being. It was unbearable and stupid, but significantly different than the other East-European régimes: "Goulash Communism", "the Happiest Block in the Gulag", call it what you like. But culture mattered. Censorship was lax, the tiny opposition movement was tolerated, and the government constantly wanted to provide citizens with small improvement. (See the Introduction.) In the 1980s Hungary became hugely indebted. Real reforms were not possible, so the social benefits were paid by Western banks.

Typically, it was no revolution of any kind that brought democracy back to Hungary. In the wake of Gorbachov's changes, the Communist state simply "melted down". Hungary became a democracy again, a stable one. Privatisation was quick, and for a decade Hungary developed faster than its neighbours. Alas, not any more. In 1999 Hungary joined NATO and on May 1, 2004 Hungary became part of the EU. On December 21, 2007 it joined the Schengen system. The euro is expected during the late-2010s. Most Hungarians have expected a different Brave New World. But practically nobody wants the Communists back. They usually get about one percent of the vote at the general elections. To get in Parliament they would need five percent.

PERIODS OF HUNGARIAN HISTORY

895–896	The Settlement (Hungarian tribes reach the Carpathian Basin)
955	Raids and incursions into Western Europe
1000	St. Stephen converts Hungary to Christianity
1000–1541	Independent Hungarian Kingdom
1241–1242	Mongolian Invasion
1458–1490	King Mátyás (Matthias Corvinus)
1526	Battle of Mohács: utter defeat of the Hungarian army by the Turks
1541–1686	Turkish occupation
1703–1711	War of Independence led by Ferenc Rákóczi II
1848–1849	Revolution and War of Independence
1867	The Austro–Hungarian Compromise was signed
1867–1918	The Austro–Hungarian Empire
1918–1919	Hungarian Republic

1919	Hungarian Soviet Republic led by Béla Kun
1920	The Trianon Treaty assigns three fifths of the country to Hungary's neighbors
1919–1945	Kingdom Without A King (Admiral Miklós Horthy as Regent)
1941	Entry into World War II as a German ally
1944	Attempts to negotiate an armistice
1944	German invasion
1945–1948	Hungarian Republic (Multi-party parliamentary democracy)
1948	"Year of the Turnover" (Communist coup d'état)
Oct. 23, 1956	Revolution
Nov. 4, 1956	János Kádár returns in Russian tanks (from the city of Szolnok)
1956–1958	The Revenge (more than 400 revolutionaries, including Prime Minister Imre Nagy and his circle, were executed)
1963	Amnesty for most political prisoners
1968	New Economic Management (businesses and employees are rewarded for achievements)
1972–1973	Reform refrozen (harder line Communists take the upper hand)
1979	Stagnation starts
1982	"Small business revolution"
1984–1986	Debts doubled, but policies to boost economy fail
May 1988	Kádár, ailing and out-maneuvered, is deposed after thirty two years in power
March 25, 1990	First democratic elections take place. József Antall is elected prime minister of a centre-right government

1990–2000	Árpád Göncz is elected president by parliament (his second term was 1995–2000)
1990	Gábor Demszky is elected mayor of Budapest for the first time
Dec. 12, 1993	József Antall dies, Péter Boross becomes prime minister
1994–1998	Gyula Horn is elected prime minister of a Socialist–Liberal government
Oct. 1994	Gábor Demszky is elected mayor for the second time, this time by popular vote
1998–2002	Viktor Orbán is elected prime minister of a centre-right government
Oct. 1998	Gábor Demszky is elected mayor for the third time
April 12, 1999	Hungary joins NATO
June 6, 2000	Ferenc Mádl is elected president by parliament
May 27, 2002	Péter Medgyessy is elected prime minister of a socialist–liberal government, by a very small majority
Oct. 2002	Gábor Demszky is elected mayor for the fourth time
May 1, 2004	Hungary joins the European Union
April 23, 2006	Ferenc Gyurcsány becomes prime minister of the unchanged Socialist–Liberal coalition
June 7, 2005	László Sólyom is elected president by parliament
2006	Ferenc Gyurcsány is re-elected as prime minister
Oct. 2006	Gábor Demszky is elected mayor for the fifth time, by a very small margin
Autumn 2006	Street demonstrations, after the "secret speech," became public. The public television's headquarters is sieged

May 2010	Victor Orbán is elected prime minister again, with a more than two-thirds majority
Aug. 5, 2010	Pál Schmitt, a former Olympic champion, begins his term as President of the Republic
Oct. 3	István Tarlós elected mayor of Budapest

NAMES ON STREET SIGNS AND STATUES

This is a selective list of people whose names we have come across on street signs. A law prevents streets from being named after people who have died less than 25 years ago.

Ady, Endre (1877–1919) Poet, journalist, founder of modern Hungarian lyric poetry, central figure of intellectual life at the beginning of the century.

Anonymous (late 12th century) Chronicler, author of the earliest Hungarian historical work (the Gesta Hungarorum). See Vajdahunyad Castle in Walk Four for more on him and his statue.

Apáczai Csere, János (1625–1659) Hungarian theologian in Transylvania, writer, teacher, author of the Hungarian Encyclopedia.

Arany, János (1817–1882) The greatest Hungarian epic poet. His statue is in front of the National Museum.

Árpád, Prince (?–approximately 907) Leader of the alliance of tribes which conquered the territory of present-day Hungary, chieftain of the tribe known as the Magyars, ancestor of the Hungarian kings.

Aulich, Lajos (1792–1849) General, Minister of Defense during the 1848 War of Independence, one of the thirteen generals executed after the defeat.

Babits, Mihály (1883–1941) Poet, literary translator, novelist, major figure in literary life.

Bajcsy-Zsilinszky, Endre (1886–1944) Political writer, politician, a leader of the resistance during World War Two; executed on Christmas, 1944.

Balassi, Bálint (1554–1594) Great poet and womanizer of the Hungarian Renaissance, and one of the first to write poetry in Hungarian, rather than Latin. His statue is on Kodály körönd.

Baross, Gábor (1848–1892) Politician known as the Iron Minister, initiated the nationalization of the railway system and the organization of cheap transport. His statue is in the square named after him – in Pest, in front of Keleti pálya-udvar (Eastern Railway Station).

Bartók, Béla (1881–1945) Composer, pianist, musicologist, teacher, major figure in 20th century European music. Died in New York and declared in his will that no street could bear his name while there were still Hitler and Mussolini Squares in Budapest.

Báthori, István (1533–1586) Prince of Transylvania, King of Poland from 1576.

Batthyány, Lajos (1806–1849) Landowner, politician, first prime minister in 1848; Executed after Hungary's defeat in the 1848–1849 War of Independence.

Bem, József (1794–1850) Polish army officer, Hungarian general, leading figure in the 1848–1849 War of Independence.

Blaha, Lujza (1850–1926) Leading actress, prima donna, the "Nightingale of the Nation".

Boráros, János (1755–1834) Chief Justice, later mayor of Pest, opened Városliget to the public.

Bródy, Sándor (1863–1924) Writer, dramatist, muckraking journalist, persuaded the Hungarian public to appreciate naturalism.

Clark, Ádám (1811–1866) Scottish architect who settled in Hungary, directed the construction of Lánchíd, designed the tunnel.

Csokonai Vitéz, Mihály (1773–1805) Poet, dramatist, teacher, major figure of the Hungarian Enlightenment.

Deák, Ferenc (1803–1876) Politician, lawyer, the "sage of the nation", played a decisive role in the Compromise with the Habsburgs in 1867. His statue is in Roosevelt tér.

Dürer, Albrecht "Ajtósi" (1471–1528) German painter and graphic artist. His father emigrated to Nuremberg from a Hungarian village called Ajtós. The name Dürer (door-keeper) is a literal translation of the village's name.

Eötvös, József (1813–1871) Writer, poet, politician, introduced Public Education Law. His statue is outside the Marriott Hotel.

Eötvös, Loránd (1848–1919) University professor of physics, minister, son of József Eötvös; he invented an important instrument which is still used in geological research.

Erkel, Ferenc (1810–1893) Composer, conductor, pianist, founded the national opera, composed the music for the national anthem.

Erzsébet (Elizabeth, or "SisSi"), Queen (1837–1898) Wife of Franz Joseph, the Austrian emperor and king of Hungary. She learned the Hungarian language and spent a great deal of time in Hungary.

Gárdonyi, Géza (1863–1922) Writer, poet, teacher; still one of the most widely-read writers in Hungary.

Hunyadi, János (approximately 1407–1456) Regent, army leader, father of King Matthias; his victories over the Turkish army temporarily held up the Turkish onslaught. His statue is in the Castle district, at the Fisherman's Bastion.

Innocent XI (1611–1689) Pope (born Benedetto Odescalchi), called for the liberation of Hungary from Turkish rule. His statue is in the Castle district in Hess András tér.

Jászai, Mari (1850–1926) Great Hungarian tragic actress, played many leading Shakespearian roles in the National Theatre.

Jókai, Mór (1825–1904) Prolific novelist, the greatest figure of Hungarian romantic prose, sometime member of parliament; as a hero of the 1848 Revolution, he kept its spirit alive.

József, Attila (1905–1937) Poet, the greatest figure in 20th century Hungarian poetry. His statue is near Parliament, on the Danube bank.

József, Palatine of Hungary (1776–1847) Austrian regent who promoted the development of Pest. His statue is in József nádor tér, which is named after him.

Julianus the Monk (?–approximately 1289) Hungarian monk and traveller who found the ancestral home of the Hungarians in Asia and warned of the Mongolian invasion. His statue is behind the Hilton Hotel (in the Castle district).

Kapisztrán (Capistrano), (St.) János (1386–1456) Monk, inquisitor, army commander who played a major role in the victory over the Turks in 1456.

Karinthy, Frigyes (1887–1938) Writer, poet, classic Hungarian humourist, legendary jester.

Károlyi, Mihály (1875–1955) Landowner, politician, the first president of the Hungarian Republic in 1918. His ashes were ceremonially brought back from Paris in 1962. His statue is to the right of Parliament.

Kodály, Zoltán (1882–1967) Composer, musicologist, music teacher, colleague and friend of Bartók.

Kossuth, Lajos (1802–1894) Lawyer, journalist, politician, outstanding figure in the Reform Age before the 1848 War of Independence, Hungarian leader (as Regent) during the war; died in exile in Turin.

Kosztolányi, Dezső (1885–1936) Poet, novelist, literary translator, journalist, one of the first to use urban life as a subject for novels. See "Reading: On the Spot and Take Away".

Lechner, Ödön (1845–1914) Architect, philosopher of architecture, master of Hungarian art nouveau.

Liszt, Ferenc (1811–1886) Romantic composer, pianist, founder of the Academy of Music.

Madách, Imre (1823–1864) Dramatist who lived in isolation in the countryside, author of The Tragedy of Man (a classic Hungarian drama). His statue is on Margaret Island.

Mikszáth, Kálmán (1847–1910) Novelist, polemicist on social issues, prolific literary figure who revived popular prose.

Munkácsy, Mihály (1844–1900) Realist painter well-known in Europe. His paintings are in the National Gallery.

Nagy, Imre (1896–1958) Communist politician turned revolutionary. See Walk Two for more. His statue is on Vértanúk tere.

Pázmány, Péter (1570–1637) Cardinal-Archbishop of Esztergom, writer, leading figure of the Counter-Reformation in Hungary. Budapest University used to bear his name, but after 1990 the re-founded Catholic University is named for him.

Petermann, Judge (late 13th century–early 14th century) Hungarian judge in Buda from 1302 to 1309 during the time when the citizens of Buda excommunicated the pope.

Petőfi, Sándor (1823–1849) Prolific Romantic poet and revolutionary politician. His statue is on the Danube bank (north of Erzsébet híd, in Pest).

Rákóczi, Ferenc II (1616–1735) Hungarian prince who became the regent and led the War of Independence between 1703 and 1711. Died in exile in Turkey.

Savoy, Eugene of (1663–1736) Franco–Austrian prince, general, liberator of Hungary. His statue is in front of the Royal Palace.

Semmelweis, Ignác (1818–1865) Professor of Medicine, the "saviour of Mothers", the first surgeon to realize the importance of antisepsis.

Széchenyi, István (1791–1860) Hungarian count, politician, writer, called "the greatest of Hungarians", prime mover behind innumerable Hungarian public institutions and enterprises. His statue is in Roosevelt tér.

Szent István, St. Stephen (approximately 977–1038) King, founder of the Hungarian state, converted to Christianity in 1000. His statue is in the Fisherman's Bastion.

Szondi, György (?–1552) Soldier, commander of a castle which he defended with a garrison of one hundred and fifty Hungarians against 10,000 Turks. He died there with all his soldiers. His statue is in Kodály körönd.

Táncsics, Mihály (1799–1884) Politician, journalist, several times imprisoned for his ideas in the street which now bears his name.

Vak Bottyán, János (approximately 1643–1709) Legendary military leader of the Rákóczi War of Independence, a talented strategist. He lost one eye in battle, hence his nickname of "vak" (blind). His statue is in Kodály körönd.

Vörösmarty, Mihály (1800–1855) Romantic poet, author of one of the most influential patriotic poems of the last century. His statue is in Vörösmarty tér.

Wesselényi, Miklós (1796–1850) Political writer, reformer, "hero of the flood" of 1838, a leader of the anti-Austrian opposition before the Revolution.

Ybl, Miklós (1814–1891) Leading Hungarian architect; designer of the Opera House, the Basilica and many other public buildings; master of the neo-Renaissance style. His statue is on the Danube bank at the foot of Castle Hill.

Zichy, Mihály (1827–1906) Painter, graphic artist, welcomed in several European royal courts. He died in St. Petersburg.

Zrínyi, Miklós (approximately 1508–1566) Hungarian nobleman who was killed at the siege of Szigetvár defending the castle. His statue is in Kodály körönd.

Zrínyi, Miklós (1620–1664) Army commander, poet, "hero of the sword and the lute", wrote a famous epic on the heroic deeds of his great-grandfather (above). His statue is in front of the Vígszínház.

The word "naff" – what the hell does it mean?

You may have noticed that I use the word "naff" quite a bit throughout this book. It is a British slang word for something that is liked by too many people, or liked by too few people. It is not just related to taste, like the American word tacky. *Hungarian:* ciki. *French:* ringard. *German:* ätzend.

The classic definition from the Dictionary of Contemporary Slang (street-speak and vulgar language, swearing and obscenities) is the following:

NAFF adj. tasteless, inferior, shoddy, and unappealing. Naff had existed in working-class slang for at least 40 years by the time it became a vogue word in the later 1970s. It had been used in the jargon of prostitutes to mean nothing or negligible. In the theatrical, criminal and street-trading milieus it meant third-rate or poor quality. The word's sudden popularity occurred probably because it was seized upon by TV scriptwriters (particularly Dick Clement and Ian la Frenais in the comic series Porridge) as an acceptable euphemism for fuck in such forms as 'naff-all' (meaning fuck-all), naffing and naff off. Naff's ultimate origin, which seems to be 19th century, is nonetheless obscure. It has been claimed that it is a back slang form of fann(y) (in the sense of females sex organs) or an acronym or alteration of a phrase involving the word fuck ('not a fucking fart' or similar). Neither etymology is attested (or particularly convincing), and the similarity to NAFFI is probably coincidental.

When it was most fashionable, in 1983, an utterly funny book was published from the authors Dr. Kit Bryson, Selina Fitzherbert & Jean-Luc Legris, entitled The Complete Naff Guide: Where not to go, how not to speak, who not to be – a definitive handbook for the socially aware *(Arrow Books). Their definition, after hundreds of examples: "To be naff is to be unstylish, whatever that may mean."*

A CITY INHERITED

FOR THOSE WHO ARE HERE

"Full House at the Dunacorso", a photo taken by
Ernő Vadas in 1930. In the top left corner you have
a glimpse of the original Erzsébet híd, which was
completed in 1903 and not rebuilt after World War
Two. As you can see, the chairs were laid in six rows
on the promenade. You had to pay for them, like with
the deckchairs at the seaside. Ernő Vadas (1899–1962)
was a successful photographer with a distinct style
called "Hungarianesque". He was also published in
US magazines.

THE WALKS

The following five walks will show visitors Budapest's most important attractions while providing a sense of orientation and an in-depth look at the city.

FOR WEEKEND VISITORS: WALK ONE

The magnificent view from the top of Gellérthegy and a tour of the Parliament building are activities worth adding to this route. The route itself cannot be covered by car since most of it takes us through pedestrian areas.

FOR THREE OR FOUR DAYS: THE FIRST FOUR WALKS

These routes include all of Budapest's important sights. If you complete all four walks you will have a clear idea of the structure of the city. Parts of the routes can be covered by car or bike to save time.

FOR FURTHER DISCOVERING EVERYDAY LIFE: WALK FIVE

There are few tourist attractions included in Walk Five, which provides a glimpse of the life in the districts along the Nagykörút. This walk is, in a way, a cross between the first four walks and the chapter "For Serious Addicts". It makes no sense to follow this route by car.

THE BEGINNING AND THE END: VÖRÖSMARTY TÉR

It was a clear choice to make Vörösmarty tér the beginning and end point of all our walks. Even Walk Six can leave from here if you have a bike. The square is in the heart of the city, near the river, the big hotels, and the junction of the three metro lines. In the middle of the square is a statue, which was erected by public subscription, to the memory of Mihály Vörösmarty (1800–1855), who was an important romantic poet. Carved from Carrara marble, it must be covered in ugly transparent plastic from late autumn until early spring to protect it from cracking.

During the winter the middle of the square looks as if Christo the packaging artist has been working here.

The poet himself is the centre of the composition, while the figures around him are reciting his famous patriotic poem, whose opening line is carved into the pedestal of the statue – "Be faithful to your land forever, O Hungarians." Below this line, the black, round spot contains the most precious of all the donations that were collected to build the statue: a church beggar from Eastern Hungary offered the lucky coin she inherited from her mother.

A Celebrated Coin, the Donation of a Church Beggar on the Facade of the Vörösmarty Statue

The dominant building on the square has just been replaced. In the early 19th century a German language theatre stood on the site which was capable of seating 3,500 (hardly anyone spoke Hungarian in Pest at that time). Later it was a department store. A photograph of these buildings can be seen on the thick poster-pillar behind the statue (the building with the pediment is the theatre, and the department store was the building called Haas Palace). A new high-tech, glass-covered luxury office and residence complex was completed in 2007. Opposite this high-tech tour de force there is an Edwardian corner block. Its ground floor was occupied until recently by the Luxus department store, which for decades was the only place to buy "import quality" clothes.

Café Gerbeaud *(V. Vörösmarty tér 7.)* ••• is the square's greatest attraction, it has occupied this spot since 1858. Apart from a terrace, the café has three separate shops. The one on the left (with an entrance on Dorottya utca) is a separate café which is not always open and can be rented for special functions. The main shop opens from the square itself and is always full of tourists.

The entrance to the right of the building is now a luxury restaurant that tries to mix tradition and innovation, gilded mirrors and flat screens (there are four of the latter.) It is called Onyx.

It is worth walking through all of the rooms at Café Gerbeaud to look at the 19th century decoration and furniture, which is quite remarkable and varied. Remember that it is impolite not to check your coats in the cloakroom. After all, you are a traveller or a tourist? Don't spoil the elegance of the place by leaving coats on the chairs.

The confectioner's occupies the ground floor of two neighbouring buildings, which is why the rooms are so different. If you can find a table near the corner window in the vaulted section on the right (when you are facing the café from outside), you will feel and hear the trains of the old underground line thundering underneath. In one of the high rooms, with a richly decorated flat ceiling, there is a portrait of Émile Gerbeaud, the Swiss confectioner who bought the shop in 1884. He started out by selling his cakes at reduced prices since only the very well-to-do could afford pastries. He invented *konyakos meggy*, a Hungarian bonbon which is dark chocolate filled with a sour cherry soaked in cognac. The story goes that he smashed the punch cakes whose colour was not what he had prescribed. The service in Gerbeaud is still very polite, although a little impersonal and occasionally slow. The waitresses these days are too busy to chat about the guests in code-language as their old-time counterparts once did. The dessert choice, however, is first class (unlike the layout of the menu). In addition to Hungarian specialties, Viennese classics are also available.

During the long Communist years Kis Gerbeaud, the little shop in the right wing of the building, was once a world apart. In the place of Onyx (a great restaurant with one Michelin star!), there used to be an eminent meeting place for the "Gerbeaud ladies" – a group of older women who had once lived better lives. They wore lots of jewelry and drank coffee with whipped cream. It is difficult for me to recognize Kis Gerbeaud now since it has changed so much since my ersatz-grandma aunt, Mrs. Rudolf Bozóki (née Irén Engländer, 1904–1976) dragged me there almost every first Tuesday of the month. She boasted about my reasonably good grades to her fellow Gerbeaud ladies, and invariably, stuffed me with a cake called "corner block" (sarokház), a chocolate cake with lots of whipped cream. The ladies wore heavy perfume, had relatives in the States and Britain, and shared their bad news about every conceivable subject. And they had a terrific time, in the centre of a Central European city that had seen better days.

This photo was taken in 1874 by an unidentified photographer. Matthias Church was then an "ugly duckling" of a Gothic church, surrounded by mediocre buildings. Twenty years later, the visionary architect/retro-designer Frigyes Schulek gave Budapest what it badly needed: a totally new, representative Medieval Gothic Church, partly authentic, partly fake. It is the wedding venue of very rich Hungarians, including some Habsburgs.

WALK ONE

THE CASTLE AREA AND VÁCI UTCA

This walk takes us across the river to Buda where we will look at some houses dating from the Middle Ages and at an old church which King Matthias would not recognize, even though he was married there twice. We will visit the Royal Castle, which finally has a proper dome. We will then cross the river back to Pest via a modern bridge and plunge into the busy city centre, where we will even visit a charming flower shop.

Time: seven to eight hours.

Since this walk is so long, I have recommended places to sit down for coffee or a meal along the way (see separate listings in the "A City to Enjoy" section).

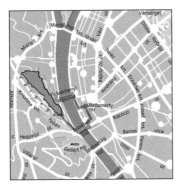

The Promenade (Duna-korzó) ••• When viewed from the river in the second half of the 19th century, neo-Classical Pest was hidden behind large hotels. Here, on the river bank stood the Carlton, the Bristol, the Hungaria and the Ritz. They were the same height as the only building remaining from that period, the Thonet House on the corner of Vigadó tér. Only one of these hotels survived the war, but even that was later pulled down. The pedestrian promenade in front of these hotels, the Dunakorzó (or the "Korzó" for short), was popular for strolling until tram tracks were laid along the old walk.

This row of hotels contained no fewer than nine cafés, which all overlooked the river and had terraces that merged into one another. All types of Budapesters from all neighbourhoods strolled here from spring to autumn. It was a tradition that had survived from the time when Pest was a small town, when there was always a place to go to meet friends and to socialize. Budapest once had four such promenades, but this was the most important and the busiest (it even had four rows of benches). The other promenades were on nearby Váci utca, on Bástyasétány ("bastion promenade") in the Castle, and on Stefánia út near Városliget (which was for luxury coaches). Dunakorzó, where quasi strangers walked together or even talked to each other, was the most relaxed. There is a story of a famous bohemian writer, Jenő Heltai (1871–1957) who was once accompanied by a young man on the Promenade. They strolled along together chatting. Suddenly the writer was greeted by a passer-by. The young man asked who it was. "How on earth should I know?" replied the writer. "I do not even know who you are!"

Evenings were especially beautiful here when all the cafés were illuminated and the best gypsy and jazz bands played. At a safe distance from the bright terraces sat people who came from the suburbs to listen to the music, but could not afford to sit in the cafés.

Since a row of hotels was built in the 1970s, the Promenade is beginning to come to life again after its apparent death. Although it is mainly tourists who stroll here now and frequent the restaurants and cafés along the Korzó, the locals seem to be slowly returning, especially the older generation. At night, however, sleaze dominates the Promenade, with all three sexes offering themselves for sale. The lovers of the Dunakorzó would like to drive the noisy Tram 2 underground and have the promenade widened. But there is no sign of this expensive proposition being adopted.

The Cutest of Cute Little Princesses ••• In Vigadó tér, by the Tram 2 stop, the little bronze statue by László Marton (1990) perching on the railing has sat there for only a few years. But some tourists might think it was a hundred years old. When it appeared the statue made most sculptors furious and many artists and critics called it downright kitschy. But tourists, including Prince Charles, loved it (so much so that he acquired a copy and invited the artist to London, where a show was devoted to his work). In most months you'll have to search for the princess behind makeshift stalls filled with gadgets and bric-à-brac. Look for Marton's Liszt statue in Walk Five.

Hotel Intercontinental and **Atrium Sofitel Hotel 1E–F •••** These hotels, which are at the Pest end of the Lánchíd, were built almost simultaneously in the early 1980s, bringing the Danube bank back to life. They are far too big, they have spoiled the inherent scale of the riverbank, and they are insensitive of the buildings of the inner city. They do not even match with the style of the Marriott Hotel (to the south of them), which was built fifteen years earlier, an eternity in the field of Budapest hotel architecture. When completed, the **Hotel Intercontinental** (József Finta, 1981) was said to look like a cassette recorder of the day, standing on its side. It still reflects the afternoon sun from many angles, which it was also praised for. Luckily, when the hotel was renovated in 2000 its giant coloured wooden relief (Pál Kő, 1981) in the foyer was preserved, along with its poets and writers recognizable to educated Hungarians. It now faces the elevators.

The 356 room **Atrium Sofitel Hotel** (Lajos Zalaváry, 1982) is a hive-like building that reveals its true self from the inside. All guest rooms open onto a circular gallery that surrounds a central courtyard, hence the name Atrium. Over the atrium hangs a replica of the first Hungarian-built airplane. Its foyer has been revamped a couple of times since it opened. Since 2006 it is called the Bibliothek Lounge, a friendly and tasteful space with

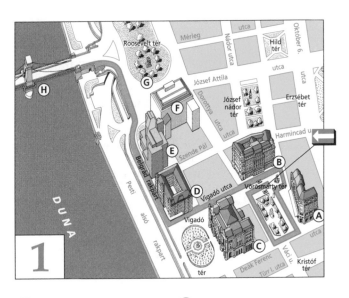

A Elegant shops		**E** Hotel Intercontinental
B Café Gerbeaud		**F** Hotel Sofitel
C Vigadó Concert Hall		**G** Statue of Ferenc Deák
D Thonet House		**H** Lánchíd (Chain Bridge)

dark brown shelves and hundreds of books. It could stay like this for many years, if the management changes the books.

There is a statue of József Eötvös, a 19th century writer and politician, at the entrance to the Intercontinental Hotel. There is a small tablet saying "Erected by the Nation", which was added by Hungarian secondary-school pupils and teachers on the occasion of Eötvös' centenary.

There was a pontoon bridge over the Danube from spring to autumn from the Middle Ages onwards. During the winter the river froze and carts could pass across the thick ice, but there were also times when many citizens got stuck on the wrong side when the thaw set in. In the winter of 1800 the entire magistracy of Pest went to Buda for the wedding of the Austrian governor and were not able to cross the river again for weeks.

It was thought to be impossible to build a bridge of wood and stone over a river of this width until Count István Széchenyi founded a society for building a bridge to span the Danube and connect Pest and Buda. Inspired by having to wait at the river bank for a week while travelling to his father's funeral when he was a young hussar captain in 1820, Széchenyi comissioned a British architect, William Tierney Clark, and Scottish master builder, Adam Clark (no relation). The iron was also imported from Britain. The building of the bridge was an example of an early public-private partnership, as it was partly financed by tolls. After protracted and fiery debates, Parliament passed a law declaring that the aristocracy too should pay the bridge toll, which was enforced until 1870. Some members of the Upper House declared that they would rather make a two-day detour to the south and cross the river by ferry, so intent were they on maintaining the noblemen's exemption from tax.

Chain Bridge (Lánchíd) 1H–2A ••• Linking Roosevelt tér in Pest and Clark Ádám tér in Buda, the Lánchíd was built between 1842 and 1849. The span between the pillars is 202 metres and the original structure weighed 2,000 tons. It was not quite finished when Austrian troops withdrawing to Buda towards the end of the Hungarian War of Independence tried to blow it up. They failed, however, to lay the charges properly and no damage was done to the bridge. Meanwhile, the colonel who gave the order to destroy the bridge was blown to pieces.

When the bridge was ready, its creator was so proud of it that he declared he would drown himself if anyone could find any fault with his masterpiece, begins an old anecdote. So the people came and examined every little part of it, but in vain.

They could not find anything wrong with the bridge. Then one day an apprentice cobbler (the proverbial hero of Hungarian stories like these) discovered that the lions at either the end of the bridge had no tongues. So Adam Clark committed suicide, the story went.

In fact, the lions were made later than the bridge itself, and the sculptor gave his word that they do have tongues (which you can only see if you stand directly opposite them). In January 1945 German soldiers were, unfortunately, rather better at preparing demolition charges for bridges. They pushed a button and dropped the central span of the Lánchíd into the Danube. During the renovation of the bridge in 1987, sixty tons of paint were used and most of the 100,000 rivets were replaced.

The Tunnel under Castle Hill was built in 1857. The joke at the time was that it was built so there would be a place to push the bridge when it rained. The Tunnel was also built by Adam Clark, a fact that indicates that he did not commit suicide, rather

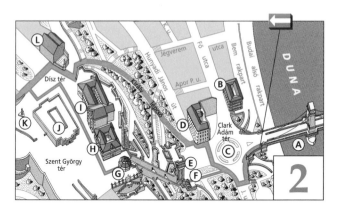

A Lánchíd	**E** The entrance to the Tunnel	**I** Castle Theatre
B Fő utca 1.	**F** Lower terminal of the Cable Car	**J** Ruins of the former Ministry of Defence
C Flowerbed that used to form a red star for decades	**G** Upper terminal of the Cable Car	**K** Statue of a Hussar
D Hunyadi János út 1.	**H** Sándor Palace	**L** Batthyány Palace

married here and built a fine home for himself and his family in Buda. He died in 1866 at the age of 55. The square on the Buda end of the bridge was named after him in 1912 and was one of the few streets named after a foreigner that was not re-named during the Communist period.

Cable Car (Sikló) 2F–2G ••• The cable car is located at the base of the Castle on Clark Ádám tér. With a track almost 100 metres long and a 48 percent gradient, the cable car opened for service in 1870. The idea was to provide cheap transport for clerks working in the Castle District. Originally it was operated with a steam engine, but switched to electricity when it was rebuilt in 1986. It still uses a cable, however, with the car going down counter balancing the car going up. The two carriages are named Elizabeth (the left one) and Margaret (the right one), after the bridges, no doubt. The cable car runs from 7:30 a.m. to 10 p.m. daily (but is closed every other Monday). At the lower terminus there is always a long queue, so you can take the Király lépcső (steps) as an alternate route up to the Castle. Castle Hill rises only 50 to 60 metres above the riverbank, so you can walk to the top in 5 to 10 minutes. If you make a little detour to the left at the first point where the paths cross, you can admire the fine proportions of the Lánchíd from above the tunnel. You'll also see the cable car from a little bridge over the tracks.

Castle Hill (Várhegy) ••• This flat 1.5 kilometre long crag is packed with houses and could be compared to a floating stone galley. At first sight the district may look poor and provincial compared to other historic districts in Western Europe that have remained substantially intact since the Middle Ages, but upon closer inspection it offers delightful sights and stories. Apart from some stately town houses, most of the buildings are simple plastered burgher's houses. The streets, which lead from the old castle gates, follow the shape of the hill.

After an unexpected and devastating Mongol attack in the mid-13th century citizens of Buda began moving up the hill. Later, the Royal Court was established on the hill and the long golden age of the district began. Buda became an important European city in the 15th century when its population is estimated to have been about 8,000. It was a melting pot of different nations: "Pontiffs of Italian culture live in the neighbourhood of noblemen used to the rough life of soldiers. Swiss ambassadors open their doors to Turkish aristocrats," wrote a historian at the time. Buda started to decline when the Turks ruled between 1541 and 1686, but the siege and bombardment that happened just 75 days before its liberation in 1686 left it in ruins. The Austrian authorities counted 300 inhabitants in the remains of the city. There were no Jews among the survivors. The numerous and once prosperous community which had enjoyed the religious tolerance of the Turks was massacred by the Christian liberators because it sided with the Turkish defenders of the city.

After the Turks left, reconstruction followed the old street layout, but with houses being built only two stories high rather than three. A Baroque city slowly came into being, hiding the old ruins behind its thick walls. The Castle became a district of government. It was besieged again in 1849, and again reconstructed. Later, most of the government ministries moved here. After a long period of peace, it was battered to pieces yet again in January 1945 when the Germans and Russians met there, before the eyes of an anguished civilian population. The German forces were completely surrounded, but held out for seven weeks (December 24, 1944 to February 12, 1945). This was the city's thirty-first siege.

The latest reconstruction lasted for a long time – too long for the ministries, which moved out and allowed museums to take their places. Most of the district's houses are used as residential flats, some of which have only been modernized in the past few years. Cars have recently been banned from the entire area, with the exception of residents, guests of the Hilton Hotel, and taxis. The Castle has become quiet again. According to an architect/writer, the spirit of the city came here in its retirement. There is a peacefulness up here that cannot be found anywhere else in Budapest. The Venice Charter of landmark preservation regulating the reconstruction of historic buildings says: "if a building has several architectural layers, the reconstruction of the remains of some earlier state can be permitted solely on condition that in so doing only parts of lesser value are demolished while the reconstructed part should be of great historical, archaeological or aesthetic value."

The whole city of Buda is a good example of such reconstruction. While the rubble was being cleared away after the war, many remains dating from the Middle Ages came into light and were left intact. Regarding the Castle, from what we have left it seems certain that the walls of the buildings were painted different colours everywhere, with black, white and green patterns being dominant. Even the doorways of the ruined houses held surprises. Dozens of *niches* were discovered, whose function is still not clear to archaeologists. Some think they were resting places for night watchmen, others say they were used as stalls by broadcloth traders. Sixty-three such niches can now be seen in the Castle District. The oldest ones, from the 13th century, are finished in a simple round arch, while the later ones were

WALK ONE

WALK ONE

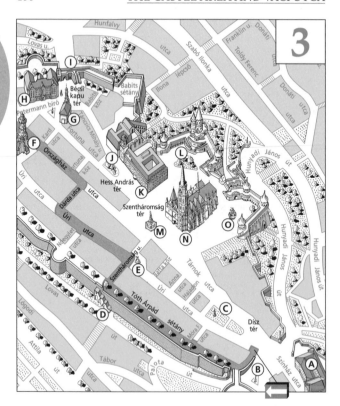

A	National Dance Theatre (former Castle Theatre)	H	National Archives
B	Statue of a Hussar	I	Vienna Gate (Bécsi kapu)
C	Memorial to the soldiers of 1848/49	J	Statue of Pope Innocent XI
D	Steps up to Castle Hill	K	Hilton Hotel
E	Statue of András Hadik, general of Hussars	L	Fishermen's Bastion
F	Mary Magdalene Tower	M	Holy Trinity Column
G	Lutheran Church	N	Matthias Church
		O	Statue of St. Stephen, first king of Hungary

increasingly richly decorated. Perhaps there was some kind of competition between the residents of old Buda to have the most beautiful niche.

The walls of the Castle are well preserved nearly everywhere. Except for some short sections, you can take a walk around the top of Castle Hill. The tablets on the walls of the buildings indicate which century they were built ("Sz." written after Roman numerals signifies century). Tablets also name any previous buildings that stood on the site (Helyén means "on the site of").

Let's start our walk at the statue of András Hadik and move on to the section that overlooks Buda. If we start from the gate called Fehérvári kapu and head to the round bastion nick-named the "sour soup bastion" (Savanyúleves rondella), we will be walking where the Buda side promenade was once located. Nowadays, it is fairly quiet. The greatest attractions of the Castle District are its unity and discovering it under one's own steam. For this reason, I was reluctant to be categorical about laying out the route.

The Statue of András Hadik 3E ••• The nickname of this dare-devil general of humble origin (1710–1790) was "the most hussar of hussars". He was the commander of the Buda Castle and a favourite of the Empress Maria Theresa. In October 1757, with a small force, he besieged Berlin and made it pay a ransom. He also demanded 50 pairs of gloves for the empress (which were found all left-handed at closer inspection). The statue (by György Vastagh Jr.) was unveiled in 1937. Experts say that it is a perfect image of the ideal, effortless, and elegant cooperation between horse and rider. In the pediment there is a glass case with the names of the heroes of the Imperial and Royal 3rd Hussar Regiment. If you look very close, you'll see that the horse's testi-cles are shiny yellow. Generations of engineering students have touched the parts on the morning of difficult exams. It allegedly brings luck.

A rest
Café Miro
I. Úri utca 30.

Úri utca 31 ••• This three-storey building has an almost com-pletely Gothic façade. In its present form it may date back to the second half of the 15th century, during the reign of King Matthias, but the core structure may be even older. The façade, which had been rebuilt several times, collapsed during World War Two, revealing some medieval remains. This building is also the only evidence that there used to be three-storey houses in

Buda. Enough of the wall painting was left to reconstruct the original decoration, but the function of the five protruding windows remains unknown. There are niches in the doorway, and the staircase was restored in a Baroque style.

Országház utca 18–20–22. ••• These three houses, built in the 14th and 15th centuries, reveal how most of the Castle District might originally have looked in the Middle Ages. They also explain why this street used to be called Olasz utca (Italian Street). On the gate of the middle house the initials stand for the name of Johann Nickl, the butcher who had the house rebuilt in 1771. The present tenant of number 22 does not want to lean out of the windows, as was customary in the Middle Ages when there was a knock at the door, so he put a car rearview mirror on his window and keeps his house locked.

Mary Magdalene Tower (Mária Magdolna-torony) 3F ••• On the corner of Országház utca and Kapisztrán tér, this 13th century Franciscan church was where Hungarian speakers worshipped in medieval times. Under Turkish rule this was the only church allowed to remain in Christian use, while all others were converted into mosques. The chancel was used by Catholics, while the nave was Protestant. In the end, it too was converted into a mosque. Both the chancel and the nave were destroyed during World War Two and have not been rebuilt, except for one stone window as a memento. There are plans to rebuild the whole church, but it's unlikely to happen because of the cost.

"The Flying Nun" ("A repülő apáca") ••• Quite a few street names have become protected by the city. For some, artists have been commissioned to make allegorical figures to illustrate them. This one – on the corner of Országház utca and Petermann bíró utca (a street named for the first known elected official in Buda, who served in the early 14th century) – was created by Miklós Melocco in 1977. According to the memorial plaque next to the figure, the convent of the Order of the Poor Clares, in which Parliament at one time held its sessions, stood nearby at Országház utca 28. The building is now used by the Hungarian Academy of Sciences and Letters. Some further protected street signs are at Dísz tér 8. and Fortuna utca 4.

Military History Museum (Hadtörténeti Múzeum) 4B *I. Tóth Árpád sétány 40*, www.militaria.hu, open Tuesday to Sunday 10 a.m. to 6 p.m. (April to October) and Tuesday to Sunday 10 a.m. to 4 p.m. (October to April). ••• This building, with remarkable twin windows, was built as an army barracks in the 1830s. On both sides of the entry gate, cannonballs can still be seen lodged into the wall. They have not been removed out of respect for the Hungarian army, which liberated the Castle in the spring of 1849. On the round bastion, cannons from the Turkish era are exhibited, some of which have richly ornamented handles in the form of bird's heads.

The museum has a specialised military collection: weapons and uniforms of all kinds and a controversial 20th century history to look back on. But museum-goers here are varied, with boys and old warriors represented in the highest numbers. The museum perhaps shows the least inclination of Budapest's museums to be transformed into a modern educational institution: modern technology is slow to penetrate here. Critics also say that complicated problems are rarely portrayed objectively here, with both majority and minority standpoints included. It is no small feat to honor all historic heroes in this country that ended up on the wrong side in both world wars.

Hospital in the Rock *I. Lovas út 4/c.*, www.sziklakorhaz.hu •••
It is a nearby, related museum – a secret nuclear bunker and hospital, opened in 2008. Incredibly authentic!

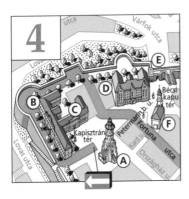

Tomb of a Turkish Governor ••• Near the left wing of the museum there is a small tomb with the following inscription in Hungarian and Turkish: *It was near this site that the last governor of the 143-year-long Turkish rule in Buda fell in a battle, at the age of 70. He was an heroic enemy. Let him rest in peace.*

A Mary Magdalene Tower
B Military History Museum
C District Hall of the Castle
D National Archives
E Vienna Gate (Bécsi kapu)
F Lutheran Church

Let's walk back into the centre of the Castle district, past a modern building (*Petermann bíró utca 5–7.*) that is in ideal harmony with its surroundings (designed by Csaba Virág, 1979). The giant transformers of the National Electric Supply

Board sub-station needed the hard rock of the hill, which is why they are located here. The next building, the National Archives (*Bécsi Kapu tér 2–4.*) designed by Samu Pecz, 1913–1920, does not give rise to such a question. The only question here is why it should be so big. Quite a few medieval houses had to be demolished to clear the site, which once had a large tower that was demolished during World War Two and was never rebuilt. And in early November 1956, when the Soviet troops re-entered Budapest, thus putting an end to the short-lived revolution, some freedom fighters fired their weapons from the windows of the building. Tanks fired back, and in the ensuing fire some invaluable documents were destroyed. The Russian soldiers did not know which building they were aiming at, they did not really know which country they were in. Some of them allegedly thought they were in Egypt, at the Suez conflict.

District Hall of the Castle (Polgármesteri Hivatal) 4C *I. Kapisztrán tér 1.* ••• This run-of-the-mill neo-Classic block was built around 1835. In 1869 it was converted into a large printing house (the State Printing House), which worked for the ministries located in the Castle District. It operated like that until it was bought by the local government in the mid-1990s, when it was beautifully restored and converted into a district hall (by Ilona Kremnicsán, 1997). It somewhat stressed local finances, but Tamás Katona (the mayor at the time) was a former historian specializing in the 19th century, and he insisted on it.

One can walk into the covered courtyard, which is a great venue for public ceremonies and concerts. It is decorated with high quality oversized historical paintings and some of the original statues from the top of the old Pest City Hall, which was demolished to make way for the Erzsébet híd. Inside there is a high-tech lift, as well as some restored wrought-iron from the heyday of the printing house era.

The landmark preservation authority did not let the builders attach a balcony to provide a speaking platform for the mayor, arguing that it would be a fabrication. A renowned specialist who obviously agreed, commented in a review: "It is possible to add things to a landmark building, especially things that are needed. It is possible to decorate it with some false jewels. But one must not put a wig on a landmark."

Vienna Gate (Bécsi kapu) 4E ••• Bécsi kapu tér was called the "Saturday Market" in the Middle Ages. This was the market at which non-Jewish merchants bought and sold goods. It is the northern gate of the Castle District, and is where all four streets that run the length of the hill converge. From this square it takes only a few minutes to walk to the busy centre of Buda, Moszkva tér. If a child talks back to his parents they usually scold him by saying "Your mouth is as big as the Vienna Gate".

You can walk up to the top of the gate. Enjoy the panorama of Buda and the view of the late 19th century Lutheran church in the square below. Parliament can also be seen from an unusual angle from here. To the right of the gate, next to the bastion wall, there is a small grove of trees. This is called the Europe Grove because the mayors of cities all over Europe brought and planted rare trees here in 1972. There are 16 types of trees here, among them are a Turkish hazel, a Japanese cherry and a cherry laurel.

Bécsi kapu tér 7. ••• This building, which stands on the site of a medieval house, was rebuilt in its present form in 1807 by a priest and teacher who lived here. He also commissioned the portraits of Virgil, Cicero, Socrates, Livy, Quintilian and Seneca to be seen on the façade on the first floor between the windows. There are beautiful grilles on the windows and on the door of a staircase in the gateway. In the first half of the 20th century Baron Lajos Hatvany (1880–1961) lived here. He was an erudite patron of literature and the arts, who spent most of the profits from his sugar factory to support some of the greatest figures of early

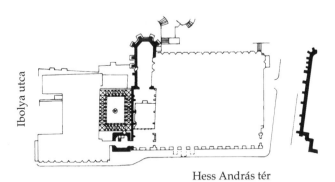

Hess András tér

Hotel Hilton

20th century literature. In 1935 and 1936 Thomas Mann was his guest here on three occasions – on one of them, the Hungarian poet Attila József was also among the guests. He was so short of money that he could not afford tram and cable car tickets, so he walked here from his far away Pest home.

Hotel Hilton 5B *I. Hess András tér 4.* ●●● This hotel, which was designed by Béla Pintér, was the most elegant in Budapest when it was completed in 1976. It was given a warm welcome, by both architects and experts on historic buildings, for its seemingly perfect mix of old and new. One side of the hotel is the wall of the former Jesuit cloister, which was built in a late rococo style and decorated with plaits. The Gothic remains of a Dominican church are also enclosed by the modern hotel in such a way that they can be visited, and open-air music performances are

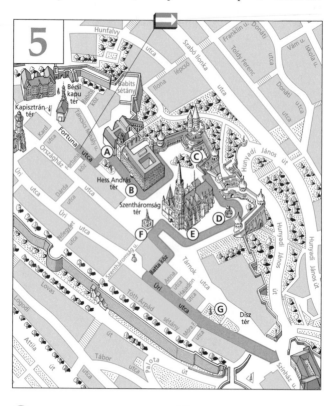

A Statue of Pope Innocent XI		**D** Statue of St. Stephen, first king of Hungary	
B Hilton Hotel		**E** Matthias Church	
C Fishermen's Bastion (Halászbástya)		**F** Holy Trinity Column	
		G Memorial to the soldiers of 1848/49	

held there in the summer. At the opening ceremony, the president of Hilton International called this hotel the most beautiful pearl in the whole string. Matthias Church reflected in the large glass panes of the hotel has long been a favourite subject of amateur photographers.

Fishermen's Bastion (Halászbástya) 5C ••• This lookout terrace, which is totally unfit for defense purposes, has five round towers and a main tower with several floors. In the Middle Ages the fish market was nearby and this part of the wall was traditionally defended by the Guild of Fishermen, hence the name. But this structure was only built between 1890 and 1905.

While the tourists are at the dinner table, the Halászbástya is visited by teenage couples intent on a first kiss.

Matthias Church (Mátyás-templom) 5E *I. Szentháromság tér* ••• The official name of this church is the "Church of the Blessed Virgin in Buda", but it is universally known as the Mátyás (Matthias) Church. Its popular name derives from the fact that the great Hungarian king Matthias held both of his weddings here. Originally, it was the church of the German burghers. The main eastern gate and the long apse date from the 13th century, and the latter was built after the French pattern ending in a regular seven-sided polygon. The central part of the church was built around 1400. In Turkish times all of the furnishings were removed and the decorated walls were whitewashed. Later, it was converted into a Baroque church and by the middle of the 19th century it looked rather miserable. *(See the photo on page 91.)*

Between 1873 and 1896 it was restored by Frigyes Schulek, who preserved all of the original elements that were found as the walls were pulled down. His dream was to make a new building that would retain what was inherited from the past. The row of chapels along the north wall was added by him, and one holds the tomb of Béla III and his wife Anne of Antioch, which is the only tomb of a medieval king to have survived. The 80-metre spire has a rectangular ground and first floor, above which it becomes octagonal. Schulek kept the original tower intact up to the third floor, but from there finished it according to his own plan. At the end of the 19th century the walls were also repainted based on fragments found during the restoration.

There is a clash of opinion on the artistic value of the church. Some regard it as a masterpiece of European eclecticism, and of art nouveau, in respect to the wall paintings. Others claim that it is no more than over-decorated stage scenery. Both may be right.

The building is evidence of all the knowledge the hardworking 19th century had of the Gothic period. But at the same time, it is able to quickly arouse emotions, rather like a momentarily glimpsed set in a film. Anyway, the average man in the street likes this church a lot.

Holy Trinity Column (Szentháromság-szobor) 5F ••• In the middle of Szentháromság tér, which is the highest point of Castle Hill, this 14-metre-high monument was erected between 1710 and 1713 by the inhabitants of Buda to fend off another plague epidemic. In the Middle Ages, the square here was much smaller, only 10 metres wide.

House of Hungarian Wines ("Magyar Borok Háza") *I. Szent-háromság tér 6.,* www.magyarborokhaza.com, *open daily noon to 8 p.m.* ••• Unless you hate wine, make sure you pop into the House of Hungarian Wines, which is evocatively installed in the cellars of this Neo-Gothic building which was the pre-war Ministry of Finance. With tasteful and informative décor, there is text in four languages. For a reasonable sum you will be guided around the cellar which has a representative selection (several hundred different types) of wine from all of Hungary's wine regions. You'll be offered a choice from the 80 different wines for tasting – but, naturally, it doesn't include the most precious bottles. All exhibited wines are also for sale.

If you are a Hungarian-based business with frequent visitors from abroad, you might be tempted to rent some handsome storage space of your own, from where you can offer your own wine to your visitors whom you especially want to impress.

The Old Town Hall of Buda (Collegium Budapest) *I. Szent-háromság utca 2.* ••• The first session of the City Council was held here in 1710. A prison, which had such a low ceiling that even the shortest man could not stand upright, was once in located in the yard. In 1873, the year when Buda and Pest united, the building lost its function. The statue at the corner of the building is a copy of the original which was made by an Italian sculptor in the late 18th century and represents Pallas Athene (the guardian of towns).

The building is much admired for the fine proportions of its windows and for its inner, forked staircase, which is trod these days by foreign scholars. The place now functions as the Collegium Budapest, which is an institute for advanced studies founded by and similar to Berlin's Wissenschaftskolleg. The scholars come for six months or a year and work in the house, but

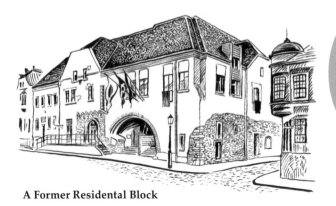

A Former Residental Block

live nearby in an attractive hostel that is, as we say in Hungarian, just a spit away on the hills of the Castle.

I was once invited to have lunch with the dean. Expecting a sort of high table, I instead found myself in a noisy, lively cafeteria in the heart of an institution that looks like one of the smaller Oxford colleges. This cafeteria hosts small and well-curated exhibitions.

A Former Residential Block *I. Szentháromság utca 1–3.* ••• In some places unadorned modern buildings were built on the site of buildings destroyed in the war. But today only "non-polluting modern" buildings, which harmonize with their environment, are permitted to be built in the Castle. The planning rules are strict and in the case of this corner house (György Jánossy, László Laczkovics, 1981), the bulk, the height, and even the roof structure were strictly prescribed. Traditionally the aesthetic of Hungarian towns favours verticality, with lines running upwards. This explains why the architects omitted the third horizontal line under the roof. Thus, the pillars in a way repeat the vertical directions of the church opposite, only on a smaller scale. The broken façade echoes the medieval site. Other successful modern buildings in the Castle District are *Úri utca 4.*, *Úri utca 10.*, *Úri utca 32.*, *Fortuna utca 16.*, and *Tóth Árpád sétány 30.* One of the best buildings erected after World War Two is *Fortuna utca 18.* (on the corner of Kard utca) which was built by Péter Reimholtz in 1999.

In medieval times Tárnok utca was the site of the German burghers' Wednesday market. Ordinary bread was sold from tables, black loaves were sold from mats. Until the middle of the 15th century, bread was unleavened. There was a wide choice of game and fruit. Only live fish were sold, and on the second day their tails had to be cut off to show they were not quite fresh. Peaches and grapes could only be sold by special permission of the council, as they could be used to make alcohol.

The House of a Medieval Warlord *I. Úri utca 19.* ••• This house is presumed to have belonged to an infamous 15th century Italian aristocrat and in Turkish times it was occupied by monks. The only "bridge of sighs" which has survived, is

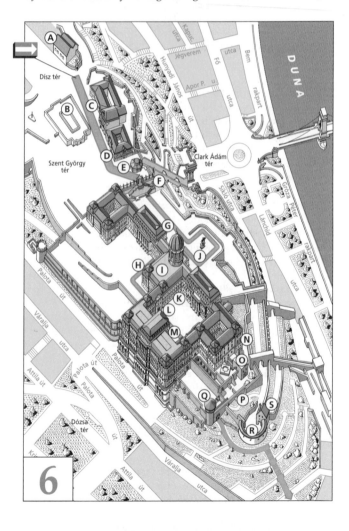

located here, although various documents mention that once there were several such bridges in the town. The house was rebuilt in its present form in the 1830s and a tomb and a sundial remain in the courtyard.

Entrance to the Catacombs *I. Úri utca 9.*, www.labirintus.hu, open daily 9:30 a.m. to 7:30 p.m. ••• There is a 10-kilometre-long underground labyrinth under Castle Hill where evidence of human occupants dating back half a million years has been found. The caves were first connected to the Turks for military purposes. In the 1930s an air-raid shelter for 10,000 people was created in the labyrinth by using concrete reinforcements. Today a section of about 1.5 kilometres can be visited.

Water always drips in limestone caves and this one is no exception. After a heavy rain, the dripping resembles a shower in some places. The temperature is 14 degrees Celsius and the humidity is about 90 percent. Only a street sign on the wall reminds us of the time during World War Two when thousands of people lived through the siege down here. Some say that the postman even came down to deliver their letters. There is another entrance at *Lovas utca 4.*

A Batthyány Palace

B Ruins of the former Ministy of Defence

C Castle Theatre

D Sándor Palace, office of the President of the Republic

E Upper terminal of the Cable Car

F Statue of the legendary Turul Bird

G National Gallery (Royal Palace, Wing B)

H Matthias Well

I National Gallery (Royal Palace, Wing C)

J Statue of Eugene of Savoy

K National Gallery (Royal Palace, Wing D)

L Lions

M National Széchényi Library (Royal Palace, Wing F)

N Budapest History Museum (Royal Palace, Wing E)

O Gothic Great Hall

P Palace Gardens

Q "War Hammer" Tower

R Southern Round Bastion

S Tower of the "Gate of Sighs"

National Dance Theatre (Várszínház) 6C *I. Színház utca 1–3.,* www.nemzetitancszinhaz.hu/english. ••• This building was completed in 1736 in a late-Baroque style as the church of the Order of Our Lady of Mount Carmel. In 1784 Joseph II dissolved this religion's congregation, just as he did most others. The monastery was converted to a casino, and the church gave way to a theatre. The latter was designed by Farkas Kempelen, who was also the inventor of the famous chess automaton.

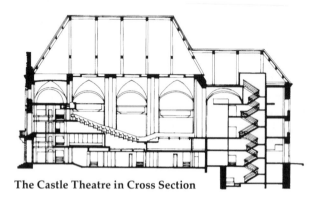

The Castle Theatre in Cross Section

The theatre had a wooden structure and could seat 1,200 people. Performances were held in German, but the first play written in Hungarian was also performed here. The theatre has been rebuilt several times, but the wooden structure remained until 1924 when a part of the gallery collapsed. The next performance was not until 1978 when a new theatre, made of marble and concrete (but seating only 264 people), was opened. Unfortunately, the dress circle and the foyer are not separated, so even the slightest sounds from outside can be heard. And there are always some sounds from outside. For more than two decades this theatre was used as the studio of the National Theatre. But since 2002 it has housed the National Dance Theatre, which hosts productions from Hungary and abroad.

The President's Office at Sándor Palace (Köztársasági Elnöki Hivatal) 6D *I. Szent György tér 1–2.,* www.keh.hu. ••• Sándor Palace is one of the finest landmarks of Hungarian Classicism (Johann Aman and Mihály Pollack, 1806, conversion by Miklós Ybl, 1867). The palace, which is in a fabulous location, was converted to the prime minister's office in 1867. It operated as such until 1944 when it was almost completely destroyed during the siege. For almost 60 years it was a mere ruin with an uncertain future. Then in 2000, the government (which at the time was one highly sensitive to symbolism) decided to recreate the prime minister's office here. No expenses were spared, but as one critic said: "it was no reconstruction, rather recreation". But it was a wonderful job, in every respect. (Architect: Ferenc Potzner, interior designers: Éva Magyari, Béla Pazár, ornaments: Kornél Baliga.)

To put the prime minister's office there, far away from the ministries and Parliament building, was strongly criticized, however. The president of the republic move here instead. His study is on the riverfront, near the balcony on the left, and there is a vast painting on his wall of count Lajos Batthyány, the first Hungarian prime minister, who was shot dead by the Austrians on October 6, 1849. Unfortunately, the palace can be visited by ordinary mortals only during the European Heritage Weekend, which is the last weekend of September. The changing of the guard happens daily at noon. By way of the fine web site, you can take an extraordinary virtual tour of the inside of the palace.

Royal Palace (Királyi palota) 6G, I, K–O ••• Since the Royal Palace is also a pseudo-historic building which incorporates many of the original parts, its history is similar to that of the Matthias church (although the palace is younger than the church). Even though between 1892 and 1918 the Buda Castle was officially one of the royal seats, the royals have never been residents here, only visiting guests.

The first palace on this site was a gothic and renaissance one which was added onto for 300 years. It was totally demolished by the Christian army that liberated Buda from the Turkish occupation in 1686. In 1715 work started on a completely new, and much smaller Baroque palace. By 1779 the palace had expanded and after some minor reconstruction, it had almost doubled in length by the end of the 19th century. A huge wing was added to the back and it is now 304 metres-long. All the halls on the ground floor opened into one another. The neo-Baroque palace, which also had some art nouveau elements, had a false dome with an attic underneath. The reconstruction by Miklós Ybl and Alajos Hauszmann was finished in 1904.

At the end of World War Two, the palace was the last stronghold of the besieged German troops. The roof fell in completely and most of the furniture was destroyed. At the end of the 1940s, experts decided that the palace should not be restored in its original form, although it would have still been possible to do so using the ruins and the plans. They declared that they wanted to return to an earlier, 18th century version of the palace, but at the same time they wanted to retain the dimensions of the 1904 version. Finally they built a Baroque façade that had never existed before and added a newly designed, though pleasing, real dome to the building. The architects of the time saw no value in the eclectic style, even though this is now considered to be the richest aspect of architecture in Budapest.

Budapesters knew nothing of this dilemma. They were just happy to take possession of the Castle again, step by step. Nowadays the building houses two large museums and the National Széchényi Library.

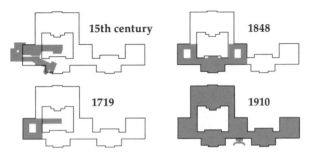

How the Royal Palace was Built

Looking down from the western side of the palace to the foot of the walls, you can see that archaeological excavations are still going on. They were, in a way, made possible by the devastation of the war and by the slow pace of reconstruction afterwards. Although archaeologists have not found the first 13th century palace, some remarkable finds have been made from the time of the 14th century Anjou dynasty. The stripes in the pavement of the courtyard mark the courses of earlier walls.

The Statue of Eugene of Savoy 6J ••• Opposite the front entrance of the palace, overlooking the Danube, is a bronze equestrian statue of the famous commander, Eugene of Savoy (József Róna, 1900). He led the armies that liberated Hungary and expelled the Turks in 1686. The commission for the statue was originally given by the town of Zenta, which was the scene of a last, decisive battle. But the town went bankrupt and could not pay the artist. Hauszmann, the architect who completed the enlargement of the palace, discovered the statue in Róna's studio. He persuaded the prime minister to raise funds from the emperor to buy the statue. Emperor Franz Joseph agreed to give the money and, most significantly, he ordered that the statue be erected in place of an equestrian statue of himself that had previously been planned for the spot.

National Gallery (Nemzeti Galéria) 6G, I, K Royal Palace, Wings A, B, C, and D, www.mng.hu, open Tuesday to Sunday 10 a.m. to 6 p.m. ••• The art of a small country is always a private affair, and this is especially true of the art of the past. Still, those who spend an hour strolling through the 19th century Hungarian Painting exhibition will not regard it as a waste of time. Do not bother with the strangely spelled names and unknown historic figures. The paintings in this exhibition, which takes up one floor of the gallery, breathe a definite awareness of life. There is a Hungarian word, *honfibú*, for this feeling, but such a word seems to be missing from other languages. It can best be described as "patriotic sorrow". There is the grief of generations behind this word, the grief common to all Hungarians for their ill-fated country.

Hungarian painting developed its unique character during the Romantic era. It is a deeply sentimental way of painting, and even has some elements of Romantic horror. Late 19th century painting may seem familiar to foreign visitors – impressionism and other developments became popular in a rapidly developing Budapest, which, like Vienna, was a flourishing intellectual centre. Hungarian painting has one mysterious, lonely genius – Tivadar Csontváry Kosztka (1853–1919) – and three of his major paintings are on the staircase landing between the second and the third floors (where the light is dim enough to conserve them). He first took a pencil in his hand when he was 27 years old when an oxcart stopped outside a village chemist's shop where he worked, and he sketched the dozing oxen on the back of a prescription form. (At least, he claims that in his autobiography.) He then started to draw and paint and sent his first drawings to a famous art teacher in Budapest. Later he studied in Rome, Paris and Munich. He was already a well-known artist at the beginning of the 20th century, although he was frequently attacked for his style. He had four exhibitions in his lifetime. After his death, his family had already agreed with some carriers to sell his large canvases as tarpaulin when a 24 year-old architect turned up and invested his inheritance in the paintings. Despite efforts to introduce him to the world, Csontváry remains practically unknown outside of Hungary. Most of his paintings can be seen in a museum named after him in the city of Pécs, about 200 kilometres south of Budapest.

Matthias Well (Mátyás-kút) **6H** ••• This bronze statue of King Matthias (Alajos Stróbl, 1904) portrays him as a huntsman in the company of his shield-bearer, his chief huntsman and his Italian chronicler. Notice the dogs, which have the nicest ears of any hunting dogs. On the bottom right, Szép Ilonka ("Helen the Fair") can be seen. She was a girl of low birth who fell in love with the king while he was hunting, not knowing who he was. The predictable end of the story was not preserved for posterity. The memory of King Matthias was well-preserved in hundreds of folk tales for many centuries, as a just and great ruler, who often punished aristocrats and officials and who bullied "plain folks". Historical evidence shows a different picture. At the zenith of Hungarian power he managed to centralize his government and probably wasted too much energy on wars and on the wrong campaigns. Though he did not underestimate the Turkish threat, he aimed at becoming the Holy Roman emperor, which is why he conquered Vienna and transferred his royal seat there. Hungary lost its independence for many centuries in the early 16th century, not long after Matthias' death in 1490. His greatest achievement was bringing Renaissance splendour to Buda by way of his second, Italian wife, Beatrix of Aragonia, the daughter of the king of Naples. He established the legendary library of finely illustrated "Corvinas". It is estimated to have consisted of about 5,000 volumes, a very large number in that age.

Lions **6L** ••• The lions guarding the entrance of Oroszlános udvar (The Lion Courtyard) were carved by János Fadrusz in 1904. Two of them are trying to discourage visitors with their grim looks, while the other two, which are inside the gate, roar angrily at those brave enough to enter. The huge door in the gateway between the lions leads to an elevator which leads to the bottom of the wing overlooking Buda, to the stop for bus number 16. The entrances to the National Library, the Budapest History Museum and the National Gallery are in the courtyard.

National Széchényi Library (Nemzeti Könyvtár) **6M** *Royal Palace, Wing F,* open Tuesday to Saturday 10 a.m. to 8 p.m. ••• This library has about eight-million volumes which include books, periodicals, musical scores, multimedia products and other ephemera. Among these are the few codices which have not been dispersed from King Matthias's celebrated library. These codices are called "Corvinas", after the bird on the king's coat of arms (corvus means raven in Latin). There are 70,000 books shelved in the reading rooms. The spacious Main Reading

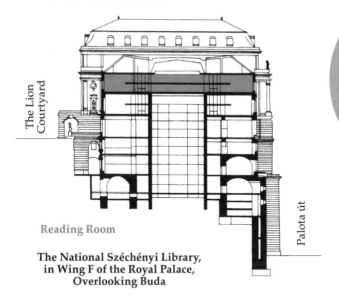

The Lion Courtyard

Reading Room

Palota út

**The National Széchényi Library,
in Wing F of the Royal Palace,
Overlooking Buda**

Room, which consists of several smaller rooms, is not very elegant, but has ideal working conditions thanks to the abundance of natural light from the windows. The books are transported by small carriages which run between the glass roof and the mock-ceiling. The carriages are rather noisy, if they happen to be working.

The library has several special collections, from manuscripts to posters and maps. The most interesting perhaps is the intriguingly named "Special Collection of Documents about Historical Epochs" (Kortörténeti Tár). It is the bulk of the former "prohibited works", which consists of right-wing émigré literature and samizdat publications. It was only made accessible to the general public in 1988. For some reason back then these books were simply not put back on the shelves where they would normally belong.

The library's interior was restored in the 1970s and 1980s. The building has two floors above the courtyard level, but the ground floor is really the fifth floor of the library. This is the so-called Ybl Wing, which was added between 1890 and 1902 and extends over the edge of Castle Hill. About 800 people can read in the library, but it does not lend items.

The library was not happy about the many students who flooded it during exam periods until recently: their lifestyle, joie de vivre and hormones did not mesh with the hard-working concentration of scholars, who are the main clientele. So they banned the entry of "alien books" (meaning books not belonging to the Library), which decimated the number of students.

Budapest History Museum (Budapesti Történeti Múzeum)
6N *Royal Palace, Wing E*, www.btm.hu. ••• This is a most carefully arranged and intimate exhibition illustrating Budapest's 2,000 year history with clear maps and a reconstruction of the medieval Gothic palace. Recently the "History of Budapest" exhibition was extended to the present day, using modern display techniques and drawing on help from stage designers and other visual artists. It puts the city's history powerfully into context, rather than just showing the objects (which contrasts the grand display at the National Museum). Moreover, the glass-topped Baroque courtyard is a wonderful reception and concert area (János Balázs, Irisz Borsos, 1997).

After World War Two, excavations began around and under the ruined Baroque palace on an area covering 30 acres. Despite the rich architectural finds, it is difficult to imagine a medieval palace of the scale that this one once was. The largest of its halls was 70 × 17 metres, which was big enough for tournaments to be held here. Compared to this, the ten or so surviving rooms seem humble, but they are nonetheless fascinating. The palace from which they were resurrected was once famous all over Europe and praised in the writings of travellers and ambassadors. In the second half of the 15th century, King Matthias even enjoyed a larger income than both the English and the French kings. Almost all of the restored rooms were outside the main building: a cellar, an ice-cellar, a cistern and corridors. Only two major sights can be found inside what is now the history museum: the Gothic Hall, which presumably was part of the queen's apartments, and the crypt. This is where the so-called Gothic Statue find were originally exhibited, when after a very unquiet life, they were discovered in 1974. They have since been moved to a more prominent place on the ground floor.

Sometime at the beginning of the 15th century, because of some hasty construction work, about 50 stone statues were considered to be a surplus and were thrown into a yard that was later filled in. The statues, all dressed in French-style clothes, probably portrayed the courtiers of the previous king. "Playboys of the trecento", the archaeologist who led the excavations called them, though some other experts have dated them to the early 1400s, well into the quattrocento. So it is only these dumped statues that have come down to us. Most of the most important ones did not survive Turkish rule. The secular statues are in the Gothic Hall (Room 11), and the ones with religious subjects are exhibited in the crypt (Room 16).

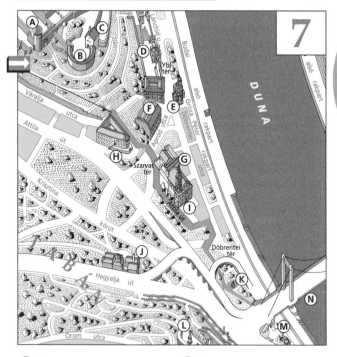

A	"War Hammer" Tower	**H**	Deer House
B	Southern Round Bastion	**I**	Tabán Parish Church
C	Tower of the "Gate of Sighs"	**J**	Rác Baths
D	Entrance to Royal Gardens Bazaar	**K**	Statue of Queen Elizabeth, wife of Francis Joseph
E	Casino and Restaurant	**L**	Statue of St. Gellért
F	Medical History Museum	**M**	Rudas Baths
G	The house of Benedek Virág, an 18th-century poet	**N**	Erzsébet híd (Elizabeth Bridge)

From spring until autumn visitors can visit a small garden, which is arranged in a medieval pattern, and from there they can get to the Castle walls. The southern courtyard of the Castle can be reached by going through the front hall of the History Museum. From there, we leave the courtyard through the Ferdinand Gate.

The museum has two other major branches located elsewhere: **The Kiscelli Museum** and **The Municipal Gallery**, which house the Budapest history collection after 1686 (*III. Kiscelli út 108.*, www.btm.hu/kiscell/fooldal/kiscell.htm, open Tuesday to Sunday 10 a.m. to 4 a.m.) and the Aquincum Museum, which includes a Roman collection and a historic theme park (*III. Szentendrei út 139.*, T: 250-1650, open spring to autumn).

A rest
Tabáni terasz *I. Apród utca 10.*

Deer House (Szarvas-ház) 7H *I. Szarvas tér 1.* ••• This triangular café was built at the beginning of the 18th century in late-Rococo style. The building now houses the Aranyszarvas Restaurant, known for its game dishes, and the original café sign can still be seen above the gate. Until the 1930s the northern slope of Gellért

Balázs Stumpf-Biró, one of the souls of the city and a self-made alternative guide

"Budapest". It's my favourite word, and just as meaningful for me as "mother" and "love". I could spin many tales about the city, but instead let me offer you a few pearls:

1. *Buy a fresh edition of this book. It's the best guide ever (and not just for Budapest)! Read it from cover to cover and follow the advice provided in every respect.*

2. *Have lunch at the Frici Papa kifőzdéje and observe the other people eating. "Uncle Francis's eatery" is a little neighbourhood restaurant in Terézváros. Here you will encounter authentic Hungarian cuisine: huge portions at ridiculously cheap prices. It's crowded at lunch time, but it's acceptable to sit next to strangers and to ask for a big glass of tap water. (VII. Király utca 55.)*

3. *Look at the mysterious gate at Kazinczy utca 55. This house, in a small street in the heart of the old Jewish Quarter, is where a type of Hungarian playing card was invented. On the old gate you can see a beautiful, mysterious piece of ironwork: the Egyptian sign of life embedded in the Jewish star and swastika, surrounded by Uroboros (an ancient snake), who is biting his own tail. Next*

Hill was packed with small old houses with wine cellars which served as pubs. This was the Tabán neighbourhood, a popular place of entertainment. All of the houses that once stood here were demolished for public health reasons, but the Szarvas ház and the yellow building opposite still preserve the atmosphere of the old district. These days this would be considered a serious city planning mistake by preservationists, and it could serve now as a sort of "Budapest Montmartre". The hotels that were planned to be built here were not realized, until now.

The Statue of Queen Elizabeth, Who Allegedly Loved the Hungarians 7K ••• The whole nation mourned the death of Franz Joseph's wife, Elizabeth, when she was assassinated at Lake Geneva by an anarchist in 1898. She was said to be a great friend of Hungarians and even spoke our language. This statue originally stood on the other side of the Danube until the early 1960s when an open-air Roman archeological museum was built on the site. It was erected again here in 1986. Before the war, a statue of the ultra-right wing leader whose policies led Hungary

WALK ONE

door is a pub from the old days where you will still find the best Wiener Schnitzel ever.

4. *At the corner of Rumbach Sebestyén utca and Madách Imre utca (where Budapest's first stand-up comedy venue, Café Godot, is located) you can see the Buda Citadel peacefully lying on the roof of Pest's City Hall from under the arch of Madách tér. It looks like Buda in Pest.*

5. *Ask for "sós rakott palacsinta tejföllel" (savory layered-pancakes with sour cream) at Nagyi Palacsintázója (Granny's pancakery) on Batthyány tér, and enjoy its typically Hungarian flavours. Try the sweet versions as well if you have any space left. (I. Batthyány tér 5.)*

P.S.: Don't forget to check out the hidden and ever-changing kerts (garden pubs or courtyard pubs) of Pest if you visit us in the summer. Some names to watch out for are Szimpla Kert, Szóda Kert, Konzikert, Fészek Kert, Corvintető, Fecske, and Kuplung. If you are lucky, they will still be around. If they are not, new ones will have appeared. Not all of them are advertised, so just follow the crowds.

Best wishes, from your guiding light. www.privateguide.hu.

directly into alliance with Nazi Germany sat on this spot. This statue was blown up by Communist resistance fighters at the time of the German invasion. A tablet on the ground near the statue of Queen Elizabeth commemorates this.

Elizabeth Bridge (Erzsébet híd) 7N, 8A ••• The Erzsébet híd links Március 15 tér in Pest with Döbrentei tér in Buda. This suspension bridge was built in 1964 (designed by engineer Pál Sávoly) to replace the original bridge, which was also named in honour of Queen Elizabeth and was destroyed by the Germans in January 1945. The damage was more serious than it was for the other bridges, and reconstruction would have cost too much.

The two towers of the present bridge are joined by suspension cables, each consisting of a bundle of 61 separate cables. The vertical suspenders are not fastened to the cables, but kept in place by the weight of the bridge. The present bridge, built between 1960 and 1964, imitates the arch of the old one, which is

---

Váci utca, Southern Part, 5:10 p.m.

The autumn sun is just deleting the last trace of lettering from a makeshift note on the former Glass Statue Shop: "The Store is Closed for Reconstruction".

Former State Secretary for Culture Mr. I is leaving a boring, predictable conference at New City Hall. He feels disillusionment and ponders how one would say in Czech "once a state secretary, always a state secretary".

Vam Design owner Mr. V. is complaining again about the City Council authorities upstairs: no conspicuous sign allowed, no "designer" designer sign.

Mr. Flaschner, knife store owner is signing a letter to refuse a takeover bid for his shop. He is here to stay. An amorphous piece of plaster from the wall of the Church of Blessed Mary Virgin (popularly called the Church of the English Ladies) has just fallen and just missed the accountant of Fat Mo's Club, on the way to work. A 4-year old beginner reader is making a desperate attempt at deciphering the inscription on the wall of my former school: "Charles XII, king of Sweden, on the way to Turkey, had a rest on December 14, 1714, here".

You can hear rents rise by the minute.

No one can tell the good effects from the bad.

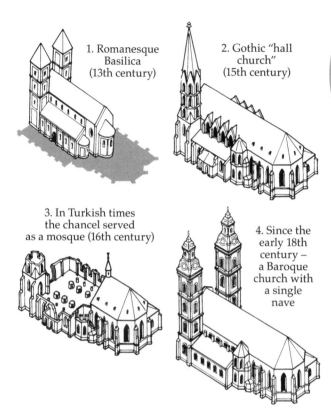

1. Romanesque Basilica (13th century)

2. Gothic "hall church" (15th century)

3. In Turkish times the chancel served as a mosque (16th century)

4. Since the early 18th century – a Baroque church with a single nave

Phases of Building the Inner City Parish Church

perhaps why residents of Budapest like it so much. The opening of the bridge was on the afternoon of November 21, 1964 and turned into an impromptu festival despite the drizzle. I went to see the new bridge with my piano teacher, who cancelled our lesson for the occasion. The new Erzsébet híd has virtually become the symbol of the capital, the first modern, yet beautiful, attraction of the city.

Inner City Parish Church (Belvárosi plébániatemplom) 8B
V. Március 15. tér ●●● Walking across the Erzsébet híd from Buda, it's hard to believe that there is a centaur-church behind the non-descript Baroque façade of the Inner City Parish Church, which from the waist has a Gothic chancel.

WALK ONE

8

This building has had a more eventful history than any other in Pest. Remains have been found here dating from the late-12th century, and each later century has left its mark on the building, which also served as a mosque in Turkish times. At the end of the 19th century, when the original Erzsébet híd was built, some city planners proposed to demolish the church since it was in the way of the new bridge. Until the 1930s it was surrounded by small shops.

Váci utca begins at Vörösmarty tér and stretches south to Vámház körút, which is where Szabadság híd (Liberty Bridge) is located. In the Middle Ages this was the entire length of Pest. The street essentially has two very different parts: the section to the north of Erzsébet híd and the section to the south of the bridge. The northern part is an over-crowded, commercial, naff, touristy pedestrian zone. The southern part

A Erzsébet híd

B Inner City Paris Church

C Piarist School

D Entrance to Haris köz

E Millennium Court

F Péterffy Palace

G Hotel Taverna (Mercure)

H Fontana Department Store

I Statue of Fisher Rézi, symbol of the fishermen's guild

J Statue of Mihály Vörösmarty, the romantic poet

K Vigadó Concert Hall

L Hotel Marriott

M A detour to southern Váci utca

WALK ONE

has also been pedestrianised some years ago and is fast losing its character. According to a local history monograph, once the two parts of the street resembled each other just as little as a famous over-adorned prima donna and her sober, humble, housewife sister. Nowadays, unfortunately, they are rather like two twin sisters, one trying to imitate the bad taste of the other. And maybe both of them are trying to imitate the style and manners of a cousin living in London or Paris.

By the end of the 18th century the street had already developed into a fashionable shopping street and was becoming richer and more handsome right up until World War One. Ten of the buildings still standing today used to witness mornings when the tenants were woken by the loud gossiping of maids waiting for the horse-drawn rubbish cart, and reliable "civil servants" in uniform caps (that is, porters) stood on the street corner all day waiting for customers. The shops were forever changing hands, as the landlords were continuously raising the rent.

Today, the same thing is done by the District Council: the idea behind the ever-increasing rent is that only quality shops should be located here. At the beginning of the 1970s, the steam-roller of modernisation hit the street and all shops were given uniform "modern" shop windows, regardless of the style of the buildings.

The southern part of Váci utca has still not fully adjusted to

"New" City Hall
in Váci utca 62–64.

the street's new role. There is a sort of Sleeping Beauty quality lin-
gering there. It is a pity that no visitors are allowed in the new City
Hall building at Váci utca 62–64. (See illustration on the former
page.)

Millennium Court 8E *V. Pesti Barnabás utca 4.* ••• Ringing
in the old and the new keeps us very busy in Budapest nowadays. This hotel follows the luxury hotel trend of offering
a home to people who do not wish to live in a hotel, but are
not willing to buy or rent a flat of their own. The design (József
Finta and Associates, 1997) preserves the original façade, which
is more than 100 years old, of the former Iron Court, which was
a mixed office and shopping complex. The Millennium Court
apartments, which are all unique, offer all amenities (even
washing-machines). Adjacent is one of the few remaining 18th
century secular buildings in Pest, which houses a restaurant
called Százéves ("100 Years Old"), though it has already passed
150 years of existence.

Haris köz 8D ••• At the beginning of the last century the owner
of a piece of land in the neighbourhood of Váci utca had the idea
to build a street on the site of his old arcade, then called "bazaar"
between Váci utca and Petőfi Sándor utca. Thus he could have
more profits from the lease of the apartment and the shops. So
as not to forfeit his ownership, law dictated that he had to close
his private street every year for one single day, thus flaunt his
ownership. The last time that happened was 1949, when the piece
of land was nationalised along with the street.

The Former Queue at the Adidas Shop *V. Váci utca 24.* ••• In
previous times, if there was a queue in Budapest it was either for
bananas in the winter or for a famous novelist autographing his/
her new book. The constant interest and long lines at this particular Adidas shop was due to its somewhat lower prices since the
wholesale firm acted as a retailer here. But why not open another
shop, and another and another, until there is no queue?

(I kept this entry from the first edition of this book in 1989. Since then,
of course, Adidas has opened another shop, interestingly enough, on
Váci út. But the queue remained here for almost a year, and then gradu-
ally disappeared. Nowadays in Budapest you can buy everything. The
forint became convertible, which seemed unbelievable at the time of
queues, since queues were obviously the consequence of non-convertible
money, and non-convertible money was the consequence of the Wall.
Can you follow me?)

Philanthia Flower Shop *V. Váci utca 9.* ••• This shop's art nouveau décor does not suit the classical façade of the building, but it has miraculously survived various hard times. The shop's name is Greek for "the love for flowers". It would be nice to praise the selection of flowers, to say it is special – but it is not. Maybe one day they'll get rid of the chandeliers. How could they subject the interior to them?

The Site of Vác Gate ••• The white line on the pavement on the corner of Váci utca and Türr István utca marks the site where the city's northern gate (Váci kapu) and its medieval city wall once stood. According to contemporary sources, there were "deadly bustles" around the gates. In 1789 it was quietly pulled down (and it had nothing to do with the events in France that year.)

This has been a long walk. If you do not want to go back to Gerbeaud, you can have coffee at **Anna presszó** (*V. Váci utca 7.*) or **Muskátli** (*V. Váci utca 11/a*). The latter was the haunt of young artists who wanted to save the world at the beginning of the 1960s, before the Hungarian beat movement. *(See the photo on page 19.)* They either do not come here any more or have become so conventional that you would not recognize them.

WALK ONE

"István Bethlen, Prime Minister, arrives to Parliament, 1925" in this carefully composed image by Martin Munkacsi (1896–1963), taken more than a decade before his spectacular American career began. The prime minister seems to be fully in charge, obviously untorn by the ongoing scandals and the terrible post-war inflation.

WALK TWO

THE CITY AND THE VÍZIVÁROS AREA

This walk takes us through Pest, passing behind the Parliament building. As the whole of the building can only be seen from a distance, we will cross over to Buda, visit a Turkish bath and walk under the chestnut trees lining the riverbank. We will also peek through some gates to look at the courtyards behind them.

Time: about 7.5 hours, including stops for refreshments.

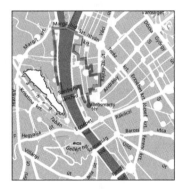

József nádor tér was one of Budapest's most attractive squares before the invention of the automobile. It is named for Archduke Joseph, the seventh son of the Habsburg Emperor Leopold, who was the governor or palatine (*nádor* in Hungarian) of Hungary for more than fifty years beginning in 1796. He showed great interest in city planning – his ambition was to create a city to live up to his standards. His statue is in the middle of the square. The original plan was that he should face the opposite direction because of the great construction work he helped so much, that of Leopold Town (Lipótváros).

A Romantic Building with a Story *V. József nádor tér 1.* •••
This Romantic-style building, which was originally a residential building (Hugó Máltás, 1859), was completely refurbished by the Postabank Corporation in the early 1990s. Postabank's eccentric founder, who was CEO for a decade, behaved like a modern Hungarian version of Andrew Carnegie. He had a spacious office on the top-floor which was built as an addition in 1922. The carefully furnished room included some rare and valuable Hungarian and foreign books and some excellent artwork.

To make up for the lack of a panoramic Castle view, there was a large photograph of the view that would have been seen from the room if the rest of the building were pulled down. There was a similar trick in the inner courtyard: a gigantic mural depicting the panorama of Váci utca as it would look if the adjacent building, which was Café Gerbeaud, were not there. The bank was sold to another in 2003, and the building has changed hands since. I wonder what happened to the interior.

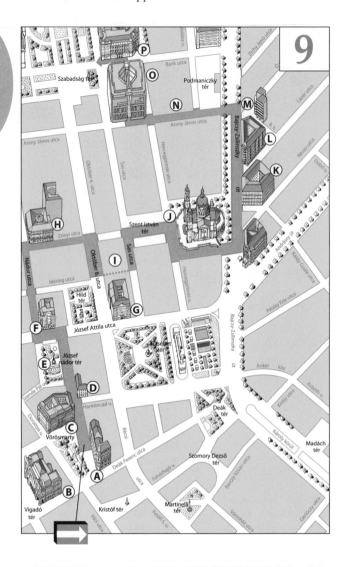

Gross House *V. József nádor tér 1.* ••• This typical neo-Classical apartment building (János Hild, 1824) housed the famous Blumenstöckl pub at the beginning of the 19th century. At the pub, guests could choose from three set meals. The most expensive was an all-you-can-eat meal for two forints. (That was a different forint, of course. The present one was introduced in 1946.) Anyone who told a bad joke or argued loudly had to put a fine into the money-box that had a Saracen head.

Central European University (CEU) (Közép Európai Egyetem) 9H *V. Nádor utca 9.,* www.ceu.hu. ••• This neo-Classical masterpiece was completed by Mihály Pollack in 1826 for Count Antal Festetics. The street was then called Tiger Street. Pollack (1773–1855) designed at least 186 buildings, among them the National Museum. You can walk through the circular entrance hall unhindered (at least as far as the receptionist) which is enough to see the 1990s extension that is much bigger than the original, and yet is invisible from the outside. Students do not live in this building, but five kilometres away. CEU is slowly taking over the whole block. Deep inside the complex, there is a huge library which was converted from a garage.

Budapest-born philanthropist George Soros spent his adolescent years in hiding in his home town, helping his father save Jewish lives. He emigrated to Britain in 1947 at the age of 17 and was going to become a scholar and a philosopher. He was a follower of Karl Popper, whose ideas about the "open society" proved to be formative and decisive for Soros. In 1956 he moved to the United States. He was over forty when he found his real vocation as an "alchemist": a prime mover in long-term monetary markets. A passion for "opening up" Central European societies

WALK TWO

A Elegant Shops		**J** St. Stephen's Church, the "Basilica"
B Vigadó Concert Hall		
C Gerbeaud		**K** Bajcsy-Zsilinszky út 17.
D Bank building		**L** Bajcsy-Zsilinszky út 19/a
E Statue of József nádor, Habsburg Palatine		**M** Bajcsy-Zsilinszky út 19/c
F József Attila utca 16.		**N** Open Society Archives, Fruccola Salad Bar
G Derra House		**O** Bank Centre office block
H CEU Building		**P** Hungarian National Bank
I Október 6. utca 3.		

and democratizing them began to obsess him in the early 1980s. In 1984 he set up his foundation in Budapest, which was followed by many more in other countries in Central and Eastern Europe, and even in Central America. This university is said to be the largest single long-term charitable commitment of his anywhere in the world. He hopes it will play a pivotal role in educating the future elites of the region. Soros himself, now over eighty (though he looks considerably younger), often comes to attend the university's events. The meetings are held on the first floor above the circular entrance hall, which holds the statues that represent the four seasons. Soros still speaks impeccable Hungarian.

"Piranesi House" – The Favourite Building of this Book's Illustrator *V. Zrínyi utca 14.* ••• This building was converted to its present form in 1879. It is heavy, bombastic, but still somehow majestic even though it blocks the light, takes up a lot of space, and attempts to impress with its fireworks of forms and shapes (which is enough material for an architecture student to fill two sketchbooks with). It has been illustrator András Felvidéki's inspiration for several of his works. It reminds him of Piranesi, the great 18th century artist who portrayed Rome in hundreds of etchings. (The Museum of Fine Arts has a huge collection of original Piranesi prints.)

Október 6. utca 3. 9I ••• This house with the passageway was built between 1844 and 1845 and has recently been restored. If you include the two small spiral ones hidden at the sides, it has four staircases. The statue in the garden honours Béla Czóbel (1883–1976), who was a great post-impressionist painter who once lived in the building and had an atelier that overlooked the inner courtyard. During the daytime the building's gate is open, unlike the other ones which are carefully closed since they are private property. It reminds one of the Budapest of the 1970s, when all Budapest buildings were accessible. True, the crime rate was much lower then, which was a good side-effect of totalitarianism.

Budapest Cathedral: The "Basilica" 9J ••• Located on *Szent István tér*, St. Stephen's is the largest church in the city. It can hold 8,500 people and has a 96 metre-high dome. The name, however, may be misleading since strictly speaking, basilica means a church of a totally different shape (it technically is a "basilica minor"). Until 1993 there was no bishop seated here, but when the Archbishop of Esztergom became the Archbishop of Esztergom and Budapest, the church could properly be called a cathedral.

Bajcsy-Zsilinszky út

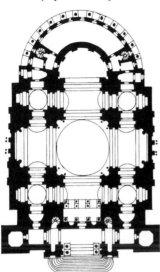

Alpári Gyula utca

**St. Stephen's Church,
the "Basilica"**

It took so long to build the church that people used to say: "I'll settle up when the basilica is finished". Work on the building began in 1851 when Pest was still a small town. The architect, József Hild, died in 1867, and was succeeded by Miklós Ybl, who later designed the Opera House. On examining what he had inherited, Ybl was astonished to find cracks in the walls. He had a fence built around the half-completed church and had watchmen guard it. Eight days later, at 3 a. m. on January 22, 1868, the dome collapsed. You can imagine how empty the streets were back then, since a baker's apprentice was the only eyewitness to the disaster. He gave an eloquent account of what he had seen to the newspaper reporters: "*I can see small clumps of stone starting to roll down from the top of the dome. As they are falling slowly downwards, tumbling in the air, a kind of groan-like sigh permeates the air, and the whole dome begins to tilt. First in absolute silence, then with a horrible roar.*" More than 300 windows were broken in the area. Inferior building materials were blamed.

Ybl drew up new plans and work started again, almost from scratch. But he did not live to see the church finished and decorated, since he died in 1891. In 1906 the internal decoration was finished by József Kauser. Emperor Franz Joseph spoke at the inauguration ceremony and, it was rumoured, cast suspicious glances at the dome, which is 22 metres in diameter. For many years the general opinion was that the Basilica was too gloomy. Since a complete, and wonderfully done, renovation was completed in 2003, many in Budapest have changed their minds.

Behind the main altar stands a statue of St. Stephen, King of Hungary, by Alajos Stróbl. St. Stephen (1000–1038) is the patron saint of the church and there is another statue of him above the main entrance. The mosaics were designed by Hungarian painters and made in Venice by Salviati e Jesorum. The neo-Renaissance ground plan is in the form of a Greek cross. The façade facing busy Bajcsy-Zsilinszky út is not the main one, rather the main one is on Szent István tér on the opposite side.

The basilica is a rare example in city planning since during the time it took to build it, the city's structure changed. When the second plan was made after Hild died, a "second façade" was already needed. Ybl cleverly solved this problem by enriching the walls outside the chancel with an elegant Ionic colonnade and statues of the twelve apostles.

The Holy Dexter (Szent Jobb), which is the right hand of St. Stephen, is the most revered relic of the Hungarian Catholic Church. There is a gap in the story of the relic, between the death of the king in 1038 and the first time the relic appeared in 1090, but it is a relatively short one. Empress Maria Theresa received it as a forced gift from the Dominican monks of Raguza (now Dubrovnik) in 1771 in return for some defense against the threat of the Russian fleet of Admiral Orloff. The relic was then brought to Vienna, where the archbishop, the court librarian and the great historian of the day, György Pray, were asked to declare whether it was authentic or not. They decided it was, especially since Pray found a small piece of old parchment with the following Latin words: Dextera beati Stephani regis et confessoris gloriosi. It can be visited in a chapel to the left of the main altar. Drop a coin in the slot, and the relic lights up (if not, the guard gives the case a knock, and behold, it lights up). Every year on August 20, a national holiday celebrating the feast day of St. Stephen, the relic leaves the cathedral to be paraded in a traditional procession.

Under the church there is a large cellar where many important city documents and some valuable art treasures survived the last war. The windows of the church overlook Bajcsy-Zsilinszky út. In the second half of the 1960s some unknown student elements painted LENIN, MAO, CHE on the windows with large letters. Since they did not have spray cans then, they must have had to carry buckets of paint to the spot. Before the completion of the recent renovation, you could still decipher the fading graffiti on the wall. (After reading these lines, a friend of mine, who is a well-known scholar and critic, called me and claimed responsibility.)

The chancel is also worth looking at from the other side of the road, for example from the café on the other side of Bajcsy-Zsilinszky út at the corner of Révay köz. These few metres do make a difference. Or you can look at the basilica again from an unusual angle, while sitting comfortably on the terrace of the small café on the corner of Lázár utca, which often changes owners and names. To read why it is an absolute must to go up to the dome, *turn to page 46.* Check the website, www.basilica.hu, to see some photos of the collapsed dome.

A Nice Block of Flats 9K – M *V. Bajcsy-Zsilinszky út 19/a, 19/b, 19/c.* ••• In the 1930s modern architecture made a breakthrough in Hungary (for the second time) and the city underwent a construction boom. The aim was to achieve the optimal use of space while creating healthy, cleverly arranged flats. This block is an example of how well this style could be integrated into its surroundings, which were 50 or 100 years older (Jenő Schmitterer, 1940). All three gateways hold their own surprises. The 19/a building has lead glass windows on the ground floor and interesting lamps on the capitals of the columns. The gateway of 19/b has pleasant proportions, and on the ceiling behind the entrance the present tenants have managed to solve the problem of "squaring the circle" (a Hungarian catchphrase: doing something apparently impossible): they added a square-shaped ordinary lamp to the circular design. The third building is the one currently in the best state. It has the best preserved lighting fixtures, and even the mosaic glass has survived, redolent of the atmosphere of the old times. All of the tranquility and elegance of this style is summarized in the stone giant resting on the edge of the roof of the 19/b block. It can only be seen from a distance, so do not forget to look back.

Podmaniczky tér was once occupied by houses, but they were destroyed during the war. The square holds the Arany János utca metro station (M3), and is becoming a new gateway to the city. At the request of the Budapest City Preservation Society, it was named after Baron Frigyes Podmaniczky (1824–1907), who was a leading figure in city planning during the second part of the 19th century. His nickname was "the Chequered Baron", since he loved chequered suits. He loved Budapest so much that he allegedly never left the city, not even for a summer holiday. When he was very old, once he appeared at the city council meeting, and cast a vote – forgetful of the fact that he had retired long ago. Nobody dared to remind him of the fact, but his vote was disregarded.

The Most Complex Public Landmark Ever – a Bench and a Clock ••• In the middle of Podmaniczky tér, Baron Frigyes Podmaniczky, the doughty 19th century campaigner for new urban projects, holds the statue of Pallas Athene which has become the symbol of Budapest's conservationists. The original, life-sized version of this Athene statue (now in a museum) has a lance in

WALK TWO

her hand. This missing lance refers to the subtitle of a television programme anchored by the maverick Mihály Ráday, president of the Budapest City Preservation Society: "Our Grandchildren Will Not See It, OR THE LANCE IS SOMETIMES STOLEN FROM THE HAND OF PALLAS ATHENE". I told you it was a complex landmark. *See also Mihály Ráday's "Budapest Bests" on page 60.* (Pál Kő, sculptor, 1990)

A Complex Landmark in the Underground – a Bench and a Poem "Upon my soul / More Desire / I don't have Just / I wish I had / a Bench / Down / at the Metro Station / Named after / János Arany." This poem is written on a clumsily designed brass plaque over the copy of a late-19th century bench in the Arany János utca metro station. It is named for János Arany (1817–1882), the great 19th-century epic and lyric poet, critic, moral authority, secretary of the Hungarian Academy of Sciences and Letters, etc. The plaque cites a poem, Hiúság ("vanity"), by Sándor Kányádi (born 1929), which was written in 1983. In the poem he tells his son that his greatest ambition is to have a bench at the metro station named after János Arany. This bench was unveiled by the city on May 14, 2003 on the poet's 74th birthday. It was proposed by some retired literature teachers who love poetry.

Open Society Archives (OSA) 9N *V. Arany János utca 32.,* www.osaarchivum.org ••• One of the most prominent private academic institutions is partly an archive, partly an exhibition space – basically it serves to maintain the proper historical memory of Hungarian society. One of the means to this is its incredibly complex website, which is continuously being further developed. It is a great example of the democratisation of knowledge. Despite that, it is worth visiting the building. On the facade a large sign says: "Goldberger". The pre-modern building was erected for the staff of the company called Goldberger Samuel and Sons (Dávid Jónás, Zsigmond Jónás, 1911.) The central space of the building is called Galeria Centralis. It aspires to show things that have hitherto seemed impossible to present in a sensual and physical form.

Fruccola 9N *V. Arany János utca 32.,* www.fruccola.hu ••• To the left of the archive's entrance there is a high-class, very original salad and sandwich bar (open 7 a.m. to 7 p.m. every weekday). It has a nice website (only in Hungarian) that gives its mission statement (unusual for a salad bars): "Our mission is to prepare the yummiest juices in the region, to win prizes, and to become famous in order to get a banana-shaped yacht painted yellow to live on. And we would have a great time!" It is not a weird place for nerds and bluestockings, not at all. It provides the best serious magazines in town, from *The New Yorker* to *A10* and *Monocle*.

Bank Centre 10A ••• This office building is located between Bank utca, Sas utca, Arany János utca, and Hercegprímás utca. When the architect, József Finta, showed me around, he said that it was the first building for which he'd been allowed by the developer to choose the quality of materials that he wanted. Finta argues that the city should grow upwards by two or three floors in this area. The glass-walled higher levels are deceptive: this is a bigger building than it appears. You can walk through the building, which also has some fine shops and the finest wheelchair lift in Central Europe in the lobby. The cafeteria/restaurant in the basement is an affordable and nice place for a rest. The restaurant only serves lunch on weekdays, but the building is open all day, until late in the evening.

Hungarian National Bank (Magyar Nemzeti Bank) 10B
V. Szabadság tér 8–9., www.mnb.hu ••• The stately bulk of the National Bank (Ignác Alpár, 1905), which was originally the Austro–Hungarian Bank, shows how eclecticism was already lightening up under the influence of art nouveau. Between the first-floor windows a fine relief shows people working, from peasants to mint workers to a tycoon signing a cheque. On the southwest corner, towards the square, you can see Hamlet pondering whether to be or not to be, actually holding the skull of "poor Yorick". The bank's president is elected by Parliament for a term of six years, which is to avoid immediate replacement after changes in the government. Some analysts say that the term should be made similar to that of the president of the National Audit Office (Számvevőszék), which is 12 years. The inside of the building cannot be visited, except during the European Heritage Days (the third weekend in September). But the visitor's centre can be visited free of charge daily from 9 a.m. to 4 p.m. (until 6 p.m. on Thursdays, groups more than 10 should register in advance.) It's partly a museum and partly an interactive educational centre with a cinema and a playhouse. You can watch a detailed film on the interior and exterior of the bank, and you can print out a banknote with your own portrait on it.

A Statue to Think About ••• In front of the Bank Centre, towards the National Bank on Szabadság tér, there is an abstract statue by Ádám Farkas, professor and former dean at the Academy of

Fine Arts. The statue is in three parts. If you come from the direction of Hold utca, it obviously forms a lion, but only from this direction.

I asked the sculptor if this was intentional. He said, with a characteristically cunning smile: "*Yes and no.*" He is the president of the Japanese–Hungarian Artists' Club. Maybe he was elected because of his calm, cunning smile. Or maybe he acquired it during his visits to Japan.

Szabadság tér (Liberty Square) is one of Budapest's hidden treasures. It does not sit on any major streets or boulevards, you just come across it, as if by chance. It has been especially charming since the enormous underground garage was completed in 2003, and cars were forced to park underneath. The explanation for this unusual city development is a former Austrian barracks here called the "Neugebäude" or "New Building", which was built in 1786. The barracks covered the entire area bounded by the present Hold utca, Báthory utca, Nádor utca and Bank utca. The intention was to build the barracks far from the city of Pest, on the barren land to the north. Nobody expected the city to grow this far, even in hundreds of years. But it did, within decades. Demolition of the barracks started in 1897 and the square and neighbouring streets were built as a homogenous unit in its place. Today there is a pleasant park in the square which is surrounded by banks, office buildings and the American Embassy. The above ground garage entrance is a pavilion that includes a nice café, which is a welcome addition to the social climate of the City (in the London sense of the word).

A rest

Café Farger
V. Zoltán utca 18., corner Szabadság tér

Statue of General Bandholtz 10C ••• In Szabadság tér, near the embassy, there is a statue of a stocky man theatrically standing on a pedestal. He is the American General Harry Hill Bandholtz who, as an officer of the Entente force in 1919, saved the treasures of the National Museum by "sealing" the doors with the only thing he could find: paper customs seals. These bore the coat of arms of the United States and they kept Romanian soldiers, apparently few of whom spoke English, from looting the building.

American Embassy 10E *V. Szabadság tér 12.* ••• Among the eclectic palaces surrounding Szabadság tér, the art nouveau American Embassy stands out. Cardinal Mindszenty spent the years from November 4, 1956 to September 28, 1971 in this building. Mindszenty had been imprisoned and tortured in the 1950s (needless to say, under false charges). In 1956 he was freed, but the invasion of Hungary prevented him from leaving for the

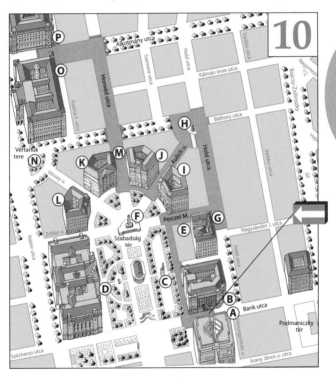

A Bank Centre office block	**G** Post Office Savings Bank		
B Hungarian National Bank	**H** Batthyány Eternal Flame		
	I J K L Office blocks		
C Statue of General Bandholtz	**M** Honvéd utca		
D Former Stock Exchange, later Public Television	**N** Statue of Imre Nagy		
	O Ministry of Agriculture		
E American Embassy	**P** Ethnographical Museum		
F Soviet War Memorial			

West. The ambassador let him use his own third floor office and in 1971 he was forced to leave Hungary. He was an obstacle to the reconciliation between the Vatican and Hungary, a controversial one especially from the former side.

Post Office Savings Bank (Postatakarék) **10G** *V. Hold utca 4.* ••• *"Hungarian style has no past but it does have a future"*, said Ödön Lechner (1845–1914), one of the most influential architects of Hungarian art nouveau. When he finished this building in 1901, it received a warm welcome from his contemporaries who admired the simplicity of its handling of space and its use of Hungarian folk ornamentation. The beautiful plainness of the main walls gives no indication of how restlessly alive the building is inside and at the roof level. The building's greatest attraction is undoubtedly its roof of green, yellow, blue and brown hexagonal tiles, hidden behind the yellow majolica waves that crown the top of the main walls. The roof is full of flowers familiar from folk embroidery, angel-wings, Turkish turbans and scary dragon tails. This, however, can only be inspected from farther away. A disciple of the architect once asked him: "But tell me, master, why did you build a roof so ornamented, as no one will ever see it from street level?" Lechner answered: "the birds will." When Lechner died, all unionised building workers stopped work for five minutes.

Batthyány Eternal Flame (Batthyány-örökmécses) **10H** ••• On October 6, 1849, shortly after the suppression of the Hungarian insurrection against Habsburg rule, thirteen Hungarian generals were executed and the prime minister of the Revolutionary Government, Count Lajos Batthyány, was shot and killed on this site, which (as we saw above), was then the army barracks. Batthyány is commemorated by a permanent flame inside a red cup (Móric Pogány, 1926). Some years ago people living nearby were shocked to see that the flame – at the crossing of Báthory utca, Aulich utca and Hold utca – had gone out. They wrote indignant letters to a newspaper, and the permanent flame was quietly relit. In the dying years of the Communist régime, the police used force to break up several demonstrations here.

Café Szabadság **10H** *V. Aulich utca 8.*, www.szabadsagkavehaz.hu ••• This café of historical importance reopened late in 2008. Almost all of the original space was reclaimed, and someday maybe the missing section will be returned from the adjacent bank. They capitalize on the fact that Endre Ady (1878–1919), the iconoclastic, larger-than-life poet used to come here. It was not his favourite café, but he definitely wrote an important and mysterious poem here: *"Struggle with the Pig-Headed Warlord"* (1906). That's why in the rear you can spot the lifesized poet scribbling something, probably this very poem, at a table. The exorbitant sum the owner poured into this project may never come back. Unfortunately, the laudable zeal in resurrecting this café did not come with good taste (note the kitschy, pseudo-authentic paintings created yesterday, the chandeliers and the massive, marble and granite-clad toilets). Don't miss the upstairs, where you can smoke and see an untouched part of the ceiling. It's a great hiding spot for secret lovers.

Bedő House – Museum of Hungarian Art Nouveau 10M
V. Honvéd utca 3., www.magyarszecessziohaza.hu, open Monday to Saturday 10 a.m. to 5 p.m. ••• The year 2000 was a great year for Budapest's art nouveau fans. The renovation of their favourite building (Emil Vidor, 1903), which is one of the best kept secrets of the Lipótváros (Leopold Town) neighbourhood was completed. Inside there are fine details; stained glass windows in almost every apartment; nice, green doorframes; and brass peepholes on the front doors. The family of the one-time owner of the building still lives on the first floor. Tivadar Vad, a building contractor who had worked on the opposite bank and did a great job, was asked if he was interested in renovating this one as well. He was, in return for the ownership of the loft space. How could he have avoided a task like this since he was a lover and collector of Hungarian art nouveau? He rented, then bought the ground-floor shop space, which had been spoiled by a series of brutal and unprofessional alterations. He renovated it, had the portal reconstructed on the basis of a single photograph, and filled it with his own collection of furniture, textiles and glass. He created a three-level café and collection, which is practically a museum, even though it lacks detailed signs, and a catalogue.

The author works in that block, in a loft space – isn't he lucky?

This part of the fifth district, called Lipótváros (named for Leopold II, Emperor of Austria, king of Hungary) swarms with people during the day, but is almost completely dead in the evenings. Its main street, the broad, elegant Alkotmány utca, does not really lead anywhere and so has little traffic. But this is the route taken by all important guests when visiting the Parliament.

The Statue of Imre Nagy 10N ••• Imre Nagy (1896–1958) was a communist all of his life and allegedly had a dark career in the Soviet secret police in the 1930s. During the 1950s he was made prime minister in the very relative thaw in 1953. He was demoted

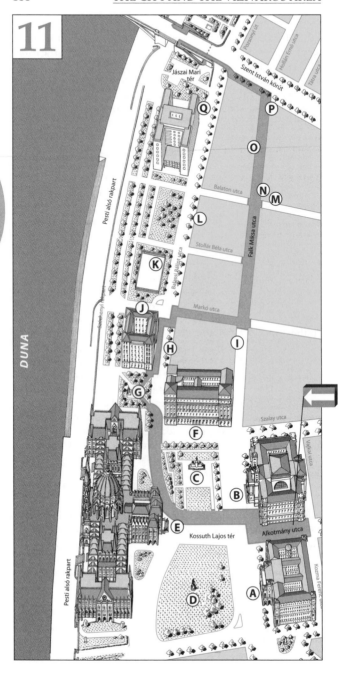

in 1955, and then during the 1956 revolution he was made prime minister again. But he was so used to greeting people as "comrades", that he also did so when talking to the revolutionary demonstrators here in Vértanúk tere (Martyrs' square), who did not really like it.

He became a symbol of freedom when he was forced into exile in Romania, but was tried and executed in Hungary in 1958. During his trial he could probably have saved his life had he cooperated with the new régime, but he did not revise his opinions. He had become first and foremost a lover of liberty and independence, though he still considered himself a communist. He was buried face down in an unmarked grave, which was later found only with great difficulty. His name was simply not mentionable in public between 1958 and 1988 and his reburial in July 1989 marked the birth of a new democracy. Tens of thousands came to Heroes' Square, where two de-constructivist artists, Gábor Bachman and László Rajk, dressed up the Műcsarnok Exhibition Hall in black draperies. Imre Nagy is buried now in Plot 301 of Új Köztemető Cemetery, under the magnificent monument designed by György Jovánovics (see page 284).

This statue (Tamás Varga, 1996) on Vértanúk tere (on the corners of Nádor, Vécsey and Báthory utca) was erected on the centenary of Nagy's birth and was given little praise when unveiled. Critics found the symbolism – a bridge – cheap, as it represents a transition from totalitarian notions towards democratic ones. And everyone found the figure idealizing to the point of falsification. The martyr prime minister was a typical, stocky, overweight Hungarian peasant type, quite unlike this melancholic, café-type portrayed in the statue, who is looking vaguely in the direction of the Houses of Parliament.

WALK TWO

A	Ministry of Agriculture	**J**	Residental block
B	Ethnographical Museum	**K**	Playground
C	Statue of Lajos Kossuth	**L**	Cirko-Gejzír Art Cinema
D	Statue of Ferenc Rákóczi II	**M**	Nagyházi Gallery
		N	Wladis Goldsmiths
E	Houses of Parliament	**O**	Virág Judit Gallery
F	Kossuth Lajos tér 13–15.	**P**	Kieselbach Gallery
G	Statue of Mihály Károlyi	**Q**	The White House, office block of Parliament
H	Szalay Confectioner's		
I	Pintér Antik		

Houses of Parliament (Országház) 11E *V. Kossuth Lajos tér,* www.mkogy.hu/guide, free admission for European Union citizens. ••• It's "a Turkish bath crossed with a Gothic chapel," scoffed Gyula Illyés, a great 20th century poet, referring to the Parliament building. Work on the Parliament started in 1885 and an average of 1,000 people per year worked on it for 17 years. Its designer, Imre Steindl (1839–1902), started as an apprentice stone carver, but went on to study architecture in Vienna and Budapest. He was 44 years-old when this work started. By the time it neared completion he was so ill that he could direct the work only from a chair carried to the spot. He died just a few weeks before the building was completed.

The building is 268 metres-long, 118 metres-wide, and has a spire that reaches 96 metres above the ground. There are 691 rooms and the length of all of the stairs put together is about 20 kilometres. The building's structure is readily apparent, especially if seen from across the river. On either side of the central hall under the dome, the council chambers of what were formerly the Commons and the Upper House are situated. "I did not want to establish a new style with the new Parliament because I could not build a monumental building of this kind, one that would be used for centuries, with ephemeral details. My desire was to combine this splendid medieval style with national and personal features, humbly and carefully as is required by art," the architect declared in his inaugural address at the Hungarian Academy of Sciences. He must have meant Gothic when speaking of "style", even though the ground plan of the building shows Renaissance features and the way space is organized inside is very often Baroque in character. It is thus a summary of Hungarian eclecticism.

The novelist Kálmán Mikszáth attended the first session in the building as a minister of parliament (MP) and summarized his impressions by declaring: "Dazzling, true, but still gaudy." The writer said this about the inside of the building, since the outside was covered with white, Hungarian limestone. As it turned out, the stone was not hard enough. Renovations of the façade began in 1925 and are still in progress. Since the first edition of this book, much has happened to this building. The red star (which was obviously not part of the original design) has, of course, been removed from the spire. But more importantly, since 1990 there is real work being done inside – Italian-style politicking. As there is only one chamber (there's no upper house), one of the two large halls is rarely used. Since five percent of the popular vote is required to secure seats on the party list under the Hungarian electoral system, it is unlikely that there will be more than four or five parties in the House. (This system

1. Munkácsi Hall
2. Assembly Hall (original Lower House)
3. South Lounge
4. Office of the Prime Minister
5. Cupola Hall
6. Office of the Speaker of the House
7. North Lounge
8. Former Upper House (used for conferences)
9. Hunter Hall

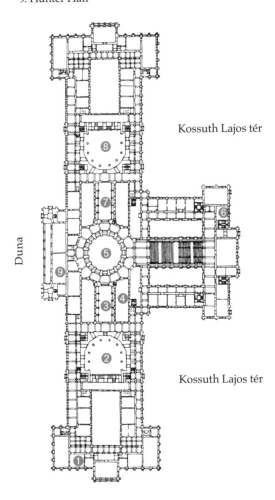

Kossuth Lajos tér

Duna

Kossuth Lajos tér

The Houses of Parliament

was copied from Germany, along with the "constructive no-confidence vote" that assures a stable government.)

THE HOLY CROWN

On January 1, 2000, which marked the 1000th anniversary of the establishment of the independent state of Hungary, the Holy Crown of Hungary and most of the regalia (the scepter, the sword, and the orb) were removed from the National Museum and solemnly transferred to a glass case under the Parliament's dome. This was much criticized by those who thought the crown already had a very good place in the National Museum, but was supported by the voters of the heritage-ticket government.

The crown has had a particularly spectacular history, having been lost, stolen or misappropriated at various times in history. Although it was made in the early Middle Ages, the crown probably has nothing to do with the actual one that was placed on the head of King Stephen, the founder of the Hungarian state, in 1000. The last Hungarian king crowned with it was the Habsburg Charles VI (who was Charles IV as a Hungarian king) in 1916. After World War Two the crown was taken out of the country by fleeing Hungarian fascists. It was held in the United States for decades until President Carter decided to return it to Hungary in 1978. Secretary of State Cyrus Vance, escorted by a large American delegation, brought it back to Budapest.

LIFE IN THE PARLIAMENT BUILDING

Life is quite busy in the House and the whole building, except for January, July and August. You can get an idea of how busy the day will be by looking at Kossuth tér, where only MPs can park. Parliament is the workplace not only of the 386 representatives (half are elected in their constituencies, and the other half are appointed by their party; citizens cast two votes at the general elections, for a person and for a party) but also of the prime minister. The tone of the skirmishes here is reminiscent of the British Parliament. Opposition leaders often disrupt the work of the House with their belligerent "before the agenda" speeches on Monday afternoons. MPs often read newspapers, talk on mobile phones, and even nap (which is always recorded by the press). Hungarian citizens don't really understand how Parliament operates. When TV news programmes show House debates with few MPs attending, they think the others are remiss in their duties, though they may be in committee meetings where the bulk of the work gets done. Also, polls show that voters hate debates. They think "good Hungarians should agree with each other".

There are guided tours of Parliament, but only in groups and only when there is no plenary session. Groups form at Gate X, which is the first gate to the right of the main entrance with the lions.

Ethnographical Museum (Néprajzi Múzeum) 11B *V. Kossuth Lajos tér 12.*, www.neprajz.hu, open Tuesday to Sunday 10 a.m. to 6 p.m. ••• With a strong resemblance to the less-elegant Reichstag in Berlin, this 125 meter-long neo-Renaissance palace was built to house the Supreme Court and the Chief

WALK TWO

Szalay utca

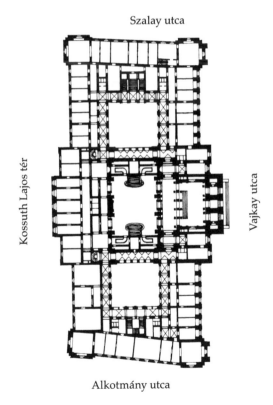

Kossuth Lajos tér

Vajkay utca

Alkotmány utca

Ethnographical Museum, Formerly the Supreme Court

Public Prosecutor's Office (Alajos Hauszmann, 1893–1896). But building another dome opposite the Parliament seemed out of the question. Of the many statues on the building, the most interesting is probably the three-horse-driven Roman chariot, called "triga", by Károly Senyei. It was hammered from three millimeter-thick copper panes, after a model one third of the size. In the middle of the tympanum (the triangular space on top of the columns) there is an imagined scene called "Court Procedure", with the judge in the centre.

WALK TWO

From the ticket office, you enter an astoundingly large and richly decorated hall where it is well worth looking around, as well as up at the ceiling. At the back, there are some chairs around a large table where you can sit down. From here you can admire the first floor ceiling, the large painted windows and the splendour of the staircase. The ceiling fresco shows Justitia, the goddess of justice, sitting on her throne among the clouds. The allegorical groups beside her represent justice and peace on the right, and sin and revenge on the left. Károly Lotz worked on this fresco for ten months. The museum is a pleasant place, which has recently attracted attention for its daring, unusual exhibitions, such as presenting an ironic history of the pastoral image of Hungary which has been propagated since 1896. In 2001 it hosted an exhibition on time, called "Images of Time", where even office corridor space was used to hold the part of the show portraying museums as sorts of time machines. Another exhibition that attracted many visitors and earned the praise of museum professionals was entitled "Plastic" and explored how generations of Hungarians used this modern material in their homes. It was accompanied by smaller exhibitions on LPs and other plastic objects.

Tympanum

Kossuth Lajos tér ••• There are four traditional statues in Kossuth Lajos tér: Kossuth and Rákóczi in front of the Parliament and Attila József and Mihály Károlyi near the river on either side of the Parliament (see "Who was Who", page 75–80). Kossuth tér is also a receptacle for every conceivable kind of

miscellaneous plaque and monument: the good, the amateur-
ish and the naff. The otherwise strict rules that authorise the
erection of public monuments were not enforced around the
time of the government changes between 1989 and 1992. There
is a black granite slab with an eternal flame in memory of the
1956 Revolution. There are about a hundred larger than life size
rifle bullets in the wall of the Ministry of Agriculture (opposite Parliament) commemorating the tragic and mysterious shots
that were fired on the peaceful crowd demonstrating here on
October 25, 1956.

The most visited monument nearby is called "Shoes" (on
the Danube Promenade), a memorial at the Danube to the
victims of the Holocaust. It is on edge of the embankment
south of the Parliament building. *(See details on page 292.)*

An Elegant Apartment Building 11F *V. Kossuth Lajos tér
13–15.* ••• This site was long-vacant until the city authorities gave the permission for a building to be built, but with
dozens of restrictions. All the building's measurements, even the
number of windows, were prescribed to preserve the square's
unity. The building (Béla Málnai, 1929) is a rare mix of tradition
and innovation: neo-Baroque façade and modernist interior. The
favoured style of the period's ruling elite was the neo-Baroque.
(Historian Gyula Szekfü ironically described the interwar years
with the term "neo-Baroque society".)

Szalay Confectioner's (Szalay Cukrászda) 11H *V. Balassi Bálint
utca 7.* ••• Even during the time of catch-all nationalization
after World War Two, some confectioners remained in private
hands. They earned legendary reputations, even though all
that their proprietors did was carry on as masters of the old-
school, wholeheartedly filling pastries with custard and churn-
ing the ice cream. "He spares no time, ingredient and energy,"
the older generation remarked of these private confectioners,
who once knew their customers personally. There was little
staff turnover, and in most cases, relatives took over if there
was a vacancy. The shop fittings also remained the same, and
today they look movingly obsolete in spite of efforts to mod-
ernize them. You would not suspect that this strict, tall, bald
man, Mr. Szalay, is a living legend. Perhaps the legend is not
really about him, but about his cakes. Until 1949 he had a bigger,
more elegant shop nearby (*V. Szent István körút 7.*), which is now
called Európa Café. The family could not repurchase the place
from the state in the early 1990s, though they wanted to. So they
stayed in the present shop which has been in operation since the
early 1950s.

WALK TWO

At the launch of the Hungarian edition of this book, which was on the 125th anniversary of the birth of modern Budapest, I was given a surprise gift from all three generations of the Szalay family. It was a large cake with the key to the city on top, and it was the only present that I have ever accepted from a business featured in this book.

A rest
Culinaris Shop and Bistro
V. Balassi Bálint utca 7.

WALK TWO

A Playground 11K ••• This playground between Balassi Bálint utca and the river is in another world from those in the grim 1950s when playgrounds only held three things: swings, see-saws and sandpits. Swings were always painted red and parents constantly argued with their kids about fastening their safety chain and not standing up on them. The see-saws provided opportunities for socialising. You could "send your partner on a summer holiday" (which meant keeping him in the air for a long time), or you could let him down fast to "make him jump". But the real area for socialising was the sandpit. Unfortunately, the old park-keeper (which was common in all Budapest parks in those days) would not allow us to bring water in the sandpits. "Watering again, are you!" he used to shout, waving his stick with the nail at one end for collecting dry leaves and litter. At that time there was much less for kids to do, and there wasn't a single slide in town. Nowadays, Budapest is being converted into a city of playgrounds. The best ones are fenced off and closed at dusk.

Falk Miksa utca Antique Row ••• Miksa Falk (1828–1908) was a journalist and politician who taught Queen Elizabeth, wife of Franz Joseph I, Hungarian language and literature. The street was first named after him in 1910. However, in 1943 his name was not good enough any more and the name of a recently deceased supreme court chief justice took the upper-hand. Two years later, Falk gloriously returned, but only until 1953 when he left again and the name "People's Army" arrived on street signs.

Falk's name returned in 1990 when several hundred old names were restored. Also that year the rather severe rule was passed that no street could be named after someone who had died less than 25 years earlier. (When Ferenc Puskás, the great soccer player died in 2006, this rule was softened and honorary citizens of Budapest are now exempted.)

The old-new name easily stuck because in the early 1990s antique shops began to proliferate on the street. Originally there was only one: the large and naff state-owned shop called BÁV, which used the Venus de Milo as its trademark, and sits on the corner of the Nagykörút. In the mid-1990s the shop was given a tasteless facelift and since then no decent local or expat is likely to shop there. The excessive use of brass rails is an obsession with some nouveau riche businesses owners. Maybe because brass resembles gold? But before you get to the anticlimactic end of the street, it is worth visiting the four key players on the scene, whose listings follow, though the others are interesting too. Opening hours are quite standard here, 10 a.m. to 6 p.m. on weekdays, and until 1 p.m. on Saturdays.

Pintér Antik 11I *V. Falk Miksa utca 10.*, www.pinter-antik.hu ••• This shop is a revelation for the uninitiated. The two modest windows hide an 1,800 square-metre labyrinth holding a universe of treasures. Pick up one of the shop's postcards featuring its amazing ground plan when you enter. Péter Pintér is a mid-career dealer who began selling antiques in the early 1990s in a similarly large space in a no-name area along the Outer Boulevard. His clients were loyal and followed him to his next and bigger Józsefváros shop, and then to this final shop, which is one of Budapest's finest. The variety here is tempting for people from various walks of life – for its style, quality and state-of-repair. The varied space has been restored with an imaginative vein. For instance, there is a small circular café space with a new floral painted ceiling, there are parts paved with cobblestones, and there is a central spot with a classic street sign that says "Pin tér" ("Pin Square"), which is a pun on the owner's name. His wife, Sonja Pintér, opened a contemporary gallery/shop in another part of the shop, which has changing exhibitions, all of which are fit for a home in the elegant surrounding blocks. Pintér is open until 2 p.m. on Saturdays, which is when his most precious diplomatic and fast-lane clients visit his shop, and practically all of the other major shops on the street.

Cirko-Gejzir Cinema 11L *V. Balassi Bálint utca 15–17.*, www.cirkofilm.hu ••• This independent two-screen art cinema moved here in 1998 from another Pest venue. There are five employees and 10 volunteers who keep the institution in motion, for 35,000 to 40,000 visitors a year. Director Péter Balassa claims to be able to judge whether a film will attract 500 or 5,000 viewers here. Films focus on European and South American films, as well as festival winners. It is a trendy, attractive place, with a fitting website. All films are subtitled, needless to say.

Nagyházi Gallery 11M *V. Balaton utca 8.,* www.nagyhazi.hu ●●● This shop has forever changed the streetscape. One of Budapest's most important antique shops, it holds regular auctions and occupies a bigger space than is usual for a business which was neither a former state-owned one nor a foreign chain. It is a low-key business with high standards, and is priced accordingly. It sells furniture, paintings, chandeliers, and various peasant textiles such as blankets, skirts, and folk costumes (both old and recent). The staff are always friendly, even to obvious non-customers. The gallery commissioned a well-known playful goldsmith (Vladimír Péter, 1997) (see below) to design a witty and brilliant sign for them. It's on the corner of the building, and is visible from both Balaton utca and Falk Miksa utca.

Wladis Goldsmiths 11N *V. Falk Miksa utca 13.,* www.wladisgaleria.hu ●●● Vladimír Péter is a professor at the Moholy-Nagy Arts University (MoME) who has taught generations of his students to respect precious metals and to blend the old with the contemporary. This atelier/gallery/shop is a work of art in itself. The small, bearded, long-haired owner tends to be here on Tuesday afternoons.

Virág Judit Gallery 11O *V. Falk Miksa utca 30.,* www.mu-terem.hu ●●● The inauguration of this space was a major social event in the spring of 2001. The formerly derelict cellar, which was used for storing coal and was once flooded with sewage, was converted into a gallery worthy of Manhattan. The space was designed by the owners, Judit Virág and István Törő. The former was the first chartered auctioneer in Hungary. She did her job with such gusto that it helped develop the antique art market at an unprecedented pace. She was also the first to include post-1945 masters in her auctions *(see "Art to See, Art to Buy", page 319.)* The auctions that the gallery holds cannot take place in-house since they attract several hundred people. They are usually held in the Budapest Convention Center. Apart from paintings, the gallery also deals in Zsolnay ceramics. Year after year it sets record prices among its quite harsh competition.

Kieselbach Gallery and Auction House 11P *V. Szent István körút 5.,* www.kieselbach.hu ●●● Tamás Kieselbach is not just an important art dealer and a self-made billionaire gallerist with a large, well-known space on the corner of the Nagykörút and Falk Miksa utca. He also aims to form public taste and to do

WALK TWO

things that are usually done by museums in other countries. His book, Modern Hungarian Painting (also in English) comes in two volumes which weigh seven kilograms each (volume one covers 1892–1919 and volume two covers 1919–1964). It took five years for him to research 70 museums and 180 private collections, from which he short listed some 70,000 paintings. Volume one includes some 1,000 illustrations, while volume two includes 1,500. This gargantuan and fresh look at modern Hungarian painting is still in print. Mr. Kieselbach is a soft-spoken, serious man who dresses in such a classic way that he emanates respectability. His exhibition openings are as civilized as if there had been no tragic half-a-century pause in the history of Hungarian art-dealing. The gallery is located in the former Café Luxor, whose praises were sung by famous writers and poets.

White House 11Q, 12A *V. Széchenyi rakpart 19.* ••• For decades this building was the dreaded power centre from which the country was governed. The dictator/reformer/father figure János Kádár ruled from here for 32 years. Characteristically, we did not see his office until 1986, and then only because it was on the cover of Time. There was a large oil painting hanging over his desk: "Lenin, playing chess". Kádár genuinely liked the game, and was a brilliant tactician in power struggles inside the Party. In an Orwellian way, there was the state coat of arms on this building, the Party headquarters, and a large red star on top of the Parliament, and not vice versa.

These days, the White House also houses the offices of MPs. But unlike the United States Capitol in Washington DC, there is no special underground train to carry MPs to the floor when there is an urgent vote. You can't visit our plain and rather bleak White House. If you could, you would now see the gigantic mural by Aurél Bernáth (1895–1982), a great 20th century painter, at the far end of the vast lobby. After 14 years of being covered with an oversize curtain, you would now be able to see its depiction of hard-working Hungarian comrades, peasants and intellectuals. In 2004 a member of parliament proposed the removal of the painting on political grounds. As it turned out, it is on the landmark preservation list.

Margaret Bridge (Margit híd) 12B, 13A ••• The Margit híd links Pest's Jászai Mari tér with Buda's Germanus Gyula tér. Built between 1872 and 1876, it was the second permanent bridge over the Danube and was designed by Frenchman Ernest Gouin and built by a Parisian building firm. It turns at a 150 degree angle in the middle, partly so that all the piers would be at a right angle to the stream, and partly so the bridge would continue the line of the Nagykörút. The bridge has a branch that leads to Margitsziget (Margaret Island) starting out from the middle pier. Although this branch was included in the original plan, it was only built in 1901. This bridge was the scene of the greatest disaster in the history of Budapest. During afternoon rush hour on November 4th 1944, when hundreds of people were crossing the bridge on foot and by tram, the charges placed by the Germans on the section of the bridge between the island and Pest went off, presumably by accident. The number of casualties will never be known, but it ran into the hundreds (and there were 40 German soldiers among them). The subsequent inquiry found a leaking gas pipe and a cigarette thrown into the water was the most probable cause. The thorough renovation in 2009–2011 included recreating many of the original ornaments. The x-shaped forms were placed again under the pavement (they had no role in supporting the bridge, they are just nice to look at).

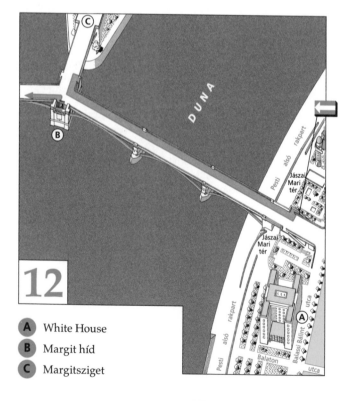

A White House
B Margit híd
C Margitsziget

Margaret Island (Margitsziget) 12C ••• Margitsziget lies in the Danube between Margit híd and Árpád híd. The island was formed over the last million years and is one of Europe's finest parks. With a length of 2.5 kilometres and a width of 500 metres at its widest point, at a leisurely pace it can be strolled through in about two hours. However, it is worthwhile spending half-a-day here. Most probably a bridge connected the island with the Buda bank even in Roman times. In the Middle Ages it was called the "Isle of Rabbits" and was a royal hunting reserve. The present name was given in the late 19th century in honour of Princess Margit, daughter of King Béla IV, who lived in a convent on the island. During the Turkish occupation the whole island functioned as a harem. There are more than 10,000 trees on the island – mostly plane trees which were planted by various Habsburg gardeners to counteract the ravages of floods. János Arany (1817–1882), one of the greatest 19th century poets, wrote his touching final poems of the series Under the Oak Trees here. Although there are some oaks on the island as well, gardeners say that the poet's favourite oaks were probably plane trees. Until the end of World War Two the island was owned by a private company and maintenance was financed by charging entrance fees. Attractions on the island include a swimming pool, a strand, competition tennis courts, an open-air theatre, a smelly collection of exotic birds, a rose garden, a Japanese garden, and a sculpture garden. The famous old Grand Hotel, now called the Danubius Grand Hotel, sits at the northern end. The hotel's terrace is a pleasant place to sit and enjoy the shady trees, the tranquility, and the elegant ambience – everything which makes the island worth visiting.

Access: Buses 26 from Nyugati pályaudvar (Western Railway Station) run to the island and make several stops within the island before ending up at the Árpád híd metro stop. Trams 4 and 6 stop at the island's entrance in the middle of Margit híd. Cars are allowed access only from Árpád híd and only as far as the hotel parking lots. There are minibus tours on Saturdays between 10 a.m. and 6 p.m. between May 1 and September 30. Two enterprises hire-out special converted bicycles, called sétacikli and bringóhintó. You have to deposit a personal document and sign a declaration that the bikes were in good condition when hired. Leaving the island, it is worth stopping at "elbow" of the bridge. There are so many gulls flying above the water that smashes against the piers that they sometimes get entangled in fishing lines. From here, the views of Buda and Pest merge into one another, with the Danube curving gently in the middle, embracing the city.

WALK TWO

**The Przemysl Memorial 13B ••• ** When you cross Margit híd and arrive in Buda, to the left is one of the most masculine lions in Budapest. It symbolizes the 1915 Hungarian defenders of Przemysl, a fortress in Southern Poland. A Hungarian soldier modeled for the statue in 1932. Memorials to the Hungarian victims of World War One have been erected at various places in the city, mostly through public contributions.

Margit körút (Margaret Boulevard) begins on the Buda side of Margit híd. After about 200 metres, the road takes a sharp turn to the left, still further it turns right and finally runs into busy Moszkva tér, the centre of Buda (and the epitome of the city's traffic problems). The winding Margit körút follows the line of a hill, Rózsadomb (Rose Hill), on which first summer houses, and later elegant villas were built. In the 1960s and 1970s hundreds of cube-like apartment blocks were built next to the old, low buildings. The eastern slope of the hill is practically full of buildings. The other sides – Endrődi Sándor utca, Gárdonyi Géza utca, and Törökvész út – are the scenes of busy construction work. For Budapesters, Rózsadomb has become a social category. If someone builds a house or buys a home in this expensive area, people just say that "they moved up to the hill". Rose Hill remains the symbolic address associated with wealth, though the real wealth has moved out to the new suburbs of Adyliget and Budakeszi. To continue on Walk Two, you should turn left on Frankel Leó út, a busy street full of shops. The corner BÁV shop heralds the establishment of a rival Buda "antique row". The functions of the street's shops change from year to year. There is no more betting office or skate sharpener here, but there is a lovely small café, a shoe shop that sells in big quantities and a hostel for nurses. There's also the evergreen Bambi café, which is just as it has always been, with its trapezoid-shaped cashier and the figure of the Disney deer that inspired its name. The notice above the soft-drink refrigerator can be commonly seen in other such places: DRUNK ELEMENTS WILL NOT BE SERVED. The one above the cashier better reflects the spirit of the place: ONLY FOOD SERVED TO THE TABLE MAY BE CONSUMED THERE (which must mean that things sometimes happen differently here). I wonder if the pensioners passing time there have been offering each other their own home-baked food.

A rest
Café Bambi
II. Frankel Leó út 2 – 4.

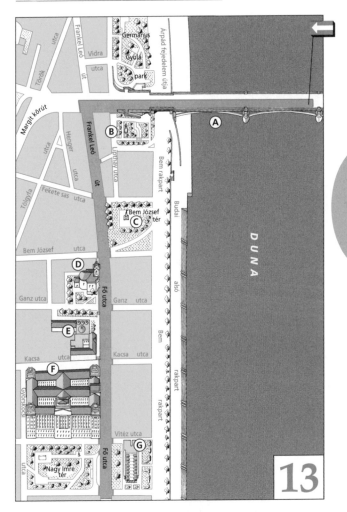

A Margit híd

B Przemysl Memorial

C Statue of General Bem

D Florian Chapel

E Király Baths

F Military Tribunal

G Point House

Statue of General Bem 13C ••• This statue on Bem József tér depicts the Polish General József Bem, who was one of the most successful generals on the Hungarian side during the

1848-1849 Hungarian Revolution and War of Independence. He was revered by Hungarian soldiers, who called him "Father Bem" (Bem apó). The statue (János Istók, 1934) depicts the small figure of the general, with his wounded arm in a sling, commanding his troops into attack at the bridge of Piski (now in Romania) on February 8, 1849. The inscription says: *"The Battle of Piski"*. And underneath: *"I Shall Recapture the Bridge Or Die/ Forward Hungarians/If We Do Not Have the Bridge, We Do Not Have the Country."* The bridge was recaptured, Bem defeated general Puchner. But, as often happened in the last centuries: *"We won the battle, it was only the war we lost."* After the crushing defeat by the combined forces of the Tsar and the Habsburgs, Bem escaped to Turkey. He converted to Islam and became governor of Aleppo under the name of Murad Pasha. This statue has played an important role in anti-government demonstrations during World War Two, in 1956, and in 1989–1990.

Florian Chapel (Flórián-kápolna) **13D** *II. Fő utca 90.* ••• We are now entering Fő utca, which epitomises almost the entire history of the country with its many important buildings from various epochs. Before the Danube quay was built, the river had flooded several times and covered the area with silt. As a result, the older buildings on this street are considerably below street level. This entire chapel, which was built by a baker in the mid-18th century, was lifted 140 centimetres in 1938. A modern painter, Jenő Medveczky, painted the frescoes in the same year. Now it serves as the parish church for the Greek Uniate community in Buda. I once saw a touching scene here of an old lady dusting the chapel's ceiling with immense affection and thoroughness. She was using a long pole made up of several shorter ones joined together.

Király Baths (Király fürdő) **13E** *II. Fő utca 84.*, www.spasbudapest .com, open Monday, Wednesday and Friday 7 a.m. to 2 p.m. (women) and Tuesday, Thursday and Saturday 9 a.m. to 6 p.m. (men). ••• This bath house was built by the Turks around 1570 inside the walls of Water Town so the troops could enjoy the benefits of a bath, even during a siege. The classical wings were added between 1717 and 1727 and the bath house took its present name (Király means King) from the König family, who owned it for a time. The thermal bath is a fine spectacle. After buying your ticket, go up the spiral staircase and follow the signs for the "Gőzfürdő" (steam bath). The attendant will hand you a cotton apron to wear and will direct you to an empty cubicle. Lock your cubicle door and tie the key to your apron string. Memorize your cubicle number and then head to the bath (where you must first shower). The actual Turkish bath is a pool through a low door, under the octagonal roof that you saw from the outside. The pool is notable for the mysterious beams of differently coloured light shooting through the hexagonal openings in the dome, illuminating the steam. Once you are finished going in and out of the steam rooms (which have different temperatures) and the waters (which are between 26 and 40 degrees Celsius), the next stop is the towel room. Leave your apron at the entrance, take a towel and dry yourself. Leave your wet towel behind, take a dry one, and follow the signs for the "Pihenő" to the first floor and have a rest. Notices on the wall say "silence, please" and "time of rest: 15 minutes" (the latter is never taken seriously). When you return to your cubicle, you'll have to ask the attendant to open it for you – like a safe, it needs two keys to open. It is customary to leave a tip for the attendant. Apart from the thermal bath, there are bath tubs, a sauna and several other facilities. In one corridor there are some old-fashioned red scales, the sort that were once found all over Budapest. Originally the price was one 20-fillér coin, then it was two 20-fillér coins. Then the scales disappeared.

Fő utca is the main street in the Víziváros (Water Town) neighbourhood. Looking up into the streets to the right (such as Kacsa utca), you'll see magnificent views of the slope of Castle Hill and get an idea of the poetic disorder of the district's past. Nagy Imre tér, however, could well be a museum of modern architecture. The severe building at Fő utca 70–72. is the Military Tribunal (13F) which was built in 1915 and perfectly exemplifies the primary aim of such buildings: to serve as a deterrent. When the façade was rebuilt it was perhaps felt that three revolving doors in the façade were too many, so iron bars were placed on the side doors. The revolving door in the middle was replaced with a simple narrow door, which is not in the least in proportion with such a large building. It seems as if it would be truly impossible to slip out of this place unobserved.

The building opposite (Fő utca 69.) is a typical 1930s apartment building, while the red brick building opposite the side wall of the Tribunal (on the other side of Nagy Imre tér) was built between 1941 and 1942 and was the first building in Budapest to have ever been built during the winter. After World War Two, there were plans to develop the river bank with tall buildings. All that was realized of the plan was one high-rise building, the "Point House" (Fő utca 61.), which was built in 1948 and was so called because all of the flats open from one single staircase in the middle of the building. But rumour had it that the name originated because there was no point in the building since it cost twice the price of a traditional building (14A).

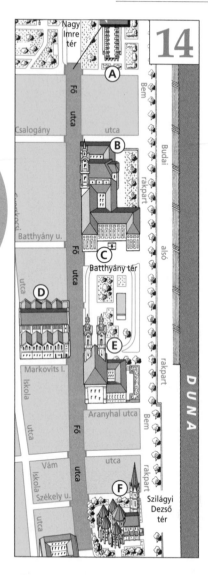

We have now arrived at one of the highlights of this walk, Batthyány tér. Apart from some fine buildings, the attraction lies mostly in the fact that the square lies directly opposite the main façade of the Parliament building on the other side of the Danube. A quite unusual view of the Parliament can be enjoyed from the first floor of the old Market Hall (**14G**), from the windows of the café or the bookstore.

This sleepy little square suddenly came to life in 1972 when a metro stop on the red line (M2) was opened here. The terminus of the suburban train (the HÉV) is also here, under the square. You can cut this walk short and return to Vörösmarty tér by taking the metro to Deák tér, which is a short walk from Vörösmarty tér.

A Point House

B St. Elizabeth Parish Church

C Statue of Ferenc Kölcsey, the romantic poet

D Market Hall

E Church of St. Anne

F Calvinist Church

A World Famous Lavatory (nyilvános vécé) ••• To paraphrase the Emperor Vespasian's famous dictum: "A little money takes away all the smell." A few steps from the metro entrance under Batthyány tér, this institution – which has always been a busy, but scruffy place – was leased out in the late 1980s to a private entrepreneur who added tropical décor, soft music and two chairs. The original owner in the mid-1980s was heralded as a symbol of New Hungary and interviewed by journalists from almost every leading newspaper. (There are no more tropical posters today.)

Hikisch House (*I. Batthyány tér 3.*) was built in 1795 and was then the residence of an architect. Like every other old build-ing here, it is below street level of the square. On the façade there is a relief with four cherubs, symbolizing the four seasons.

Former "White Cross" Inn (*I. Batthyány tér 4.*) was once a ball-room in the middle of this building which hosted theatrical per-formances. The ironwork on the balcony on the left is Baroque, on the right it's Rococo. To emphasize his puritanical character, Joseph II (1780–1790), who was called the "King with a Hat" since he was never crowned, stayed here twice rather than staying in a palace. You will be surprised at the large and won-derful courtyard hiding behind the gate. The Casanova Piano Bar, located inside, entices those who like that kind of thing. They say that Casanova himself was once put up at this inn. The tradesmen's entrance to the Market Hall is to the left of the building's back gate.

Church of St. Anne (Szent Anna-templom) **14E** ••• This church on Batthyány tér is finely proportioned in every detail. To my mind, it is one of the finest buildings in town (Kristóf Hamon and Máté Nepauer, 1740–1762). Inside, the Italianate nave is in the shape of an elongated octagon. One of the builders was Kristóf Hikisch, who lived in this square, and whose house we have already seen. Over the years this church has been the victim of earthquakes, floods and wars.

Café Angelika *I. Batthyány tér 7.*, T: 201-0668, open daily 9 a.m. to midnight. ••• One of the most pleasant cafés in Buda, the Angelika opened on the ground floor of St. Anne's presbytery at the beginning of the 1970s. In the pre-1999 editions of this book, the place was described this way: "Under the vaulted ceiling, most of the regulars are from the traditional middle class of Buda, attracted by the slightly snobbish decoration and

WALK TWO

the pleasant staff. It's a place where ladies wear their hats as they take their coffee, and where the wayward boss takes the secretary."

The Angelika fundamentally changed in 2001 when the Café Miro (of Castle area fame) management took it over. They replaced the furniture, which is playful and white, though some-what oversize for the relatively scarce inner space. They built a large, adventurous terrace, which features plateaus of varying height and panoramic views of the Parliament. The terrace is not fully covered and when it rains, the whole place is paralyzed while the staff run and gather the pillows and cushions from the rain. All in all, it is still a good place for wayward bosses and their companions, especially in the summer when they will be the only patrons in the cool innermost rooms since everyone else will be on the terrace.

Further down Fő utca, we pass a neo-Gothic Calvinist church with an extremely complex ground plan on the left (Samu Pecz, 1896). Soon after, we will arrive at Corvin tér, which is dominated by a concert hall (the so-called Buda Vigadó) and some charming Baroque blocks of flats (Corvin tér 2, 3, 4 and 5) which have been incorporated into the Art'otel.

Art'otel 15C *I. Bem rakpart 16–19.* ••• This is a quite origi-nal, four-star hotel on the Buda quay (almost directly opposite Parliament). It was built on the site of a fondly remembered open-air cinema and incorporates four restored Rococo houses on the rear side. The hotel chain engages contemporary artists to design its interiors. Here, the American artist Donald Sultan (born 1951), who was one of the stars of the 1990s, has designed everything, even the carpets and the coffee service. If I were travelling to Budapest, however, I'd rather see the work of a local artist. These days in Budapest the symbiosis between the old and the new is truly interesting, and the combination here of vaulted ceil-ings with a contemporary elevator is truly striking. The hotel's Chelsea Restaurant can be accessed from Fő utca, from where our walk continues.

Opposite the hotel's rear is a medieval church of the Capuchin order, which was rebuilt in the Romantic style. The streets lead up the hillside to the Castle. We turn left on Halász utca and walk along the Danube quay. On the corner of Pala utca and Fő utca there is a late-Baroque building which once belonged to a Greek merchant (which is why schol-ars call it the Kapisztory House). The affluent Greek minority found refuge in Hungary from the Turkish rule which lasted much longer in the Balkans (well into the 19th century) than it did here. Greeks were prominent both in Buda and Pest, with a role somewhat similar to the Jewish minority. But they were not treated with suspicion since they were Christians.

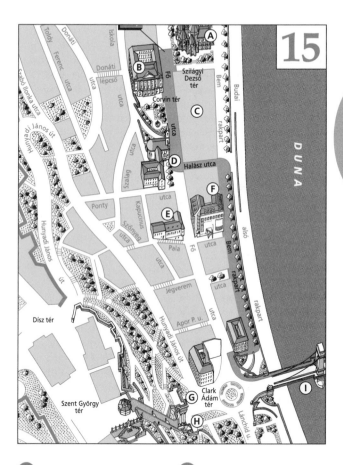

A Calvinist Church		**F** The French Institute
B Buda Vigadó		**G** The entrance to the tunnel
C Art 'otel (Main entrace from the riverside)		**H** Lower terminal of the Cable Car
D Church of the Capuchins		**I** Lánchíd (Chain Bridge)
E Fő utca 20.		

The French Institute (Institut Français, Francia Intézet) 15F
I. Fő utca 17., www.inst-france.hu, open Sunday to Friday 8 a.m. to
9 p.m., Saturday 8:30 a.m. to 1 p.m. ••• When this chic institution
moved to this prime location its influence quintupled Budapest's
cultural life (apparently the institute's budget had quintupled
too.) Designed by George Maurios (1992), the building's proportions successfully respect the riverfront and it is an exemplary
addition. Its style was something previously unseen in Budapest.
All of this originality was designed to house the French School,
so that it would be cut into two with separate entrances. (The
Fő utca façade was designed for the school, and the rest for
the Institute.) The silver-coloured cylinder shape at the corner
of the façade is a boastful allusion to the auditorium inside.
Apart from being a premier cultural centre, which hosts everything from baroque music festivals to jazz events and philosophical talk shows, people like going to the French Institute
for two reasons.

First, the panoramic view from the library offers an
entirely new view of Pest. There are also wonderful lamps on
the tables. And yes, there are the books. It's a three-level space,
with books displayed on a shelf on the platform railings. There
are incredibly helpful librarians who are proud of their library,
and like to call it *"le petit Beaubourg"* ("little Pompidou centre").
Second, the ground-level Café Dumas has an exceptionally
fine terrace.

There is a monument outside the main entrance by Pierre
Székely Péter (who insisted on carving his name in that multi-
lingual way). The statue fits into the grid of the pavement in a
nice way and honours the Hungarian–French friendship. On
the western side there is a French word: *affinité* (affinity). And
on the southern surface, there is the Hungarian counterpart:
rokonszenv. On the northern side, the monument commemorates the wartime anti-fascist activities of the French embassy as
well as the inauguration of the new institute by the Hungarian
president.

Gresham Palace (Four Seasons Hotel) 16D *V. Roosevelt tér 5.* •••
When walking back to Pest, the graceful Gresham Palace sitting
opposite the Lánchíd is striking. Despite the art nouveau style
and richly decorated surface, the building's proportions are surprisingly peaceful. Gresham himself, the founder of the London
Stock Exchange, stands in a gold setting in the middle under the
roof, in the form of a relief so dominant that it can be seen from
the other end of the tunnel under the Castle. The building makes
a striking photograph if you can set it up from the Buda side of
the bridge. The figures above the first floor windows illustrate

the working life and the carefree life, the latter undoubtedly the result of buying a good insurance policy.

The building had a turbulent first hundred years. Originally, it was the headquarters of an English insurance company. The building was designed by Zsigmond Quittner between 1904 and 1906 and was approved in London. It included offices, two large

WALK TWO

A	Lánchíd (Chain Bridge)	**E**	CEU Building
B	Hungarian Academy of Sciences and Letters	**F**	Statue of Ferenc Deák
C	Statue of István Széchenyi	**G**	Hotel Sofitel
		H	Gerbeaud
D	Gresham Palace – Four Seasons Hotel	**I**	Vigadó
		J	Elegant shops

cafés, shops and luxury apartments. The old Gresham Café was so fashionable that a painting trend was named after it – the "Gresham circle of painters", the most notable of whom were perhaps Aurél Bernáth, József Egry and Ödön Márffy. They met twice a week here, from the mid-1920s until the second world war.

In 1950 the building was nationalized and the slow, but permanent, decline started and continued until the late 1990s. It only regained its original splendour after 2000, when a group of investors pumped more than 100 million dollars into the place to bring it to the standards of the Four Seasons. The hotel opened in 2004, and is easily the most elegant hotel between Vienna and San Francisco. Its re-emergence from the ashes was somewhat symbolic for Budapest. The building's renovation was not just about making up for a loss, but was about regaining the status fin-de siècle Budapest once had. The interior was rebuilt with exquisite care, and no materials were spared for the 179 rooms. They are adorned with historic Budapest photographs chosen from the Budapest Public Library's collection. There are phenomenal panoramic views of the Buda Hills from the rooms. The ground floor is also open for non-hotel guests and the café is almost afford-

Gresham Palace

able for ordinary people (especially if you visit the royally adorned toilet, which in itself makes a visit to the hotel worthwhile). The modern statues in the arcade leading up to the reception are by Armenian-Hungarian sculptor Mamikon Yengibaryan. The hotel's decoration is that perfect blend of old and new that once again has made Budapest so interesting these days.

Hungarian Academy of Sciences and Letters (Magyar Tudományos Akadémia) 16B *V. Roosevelt tér 9.*, www.mta.hu ••• This institution, like many others in Budapest, was founded in the first quarter of the 19th century in what was called the Reform Age. On the wall facing Akadémia utca, the large relief immortalizes the moment in 1825 when Count Széchenyi offered one year's worth of his income for the foundation of the Academy (Barnabás Holló, 1893). To the question of what he would live on, he answered: "*My friends will support me.*" This was the first neo-Renaissance building in the city and was built between 1862 and 1864 by Friedrich Stüler, an architect from Berlin. The six allegorical statues on the façade at the second-floor level symbolize the sciences studied in Hungary at the time. On the same level there are six statues of scientists: Galileo and Miklós Révai (an 18th century Hungarian linguist), Newton and Lomonosof near the river, and Descartes and Leibniz towards Akadémia utca. The name of the institution is inscribed modestly between the second and the third floors in golden letters. During my childhood there used to be a full stop (period) at the end of the name. But this 19th century punctuation mark disappeared because, according to the orthographical rules published by the academy: "*there should be no full stop after a title.*"

Today, the Academy has ten departments and its charter allows for up to 200 academicians who must be under the age of 75. Academicians get a monthly salary, receive all of the Academy's journals and have their taxi fares paid. This latter tradition developed in the 1950s after the Soviet model. At that time there was a car pool at the Academy, a sort of private taxi service. An innovation of the early 1990s was the re-establishment of the Széchenyi Art Academy, an organization that belongs to the academy, though membership here is unpaid. The building's richly decorated interior is, unfortunately, not open to the public and the armed guard will politely but firmly warn you off. But the academy's singular art collection can be visited on Mondays and Fridays between 11 a.m. and 5 p.m. (It is not related to the Art Academy.)

WALK TWO

A rest
Roosevelt Self Service
Corner of Vigyázó Ferenc utca and Roosevelt tér

Palazzo Dorottya *V. Dorottya utca 6.*, www.palazzodorottya.com ••• This block is a perfect combination of the old and the new. Only the outer walls of the lower three levels are authentic (from 1824), everything else was built anew, even the inner pavilion from 1894 (by Alajos Hauszmann, of New York Palace fame). This is a state of the art shopping / office / condominium complex, with split-level loft spaces, and ordinary modern homes over-looking the inner space. In the garage, even the 17th century old walls are shown (Gábor Zoboki and associates, 2009),

On the way back to Vörösmarty tér, stop for a moment at the tiny Dorottya utca Gallery. It belongs to Műcsarnok (Kunsthalle), and it traditionally presents experimental projects. Its big windows seem to keep prospective visitors away. Passersby all cast a single glance, and feel that they have seen it all – no secrets, no longing to get in.

Tram No. 6, some time in the 1950s, on the Grand Boulevard. Trams were crowded, all of the time. Note the red star and the big sign with the slogan proudly declaring that the "young workers" (stakhanovists) do their best for the success of the Five Year Plan. The crowds on trams slowly diminished in the 1970s and 1980s, when more and more cars appeared on the streets, which then caused entirely different kinds of problems.

WALK THREE

GELLÉRTHEGY AND THE OLD CITY

This walk leads through a district – the fifth district – built at the end of the 19th century. We will also cross over to Buda and climb a 141 metre-high hill before coming back to Pest (via a different bridge) to look at some early 19th century buildings. We might have some sausages along the way. The first few stops on this walk are on the Dunakorzó, the pedestrian promenade that runs along the Danube bank, which we first explored at the beginning of Walk One (see page 93.).

Time: about 10 hours.

"Vigadó" Concert Hall

17C *V. Vigadó tér* ●●●

When the hall opened in 1865, Pest was on its way to becoming a Hungarian-speaking town rather than a German-speaking one. Earlier there was a similar building here (Mihály Pollack, 1833) which had the same function. It had also housed the Lower House during the 1848–1849 revolution and war of independence. It burnt down as the result of a cannonball hitting it from the Castle in May 1849. It was called "Redoute". When construction on this new building began in 1859, the name could not be anything but Hungarian. "Vigadó" means "a place for merrymaking, for fun". The designer, Frigyes Feszl, was a demanding man and meticulously specified even the smallest details. The building is anything but uniform. The side façades are much simpler than the main facade and cleverly hide the fact that the building is not straight, but rather follows the line of the site which breaks at a slight angle. Vigadó tér was then the busiest square in Pest. Before the permanent bridges over the Danube were built, the square was where the pontoon bridge was moored. Once the Lánchíd was built, Vigadó tér became backwaters.

When the building was completed in 1865, it was received with unanimous obtuseness. Some found it to be too unusual, others called it too Hungarian. Still others criticized its lack of uniformity and said that the main façade was "bare" and the 22 metre-tall main hall was "monstrous". An architect from abroad said, and perhaps not quite in mockery, that the building was a "crystallized csardas".

Vigadó was a sort of second home for Ferenc Liszt. He played here as a pianist, and he conducted a series of premiers for some of his compositions. In 1875 he gave a concert with Richard Wagner (his son-in-law), for the benefit of the Festspielhaus in Beyreuth. In the 20th century it was a Budapest venue for Claude Debussy, Herbert von Karajan and Arthur Rubinstein. During the siege of Budapest in the winter of 1945 it was so severely damaged that its future was quite uncertain. It only reopened in 1980, with less than perfect acoustics – it could not regain its earlier status. Its second post-war renovation was still underway when this edition went to press.

WALK THREE

The Marriott Hotel 17D *V. Apáczai Csere János utca 4.* •••
This hotel, designed by József Finta and László Kovácsy, opened in 1969. The hotel was designed in such a way that all of its 39 suites and 349 rooms overlook the Danube. About a hundred years after the design of the Vigadó scandalized critics, modern day critics were again dismayed by this nearby hotel. It is generally thought that the building is too high and its proportions don't match with the city's. It is also said that the building it turns its back on the capital, looks like a fortress and at least the back, windowless side is, quite simply, ugly. As the Budapest saying goes "if you stay at the Marriott, at least you can't see it". The hotel was built at the height of the modernist rage when anything new was beautiful. It took another ten years in Hungary before the country's heritage began to be appreciated again by the ruling elites and the people in the street. A part of the original design that would have connected the hotel to the river was never built.

Greek Orthodox Church (Ortodox templom) 17E *V. Petőfi tér 2.*
••• The large group of Greek merchants who lived in Budapest in the 18th century were enthusiastic patrons of architecture. They commissioned this baroque church from the architect József Jung and it was built between 1791 and 1794. Its southern spire was destroyed during World War Two. Nowadays, services are usually

conducted in Hungarian and are always accompanied by singing (consult the notices on the front gate for the schedule of services.) The building is open to visitors from spring to autumn between 10 a.m. and 5 p.m. There has been a long-running dispute between the

- **A** Elegant shops
- **B** Gerbeaud
- **C** Vigadó
- **D** Hotel Marriott
- **E** Orthodox Church
- **F** Statue of Sándor Petőfi
- **G** Contra Aquincum
- **H** Péterfy Palace
- **I** Millennium Court Exclusive Residences
- **J** Piarist School
- **K** Inner City Paris Church
- **L** Klotild Palaces
- **M** Paris Arcade – Párisi udvar

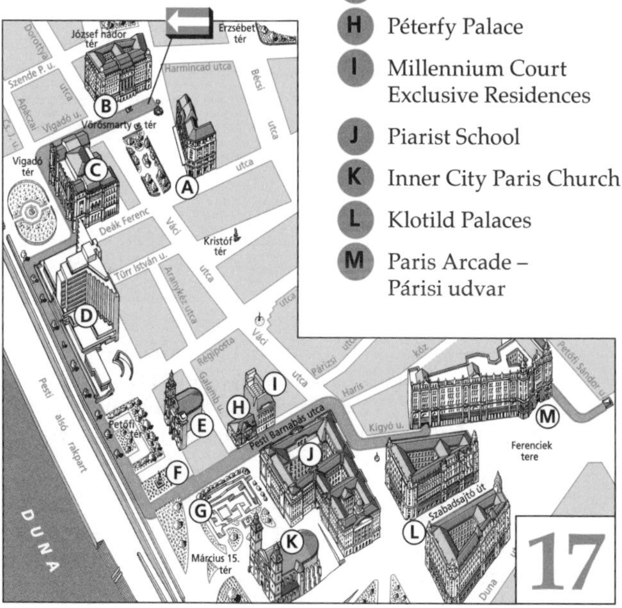

WALK THREE

Greek and Russian church authorities concerning the hierarchic place of this church. Whom should it belong to? If this is settled, perhaps someone can replace the missing spire.

Statue of Sándor Petőfi (Petőfi-szobor) 17F *V. Petőfi tér* •••
This statue (Miklós Izsó and Adolf Huszár, 1882) is a bit far from modern taste. It shows the poet at the age of 25, reciting his best-known patriotic poem, National Song, which has the famous line "talpra, magyar!" (Rise up, Hungarians!).

Petőfi (1823–1849) was a poor student and a strolling comedian in his very early years, but became the most popular poet of his time at an early age. His work was praised by literary circles as well as by regular people. He was a genius, and a master of poetic form. He introduced the vernacular into Hungarian verse, and so he inevitably acquired the title of "the Robert Burns of Hungary". His short life was a full one: his love was requited, he took part in a victorious revolution, and he became a soldier to fight for his country. He was killed in one of the last battles of the Hungarian War of Independence. Following his death, a rumour that he was still alive circulated the country for many years. It was followed up on in the early 1990s by a self-made millionaire who sent a team to Siberia to dig up a grave. The corpse they happened to unearth later proved to be that of a young lady.

Petőfi is the first poet Hungarian children study in detail at school. Despite various attempts at translation, he remains virtually unknown abroad. Today there are eighteen different streets and squares named after Petőfi in Budapest, many other things are also named after him: a museum, a bridge, an army camp and a radio channel, to mention just a few.

The Ruins of Contra Aquincum 17G *V. Március 15. tér* ●●● This open-air museum holds the remains of an old Roman fortress. The eastern border of the Roman Empire was the Danube, which means that only the Buda side was within the Roman province of Pannonia. From the end of the 3rd century this fortress – which was 84 by 86 metres wide and had walls three metres thick – served as an outpost situated opposite the nearby town of Aquincum, as the name indicates. It is documented that the Emperor Julian, and even Constantine the Great, visited the fortress. There are other, more important Roman remains in much better preserved surroundings at the Aquincum Museum in Óbuda.

Piarist School (Piarista Gimnázium) 17J *V. Pesti Barnabás utca 1.* ●●● Established in 1717, this was originally a Catholic monastery and it was the earliest catholic high school (gimnázium). The present building was designed by Dezső Hültl and built

Pest Franciscan Church

between 1915 and 1918. In the early 1950s it was confiscated and turned into the Faculty of Arts (where I was given a lengthy tertiary education).

Péterfy Palace (Péterfy-palota) **17H** *V. Pesti Barnabás utca 2.* ••• The Piarist School dwarfs this little house, which looks even smaller since it lies below street level. When Pest was still enclosed by walls, all houses were this size or smaller. This one was probably designed by András Mayerhoffer in 1756. The restaurant situated in the palace it is not 100 years old like its name (Százéves) indicates. It has been an operating restaurant for at least 150 years.

Paris Arcade (Párisi udvar) **17M** *V. Ferenciek tere 5.* ••• This building, designed by Henrik Schmal, was built in 1909. The bank that commissioned it had offices on the ground floor which are now used by the IBUSZ Travel Agency. The arcade was enlarged in the 1980s with a new passageway that branches off and opens into Haris köz. Because of bad design and cheap, un-cleanable materials, it has become a sort of a slum in a mere decade. Design students should be brought here to learn how to build (demonstrated by the old part of the building) and how not to build (demonstrated by the new part). Otherwise, the building is worth exploring.

Franciscan Church (Pesti ferences templom) **18A** *V. Ferenciek tere 2.* ••• This church shows the influence of Italian Baroque rather than the Austrian version which gave us yellow churches with towers that look like radish helmets. It also follows the medieval Franciscan pattern of having a separate bell tower cum vestry. A Gothic church was located on the site in the 13th century and the present building was finished in 1758. It is dedicated to St. Peter of Alcantara (1499–1562), who founded a branch of the Franciscan Order. His statue is in the middle niche above the choir window.

On the church's left wall, there is a large memorial tablet commemorating the catastrophic 1838 flood when the whole of the present-day inner city was under water. In some districts 90 percent of the buildings collapsed. Count Miklós Wesselényi, "the sailor of the flood", was a hero of the rescue efforts and is portrayed here in action. Dreadful as it was, this flood made it possible to build a new and safer inner city in Pest.

Café Centrál (Centrál kávéház) **18B** *V. Károlyi Mihály utca 16.,* Tel: 266-2110, www.centralkavehaz.hu, open daily 8 a.m. to midnight. ••• In the good old days, the Centrál was the grandest of

WALK THREE

Budapest's many grand cafés. Built in 1887 by architect Zsigmond Quittner, the coffee house opened at the same time and soon established itself as a writers' coffee house. The Centrál flourished between the first and second World Wars, with the writers Lőrinc Szabó and Frigyes Karinthy being among the most noted of the regular customers. Karinthy was attacked by the illness – a brain tumour – that eventually killed him here, as the first page of his famous 1939 book, A Journey Round My Skull, reveals. Other famous customers included Gyula Szini, Tamás Kóbor, Ignotus Heltai and Jenő Heltai. Jenő Heltai even lived to suffer seeing the National Paprika Growers Company moving into his favourite coffee house in 1949. The Centrál reopened in 2000 and was enthusiastically received. One of Hungary's new self-made millionaires, Imre Somody, and his wife are responsible for this. An authentic, credible, coffee house with no hint that it has been "updated" and no attempt made to create a museum piece. In 2010 the café was given a facelift, with a weird bar that blocks the entrance.

Klotild Palaces (Klotild-palota) **18C–D** *V. Szabadsajtó út 5. and 6.* ••• These twin palaces were built at the same time as the original Erzsébet híd. Built by Flóris Korb and Kálmán Giergl in 1902, they are almost mirror images of each other. In the old days, one of the most conservative cafés of the city was located here. Typists and messengers were at the disposal of patrons, and the café had its own post box so regulars could have letters sent to them here. In the 1960s and 1970s it was very popular with students. Throughout the day there were ferocious chess games in the gallery. The students disappeared when an expensive self-service restaurant replaced it, followed by a posh, tourist-oriented restaurant/cabaret. In 2000, a café-like institution was opened, which somehow could not make its way to Budapest's café map. Perhaps it was because of its mixed clientele, which made the faint-hearted classic café-types feel uneasy. One of the palaces (the right one) was being converted into a hotel with many stars when this edition went to press.

Photographs by György Klösz ••• In the pedestrian underpass at the Pest end of Erzsébet híd (between the two sections of Váci utca), there are photographs displayed that were taken by a famous 19th century photographer. Klösz's nearby studio was on the first floor of the building next to the Franciscan church. Originally taken on 18 by 24 centimetre glass plates, the photos portray the area around Erzsébet híd before and after the reconstructions that were made "necessary" because of the building of the bridge. From these photos it is evident that Budapest used to

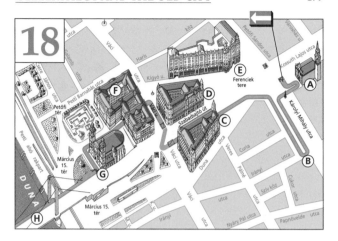

A Pest Franciscan Church

B Café Central

C **D** Klotild Palaces

E Párisi udvar

F Piarist School

G Inner City Parish Church

H Erzsébet híd (Elizabeth Bridge)

have a Prague-style Old Town, which was razed in cold blood. It was a "bad, bad decision", Budapest lovers say a hundred years later. It was "inevitable", the city planners say. The graffiti and the beggars in the underpass show how far we have come since then. Klösz's photographs appear in a continuously re-published book, Budapest Anno... (See "Reading", page 352.)

Inner City Parish Church (Belvárosi plébániatemplom) 18G
••• You may remember this church from Walk One. Then we did not pause at the statue on the chancel's outer wall. This statue of St. Florian, the saint who protects us from fires, was erected in 1723 after the great fires in Pest.

Budapest's location is so beautiful largely due to a 140 metre-high dolomite rock which descends steeply into the riverbed. The underground part of this rock reaches 1,000 metres below Városliget. The western slope descends more gently. Its area, along with that of the northern slope, the Tabán, is almost 60 hectares. Naturally, the city tries to protect every single one of the 6,000 trees here (some of which are fig trees planted by the Turks). According to the legend, the hill was the dwelling place of witches who arrived here every night, riding on the

A Erzsébet híd (Elizabeth Bridge)

B Rudas Baths

C Statue of St. Gellért

D Statue of Liberty

E Citadel

back of human beings, to get their daily wine. Nowadays there is no wine produced here, but the hill was once covered in vineyards.

St. Gellért Monument 19C ••• This bronze statue surrounded by a colonnade (Gyula Jankovits, 1904) faces the Buda end of Erzsébet híd and is interesting not so much in itself, but for its location. St. Gellért (Gerald), the Bishop of Csanád, was put into a nail-studded barrel according to the legend (although most historians say it was a wheelbarrow) and pushed over the edge of the hill by pagan Hungarians in the struggle against Christianity in 1046. It takes 20 to 25 minutes to climb the hill. The trees hide the city on the way up, so the panoramic view appears suddenly as you arrive towards the top.

The Citadel (Citadella) 19E ••• Located at the top of Gellért Hill, this grim stronghold was built after the Revolution of 1848–1849 with the military purpose of controlling the city of

Pest and Castle Hill. It became municipal property in 1894, when parts of it were symbolically demolished. There have been plans to set up a Hungarian pantheon here or to make a relief map of Hungary. During its history it has been a prison camp, a temporary accommodation for the homeless, the site of an anti-aircraft battery, and since 1961, a tourist attraction.

It is worth walking up to the upper level to look down on the city from the top, through the "symbolic damage" (in 1897 when the city of Budapest was given ownership of the fortress it decided to demonstrate that it could pull down the whole building if it had the money – it was a sort of Bastille in the eyes of Budapest people). The fourteen metre-high statue of the woman holding a palm leaf in her hands (Zsigmond Kisfaludi Strobl, 1947) is the Statue of Liberty and commemorates the liberation from Fascist rule. Liberty can be seen from all parts of the city. She has become a symbol of Budapest abroad, which is why the statue was not removed (unlike the bronze Red Army soldier with a conspicuously clenched fist who used to stand guard at the base).

Many Budapesters remember the Autumn Festival in the early 1990s when Tamas St. Auby, the avant-garde artist, "dressed up" the statue in white for three days, thus converting her into a ghost. It was a powerful image, especially at night when the ghost of Liberty was over Budapest. You can actually drive up here, since nobody checks whether you belong to the very few businesses in the area.

Instead of the usual path leading to the foot of the hill, an even more pleasant route threads between the hill's villas. Find Verejték utca, then follow Kelenhegyi út down to the Gellért Baths.

A Studio Building 20C *XI. Kelenhegyi út 12–14.* ••• This art nouveau building uses traditional materials in a bold, functional way (Gyula Kosztolányi Kann, 1903). Painters and sculptors live here even today and its architect is better known as a painter. Of his many designs, few were actually built. In 1999 the building nearly collapsed, allegedly because of some pipes built near the walls in less than thoughtful ways. Tenants had to be moved out overnight. They are happily back now.

Hotel Gellért and Gellért Baths 20D *XI. Kelenhegyi út 4.,* www.danubiushotels.com/gellert ••• Following the above route, you will see the recently enlarged open-air baths before you arrive at the hotel and the main entrance of the baths. The open-air pool stretches to the other side of Kemenes utca and is

WALK THREE

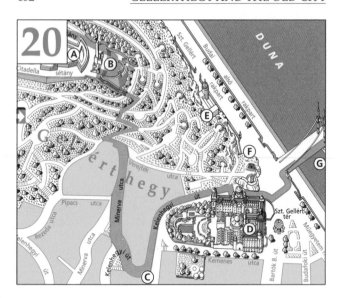

WALK THREE

A Citadel

B Statue of Liberty

C Studio Building

D Gellért Baths and
   the Hotel

E Pauline Monastery

F Grotto Chapel

G Szabadság híd (Liberty
   Bridge)

connected to the main area by an underpass. The new section
was uncommonly well-constructed with the post-modern softness matching the heavy bulk of the art nouveau building.

"*The Gellért Hotel looks like a huge white gem*", claims the illustrator of this book. "*Unlike other buildings, which go black with time,
it grows whiter and whiter.*" The hotel was built by Ármin Hegedűs,
Artúr Sebestyén and Izidor Stark in 1918 as part of a conscious
effort to make Budapest into a city of baths. If you cannot spare
the time to swim, at least walk through the separate bath house
entrance (on the side of the building) for the sake of seeing the
mosaic floor and the glass ceiling. Walk all the way back to look
at the roofed-over part of the swimming pool. Try to slip in –
you are supposed to have a swimming pool ticket. Hotel guests
have a separate lift to come down to the baths. The hotel's main
entrance faces the Danube. The lobby was rebuilt at the beginning of the 1960s in the so-called "old modern" style. Now it
is beginning to look elegant again in the same way as the 1965
Opel Rekord that fascinated me in front of this hotel one autumn

day a long time ago. This was the hotel where Budapest school-boys went to "car spot" among the latest-model cars arriving outside.

A rest
Cafe of Hotel Gellért

Pauline Monastery and the Grotto Chapel (Pálos Kolostor, Sziklakápolna) 20E–F *XI. Szent Gellért rakpart 1/a.* ••• This is another pseudo-historic building (Károly Weichinger) that fits wonderfully well in its surroundings. No one would think that it was built in 1932. For 40 years it was the dormitory for students from the Ballet Institute. I am not sure that they felt at home there. The church in the grotto, which once had a chapel too, opens from the balcony nearby and was re-consecrated and put back into use in the early 1990s. The stone cross over the entrance (the symbol barbarically demolished with hammers in the late 1940s) was re-erected in 2001 a few months after the much criticized St. Stephen statue and his horse was unveiled. You probably would not recognize the king's features since they are those of the sculptor, Pál Kő. The new statue seems to overburden the pleasant surroundings in front of the cave.

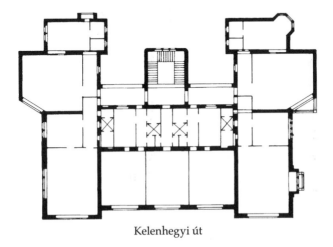

Kelenhegyi út

A Studio Building

WALK THREE

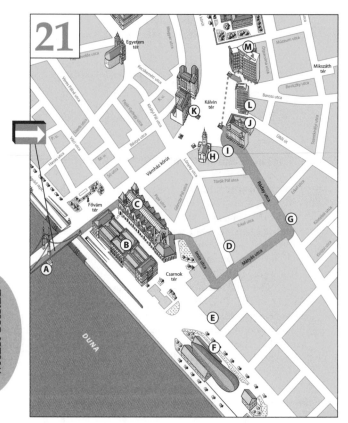

A Szabadság híd

B Corvinus University of Economic Sciences

C Central Market Hall

D A transformer station

E Corvinus University new Campus

F CET Cultural Center

G Ráday Collection

H Calvinist Church

I Former "Two Lions Inn"

J Headquarters of Aegon Insurance Company

K Hotel Korona

L M High-tech office blocks

Liberty Bridge (Szabadság híd) 20G, 21A ••• Linking Gellért tér in Buda and Fővám tér in Pest, this was Budapest's third permanent bridge. Originally called the Ferenc József híd (Franz Joseph Bridge), it was opened during the 1896 millennium celebrations in honour of the founding of Hungary. Franz Joseph himself hammered in the last silver rivet. Not by hand, naturally: he pushed a button in a tent on the Pest side to operate the 45 ton hammer. There are few things which better reveal how much the people at that time took pleasure in ornaments. It would be difficult to imagine what the bridge would look like if the designers, Virgil Nagy and János Feketeházy, had not stuck to the following principle: "When designing the bridge, we had to obey the requirements of beauty, simplicity and economy." The bridge has a modular structure, which means that if the 49 metre-long central part was removed the rest would still stand firmly. "Turul birds" – mythical birds of the Hungarians – stand on golden balls topping each pillar, with their wings stretched, preparing to take off. Some people attempting suicide also climb up here, but most are rescued by the fire brigade. The famous silver rivet with the initials F. J. was stolen during World War One, and so was its replacement. During the complete renovation of 2005–08 it was not rebuilt.

Corvinus University of Economic Sciences (Budapesti Corvinus Egyetem) 21B *IX. Fővám tér 8.* ••• This neo-Renaissance building, which was originally the main customs building, proved to be a trendsetter and influenced construction all along Andrássy út. Built by Miklós Ybl between 1870 and 1874, it has housed the university (formerly called the Karl Marx University) since 1951. It is a protected historic building, so when the university wanted to add an extra floor the request was denied and it was ordered to instead restore the building. Through the main entrance there is an inner glass-covered courtyard with Karl Marx himself sitting there in bronze. According to an old tradition, freshmen have to climb up to the statue and kiss the great theorist on his forehead to become full-blooded sophomores. A bridge, commonly known as the "Bridge of Sighs", arches over the courtyard. The cast-iron pillars are still inscribed "Ganz und Co. Ofen", the last word being the German name for Buda. It is well-worth walking up and down the elegant staircases to see the beams of light breaking through the windows at the most surprising places.

Central Market Hall (Központi Vásárcsarnok) 21C *XI. Vámház körút 1–3.* ••• At the end of the 19th century the city had five large covered market halls which were built in similar styles. All were opened on the same day. The other four are located at Rákóczi tér, Klauzál tér, Hunyadi tér and on Hold utca. This one, designed by Samu Pecz, is the largest and has six rows of stalls along the sides of the 150 metre-long hall. The structure,

WALK THREE

the lighting and the cold storage areas were very modern in their time and are still in use. Formerly, laden barges sailed right into a special entrance marked by a notice: "TUNNEL INTO THE CENTRAL MARKET HALL".

The hall's greatest attraction is its roof structure, with its amazingly large space underneath. The roof has resisted the ravages of time better than the plastered walls. Let's walk from the main entrance to the end of the hall and then go up to the gallery where you will see the most horrendously kitschy souvenirs (intended for the "other tourists") with large notices warning that they are for wholesale only.

The market is changing. The old-fashioned market-women, dressed in black or black and white, and always ready for some loud bargaining, are slowly disappearing. Instead, the rowdy, 30 to 40 year-old small businessman with his well-dressed wife at the stall, cracking endless jokes with the customers, is becoming the typical figure. There are still some – although fewer and fewer – peasant women in black skirts with scarves on their heads, Transylvanian visitors selling clothes, or provincially-dressed smallholders. They all represent the old local color.

It's worth walking around to indulge in applied people watching. Buy some sausages and pickles, just like the accidental bricklayer next to you who just left the renovation in the next block and is likely not to be registered with the National Employment Authority, since he is from Transylvania and "just visiting relatives" in Budapest.

On leaving the market from the rear triangular annex, we will arrive at an unremarkable, neglected part of Ferencváros, which is one of the great reserve areas of Corvinus University. There are plans for a new wing for the library and new lecture halls. The three remaining old market storage halls on the riverfront will be converted into a municipal cultural centre by 2010 - the accepted design shows an eccentric glass roof that connects the three buildings.

The Naffest of the Naff Public Buildings: a "Sincere" Transformer Station 21D ••• Behind the university building, this overwhelming, boring brick wall is a parody of a building. It houses a transformer station and is a typical, "unpretentious" late-1960s building (i.e. it refuses to "pretend" to be a house of any kind). Rather, it shows utter disrespect and irreverence to its surrounding environment.

Corvinus University Campus 21E *IX. Közraktár utca 6.* ••• This new campus was built in a public-private partnership, for about 4,000 teachers and students and occupies the area of about eight soccer fileds. Anyone is free to walk in, the receptionists are friendly, and you can discover the building. The main attraction is a several-floor-high light wall which is a work of art: an information board crossed with fun. It is most interesting that 17 economics professors are immortalized throughout the building, their faces with their bithdates and dates of death are printed on orange walls. It is decorative and fitting, and there is lots of originality throughout the building (Antal Lázár and associates, 2007.) To the left of the building there is a giant plastic work by György Jovánovics, entitled "Grand Corvinus Sundial" (2009.)

CET Cultural Center 21F *IX. Közraktár utca 1.* ●●● This iconic new complex was not yet completed when this edition went to press. Based on three old warehouses, designed by Kas Osterhuis, the Dutch architect, it is meant to be a new Budapest Covent Garden. The name is a pun in English and Hungarian: CET means Central European Time, but also "whale" or "cetacean", which is a hint at the shape of the building.

"Budapest's Soho": Ráday utca ●●● This old Ferencváros street has had a long history. In 1734, when estate registering was first introduced in Pest, there was only one house on it. Its present character came into being in the 1990s when district Mayor Ferenc Gegesy (who has been mayor since 1990), a lover of the arts and life, did everything he could to create a special character here by attracting cafés and cultural initiatives. The name "Soho" began to be used in association with the street around 2000. This is a loose term for the galleries, cafés and street life in the area around Ráday utca and Mikszáth tér, where the multiplication of cafés seems to be unstoppable. Some have already changed owners, décors or names, like that pleasant one on the corner of Erkel and Ráday, which belonged to the Armenian Church before World War Two. The block is also the home of two egghead celebrities of literary Budapest: the family of professor/critic/egghead/radio anchorman Tamás Tarján has lived here all of his life, while novelist/sociologist/editor Pál Závada moved here in the 1990s.

Ráday Collection and Library (Ráday Galéria) 21G *IX. Ráday utca 28.,* www.rgy.hu/general.html ●●● Few young people who flock here to spend their evenings in the cafés know who Gedeon Ráday (1713–1792) was. He was a landowner, a generous supporter of the arts and a poet. His main achievement was the compilation of his library, which was one of the foremost of his times. After his death his library was bought by the Hungarian

Reformed Church and the street was named for him in 1906. His library is now part of the 150,000 volumes of the Library of the Theological Faculty of Gáspár Károli Reformed University, where the Bible Museum is also housed.

Kálvin tér and the Eastern City Gate ••• This square was the site of one of the medieval city gates until it was pulled down in 1796. Five buildings here survived World War Two, among them: the Calvinist church (**21H**, József Hofrichter and József Hild, 1813–1851) and the old Two Lions Inn (**21I**), which operated until 1881 (*V. Kálvin tér 9*.). You can still see the two lions cowering above the main entrance on the corner of Ráday utca.

The gate is also recalled by a site-specific 80 square-meter sculpture made of red limestone from Tardos. It is officially called "In Memoriam Kecskemét City Gate", but a closer look reveals that it is an anatomically correct oversized female sex organ, which is an attempt to represent the birth of the city (or rather a mother's lap) symbolically. The sculptor, Gyula Illés, managed to outwit the prudish Communist authorities when it was erected in 1983. I still don't understand how he managed. For many people who pass here in the summer, it is just an all-too-convenient public convenience. During the winter, homeless people leave their modest belongings inside for the day.

Kálvin tér was a fine and harmonious place before 1944. Then, for decades there were four bomb sites here. The ones between Magyar utca and Üllői út are now being filled with the bold designs of Csaba Virág, who is an innovator of the older generation. He infuriated the preservation-minded Budapest public in 2000 when he and his team were said to have ordered a hasty demolition of one of the buildings facing the National Museum (technically speaking, not in Kálvin tér) whose facade he was supposed to retain.

Budapest Public Library (Központi Szabó Ervin Könyvtár) **22C** *VIII. Szabó Ervin tér 1.*, open Monday to Friday 10 a.m. to 8 p.m., Saturday 10 a.m. to 4 p.m., closed for a month during the summer around July when the exam period is over. ••• This former neo-Baroque palace was commissioned for Count Frigyes Wenckheim and his wife Krisztina, who were landowners and philanthropists. Designed by Artúr Meinig, it was completed in 1889 and is Dresden Baroque outside and Louis XV inside. With its 500 person ballroom it was considered "court worthy" and Franz Joseph I attended events here. During the short-lived Communist dictatorship after World War One, the building was confiscated and became the Carpenters' Union. A "museum of the proletariat" was planned for the space, but it never happened. The Budapest Public Library was founded at another location in 1904 by Ervin Szabó, an eminent librarian, social scientist and reformer. In 1927 the city bought the Wenckheim Palace and in 1931 the library moved here. After decades of discussions, no new library was built in the 1990s, but the old one was reconstructed and expanded. In 2002 a thorough reconstruction of the palace was completed, including the addition of two annexes. It has proved to be a real success. City developers have listened to the pulse of Budapest, and combined the old and the new.

Enter from the left side of the palace and you'll arrive in a pretty atrium, which is a covered courtyard. You can sit here and have a coffee in the café in the former stables, or you can register to use the library for a day (you cannot get past the courtyard without registering). When the library first reopened, registration wasn't necessary, but the homeless and kids hungry for Internet porn overcrowded the ground floor waiting section.

To really understand the library complex, look at the model which is in the new staircase to the left of the elevators. The two annexes are a late-19th-century former residential building (to the bottom left) and a newly built eight-storey building (to the bottom right). In the periodicals section in the latter annex, the old spiral staircases from the storage space were ingenuously inserted. The whole complex is a lively labyrinth, worth spending half a day exploring. Don't miss the glitzy art-reading room or the gold and silver parlours. By the way, this library is just the centre of the Ervin Szabó Budapest Public Library system. It consists of 61 branches throughout Budapest. The 5,000 to 6,000 people who come here annually are likely to sit down and stay for awhile. Most of the patrons are students, who tend to speak English. The terracotta palace facing the library's main entrance is the music library, which has a special collection and sophisticated music listening facilities.

Mikszáth tér and **Café Zappa (former Café Trespassers W')** •••
One of the centres of Budapest's Soho is Mikszáth tér, especially since cars have been banned from it since the late 1990s. Most of the youngsters who flock here on summer evenings haven't read any of the writings of the stocky, unattractive-looking writer portrayed in the statue in the corner of the square. He struggled much, and even divorced his wife because he was unable to support her. Later, as a successful writer, he re-married her. One of his most successful novels, *St. Peter's Umbrella*, was allegedly read by Theodore Roosevelt. At least he praised it when he was in Hungary, and he met the writer.

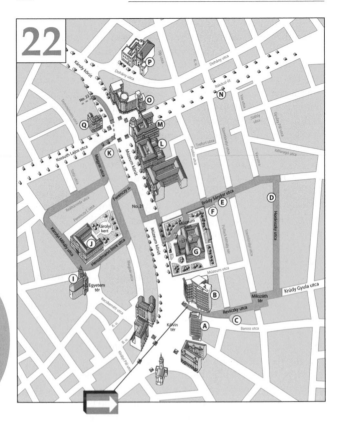

A B High-tech office blocks

C Budapest Public Library

D Atelier Pro Arts

E Hungarian Radio Building

F Gyula Andrássy German-speaking University

G National Museum

I University Church

J Károlyi Palace, now the Museum of Literature

K Hotel Astoria

L Eötvös University

M East West Center

N Uránia National Film Theatre

O Block of flats

P The Great Synagogue

Q Headquarters of the World Alliance of Hungarians (former House of "Soviet Culture and Science")

The interior of the Frank Zappa café is covered with paintings. It was a legendary place in the late 1980s during the dawn of Hungary's modern democracy. Here the idiosyncratic and innovative would-be teacher of physical education, Zsolt Palotai, became DJ Palotai and started his trend-setting career in providing live music. The café then had an entertaining name: Café Trespassers W'. This name can be traced back to a notice on a piece of broken wood which read: "Trespassers will be prosecuted". This is where the legendary alternative pirate radio station of 1989/1990 originated. It is still called "Tilos Rádió" (Radio Forbidden). But it is not forbidden these days, it's only barred from the airwaves for a month every now and then.

Atelier Pro Arts (A.P.A.) 22D *VIII. Horánszky utca 5.*, www. ateliers.hu, open Tuesday to Friday 2 p.m. to 7 p.m., Saturday 11 a.m. to 6 p.m. ••• This most improbable venture of the immigrant American non-profit consultant and businessman, John Warren Gotsch, opened in 2001. He transformed the building to a gallery with seven ateliers, six of which are given for free to young artists for six or 12 months, while the seventh is reserved for a visiting artist from abroad. The restaurant is especially pleasant in the summer when the courtyard opens.

Hungarian Radio Building 22E *VIII. Bródy Sándor utca 5–7.* ••• Hungarian Radio started broadcasting in 1925, not far from here. It moved here in 1928, originally just into the eclectic building where the main entrance is. It grew and grew, and slowly it came to include the whole block. From the side of the National Museum you can see some most improbable annexes: a neo-renaissance palazzo (where the orchestra and choir is housed) and some annexes from every modern decade. The inside of the complex is a pitiful patchwork that is hardly convenient for a broadcasting organisation. The hub of the institution is in the courtyard of the main building, a sort of large foyer built in the early 1950s, called "the Pagoda", because of its roof structure. That is where guests to be interviewed are picked up by reporters and other insiders. There are three channels of Hungarian Public Radio: MR1 Kossuth (the serious), MR2 Petőfi (light music) and Bartók (the classical music channel). Public radio was a prime mover of political changes in the late 1980s, with its muckraking fact-finding programmes. This gave way to fierce political struggles around the institution. Commercial radio appeared in the early 1990s and took a large number of listeners away.

WALK THREE

**Gyula Andrássy German University (Andrássy Gyula Buda-
pesti Német Nyelvű Egyetem) 22F** *VIII. Pollack Mihály tér 3.,*
www.andrassyuni.hu (German), www.3cgroup.hu/festeticspa-
lota ••• One of the glitziest palazzos of the mid-19th century
was built by Miklós Ybl in 1862 for count György Festetics. After
World War Two it was used for decades by the National Library
and fell into total disrepair. The renovation and conversion to a
post-graduate university happened between 2000 and 2002 and
was heavily subsidized by German-speaking countries. The
university is named for Gyula Andrássy (1823–1890), who was
prime minister between 1867 and 1871 and the foreign minister
of the Austro-Hungarian Monarchy between 1871 and 1879. He
established the Municipal Council of Public Works, and is considered to be the father of modern Budapest.

National Museum (Nemzeti Múzeum) 22G *VIII. Múzeum
körút 14–16.,* www.mnm.hu, open Tuesday to Sunday 10 a.m.
to 6 p.m. ••• In 1802 count Ferenc Széchényi, a cultured aristocrat, asked Emperor Franz Joseph I for permission to donate
his rich Hungary-related art collection to his fatherland. The
emperor graciously said yes, and the National Museum was
founded. It was the third institution of its kind in Europe in
those days. Its collection was initially made of 11,884 printed
items, 1,156 manuscripts, 142 volumes of maps and etchings,
2,019 gold coins, and a few paintings. It is the largest museum
in the country, and was built between 1837 and 1847 by Mihály
Pollack. At that time it was far from town and the weekly fair
was held in nearby Kálvin tér. Cattle sometimes wandered into
the museum garden and onto the steps.

The museum is almost 8,000 square metres and has seven
departments: the Archaeological Collection, the Medieval
Collection, the Pre-Modern Collection, the Modern Collection,
the Numismatic Collection, the Historical Portrait Collection,
and the Historical Photo Archives. A slow and painstaking
reconstruction gathered momentum in 1994–1995 and the
museum now houses the "History of Hungary" permanent
exhibition, which was opened in 1996 in the presence of former
U.S. president Jimmy Carter. The reconstruction of the rest of
the museum is still underway. The next step is building a roof
over one of the courtyards. Visiting the museum is a must for
serious travellers. Despite the high design standards, the bilingual inscriptions, and the occasionally imaginative multimedia programmes, the display is quite old-fashioned. It tends to
induce a feeling of awe rather than making people think. Some
critics say that it fails to explain context. But, it has meant that
hundreds of objects could be restored and properly and safely

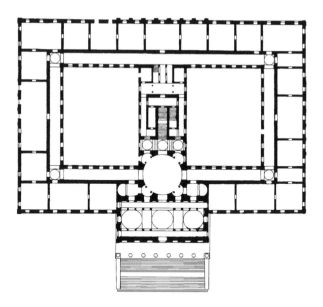

National Museum

exhibited. In due course, it could be made livelier with pro-grammable audio guides (which might include minority opinions). My absolute favourite part of the museum is in the long 19th century room: the display of all of the screws made by a particular factory, lovingly arranged on a large board. It screams: Look! We can produce all of this!

The museum played an important role on the first day of the 1848 Revolution. On March 15th a huge crowd of demon-strators gathered here to listen to the speeches of their leaders, "the Youth of March". The speakers were standing on the wall to the left of the stairs while the crowd listened, clutching their umbrellas. Not everyone recognized the day's importance. The museum's director wrote in his diary: "some noisy mob had their hurly-burly outside which disturbed me in my work so I went home." There are more than ten statues in the Museum Garden, and there is even a column straight from the Forum Romanum, which was a gift from by Benito Mussolini. That was typical of him. he must have felt: why not, when Rome had so many more of them.

The aristocracy built their beautiful town houses around the museum's garden in the 19th century. Some are still standing, like the one at Ötpacsirta utca 2., which is now the headquarters

The Statue in the Tympanum of the National Museum

of the Association of Hungarian Architects. Another building on the corner of Múzeum utca and Pollack Mihály tér, in line with the garden, is also still standing. To the left of it is a beautifully restored iron fence, which hardly compensates for the sight of the glass buildings behind it, which is the Magyar Rádió (Hungarian Radio).

The opposite side of Múzeum körút has become the rare and used book centre of Budapest. Shops have proliferated here since the mid-1990s. Múzeum körút 15. is the largest second-hand bookshop in Budapest – it was once state-owned, as were most shops between 1949 and 1989. It has a wide range of antique and foreign books (especially German ones). Head back a few buildings and take a peek into Múzeum körút 21. It has a passageway leading through the building and in the courtyard there is piece of the old city wall. A gate is cut in the wall, which originally allowed passage to the next block and to Károlyi Gardens. Unfortunately the gate is no longer open.

A Part of Pest's Medieval City Wall ••• On Ferenczy István utca between Múzeum körút and Magyar utca, part of Pest's old city wall remains. The wall once stretched in a semicircle from approximately Vigadó tér to Fővám tér. It was almost two kilometres-long and a little more than eight metres-high.

Vintage Photo Gallery *V. Magyar utca 26.*, www.vintage.hu, open Monday to Friday 2 p.m. to 6 p.m. (or by appointment) ••• Attila Pőcze – the workaholic, quiet owner of this small, professional gallery – was in his late 20s in 1997 when he decided to restore Hungarian photography's traditional prestige from this tiny space. The name of the gallery is a photography term.

"Vintage" prints are considered works of art in the photography world. They must meet three criteria: to be signed by the photographer, to be personally printed by the artist (or under his supervision), and be printed within a certain time after the exposure. Otherwise, a print is called a modern print, and has one date referring to the exposure and another to the printing. The latter is much cheaper, of course. In Vintage you can buy copies of classic interwar vintages. My favourite photographer here is Márta Aczél (1909–1997), who is still an underrated classic photographer. Pőcze represents some new talents, who are mainly contemporary artists using photography as a medium (not modern photographers proper). Look for works by Ágnes Eperjesi and Tibor Gyenis. There are always dozens of great used and rare photo books for sale. You can spot Pőcze every year at Paris Photo and elsewhere abroad.

Károlyi Gardens and Palace (Károlyi-kert és Károlyi-palota)
22J *V. Károlyi Mihály utca 16*. ••• Count Mihály Károlyi, who was prime minister between 1918 and 1919, lived here before he was forced into exile for the first time in 1919. The palace was confiscated from him for alleged high treason. He became ambassador of Hungary to France after World War Two, but resigned and stayed in France when the totalitarian madness took hold in 1949. Now the building houses the Petőfi Museum of Hungarian literature. An extensive renovation was completed in 2000 by the architects König and Wagner. All serious visitors to Budapest should find some excuse to wander the first floor of the building as far as University Church on the corner of Károlyi utca and Henszlmann utca. This is the only perspective from which the superb proportions of the church can be appreciated. Can you see the church's peculiarity? The crosses on the spires are not exactly parallel with the façade. One of Budapest's finest bookshops is located to the right of the main entrance of the Palace. The pleasant Palota könyveskert (Palace Book Garden) (V. Károlyi Mihály utca 16., open Monday to Friday 10 a.m. to 6 p.m.) sells new books, second-hand books, rare books and even manuscripts. There's also a good selection of Hungarian literature in foreign languages.

Károlyi Gardens used to belong to an aristocratic family of that name. It became a public park after World War One. Back then it was not as nice as it is now and there was no fence around it. I attended a nearby elementary school and we often came to play here and to watch the chess players. In mid-April 1966 I was beaten up here for the first (and last) time, because of a girl. It was at the hands of a much smaller, much stronger boy. I did not cry then and these, instead I went around the corner.

Egyetem tér and the New Main Street 22I ••• This vast project of urban gentrification was realized in 2009/2010, when a new and elegant axis was formed between Kálvin tér and Szabadság tér. Stretching more than two kilometres, it is in the space of a former urban highway where more than one-third of the cars spent all day looking for a parking space. Now only bus number 15 and taxis can enter here, otherwise cyclists and pedestrians rule. Pipes and roads were changed, and benches, garbage cans, street lamps and many other things were added. The slanting metal poles that prevent cars from parking are especially original. In this square there is a nice statue and a row of glass cubes that are illuminated at night. Contemporary design was used here in an unprecedented way. It is a sort of breakthrough for the city, no doubt.

An Arcade Covered with wooden bricks (Unger House)
V. Múzeum körút 7. (in the courtyard between Múzeum körút and Magyar utca) ••• Built in 1852, this building is an early work of the greatest 19th century Hungarian architect, Miklós Ybl (of the Opera House fame). In the courtyard there are two bookshops, one specialising in remainders and one in second-hand books. You can study here what Hungarians are reluctant to buy, and what they did buy, but then sold, read or unread.

Hotel Astoria 22K *V. Kossuth Lajos utca 19.* ••• This busy crossroads took its name from the Hotel Astoria, which was built by Emil Ágoston and Artúr Hikisch between 1912 and 1914 with an old-fashioned touch. The lobby is luxuriously elegant, as was the café before it was reconstructed. History books tell schoolchildren that after the secession of Hungary from the Austro-Hungarian Monarchy in November 1918, the first Hungarian cabinet met in the hotel. The modest room can be visited, if one insists.

Astoria divides the Kiskörút (the inner ring boulevard) in half, which means if you look towards the inner city you will get to the Danube, no matter which direction you walk. The busy thoroughfare leading away from the inner city is Rákóczi út, a shopping street which leads to the yellow façade of Keleti pályaudvar (Eastern Railway Station, which is visible in the distance).

The National Theatre stood here before it was pulled down in 1908. The Astoria metro station (M2) can be reached from the underpass, which is always crowded, a problem further aggravated by illegal street vendors. Every now and then "public space guards" (paid for by local governments) remove them, but gradually they return, allegedly because of petty bribes.

A Detour: Uránia National Film Theatre (Uránia Nemzeti Filmszínház) 22N *VIII. Rákóczi út 21.*, www.urania-nf.hu ●●● This unique building combines Venetian Gothic and Oriental Moorish elements. It was commissioned by a developer from eastern Hungary as a venue for concerts and dance events. It was designed by Henrik Schmahl and completed probably in 1894. It ended up opening as a cabaret, which soon went bankrupt. In 1899 it reopened and was fancifully named "Uránia Hungarian Scientific Theatre". (It was a branch of a Berlin-based organisation with the mission of popularising science. Its building still operates in Vienna.) For years, lectures and slideshows were held here. (You can see some surviving slides on the website.) It was converted to project films in 1917, and it became a proper cinema in 1930. It kept operating, only to stop during the siege in the winter of 1944/1945. But on February 4, 1945 it began showing films again, even while savage fighting was still going on in Buda.

Though cinemas were privatized after 1990, the Uránia became an exception: in the late 1990s it was "re-nationalized". After a total reconstruction, it reopened in 2002 as the Uránia National Motion Picture House. Including the two entirely new small theatre halls in the basement, there are now 547 seats in the cinema, a fancy café upstairs and a cosy one in the basement. Uránia is the elegant venue for premières of Hungarian films and festivals. It also has a busy programme of art films, as part of the Europa Cinemas network. Since 1905 part of the building has been used by the National Drama Academy.

The Great Synagogue (Dohány utcai Zsinagóga) 23D *VII. Dohány utca 2–8.*, www.synagoge.uw.hu, open Monday to Friday 10 a.m. to 6 p.m. (until 3:30 p.m. in winter) ●●● This is one of the largest synagogues in Europe. Built by Ludwig Förster between 1854 and 1859, the two onion-shaped domes are 43 metres-high. Above the main entrance the Hebrew line reads: *"Make me a sanctuary and I will dwell among them"* (Exodus 25:8). The building has three naves and a flat ceiling. It can hold almost 3,000 worshippers: 1,497 men on the ground floor and 1,472 women in the gallery. The 12 metre-wide cast iron central nave has a single span. Both Ferenc Liszt and Saint-Saëns played the famous organ on several occasions. When the synagogue was erected, the area was already built-up. Theodor Herzl (1860– 1904) – a writer, journalist and founder of the Zionist movement – was born in a building nearby on the corner of Wesselényi utca. There is a memorial tablet to him near the corner of the synagogue. The arcade and the Temple of Heroes, which can accommodate

250 people and is used for religious services on weekdays, were added when the building was enlarged by László Vágó and Ferenc Faragó in 1931. In addition to the hours of worship, the Holocaust Memorial in the back garden, which was designed by Imre Varga in 1989, stands directly above the mass graves dug during the 1944–1945 Hungarian Fascist period. Each leaf of the tree carries the name of a martyr.

Alexandra Book Mega Store 23E *V. Károly körút 3/c,* www.alexandra.hu, open daily 10 a.m. to 10 p.m. ••• The chain that owns this shop, which is the biggest bookshop in the country, did not exist ten years ago. The business grew gradually out of a micro-business in the provincial city of Pécs where business whiz kid Dezső Matyi was a street vendor with a

WALK THREE

Budapest Jews in the 20th century

When Budapest was formed in 1873 it had about 45,000 Jewish inhabitants, and by 1930 the figure had risen to 204,371. The illusion of the possibility of assimilation came between those years. Until 1914, Jewish business, social, scholarly and artistic achievements largely contributed to Hungary's progress. About 350 families were promoted to the nobility by Emperor Franz Joseph (known as King for Hungarians). All that changed during and after World War One when the Jewish population was made a scapegoat for everything: the lost war, the peace treaty, the depression, etc. First in 1920, with the Numerus Clausus legislation (which barred Jews from universities, but was abolished in 1928) and then from the late 1930s, Jewish community life was once again increasingly restricted. The three increasingly severe Jewish Laws in 1938, 1940 and 1941 gradually stripped the Jewish population of property, the right for certain social activities, and finally, even sexual intercourse between Jews and non-Jews. Needless to say, the definition of Jewishness was based on the Nazi Nuremberg laws, on a hereditary racial principle. According to those laws, in the early 1940s about 184,000 Jews lived in Budapest. Another 62,000 were considered Jews according to anti-Jewish laws, so the total Jewish population was 246,000. At the beginning of the war Hungary sided with Germany and, consequently, was not occupied until March 1944.

great imagination. Everybody was looking at the two bookstore chains that were privatized formerly state-owned companies. Alexandra (named for Matyi's daughter) is bigger now than the others. But it is more than just a business success. It grew (at least recently) through quality buyouts. It has gradually acquired some prestigious publishers and it publishes a glossy book magazine that is fast becoming much more than a PR vehicle. It has literary and other cultural lectures by the dozen every month. Alexandra is clearly more than just a business – it seems to invest in long-term expectations for the better. All in all, it is a story for a luckier country – or so it seems. If you enter this shop, you'll see some oversize pictures of celebrities who all read: authors and media people, advertising tycoons and others. In the basement there is an old-style bookbinder. It is a must to visit them.

More than 15,000 Jews from Budapest were killed in labour camps and deportations before the German occupation. After the occupation, Adolf Eichmann started a Budapest Jewish council and denied freedom of movement within the city to Jews and forced them to wear a yellow badge. A heavily guarded neighbourhood surrounded by a wooden fence and gates was formed in June 1944. It was a Jewish ghetto, the first in Hungary's thousand year history. A month later, 200,000 Jews were moved to 2,000 homes. Plans were made to deport them in July and August. Governor Horthy stopped the further deportations from Budapest on July 7, 1944, preventing most of Budapest's Jews from being deported. Meanwhile, the neutral states planned rescue actions for Budapest's Jews. Raoul Wallenberg and the other diplomatic heroes of Budapest of 1944 – Giorgio Perlasca, Carl Lutz and others – issued tens of thousands of identity documents to Jews to protect them from Nazi deportation. They are credited with ultimately saving as many as 100,000 people. By the end of December 1944, 70,000 Jews lived in the central ghetto in Budapest and tens of thousands in the international ghetto or protected houses. The Arrow Cross, the Hungarian fascist party (in power from October 15, the day Regent Horthy resigned) searched for Jews across the city and murdered them. The international ghetto was liberated by the Soviets on January 16, 1945, and the central ghetto two days later. About 94,000 Jews remained in the two ghettos at the time of liberation.

........................➤

WALK THREE

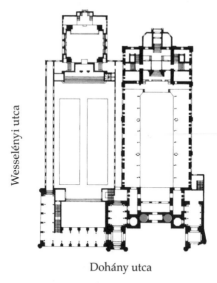

Dohány utca

The Great Synagogue – The Towers

[Continued from page 199.]

Another 20,000 came out of hiding in the city, and another 20,000 returned from labour camps and labour service detachments. Nearly 50 percent of Budapest's Jewish population died during the Holocaust. But the other half survived – unlike their brethren in the provinces, who were practically all deported and murdered.

Before the war, five percent of Hungary's population was Jewish; after the war it had dwindled to half a percent. Practically all of them live in Budapest today. After the Changes of 1989/1990, a Jewish renaissance began in Budapest, with weeklies and periodicals being published, and cultural associations and summer camps being formed. Needless to say, the hitherto latent anti-Semitism has openly re-emerged. (Only naive believers in liberty, democracy and human rights, like the author, were surprised.) Also, the scholarly debate on the history of Hungarian Jews has started: it's the one that stopped in 1948 when István Bibó, the political scientist, published his famous study on the "Question of Jewry in Hungary". There is a memorable

Spinoza House (Spinoza Ház) 23E *VII. Dob utca 15.,* www.spinozahaz.hu, open Monday to Saturday 11 a.m. to 11 p.m., closed for part of July (see the website). ••• This café and cabaret was created by the Budapest-born businesswoman and journalist, Anna Sándor. She married in Amsterdam, and, after her children were grown, set out to realize her dream of establishing a Hungarian cultural centre in Amsterdam (or the other way around). She opted for the latter and bought a neglected old bakery in what looked like an impossible address. No amount of red tape, extra cost, or government disinterest could prevent her from opening it in spring 2003. It instantly became a hit on Budapest's café map. The place serves good food (with some dishes from Spinoza's time), and has an entertainment schedule that includes serious lectures, Jewish cabaret, music of all kind, free Wednesday lunch-time concerts, photo exhibitions, and much more. Every second Tuesday of the month the Grand Budapest Round Table meets here. It includes writers, historians, journalists, a doctor, a lawyer and other professional and civilians who love Budapest and want to talk about it. If you want to meet me in person, I am always here at 6 p.m. I am also usually here on first Tuesdays of every month to edit *Budapest,* a glossy

WALK THREE

metaphor in it that is a good hint of the complexity of the problem. He says that the relation of Hungarian Jews and non-Jews is somewhat similar to that of the mistress and the maidservant. The former treats the latter as a family member, gives her everything, trusts her, but has to be disappointed all the time. And the latter works hard and shows loyalty, but still feels exploited and looked down on.

The 2000 Census also made stirs when, for the first time in many years, religion was listed as an optional question. (The government may have wanted to find reasons to underline the importance of the Christian character of Hungary.) It is obvious that, in Hungary, as in any modern country, to be Jewish is a continuous spectre – from Catholic Hungarians of Jewish origin to Orthodox Jews, with Hungarian Jews and Jewish Hungarians in between (not to speak of subtler shades).

For a very good and concise history, see "The Virtual Jewish History Tour of Budapest" by Rebecca Weiner (www.jewishvirtuallibrary.org/jsource/vjw/Budapest.html). Also, singularly wise, concise, and evocative: "The Holocaust in Hungary", by Professor István Deák of Columbia University, published in The Hungarian Quarterly, winter 2004, pages 50–84.

monthly magazine. There are also three reasonably priced rental apartments for tourists in the building.

Röser Bazaar (Röser Bazár) *V. Károly körút 22.* ••• In Farsi the word bazaar means marketplace, or a broad street. In Budapest, it usually refers to a building with a passageway full of shops and workshops and these have recently begun to come to life again. This particular one is between Károly körút and Semmelweis utca. It is nothing fancy, just a series of small shops, slowly changing owners, with a slightly changing specialization and more or less the same clientele. The most traditional shop of the neighbourhood does not belong to the arcade, in the strict sense of the word. It is to the left of the exit on Semmelweis utca. It is a shop that sells chicken and fried chicken (rántott csirke), the indispensable main course on tens of thousands of lower-middle-class and working-class Sunday lunch tables. Follow the smell, and you'll find it.

County Hall (Pest Megyei Közgyűlés) **23F** *V. Városház utca 7.* ••• If you follow this route, you can enter the County Hall building from the back, between 6 a.m. and 5 p.m. on business days. Pretend you belong here and you won't be stopped. The building consists of three parts which were completed in 1811, 1832 and 1841. This surprising oasis also once contained the county prison and the prisoner's chapel. If the gate is locked, walk around the building from the right, via Vitkovics Mihály utca, where there is another entrance.

Merlin International Theatre and Club (Merlin Nemzetközi Színház) **23H** *V. Gerlóczy utca 4.*, www.szinhaz.hu/merlin, www. merlinbudapest.org ••• This theatre is a lively egghead hangout which comprises a club and a restaurant, with sophisticated video screens that make everything visible at all tables. Plays are occasionally performed in English, but they are rarely the lighthearted entertainment that tourists or travellers might get hooked on. During lunchtime you can meet both eggheads and city hall staff here. The theatre has no company, but accepts offers from alternative companies, among them some very young, new companies.

Café Gerlóczy **23G** *V. Gerlóczy utca 1.*, www.gerloczy.hu, open Monday to Friday 7 a.m. to 11 p.m., Saturday and Sunday 8 p.m. to 11 p.m. ••• The Gerlóczy is a cross between a Parisian bistro and a carefully-developed, but regular, Budapest eatery which attracts not particularly well-off academics and lower-middle-class neighbourhood locals. It is not only for tourists, that's for

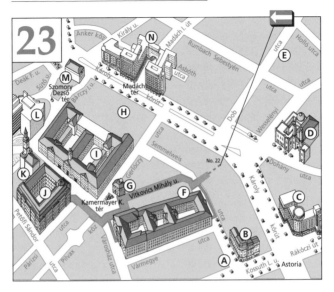

A Café Puskin

B Headquarters of the World Alliance of Hungarians (former "House of Soviet Culture and Science")

C Block of flats

D The Great Synagogue

E Spinoza House

F Pest County Hall

G Café Gerlóczy

H Merlin Theatre

I Budapest City Hall, former hospital for aged soldiers

J Main Post Office

K Servite Church

L Parking block

M Lutheran Church

N Blocks of flats, the beginning of a never completed avenue

sure. Tamás T. Nagy, a small-businessman who has gradually re-introduced quality cheese to Budapest's markets and restaurants, opened his cheese shop in the mid 1990s in the next building. This restaurant followed in 2005, a salami shop next door in 2006, and 18 rooms were added to the restaurant in the winter of 2007. You can see people from all walks of Hungarian life at this café: city council members, business people, diplomats, elderly people celebrating their silver anniversary. At noon there is a discounted lunch menu, at night there is harp music, there are oysters and there is crème brûlée. Service is attentive and nothing is naff, except for maybe the chandeliers, which are easy to change.

Budapest City Hall (Polgármesteri Hivatal) 23I *V. Városház utca 9–11.* ••• Construction of this building began in 1711. Originally it was meant to be a home for disabled soldiers covering an area of 189 by 189 metres. In the end, only the east wing was built by Anton Erhard Martinelli, the court architect, in 1747. The building housed 2,000 soldiers and Maria Theresa said it was more beautiful than her own palace in Vienna. The rest of the building was never built, simply because permission was not given to break through the city wall. Later it became the Károly Army Barracks, and it has been the City Hall since 1894. On the façade there are 47 windows in each row. The statues above the main entrance were remade in the late 1990s. The other side of the building, on Károly körút, was a row of shops after World War Two and was razed in 2005. It is awaiting redevelopment, in the framework of a large project called "heart of the city".

Main Post Office (Főposta) 23J, 24A *V. Városház utca 18.* ••• This building, built by Antal Skalniczky in 1875, is the one that blocks the view of City Hall. Let's walk through its ground floor. As soon as you enter you can count ten types of marble at the foot of the stairs. This is where poste restante letters arriving in Budapest are held and where the queue, a familiar thing in totalitarian Budapest, still exists. Post office officials must have never visited US post offices, where there is only one queue, which makes the lines move more smoothly.

Apartment Building from the early 1940s 24B *V. Párizsi utca 6.* ••• Only a few Budapesters look up to inspect the vivid, elegant façade of this building from Párizsi utca. It was built in the middle of the war, between 1942 and 1944, by Gedeon Gerlóczy. It is very difficult to imagine a war in peacetime.

A Row of Lamps *V. Régiposta utca 10.* ••• Art nouveau neglected the cult of lions in Pest. These lamps, located between the ground and first floors, are a rare exception. Rescue teams have been organized to save and repair the old lamps. On Váci utca there are too many of them, and too much antiquarianism is as bad as none.

Aranykéz utca 2. ••• At the corner of Régiposta utca, this boldly imaginative design recalls that of the Vigadó. Built by Miklós and Ernő Román in 1930, the ground floor is occupied by offices. The lift starts from the mezzanine level. The City Preservation

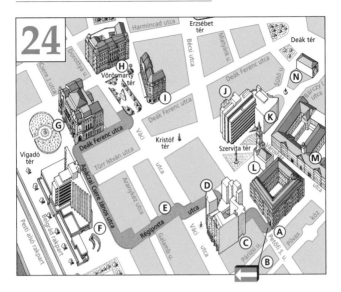

A Main Post Office

B A block of flats from the early 1940s

C Hotel Taverna (Mercure)

D Fontana Department Store

E McDonald's

F Hotel Marriott

G Vigadó

H Gerbeaud

I Elegant shops

J Office block

K Parking block

L Servite Church

M Budapest City Hall

N Lutheran Church

Association has a special task force specializing in old lifts, in an attempt to save as many as possible.

Apáczai Csere János utca was right next to the river before the quay was built. Now it is overshadowed by the back of the Marriott Hotel. The street is homogeneous, made up of entirely neo-Classical buildings, all built with taste and with their own surprises. At number 3. there is a half-naked beauty in marble, named Persephoneia, musing in the staircase and trying to hide one of her breasts behind a colourful and inadequate bunch of flowers. At number 5. there are some exceptionally pretty iron grilles, as well as wooden and stone ornaments protecting the building's corners. A building company has moved into number

7. Behind the gate, the surprise is another door and some fine statuary.

This walk took me five and a half hours and that was without going into the National Museum. Before I collapsed at the lions of the fountain on Vörösmarty tér, I had a quick bite at a snack bar on Aranykéz utca on

BUDAPEST BESTS

Tibor Frank, historian, autograph collector, Budapest patriot

For nearly half a century, I lived on Attila út (then utca), which is at the bottom of Castle Hill bordering Krisztinaváros (Christina Town) and overlooking Vérmező (the "Bloody Meadow"), which was named for the late 18th-century execution of the leaders of an anti-Habsburg uprising, which took place at this very site. When my family built the house in 1937, Vérmező was still surrounded by small, provincial-looking buildings and it functioned as a military training ground. The chief celebrity of the area was Archduchess Auguszta, granddaughter of the Habsburg Emperor/King Franz Joseph, who regularly took her horse down from her Buda palace for exercise there. She may not have noticed how she provoked the barking of author Sándor Márai's clever dog, Csutora, at the corner of Mikó utca as she rode majestically by (this was immortalized in his splendid dog novel, Csutora). Márai's sad, poorly executed, and misplaced bust stands in front of the building. This neighbourhood on the slopes of Castle Hill had a countryside feeling, like a small town in a bygone-era. This was where many eminent early-20th-century authors and poets lived, seeming to enjoy rediscovering the aura of their birthplace and their younger years, which were so far from modern Budapest in terms of time, space and lifestyle. The long list includes the poets Mihály Babits and Dezső Kosztolányi, the poet and film-theoretician Béla Balázs, the novelist Sándor Márai, the literary critic Aladár Schöpflin and the art historian and aesthetician Lajos Fülep. It must have been nice to find there – in the completely changed world of post-World War One Hungary – the ambiance of calm and the illusion of peace and happiness of what was once the Austro–Hungarian Monarchy as it had existed in cities such as Kassa, Szabadka, Szekszárd, Pozsony and Szeged. This part of the growing metropolis continued to be parochial in the 1920s and 1930s, surrounded by orchards and vineyards, inhabited mostly by the Biedermeier professional middle-class-elite, and still visited weekly by the iceman and the tinker. An unchanging 18th-century relic, the primitive, colourful and challenging Tabán the ground floor of the parking garage. It is called "Főzelék faló" – a name of which both parts are untranslatable. Food is cheap here, and the place is great for advanced people watching. Stage hands from the theatre opposite are checking out entry-level bank tellers, overheard by foundation directors and practical day-dreamers (the author of this book, for instance).

district was just a short walk away, until it was demolished for sanitary reasons in 1934. The place had its legends. Countess Teréz Brunswick, once loved by Ludwig van Beethoven, founded the first kindergarten in Hungary here (at Attila út 81), which was called "Angels' Garden". Her pretty bust is seen as you climb the Castle steps. A statue of 19th-century author and parliamentarian Károly P. Szathmáry had resided here many years before. His memorial was rumoured to have been placed there because his daughter lived next door in Mikó utca and she wanted to experience her father's glory on a daily basis. Szathmáry's noble and manly features turned originally to the southwest, while the inscription below proudly quoted him saying: Dumb is he who looks at the sun setting. There night approaches. I only watch it rising, waiting for the Hungarian dawn to emerge. When it became time to find a place for Countess Brunswick in the area around the Angels' Garden, the spot occupied by the now completely forgotten Szathmáry was desirable and so he was moved to the top of the stairs at Lovas út, where he now looks to the east (though his vision is blocked by a castle wall). His stony image may actually never see the rise of Hungary's sun. The Castle area was wrecked as a result of the Soviet siege of Nazi-occupied Budapest, in the ghastly winter of 1944-1945. As a child in the early 1950s, I saw how the worst fears of the great poet Dezső Kosztolányi came true a mere ten years after he prophesied them in 1935: The house is also sleeping, dead and dumb, As when a hundred years have gone and come, Weeds overgrow it, it collapses, And nobody could guess Whether it was home to animals or us. After World War Two a small railway had to be built to carry all the rubble from the once proud hill of the Hungarian kings down to the erstwhile military training ground, which became several metres higher as a result. Vérmező became a large park. Trees and bushes were planted on those ruins, becoming both a cemetery and a living monument to the vanished lifestyle of bygone generations, forgotten values and forlorn hopes.
(Poems of Károly P. Szathmáry and Dezső Kosztolányi translated by John Ridland)

WALK THREE

Imre Kinszki (1901–1945) was the photographer/publicist who recorded this Király utca scene. The street was the vibrant centre of retail trade, home to many lower-class Hungarian-Jewish craftspeople. Unlike many other Hungarian photographers, who become very well known, Kinszki stayed in Hungary and was killed, just as most of the Király utca residents in this photo were.

WALK FOUR

ANDRÁSSY ÚT AND VÁROSLIGET

This walk follows Andrássy út. We will look at two apartment buildings here, get a bird's-eye view of Városliget and, if we like, row on a lake (or ice-skate, if it is winter). We will visit a castle that is not part of the amusement park, and we will return by the underground metro which was built for the 1896 Millennium Exhibition.

Time: approximately 7 hours.

Former Török Bank Building 25F *V. Szervita tér 3.* ••• The façade of this building is an architectural battlefield between art nouveau and modernism. The modern elements seem to dominate now, perhaps because the astonishingly heavy Atlas statue, which once crowned the building, was destroyed by an Allied bomb during World War Two and was never replaced. Designed by Ármin Hegedűs and Henrik Bőhm in 1906, this building is typical of the era and the area, with offices on the first two or three floors and flats above that. The title of the large glass mosaic on the top is The Apotheosis of Hungary. Unfortunately, the bank's owner was not a relative of the author.

Rózsavölgyi House 25G *V. Szervita tér 5.* ••• This building, built by Béla Lajta in 1912, was commissioned by a tailor, the father of the architect. *"In Hungary the buildings speak French, German, Spanish, and English but not Hungarian,"* the architect declared. The original interior was destroyed by fire on August 14, 1961, reads a little inscription, which is only in Hungarian and is placed almost invisibly high. The building takes its name from the

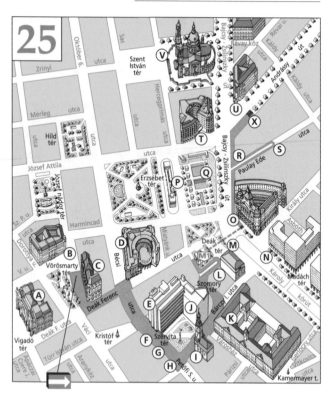

WALK FOUR

- **A** Vigadó
- **B** Gerbeaud
- **C** Office blocks
- **D** Grand Hotel Corvinus Kempinski
- **E** Office block
- **F** Former Török Bank Building
- **G** Rózsavölgyi House
- **H** Sasch Textile Shop
- **I** Servite Church

- **J** Parking block
- **K** Budapest City Hall
- **L** Lutheran Museum
- **M** Lutheran Church
- **N** Block of flats
- **O** "Anker" Palace, former Insurance Company

- **P** Former Coach Station Hungarian Design Center
- **Q** "Gödör" park and music venue
- **R** Café Vista
- **S** Vista Travel
- **T** Trade Center
- **U** Office block
- **V** St. Stephen Church
- **X** The Postal Museum

music shop on the ground floor, which was established in 1850 and is still going strong. There is a marvelous range of scores and old records. The owner claims to have scores of 160,000 pieces of music and connections with all the major music publishers of the world (rozsavolgyi@lira.hu).

Unfortunately the new buildings in Szervita tér look out of place next to the old. A government building and a multi-level parking garage have criminally shrunk the square, and a telephone exchange clashes with the church. They were all built in the 1970s. Some of them may disappear soon and give way to a celebrated design sketched by Zaha Hadid, the Egyptian-born American architect. Or it may be dropped for good.

Brammer Textile Shop 25H *V. Petőfi Sándor utca 20.* ••• The older generation simply call this place "Brammer's". Textile merchant Ödön Brammer built the shop in 1924 when he had to move from a shop which he had been running successfully for years. His textiles (with their red, white and green labels) were found in most large department stores in Western Europe at the beginning of the century. The shop's English mahogany decoration is historically protected, which means that not even a single nail can be hammered into its walls. During the decades of state ownership, the restorer wished to emphasize this by adding the state coat of arms in several dozen places on the old plaster decoration on the ceiling. They must have been put there before the protection decision took effect.

"Insula Lutherana": Lutheran Museum and Church (Evangélikus templom és múzeum) 25L, 25M *V. Deák Ferenc tér 4.* ••• This church attracts attention with its unornamented, spireless dignity. It has a memorial tablet that states "Sándor Petőfi, the romantic poet, was educated here". There used to be a gigantic bust of Luther in the tiny courtyard, standing there as if it had grown out of the ground. When I realized that the statue was no longer there I asked the staff in the Lutheran Museum about it. The Luther statue, I learned, had been left unfinished because of the war. In the early 1990s it was completed and placed in front of the Theological Academy in the 14th district. In the Lutheran Museum, which is in the school's former classrooms, a touching exhibition has been arranged. Old clergymen, now pensioners, show visitors around and answer questions. When examining one of the collection's treasures, an altar cloth from 1650, I had two questions put to me: Why do the disciples have red noses in the embroidered cloth and which of the disciples is missing?

WALK FOUR

The church, which was designed by János Krausz and built by Mihály Pollack between 1799 and 1808, did originally have a spire. But it had to be removed in 1875 when the roof structure, which the Lutherans had been forced to build as cheaply as possible, could no longer hold it. The church's interior is amazingly simple, even by Lutheran standards. The choir was built only to muffle the echo. It is open only during services, but it regularly holds concerts, which are advertised on the front gate.

Underground Railway Museum (Földalatti Vasúti Múzeum)
Open Tuesday to Sunday 10 a.m. to 5 p.m. ••• Located in the underpass beneath Deák tér, there are some old carriages sitting beside an original piece of platform from a short section of the first metro line, which became redundant when the new lines were built. A tablet in four languages near the entrance gives a short history of the "Franz Joseph Underground Railway" – the original name of the present metro line one – which opened in 1896. Walk to the end of the museum, where the story really begins: the little museum has preserved the smell of the old line. Unfortunately, you cannot go into the old carriages, but I've seen rare exceptions made.

Now let's go one stop on the yellow metro (M1), commonly called the "little metro", in the direction of Mexikói út. When you exit the station at Bajcsy-Zsilinszky út, you will be on Andrássy út, which was originally named Sugárút, or "Radial Avenue". The wide street is a masterpiece of the bold city planning of the 19th century. It was finished in 1885 after 14 years of construction during which 219 mostly one-storey houses had to be demolished. Although few of the individual buildings stand out from the homogeneous ensemble, it is one of the finest eclectic-style streets in Europe. Although not everyone shares this opinion: an American guidebook claims that the buildings here are "an architectural hodgepodge, although most of them are described as neo-Classical". I would call it neo-Renaissance (or eclectic), and not neo-Classical, which is called Classicist in Hungary.

WALK FOUR

Vista Travel 25S *VI. Andrássy út 1. (Paulay Ede utca corner)*, www.vista.hu, open Monday to Friday 9 a.m. to 6:30 p.m., Saturday 10 a.m. to 2:30 p.m. ••• World tourism has developed a lot during the last decades, but I bet you haven't seen a place as innovative as this anywhere else in the world. There are many types of travel-related services, interesting Australian aboriginal décor and a noticeable community spirit among the pleasant staff. Just one small example: the chairs in front of the plane ticket department range from first class plane seats to office chairs and wooden stools. The person who happens to sit on the latter is entitled to a discount. Discover the basement as well, complete with a video lounge and a café. The founders of this business are János Kurucz and Ferenc Pogány, a historian and a biologist, who had never worked in the tourism business before. They had just used travel services, and they wanted to provide better ones.

Café Vakvarjú 25R *VI. Paulay Ede utca 9–11.,* T: 268-0888, open daily 11 a.m. to midnight. ••• This café is a later addition to the Vista travel empire. Located some 100 metres into Paulay Ede utca, this place is a cross between a café/restaurant and a travel agency. You could spend hours here every day, planning your travels (both in Hungary and further a field) and arranging other activities. It offers a full menu and computers for checking email. Meet other travellers and locals; leave your belongings for the day; and be sure to taste the pear tart – it's a local classic. Study the notes left by previous guests, and check out the toilet doors on which "gents" and "ladies" is written in dozens of languages (from the collection of owner János Kurucz, who loves Oriental lands).

The city was so anxious to preserve the character of its beloved Sugárút that no form of public transport was allowed to ruin it, though eventually a three-kilometre long underground subway line was built beneath it. Built between 1894 and 1896, it was the second underground railway in Europe after the Metropolitan Line in London. The terminus at the other end was originally not where it is now, but above ground in Városliget. Long ago, there were lamps at the station entrances that were lit when trains were coming.

The street's many name changes are instructive: Sugár ("Radial"), Andrássy (after the 19th century statesman), Stalin (after the wise father of the world's proletariat), Magyar Ifjúság útja ("Hungarian Youth") during the days of the 1956 Revolution, Népköztársaság ("People's Republic") between 1957 and 1989, and now again Andrássy, which is the name that real Budapesters never stopped using.

An Upper-Upper Middle Class Apartment – The Postal Museum (Postamúzeum) 25X *VI. Andrássy út 3. (first floor),* open Tuesday to Sunday 10 a.m. to 6 p.m. ••• This building, built by Győző Czigler in 1886, used to be a residential apartment building that was typical of the more decorative buildings on Sugárút. There are frescos by Károly Lotz on the staircase. It was built for Andreas Saxlehner, a mineral water tycoon, and you can spot his initials on the ironwork and throughout the flat and the house. The Postal Museum is in what used to be the owner's seven-room private apartment. Apart from the movable furniture, everything is intact (only the bath tub was sent to another museum in the late-1980s). The attendants can operate the collection's individual items, such as a section of a pneumatic exchange. There is also a good view of the dome of the Basilica from an unexpected angle.

Callas Bar and Café *VI. Andrássy út 20.*, www.callascafe.hu ●●● The opening of this large and super-elegant café in 2006 heralded a new era for Budapest. Contrary to what many believed, it showed that wounds in the city's fabric could actually be healed. A long line of cafés operated in this space between 1887 and 1950. They were successively called Roma, Secession, Germania and Windsor. Later the membership renewal office of the Opera House operated here, with little windows in the place of the large portals for many years. The owner who managed to acquire this space (after a rather "complicated" story), commissioned London designer David Collins, telling him that he wanted the place to be both traditional and trendy. Collins – whose designs include Wolseley, J. Sheekey's, Locanda Locatelli, Miranda and Nobu Mayfair – studied Budapest's art nouveau, like the buildings of Ödön Lechner and the Zoo. He insisted on certain expensive materials: Edelman leather, pieces of Turkish marble for the floor (which don't look like marble at all), coconut-wood for the service counter at the bar, and many other things which amounted to a mid-size fortune. The National Heritage Authority, on the other hand, insisted on the restoration of the old proportions, and it was not against the interior designer. He happily repeated the glass and mosaic ornament patterns that survived on a very small area. (Research was done by Ferenc Vadas of the Hild-Ybl Foundation.) There is an all-day menu and a separate one for dinner. It will take years until the service is as memorable as the space.

New Theatre (Új Színház) 26C *VI. Paulay Ede utca 35.* ●●● This pre-World War One cabaret built by Béla Lajta has been modernized a few times since it opened in 1909. During a 1990 facelift, the façade was restored in an exemplary way by Kőnig & Wagner Associates. As the designer explained afterwards, the façade's restoration cost only 1/75th of the total budget. Rebuilding theatres is a costly affair, and Budapest has 16 permanent repertory theatres! The foyer, which is reminiscent of the Trump Tower in New York City, is somewhat controversial. The auditorium is marvelous, though.

State Opera House (Magyar Állami Operaház) 26E *VI. Andrássy út 22.*, Ticket office: 353-0170, www.opera.hu ●●● This is the most important building on this walk, and one of the most important buildings in the history of Hungarian architecture. Built by Miklós Ybl in 1884, work on the building lasted nine years. The architect, who also directed the construction work, is said to have personally

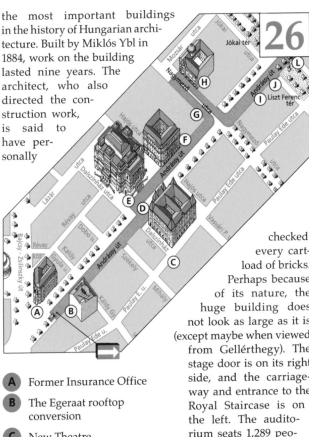

checked every cartload of bricks. Perhaps because of its nature, the huge building does not look as large as it is (except maybe when viewed from Gellérthegy). The stage door is on its right side, and the carriageway and entrance to the Royal Staircase is on the left. The auditorium seats 1,289 people. The last time that the building was lovingly restored was in 1984, its centenary.

Both inside and out, the building is decorated with hundreds of statues and paintings. In the niche to the right of the carriage entrance is a statue of Ferenc Liszt, to the left there is one of Ferenc Erkel, the father of Hungarian opera. In the first-floor-level corner

A Former Insurance Office

B The Egeraat rooftop conversion

C New Theatre

D Dreschler Palace

E State Opera House

F Cyber Café

G Mai Manó House

H Operetta Theatre

I Divatcsarnok Department Store

J Writer's Bookshop

K Statue of novelist Jókai Mór

L Statue of the poet Endre Ady

WALK FOUR

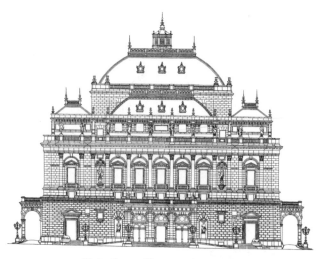

State Opera House – the Façade

niches are statues of the muses of opera: Terpsichore, Erato, Thalia and Melpomene. On the stone cornice of the terrace above the second-floor-level are the statues of (from left to right) Monteverdi, Alessandro Scarlatti, Gluck, Mozart, Beethoven (on the left); Rossini, Donizetti, Glinka, Wagner, Verdi, Gounod, Bizet (in the middle); and Mussorgsky, Tchaikovsky, Moniuszko and Smetana (on the right).

The Opera House quickly became one of the leading musical centres of Europe. Gustav Mahler was the director here for three seasons, and he personally directed two Puccini operas. Otto Klemperer was briefly the director here after World War Two. At present, the Opera House has a repertoire of more than 50 operas, which it claims is more than any other company in the world.

The box office is no longer on the left side of the building, where it operated until the mid-1990s. The original box office – which is just an entrance hall these days – was decorated in a style similar to that of the rest of the building, with brass railings intended to ensure civilized queuing. There are nearly always some tickets still available on performance days, albeit for the worst seats. When I last went to buy a ticket on a November morning I had no difficulty in getting one for the same evening. However, stamped on the ticket was: "Warning! The stage cannot be seen from this seat". Seats like that (all in the upper circle) are accessible from a separate staircase through a side entrance. Although I could not see the stage, I could hear everything perfectly. I sat close to Károly Lotz' ceiling fresco portraying Olympus and the Greek gods. The brave can attempt to go down and take better seats during the interval (although tickets may be checked). There is a shop to the right of the main entrance, which stocks good books, collectibles and CDs. If you shop during the interval, you can go back to pick up your purchases after the performance.

Lázár utca

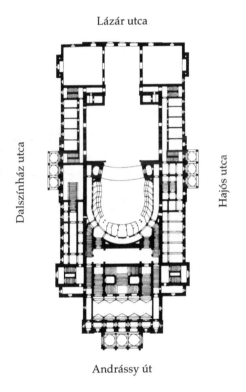

Dalszínház utca

Hajós utca

Andrássy út

State Opera House

Dreschler Palace 26D *VI. Andrássy út 25.* ••• The building opposite the Opera House, built by Ödön Lechner and Gyula Pártos in 1882, took its name from a large café which once occupied the ground floor. Six successive owners went bankrupt or committed suicide; but this may not necessarily be the reason why the café disappeared. For decades the building housed the National

WALK FOUR

Ballet Institute, whose students were on the move, in and out, at all times of the day. Soon you might find a five-star hotel here, which would be a fitting function for such a building.

Café Művész (Művész kávéház) *VI. Andrássy út 29.,* open daily 9 a.m. to midnight. ••• For decades this old-fashioned institution guarded the concept of the café lifestyle. It has become very touristy lately, especially since in 1995 when it lost its great customer and patron, Iván Mándy, who was a writer of classic short stories.

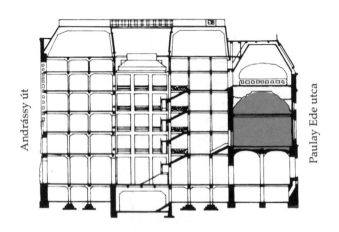

Divatcsarnok Department Store – Lotz Hall

Andrássy út is cut in half by Nagymező utca, which used to be an old market-place. The section of Nagymező utca to the left of Andrássy út is nicknamed "the Broadway of Pest". It has three theatres, a nightclub (the Moulin Rouge) and some good restaurants and cafés. The short section to the right has two theatres, an exhibition hall and a little "green house" (an old public bathroom).

Mai Manó House 26G *VI. Nagymező utca 20.,* www.maimano .hu, open Monday to Friday 2 p.m. to 7 p.m., Saturday and Sunday 11 a.m. to 7 p.m. (library closed on weekends) ••• The building that now operates as the Hungarian House of Photography was built in 1894 for Manó Mai, the imperial and royal court photographer (1855-1917) who worked and lived here. Photography was then a craft of high prestige, and this building is one of the few purpose-built, elegant, sunlit studio complexes that have

Divatcsarnok Department Store

survived and is still used for photography purposes. It has had an adventurous life since Manó Mai died: it has been a cabaret and it was later owned by the Budapest Automobile Club. It was renovated between 1996 and 1999 and re-designed by Tibor Szántó and Kálmán Újszászy. It opened to the public in 1999 as a photography gallery with three exhibition spaces, a photography bookshop and a specialized library. Notice the little cherub with the old-fashioned camera on the right side of the ground floor. Also look for the "six muses of photography" on the third floor above the library's grand balconies. In the library, ask for the balcony doors to be opened.

The building is famous for another reason: Cabaret Arizona operated here between 1931 and 1944. The space still exists in a nondescript and neglected form. It is used by the nearby Thalia Theatre and is called "Thalia Old Studio". The management of the photography house dreams about taking over the former Arizona Cabaret space and converting it to a museum and café of its own.

The Statue of Géza Hofi, Actor ••• This section of Nagymező utca was controversially redesigned in 2002. Many locals, along with the artsy folks working in the "Pest Broadway", think that it was self-indulgent on the part of designer Péter Török. They hate the never-operating pool that eats up a substantial part of the new car-free zone. The statue that was erected in 2004, on the contrary, is generally liked. It honours the eccentric stand-up comedian Géza Hofi (1936–2002), and sits in front of the Microscope Theatre where he was a star. He was a unique improviser, a crusader of the underdogs, who struggled to rise from underdog working-class status to stardom – from a tolerated one to a favoured one, in dictatorship and liberty alike. The statue by Géza Stremeny attempts to express his double character and both his light and dark sides.

A rest

Falafel Faloda
VI. Paulay Ede u. 53.

Divatcsarnok Department Store 26I *VI. Andrássy út 29.* ••• This seven-storey building, built for the old Parisian Department Store, opened in 1911. Earlier there had been a casino on the site. The architect succeeded in persuading the new owners to preserve the casino's large ballroom, which was called "Lotz terem" (Lotz Hall) and was at the back of the store between the first and the second floors and held sales and Christmas toy sales.

Alexandra Bookshop and Book Café 26J *VI. Andrássy út 39.* ••• On November 9, 2009, with a long-awaited ceremony, the renovated Parisian Department Store became accessible to the public. On the ground floor and first floor a new Alexandra Bookshop was opened, a space worthy of Rizzoli, New York or Hatchard's, London. It is an elegant, spacious, happy interior, complete with minimalistic design, and especially pretty lighting. It is a welcome addition to the neighbourhood, which was so far known only for theatres and luxury goods.

The inward-looking grand café is in the lavish Neo-Renaissance space that was built in the 1880s as the ballroom of the Theresa Town Casino. The meticulously restored and grandiose café can host about 100 guests at a time, in chairs that either torture (the black wooden ones) or pamper (the Athenaeum Club, London-type armchairs). Service is attentive, choice and price range is OK. It is a great addition to the Budapest café scene – not a revival, but a genuine addition based on old virtues.

Klassz Bistro *VI. Andrássy út 41.* ••• The name of this restaurant is difficult to translate: it is more or less "terrific," "classy" or "great." Just to the left to the nicely restored landmark department store, this ingeniously devised cosmopolitan bistro was an instant success. There are two secrets: dozens of wines by the glass are served and there is a "no reservations" policy. The back section is a wine shop, the kitchen is upstairs. Soups are a forte.

At the crossing of Andrássy út and the Nagykörút, the buildings form an octagonal square, hence its name: Oktogon. The name Oktogon was always used during those 40 odd-years when the signs read "November 7 Square" (according to the Orthodox calendar that was the day when the "Great October Revolution" broke out in St. Petersburg). At this point the road widens and makes room for four rows of trees. There is now a strip of pavement between the trees, which was once a riding track. The road was paved with wooden cubes to absorb the noise of cartwheels and hooves. Trees were planted when the street was built and were undisturbed for about 90 years until the late 1970s when some workers appeared with chainsaws one morning and removed the crowns from most of them. This shocked Budapesters, who were somewhat comforted by the Parks and Garden Department's explanation that it was a choice between pruning the trees or watching them die. It didn't prove to be enough, and most of the trees have since had to be replaced. The new-old recast lamps were erected in the late 1980s, paid for entirely by donations. A small plaque commemorates the names of the mostly corporate donors.

"House of Terror" Museum (Terror Háza Múzeum) 27D

VI. Andrássy út 60., www.terrorhaza.hu, open Tuesday to Friday 10 a.m. to 6 p.m., Saturday and Sunday 10 a.m. to 7:30 p.m. ••• This building, originally designed by Adolf Feszty in 1880, attracts attention because of its black passé

"House of Terror" Museum

partout designed by Attila F. Kovács, which especially works when it's sunny and the word "Terror" appears to be written on the wall by the sun. The building was renovated by architects János Sándor and Kálmán Újszászy in 2002 when it became a museum. The innovative institution was built with the utmost care and no effort or money was spared, as it was the pet project of the government between 1998 and 2002. The museum declares its mission as such: "Having survived two terror regimes, it was felt that the time had come for Hungary to erect a fitting memorial to the victims, and at the same time to present a picture of what life was like for Hungarians in those times... The House of Terror Museum – the only one of its kind – is a monument to the memory of those held captive, tortured and killed in this building."

60 Andrássy út has been a meaningful address with dark connotations since 1937 when the Hungarian Fascists, the Arrow Cross Party, rented an increasing amount of space there. In 1940 they made it their headquarters. The party's leader, Ferenc Szálasi, named the building "The House of Loyalty". In the autumn of 1944, when the Hungarian Nazis came to power, the basement was used as a prison. As Soviets liberated Budapest from the Nazis (without the slightest intention of leaving), the communist-dominated Political Police claimed the house in February 1945. A prison labyrinth was created by joining the cellars of adjacent buildings. The State Security Police possessed the building until 1956. When they moved out, the house was renovated, erasing all traces of its past. It was used by a state-owned company as office space.

In 2004 the museum was awarded the "Hungarian Museum of the Year" prize, for its visitor-friendly character. However, critics argue that one thing was spared: thorough historical research. The concept design was partly done by Sándor Fábry, a talk show star and screenplay writer. Fun and gags were more important than solid evidence, said the critics. Keep in mind that the museum is a love or hate affair for most Budapesters, depending on what political parties they support. One camp says that it has revolutionized the Hungarian museum scene and the way that history is taught by captivating young audiences. The other camp says that it's not a museum, but a Disneyland-like attraction. It is a must-see for the serious traveller.

Ferenc Liszt Museum and Memorial Building 27E *VI. Vörösmarty utca 35.*, www.lisztmuseum.hu, open Monday to Friday 10 a.m. to 6 p.m., Saturday 9 a.m. to 5 p.m. ••• It was only in our own time that Franz Liszt gained recognition as a significant composer, although he always had a cult following in Hungary. Despite not speaking the language, he always declared himself to be a Hungarian. His concerts in Hungary were great events. After his years in Paris, Weimar and Rome, he settled in Pest in 1875, partly because he wanted to found a Hungarian music academy in his own house. He moved into this building in 1879, occupying the first floor where the museum is now housed. In the hall you can see the copper plate which was on his door. The inscription says in Hungarian and German: "Ferenc Liszt is at home

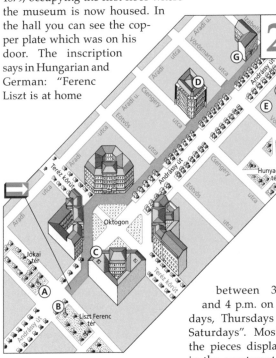

between 3 p.m. and 4 p.m. on Tuesdays, Thursdays and Saturdays". Most of the pieces displayed in the apartment are originals and include many portraits, beautifully decorated rare musical instruments, Liszt's travelling keyboard and his glass piano. Andrássy út can be viewed from the window. The building resounds with music since there are several small concert and rehearsal halls in the building. You can peep

A Statue of Mór Jókai

B Statue of Endre Ady

C K & H Bank

D House of Terror Museum

E Old Music Academy and Ferenc Liszt Memorial Museum

F Academy of Fine Arts

G Lukács Confectioner's in the CIB Bank Branch

WALK FOUR

through a ground floor window into a wind instrument workshop where the students' instruments are repaired. Liszt-related music is for sale at the entrance.

The Old Kunsthalle – Academy of Fine Arts (Régi Műcsarnok – Képzőművészeti Egyetem) 27F *VI. Andrássy út 69.* ●●● This building was erected by Adolf Lang in 1877 and was financed by public contributions. It attempts to summarize Renaissance architecture, and somewhat resembles Palazzo Bevilacqua in Verona, Italy (1530). It says on its façade that it was financed by public donations. Now it houses the offices of the University of Fine Arts, and it has recently begun organizing exhibitions again. Everything inside, even the ceiling, is made of marble – some genuine, some faux. The State Puppet Theatre gives performances in the basement, which was the site of a legendary interwar cabaret. The building to the left was also built for the arts education, which is obvious when you look at the portraits on the façade: Bramante, Leonardo, Raffaello, Michelangelo, Dürer and others. (The building was designed by Lajos Rauscher, professor of the Academy – not yet a university, needless to say.)

Café Lukács (Lukács cukrászda) 27G–28A *VI. Andrássy út 70.* ●●● The imaginative conversion of this building put an end to a decade of stagnation in the life of this café, which was one of the nicest of the handful of Budapest's truly grand cafés. It once belonged to the Lukács family but was confiscated in 1949. It closed to the public and became the cafeteria of the secret police. When I was a student, you could choose between the Baroque splendour upstairs and the 1930s elegance on the ground floor. Service was considerably slower upstairs, but there one could admire the naked porcelain lady on the marble fireplace combing her hair. You can still buy various sized copies of this statue in most large souvenir shops. In the corridor leading to the service area on the lower floor, there used to be furniture that evoked the era of Jean Cocteau. This is all gone now. But there is new life. The times they are a-changin' we sang with Bob Dylan, when I was twenty. But changes then in Hungary changed nothing. Now they do, at a Chicago pace again, in this second exuberant fin-de-siècle in Budapest's history. The new café here is a typical showcase.

Kodály körönd is one of the city's finest circles. It consists of four buildings whose shape forms a circle (körönd). Of the four, architectural experts usually favor the one at Kodály körönd 88–90. My favourite is Kodály körönd 87–89, perhaps because of its rambling turret-rooms.

WALK FOUR

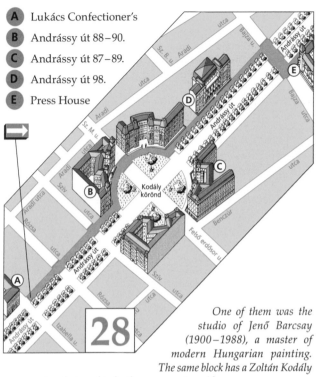

A Lukács Confectioner's

B Andrássy út 88–90.

C Andrássy út 87–89.

D Andrássy út 98.

E Press House

One of them was the studio of Jenő Barcsay (1900–1988), a master of modern Hungarian painting. The same block has a Zoltán Kodály museum in what used to be the composer's residence.

Further along Andrássy út, beyond Kodály körönd, the road becomes even airier. The houses sit further apart and hide behind front gardens. Further still, the road is lined with detached villas. Unfortunately permission was given after World War Two to build four modern buildings on this stretch. Two of them are especially out of place and are of strikingly inferior quality.

Former Press House (MÚOSZ-székház) 28E, 29A *VI. Andrássy út 101.* ••• The plans for this fine art nouveau villa are missing from the archives. All we know is that it was built sometime between 1900 and 1903 for the "timber-king of Szolnok" (a country town in south-eastern Hungary, not far from Budapest) and that for a short time it housed the Turkish Embassy. No two windows on the building are the same. My favourite ornaments are the birds under the first floor windows and the stairs leading to the twin chimneys. Above the birds there are some strange, totally non-functional iron consoles which used to hold a large sign saying "Huszonötödik Színház" (25th Theatre), referring to the 25th professional theatre company in Hungary which

WALK FOUR

performed here. In the early 1970s I often came here to watch their progressive, modern performances. The building has been owned by the Hungarian Association of Journalists for decades. There's also a chic restaurant, called Premier, which operates in the basement in the cold season, otherwise in the garden.

KogArt House 29B *VI. Andrássy út 112.*, T: 354-3820, www.kogart.hu, open daily 10 a.m. to 6 p.m. ••• Gábor Kovács, a former banker who began his career at the National Bank, became prodigiously successful in the privatisation business and in real estate. In 2003 he baffled both the business world and the arts world by holding a press conference announcing that he would donate three billion forints to a foundation promoting contemporary fine arts. He acquired this villa, which was originally built as a summer home in the late-1890s by Ferenc József Landauer, a Budapest businessman. It was redesigned by Ignác Alpár. Later it was owned by Baron Ohrensteins. From 1945 it was used by the Red Army, and later by the 6th district Committee of the Communist Party and the Youth Communist League. The latter established, financed and later tolerated the "Club of Young Artists", a legendary venue for great exhibitions and drinking parties. KogArt House opened in April 2004 ("Ko" and "Ga" are taken from the founder's name and "Rt" comes from the Hungarian word for corporation). Kovács, who considers himself a conservative gallery owner, lost some sympathy along the way by interfering with the curators whom he commissioned for the opening exhibition, and who consequently resigned. But the whole non-profit venture has put contemporary fine arts in Budapest on the map of the business elite, which is an undoubted blessing. There is also a trendy restaurant in the basement and on the terrace. There is a membership programme, and the gallery is busy planning an expansion and establishment of a permanent collection, with the help of other businesses.

Museum of Fine Arts (Szépművészeti Múzeum) 29C *XIV. Hősök tere*, T: 469-7100, www.szepmuveszeti.hu, open Tuesday to Sunday 10 a.m. to 5:30 p.m., temporary exhibitions until 6 p.m., and on special Museum Thursdays until 10 p.m. ••• This building, on the left side of Heroes' square, is one of Europe's significant fine art museums. Parliament decided to build it in 1896 for the Hungarian Millennium (the 1000th anniversary of the probable year that Hungarian tribes arrived in the territory of present-day Hungary). Their requirement was that "the museum should be monumental yet unpretentious, that it should enhance rather than rival the exhibited works". The site was donated by the city,

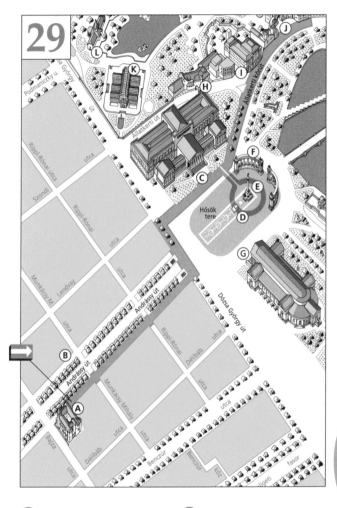

A	Hungarian Press House	**G**	Kunsthalle
B	KogArt House	**H**	Owl's Castle Restaurant
C	Museum of Fine Arts	**I**	Gundel Restaurant
D	"Tomb of the Unknown Soldier"	**J**	Zoo
E	The Archangel Gabriel and the Seven Chieftians	**K**	Palm House in the Zoo
F	Millenary Monument	**L**	Bird House in the Zoo

WALK FOUR

which didn't give up symbolic ownership and was promised 100 golden 20 crown coins per year. In the dark Communist 1950s, this was converted to 50 forints. Later it was simply forgotten about. Nine architects entered designs for the building and the resulting design was actually the second prize winner, Albert Schickedanz and Fülöp Herzog. The winning design included coloured ornaments all over the building, but was omitted because of insufficient funds. The building is an architectural allegory, representing the peaceful coexistence of various architectural styles. The main façade is a three-part Greek temple, and the rear is a significantly different large building in the style of the cinquecento Renaissance going back to Roman models. The two parts are skillfully merged, and constitute an inseparable whole.

The building has several halls of distinct styles. The finest of them is, perhaps, the colourful Ionic Pergamon Hall which has been evocatively renovated. In the rear, there are three large covered courtyards: the Roman, the Renaissance and the Baroque halls. One of them, the Roman Hall is still not open to the public. It has been used for storage since the war, and is unfit for exhibitions. These days few people know that the main reason for building these large museums was, apart from showing paintings, to present plaster-cast copies of classic statues. So, when on December 1, 1906 the museum was finally inaugurated, Franz Joseph I and his entourage could see the plaster-cast copy of Colleoni's equestrian statue in the middle of the renaissance Hall. Years later, at the end of World War Two, this hall was hit by a bomb. The roof collapsed and a well-known photo shows the Colleoni covered with snow. By that time, most of the collection, including the most precious treasures, had been carted off in a rough and ready manner by the Nazis during the last few months of the war. In 1946 and 1947 the collection returned from Germany bearing the scars of that journey. A few of the paintings never returned. The remaining parts of the plaster-cast collection are now in a provincial museum in Tatabánya.

In the pediment above the main entrance, a relief shows the battle of the Centaurs and the Lapiths during the wedding of Peirithoos and Hippodameia. It follows the reconstruction of Ernst Curtius, who was the leader of the original excavation in 1875–1881. The copies are by Ignác Langer. Behind the attractive façade, the monumental staircases and open spaces were laid out without any heed to the practical needs of the museum, which consequently had to be rebuilt several times.

The museum houses a large collection, which is based on the renowned Esterházy Collection. The collection belonged to

Prince Miklós Esterházy (1756–1833) who had acquired about 1,000 paintings and several thousand prints. His collection was bought by the Hungarian state in 1870 and was first shown at the Hungarian Academy of Sciences and Letters. It was moved here in 1906, when the museum opened. In 1957 the National Gallery seceded from the Museum of Fine Arts. Since then the former has been responsible for exhibiting works by Hungarian artists. The present director here, Dr. László Baán thinks this is an artificial separation. He would gladly reunite the two institutions. Baán has achieved a miracle in a very short time: out of a drowsy, slow and unfashionable museum, he has created a trendy, sexy institution with a record-breaking number of visitors. He has also managed to find funds for a major underground extension programme and has found sponsorship opportunities which hardly existed before.

In the spring of 2010, the museum's modernisation and underground extention plans stirred a heated public debate. The new main entrance was especially criticised by heritage crusaders. In the end, the director backed off, and the redisign is somewhat less striking. I found the process disheartening – the extention is now like a child born out of wedlock. Everybody knows about it, but it should be kept out of sight. Renovations are expected to be completed in 2013.

Városliget, with an area of about one square-kilometre, is the largest park in the city, but it does not take long to walk across it. Our route takes us down Állatkerti körút, past Gundel Restaurant (one of the most venerable in Budapest), past the Zoo (which is full of small buildings in a Hungarianised version of art nouveau) and past the Circus.

Millenary Monument (Millenniumi emlékmű) 29E–F *XIV.*

Hősök tere ••• Erected in 1896 to celebrate the Hungarian millennium, this monument was designed by sculptor György Zala and architect Albert Schickedanz and was not completed until 1929. The two were awarded the grand prize at the 1900 World Exhibition in Paris. In the monument, the Archangel Gabriel stands on a 36 metre pillar, which is in-line with Andrássy út. According to the legend, Gabriel appeared in a dream to King Stephen, founder of Hungary, and offered him the crown. Seen from opposite the angel, the monument looks a bit rigid and theatrically solemn. Facing the statue, the wings seem to cover the angel's hands as they are handing over the crown. But if you stand to the side, or even on the steps of one of the museums, the angel is balancing on a ball, nearly floating in the air and affectionately handing over the crown with almost the whole of his body. The figures around the pedestal are the legendary "seven chieftains", who led their tribes to conquest present-day Hungary.

The colonnade has two semicircles and is 85 metres-wide and 25 metres-deep. Notice the symbolic figures on top of the corner pillars. The two in the middle are especially remarkable. On the left, War whips his horses into an even more frantic gallop. Opposite him, Peace carries a palm leaf and rides gently out, his calm apparently communicated to the horses. At the far left are Work and Welfare, and at the far right are Knowledge and Glory. Some of the statues of kings on the colonnade were changed after World War Two. Those of the Habsburg's (Ferdinand I, Charles III, Maria Theresa, Leopold II and Franz Joseph) were replaced by heroes of the anti-Habsburg struggle for independence. Curiously enough, when Hungary was a sort of Soviet colony in the 1950s, the Communist government stressed the independent-tradition through books, films and statues. Contrary to expectations, the Millenary monument was not touched in the years after 1990 when Communist statues were relocated to Statue Park, a sort of Communist theme park. The anti-Habsburg indoctrination has had a lasting effect – most Hungarians disregard the development Hungary underwent in the 18th and 19th centuries, some of which should be credited to that early European Commonwealth, the Empire. By the way, some of the original statues survived the removal. That of Maria Theresa, for instance, can be spotted inside the Museum of Fine Arts, to the left of the main entrance.

Gundel 29l *XIV. Állatkerti körút 3.,* www.gundel.hu, open daily noon to 4 p.m. and 7:30 p.m. to midnight, Sunday brunch is from 11:30 a.m., the bar is open from 9 a.m. to midnight. ••• "The awareness that one has finally arrived at a setting designed primarily to minister to one's every need, a bright palace of rendered attention." This phrase from British writer John Lanchester's *The Debt to Pleasure* comes to mind whenever I enter Gundel. The restaurant Wampetics opened in this building in 1894. Károly Gundel rented it in 1910, and transformed it into a great establishment that became famous all over Europe. In 1949 the restaurant was nationalized. In 1991 Ronald Lauder, a Hungarian American businessman, and George Lang, the Hungarian-born restaurateur and gastronomic writer, acquired the famous restaurant from the State Privatization Agency. *"In order to raise Gundel to its former grandeur and make it once again one of Europe's finest and most exquisite restaurants, we shall blend with utmost care old traditions with trends of our time in just the right proportion,"* the new owners stated.

They spared no effort in finding the most suitable materials for Gundel, the best traditional restaurant between Paris and San Francisco. The raised section in one-third of the main room has no structural raison d'etre: it is just a trick to create some intimacy in what is a very large room. Above the dining room are the Elizabeth Room and the Andrássy Room, which are the settings for Budapest's most elegant banquets (a maximum of 260 people can be seated in the two rooms). In the main dining room there is a collection of paintings by Hungarian masters decorating the walls. The last page of the menu describes the collection, and gives exact locations of the paintings on a ground-plan of the room. The logo and stationery were designed by one of the most famous designers in the world, Milton Glaser. See his posters in the Colonnade Bar (which was not part of the pre-1991 ground plan) which are reminiscent of the art-deco 1920s in Chicago.

Gundel has its own wine label and a very serious wine cellar restaurant called "1894 Borvendéglő – which is accessible from both the street and from inside of Gundel. In 2004 the restaurant complex changed hands and is presently owned by a British-owned Hungarian hotel group. Between 1990 and 2007 Gundel had its own historian. Its website commemorates the career of Zoltán Halász, lawyer, historian and gastronomy author (1914-2007).

Owl's Castle Restaurant (Bagolyvár) 29H *XIV. Állatkerti út 2.,* T: 468-3110, www.gundel.hu, open daily 11 a.m. to 11 p.m. ●●● Part of the Gundel complex, this restaurant is located to the left of Gundel. It was built by one of the architects who built the Zoo, Dezső Zrumeczky, in 1913. During the 1960s and 1970s it was closed and was used as a storage space. In 1981 it was converted into a beer hall. George Lang spent a year trying to find the right role for this restaurant, which as a sister institution would not hide in the shadow of Gundel. In May 1993 Lang and Lauder opened it as an all-female-staffed restaurant, possibly the only serious restaurant like that in the world. It is grandmotherly cuisine Hungarian-style. The menu changes daily.

The Zoo (Fővárosi Állat- és Növénykert) 29J–30A *XIV. Állatkerti körút 6.,* www.zoobudapest.hu, open daily 9 a.m. to 6 p.m. (until 4 p.m. in autumn and winter) ●●● The Municipal Botanical and Zoological Gardens was originally established as a private corporation. It opened in 1865 on 16 hectares of land donated by the municipality of Pest. At first it housed only animals, but by 1872 it was also exhibiting plants. From

WALK FOUR

A   Zoo: main entrance

B   Artificial Cliff

C   Elephant House

D   Municipal Circus

E   Carousel in the Amusement Park

F   Amusement Park: main entrance

G   Széchenyi Baths

H   Vajdahunyad Castle

I   Statue of the medieval chronicler Anonymus

J   Ice Rink

K   Kunsthalle

L   Millenary monument

the 1880s it hosted peculiar "live shows" in which American Indian, African, Tamil and Inuit families were invited to reside there for months to show spectators how they lived. In the early 1900s the zoo went bankrupt, and the city took it over. It was re-established in 1907 and the buildings that we admire so much today were added by architects of the trend-setting National Romantic school, such as Károly Kós, Kornél Neuschloss and Dezső Zrumeczky. It reopened in 1912. Its highlights include the main entrance (with the stone elephants at street level and the twelve polar bears around the top), the elephant house, the bird house and the palm house. Kids always enjoy the "animal kindergarten", where newborn animals are kept together, at least those who do not eat the others.

Since 1997 the zoo's art nouveau (or National Romantic as some experts insist) buildings have been listed as national landmarks. The general director and his staff work in the painfully obtrusive 1960s bison house, which is a blatant example of the modernist craze raging then which was so insensitive to the immediate and larger environment. The Communists were not the only ones to create such things. Fundraising events are often held at the zoo. I once attended a charity concert inside of the artificial cliff, which offers space for animals on the outside and stores hay inside. Outside the large gate at the corner of Dózsa György út and Állatkerti körút there is a funny but untranslatable slang slogan: *"Állati jó hely!"*, which literally means: this is an "animally" (i.e. terrifically) good place. You can adopt all kinds of zoo animals and support the zoo in many imaginative ways. The zoo's history reflects the tragic ups and downs of Hungarian history: only 15 animals survived World War Two. The highly successful director since 1994, Miklós Persányi, spent four years away, as the Minister of the Environment. In 2007 he returned, not only to implement his public relations ideas that have put the Budapest Zoo on the map of European zoos, but also to enlarge its pleasant territory. The city of Budapest decided to relocate the adjacent amusement park to give the zoo more space. To make sure it happens, Mr. Persányi was appointed as the chairman of the board for the corporation which operates the Amusement Park.

Amusement Park (Vidámpark) 30 *XIV. Állatkerti körút 14–16.,* www.vidampark.hu, open (April 1 to June 30) 11 a.m. to 6 p.m., (July 1 to August 31) 11 a.m. to 8 p.m., (September 1 to October 31) 11 a.m. to 6 p.m. ••• The amusement park is a municipally-owned company that was established in 1950 when the elegant English Park, which had operated since the early 1900s, was nationalized and merged with the Fun Fair, which consisted of dozens of more modest attractions that had been there since the early 19th century. Most of the roughly one million annual visitors queue up to ride the Ferris wheel, which offers a full view of Városliget. It is wise to hold on tight when the creaking parts start moving. If there are only a few passengers, only every second gondola can be used. Apart from the modern rides and games, two landmarks shouldn't be missed. One of them is the carousel, which was built in 1906. Children, some not so young, go mad with indecision over which ride to choose: the fiery horse, the luxurious triumphal coach or the spinning box? There is a fresco above the animals and the operator peeps out from behind the organ. It was restored to its original splendour in 1997, with donations from the then British Ambassador and others. *(See "Budapest Bests", by Mihály Ráday, page 60.)* Another highlight is the roller coaster which is made entirely of wood. Every year about 100 cubic meters are replaced so that every six years the whole track will be rebuilt. There used to be a third legendary place: the enchanted castle. It burnt down in the early 1980s and all of Budapest mourned. A new, postmodern one was built by two contemporary architects, Ferenc Török and Antal Puhl, in 1987.

During the last years of totalitarianism in Hungary the park was a place very much on the decline. In the 1989 edition of this book, I wrote the following: "The slot machine hall has probably the most worn out American and Soviet machines in the world. If one breaks down, you must turn to one of the gentlemen wearing a blue coat chatting in the middle of the hall. He will open the machine but usually just shake his head and say 'play it on the other one', and point to a similar machine." There are no more slot machines in the park, but you can find the "biggest and only Laser Dodgem to be found in Europe, which is the biggest in the world", as the park claims. The park is quick to follow new gaming trends. A Goalstriker game was installed in 2004, in which anyone can strike penalties against a virtual goalkeeper. Invented in 1998 by a 19 year-old Briton, 20 games have since been installed around the world so Budapest players can play against those in Mexico, Canada and Cyprus. The place has been enchanted by the low-tech and high-tech alike. Ask for a map at the gate.

The zoo needs a bigger space, so the Amusement Park will be relocated in a reasonably short time. Its new place is not known yet. The protected old buildings will stay where they are – no doubt about that.

Széchenyi Baths (Széchenyi Gyógyfürdő és Uszoda) 30G *XIV. Állatkerti körút 11.*, www.spasbudapest.com, open daily 6 a.m. to 10 p.m. (the medicinal part until 7 p.m.), except for some public holidays. ••• The Széchenyi (nicknamed "Szecska" ["setch-kah"]) is one of Europe's two largest public bath houses and is visited by about two million people annually. It consists of

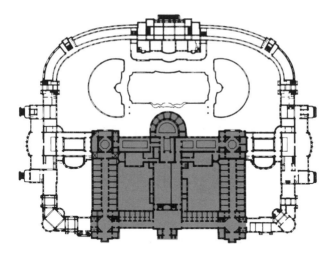

Széchenyi Baths – The Older Part (1913)

two separate parts, which are two different worlds of architecture attracting two different types of regulars. Walk around the building to see the southern wing. The stone-clad medicinal baths there were the first to be built (Győző Czigler and Ede Dvorzsák, 1909–1913). The building is one of the most relaxed ones built at the turn of the century. The main entrance's dome has a huge art nouveau mosaic inside. The floor tiles, the light fixtures, the door frames, and all of the other fittings were made with exceptional care, and were all restored by 2006. You can also walk to the left or to the right, as far as the two side domes. This is where the luxurious private thermal bath tubs are located. The numbers chalked on the doors show what time the occupant started his bath. This was an ideal place to refresh for a student in the early 1970s, after nights not spent at home, in a marble tub that one had not even imagined could exist. And, it still is.

The northern wing, which was built by Imre Francsek, opened in 1927 and its neo-Baroque interior demonstrates a modern use of space. The entrance hall is largely in its original condition. Additions such as the soft drink machines would seem to be glaring mistakes which at best emphasize the charm of the original décor. It's always busy here, and the atmosphere is quite different than that of the other wing. Behind the entrance hall there is a battered but lively restaurant from where you can see the pools. The Széchenyi has three outdoor and twelve indoors pools. The outdoor section has been open since 1963, and the pools are reached through a heated corridor. In the middle outdoor swimming pool bathing caps are required. The right outdoor pool is very hot, while the left one is an "adventure pool" with various surprise elements that alternate every 15 minutes.

The water temperature in the large outdoor pool is 27 degrees Celsius and in the warm water pool it is 38 degrees Celsius. This is where you will see the much-photographed games of water chess, which are played in the warm pool on floating cork chessboards. Of the flood of notices in the main entrance hall, those written only in Hungarian tell where to find the complaint book and specify who can be subsidised to use the baths and on what conditions. You must pay for a "full day" entrance pass, but if you leave earlier you are partially refunded. In late 2007 police reported that a huge fraud was unveiled in this and other baths in which groups were given individual tickets, but they were let in ("for speed reasons") through the handicapped gates, and the tickets were then re-sold. Water for the hippos in the nearby zoo has been traditionally provided from one of the Széchenyi's hot springs since it shows a close chemical resemblance to the water of the river Nile.

A rest

Szent István Fountain
Pavilion NE of Széchenyi Baths

The millennium of the Hungarian state was celebrated in 1896 with a huge exhibition which took up the entire Városliget. A popular attraction of the millenary exhibition was a group of temporary buildings which demonstrated the various architectural styles of the previous 1,000 years. Some of these were copies of real buildings. This mixture of buildings, however absurd the idea may now seem, met with such success that the city commissioned a stone version of one of the buildings to be built after the exhibition. Its popular name is the Vajdahunyad Castle.

Vajdahunyad Castle (Vajdahunyad vár) 30H–31A ●●● One of the main attractions in Városliget is this castle, part of which was modeled after a Transylvanian castle of the same name. The complex consists of four parts: the Romanesque, the Gothic, the Transitional and the Renaissance/Baroque. This bizarre notion was carried out by Ignác Alpár, an exceptionally talented and imaginative architect. The building, which gives a fairy tale

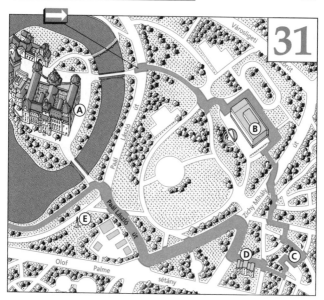

A Vajdahunyad Castle

B Petőfi Csarnok –
   Metropolitan Youth
   Centre

C Fuit Stone

D Former Metropolitan
   Museum (1885)

E Statue of George
   Washington

impression rather than a kitschy one, was completed in 1904.
Naturally, no two turrets are the same, yet the many con-
trasting forms seem to work together as a whole. The permanent stone building was built to house the Agricultural
Museum, which still occupies the castle. During the winter
the boating lake surrounding the castle is turned into an ice
rink. Opposite the main entrance is the statue of Anonymous,
one of the most popular statues in Budapest. He was the first
medieval Hungarian chronicler, but his epoch-making work was
modestly signed with the words that appear on the pedestal of
the 1903 statue: GLORIOSISSIMI BELAE REGIS NOTARIUS ("the
notary of the most glorious King Béla"). This would be sufficient
had not four kings been called Béla in the 12th and 13th centuries. His identity is still disputed by scholars, and the sculptor,
Miklós Ligeti, has given him a hood that hides his face.

WALK FOUR

Petőfi Hall (Petőfi Csarnok) 31B *XIV. Zichy Mihály út 14.,* www.petoficsarnok.hu ••• This converted exhibition hall is a youth centre that opened in 1985. It is now the stronghold of Hungarian rock and pop music. But it also hosts a flea market on Saturdays and Sundays, theatrical performances for children, a roller skating club and a Saturday evening disco. During the summer there is an open-air cinema, a new-wave fashion show, underground theatrical performances, disco-dancing competitions and a "hair show". In brief, it caters to and has caught the imagination of the young who flock to it. Upstairs, airplanes are exhibited which come from the nearby Museum of Transport (only open from spring to autumn, as the rooms are not heated for some reason).

BUDAPEST BESTS

István Rév, historian, maverick political scientist, true son of Buda

Following the imposing wall fence on busy Kerepesi út, not far from the monumental Keleti pályaudvar (Eastern Railway Station), turning at the corner of Salgótarjáni út, unexpectedly and without forewarning, the city comes to a dead-end. The walled fence along Kerepesi út borders the Kerepesi cemetery, the pantheon of the Hungarian people, but along Salgótarjáni ut, the wall protects the hibernated Jewish cemetery, one of the best-kept secrets of Budapest.

The Jewish cemetery opened in 1874, as the representative burial place of one of the largest and richest Jewish communities of Central Europe. The size of the mausolea matches the enormous size of the cemetery: there is no single burial place in Central Europe where the size of the funerary structures could be compared to the mass and height of the mausoleums and crypts of this Jewish necropolis.

The ruined medieval castle with the grates on the gate was designed by the eminent and unique modernist architect, Bela Lajta, who was the architect of the square-shaped mortuary behind the entrance. The dome of the mortuary collapsed almost half a century ago; there is only one preparation room with one large, undamaged, red marble table; and the fireplace, where water was heated is still standing. The shape of the half-collapsed mortuary can be recognized; it looks as if it were the ruins of a Babylonian fortress temple of the imagination. Above the entrance to the mortuary there is an inscription in Hebrew, a line from Psalms 90,3 with Art Nouveau fonts: "You return man to dust; You decreed: Return you mortals!".

WALK FOUR

The Statue of George Washington 31E *XIV. Városliget, Washington sétány (at the lake).* ••• According to American statistics, 3.5 million immigrants from Austria–Hungary arrived in the United States between 1871 and 1913. Half of them were Hungarians, but many others came from Bohemia – hence the old American slang word, "Bohunk". The funds to erect this bronze statue of George Washington, made by Gyula Bezerédi in 1906, were collected by the Bohunks. This was the first full-figure statue of Washington in Europe.

Palace of Arts (Műcsarnok) 32D *XIV. Dózsa György út 37.,* www.mucsarnok.hu, open Tuesday, Wednesday and Friday to Sunday 10 a.m. to 6 p.m., Thursday noon to 10 p.m. ••• The Műcsarnok

The number of the dead and the graves reached almost the full sanctioned capacity of the place before 1945; burials, with a few exceptions, ceased already before World War II. The cemetery was forgotten, perhaps this is why it survived. The Jewish cemetery survived but not the monumental structures. In the past seven decades, the peace of the dead was not honoured: almost all the graves were opened and robbed; not only the living Jewish community was decimated but the community of the dead Jews as well. Once, the cemetery was like a modern metropolis of the dead with three four-story high Art Nouveau or Art Deco mausolea in the proportion of skyscrapers. They were carved from white or black marble, designed by daring, experimental, modernist architects and sculptors. The resting place of the enormously rich Budapest Jewish aristocracy—members of the upper middle class, the bourgeoisie, politicians, artists, and intellectuals—once looked as the silent counterpart of the Gründerzeit, the last third of the 19th century, the time of the frantic construction era of the Millenary Celebrations in the second half of the 1890s. The colossal monuments are comparable to the building of the Fine Arts Museum on Heroes' Square, or the enormous building of the Hungarian Parliament. The grave robbers, the elapsed time and nature, however, did their job: all the monuments are ruined or opened. Nature took over. Compared to the Jewish cemetery at Salgótarjáni út, the world-famous Jewish cemetery in Prague is just a toy, an illustration, a theme park of long-dead Jews. "Trees and men do not grow together" – said Kaa, the half-deaf rock-python in the jungle. Here, where Budapest ends, although we are still in the city, massive trees grew over the ceiling of colossal marble monuments; flowers, evergreen, moss cover the ruined structures, nobody knows where death ends and the life of nature starts; who perished and what is being reborn.

WALK FOUR

was designed by the same architects (Schikedanz and Herzog) as the opposite Museum of Fine Arts, but ten years earlier. They were given the commission without any tender, which caused an uproar. The ground plans show the influence of the late-Renaissance, as does the fine ornamentation of the façade, which was made from "frost-resistant pyrogranite", a contemporary Hungarian invention. Funds ran short when it was time to decorate the pediment, the mosaic of St. Stephen, who was a patron of the arts. It was only put in place in 1941. During World War One the hall housed a military hospital.

This 3,200 square-metre exhibition hall was the largest in the country when it opened in 1896 at the time of the millenary celebrations. It was built for the National Hungarian Fine Art Society. At the opening exhibition (May 2 to October 31, 1896) visitors were shown works by "everybody who counted in Hungary" – painters, sculptors, graphic artists and architects. All in all, there were 1,276 works by 267 exhibitors. The function of the place was to provide an official academic representation of art. Innovators intentionally stayed away, even after the institution was transferred to municipal ownership in 1926. During World war Two the building was severely hit and was reopened only in 1950 when it was used for totalitarian purposes. Mátyás Rákosi, the Communist dictator, was said to have personally removed a painting in 1955 when visiting one of the national fine art shows on the grounds that it emanated "bourgeois notions". "Műcsarnok taste" meant conservatism for many decades until the early 1980s.

The director of Műcsarnok is traditionally the Hungarian commissioner of the Hungarian Pavilion at the Venice Biennial. Since the early 2000s there has been a tender organized for would-be curators. In 2007 the Hungarian pavilion won the Golden Lion prize for the best national pavilion, which was a surprise for the Hungarian art scene which basically disliked the project by Andreas Fogarasi, a Vienna-based artist of Hungarian descent: slow film shots in deserted Budapest community centres.

Műcsarnok hosts some events, most notably the Budapest Art Fair in mid-November when a huge tent is set up next to it to accommodate modern galleries. Aviva Fione Art Prize is a group show of Hungarian artists, the shortlisted one.

Along the side of Városliget there is a wide paved area which was called Felvonulási tér (Procession Square). Celebrations, such as those on April 4th or May 1st, were held here and involved huge crowds. It was also the scene of the military parade every five years. On such occasions there was a demonstration of fighter planes flying overhead. In

A The 1956 Monument

B Time Wheel

C ING Building

D Ice Rink Building

E Kunsthalle

F "Tomb of the Unknown Soldier"

G **H** Millenary Monument

I Museum of Fine Arts

WALK FOUR

1990, April 4th (which celebrated the liberation of Hungary by the Red Army) ceased to be a holiday, to the sorrow of many small boys who were henceforth deprived of military parades.

Opposite Városligeti fasor once stood a huge statue of Stalin (1951–1956) which was pulled down during the 1956 Revolution. From the pediment of this statue the Communist leaders waved to the crowds that marched past in tens of thousands. The pediment was also pulled down. And so was the statue of Lenin which stood near the Műcsarnok and was taken away to be repaired because of "metal fatigue" when the ancien régime was collapsing. It never returned, of course.

The 1956 Monument 32A ••• Public art in Budapest is always a matter of love or hate. Nobody doubts that the new 1956 monument, opposite Városligeti fasor, was chosen with the utmost care out of the many designs submitted. The venue is fitting: it was erected in the former place of the Stalin statue, which was pulled down on the first day of the revolution. The essence of the monument is a growing number of rusty iron columns that unite to form a shiny and pointed razor blade: one that breaks up the pavement. It is a comprehensible metaphor, which also symbolises the crowd: once you are inside, you cease to be an individual. (Designed by the I-ypszilon Group – Tamás Emődi-Kiss, Tamás Papp, Katalin, 2006).

Time Wheel (Időkerék) 32B www.idokerek.hu ••• It took about 20 years for the idea of this giant "Monument to Time" – which is to the right of the Műcsarnok, on the park side of Dózsa György út – to be realized. Designed by István Janáky and

ING Building

associates in 1999, it was finally unveiled on May 1, 2004 when Hungary joined the European Union. According to its initiator, János Herner (a publisher and historian), "it does not measure, rather represents time." The eight metre-high, 2.5 metre-wide, 60 ton granite wheel contains an ingeniously designed hourglass in which all of the identical artificial quartz globes (4.5 cubic meters in all) fall in exactly one year. Of course, this could not be left to the blind forces of nature, so a computer controls the process (when it is not out of service). The computer is needed to

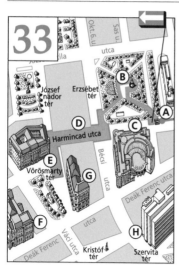

A Coach Station, the Hungarian Design Center

B Danubius Fountain

C Grand Hotel Corvinus Kempinski

D British Embassy

E Gerbeaud

F Vigadó

G Elegant shops

H Office block

compensate for weather changes and leap years. The time wheel is turned every New Year's eve in the midst of a specially organized festival. It cost about 1.5 million euros, which was almost exclusively public money. The father of the idea promised world attention for the wheel turning ceremony, which he said would be shown on every conceivable TV station, which is something yet to happen.

ING Building 32C *VI. Dózsa György út 84/a.* ••• This eccentric office building by Erick van Egeraat, a Rotterdam and Budapest-based architect, is a love or hate affair. To many people it is the symbol of the new Budapest. Before ING (the Dutch bank and insurance company) moved here, it was housed at Andrássy út 9. in a superbly converted late 19th century building with a brand new wing on Paulay Ede utca. We passed it earlier on this walk.

This is the end of our walk in Városliget. We shall return to Vörösmarty tér on the subway. You should exit at Deák tér.

Danubius Fountain (Danubius-kút) 33B ••• This fountain in Erzsébet tér has three basins topped with a male figure symbolizing the Danube. The women sitting on the rim of the lower basin stand for three of the Danube tributaries: the Tisza, the Dráva and the Száva. The lower basin was carved out of a single piece of rock weighing almost 100 tons. Transporting a rock of this size presented quite a problem at the beginning of the 1890s.

WALK FOUR

This is a copy of the original, which was built by Miklós Ybl and Leó Feszler in 1893 and destroyed in World War Two. Originally it decorated Kálvin tér, but when the square was recreated, the statue was also re-located.

This walk took me seven hours without visiting the Museum of Fine Arts or the Műcsarnok.

WALK FOUR

This amazing photo was taken for a daily paper in 1947 by Tibor Bass (1909–1973). Cows are passing the former National Theatre at Blaha Lujza tér on their way to the slaughterhouse. It is not clear whether they came from the Great Plain or only from Keleti pályaudvar (Eastern Railway Station). Anyway, shortage of wagons and lorries were serious.

WALK FIVE

MILLENNIUM QUARTER, ALONG AND BEHIND THE NAGYKÖRÚT

This walk takes us to a new riverfront neighbourhood which holds two new cultural institutions. From there we will go all the way along the Nagykörút (Grand Boulevard): from the Danube back to the Danube. We will look into some side streets and we will peer behind the plastic cover of the Corvin department store. We will visit Café New York, the Royal Waiting Room in the Nyugati pálya-udvar (Western Railway Station) and a giant shopping centre/hotel development. We will get an introduction to Újlipótváros (New Leopold Town) before we return.

Time: Most of a day, depending on how many stops you make.

From Vigadó tér, we board a 2 or 2/A tram coming from the right (in the direction of Közvágóhíd). Notice how expansive the river and its panorama are at this point. The two parts of Budapest are equally important, but totally different in character.

Directly opposite us is a large building at the foot of Castle Hill which was the Royal Gardens Bazaar. Legendary rock concerts, which affected the building's foundations, took place on the top floor during the 1960s. It awaits restoration and will soon be woken up from decades of neglect.

We will take a scenic route and ride for 10 to 12 minutes. Get off at the sixth stop, near Lágymányosi híd (the fourth bridge from where we boarded). The bridge is the newer-looking

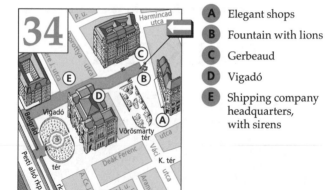

A Elegant shops

B Fountain with lions

C Gerbeaud

D Vigadó

E Shipping company headquarters, with sirens

one with the red pillars. Look for the stop "Közvágóhíd" ("Public Slaughterhouse"), which might be changed to "Nemzeti Színház" or "National Theatre", by the time you have arrived here. It's an improbable neighbourhood for building new cultural institutions (although the same thing was done in Paris when Parc La Vilette was built on the site of a former slaughterhouse).

The neighbourhood on the opposite side of the river is called Lágymányos, a part of district eleven which was once a marsh, where the campus of the Technical University is located. Behind the Lágymányosi híd you can see the tip of Csepel Island, which is the proposed site for some ambitious development. The centre of the island can be reached in 13 minutes on the HÉV commuter train (its terminus is next to the bridge). Lágymányosi híd was long overdue. It was built in an obvious location, completing the Outer Boulevard in Pest. New pillars were built alongside the existing ones of the Southern Railway Bridge. Every single route proposed for the approach roads on the Buda side was contested by locals. In the end, the worst possible solution was chosen and there was an almighty scandal. Most Budapesters, however, like the bridge, especially the big mirrors that throw an even light on the road.

Millennium Quarter (Millenniumi negyed) ••• The construction of this new quarter, which holds the National Theatre and the Palace of Arts, was not the consequence of any natural city development. It is being built in the triangular strip of land formerly used by the railway connecting Petőfi híd and Lágymányosi híd (the so-called "Expo sites"). The land was cleared and taken into direct national ownership when Hungary planned a B-category World Expo jointly with

Vienna, and then alone, for 1996. The plan was cancelled by the newly elected government in 1994, because of alleged minimal foreign interest. For five years not much happened, except for the erection of a nondescript residential building on the northern tip of the neighbourhood near Petőfi híd.

The turning point was related to another new government elected in 1998. This government decided to halt the construction of the new National Theatre that was being built in Erzsébet tér, which is in the city centre where the three metro lines meet. The foundations were already completed and the underground garage had already been built. They argued that the theatre would obstruct the fresh air coming from the river to the inner city. So, they decided on the former Expo sites, which were a little far away from the centre. The government found an ally in a visionary businessman who heads the Hungarian-Canadian Trigránit Group. Sándor Demján is a Hungarian business whiz kid, who has been nationally known since the 1970s. He built the WestEnd City Center at the Nyugati pályaudvar (Western Railway Station; which we will see later in this walk). His Trigránit Group offered to build the National Theatre, allowing it to be paid for after completion.

National Theatre (Nemzeti Színház) IX. *Bajor Gizi park 1.,* www.nemzetiszinhaz.hu ••• The peculiarities continued after the new site was chosen. An entirely new venue obviously meant that a new design was needed. But the new commissioner did

National Theatre

not want a new design contest and appointed architect Mária Siklós, who was an expert in modernizing old theatres but had never designed one herself in her long career. After the Chamber of Architects forced a quick design competition for seven invited architects, the winner was overlooked and the theatre was built according to Ms. Siklós' plans. It was inaugurated on March 15, 2002. The then Prime Minister said in an interview that he had personally chosen the chandelier in the auditorium from what was available. He may not have had a say in the design of the multitude of plastic adornments that proliferate in the over-adorned theatre. The most prominent decoration is the façade of the old National Theatre which was located at Blaha Lujza tér and pulled down in 1964 after it collapsed into a large pool of water. It is accompanied by three torches with real flames burning day and night (hinting at the widespread opinion that the Communist authorities pulled down the theatre not because of the problems building a new metro line underneath it, but to strike a blow against Hungarian traditions).

The building's questionable taste is one thing. Some approvingly say that it is a "comprehensible building", while others think the exterior is unimaginative, over-adorned, and morally obsolete (and was already like that even on the drawing board).

The traditional, rigid character of the basic setup is another controversial thing, and so are the terrible acoustics. In a letter to a newspaper, one reader seriously proposed that some dozens of seats in the 619 seat auditorium should be given to visitors with deficient hearing. The stage can be raised at 72 points, which is a unique feature in Europe. This capacity is often used, whether it's needed or not.

Further development of the area was also proposed by the builders, which would include hotels, a congress centre and another cultural institution. By 2011 only the Palace of Arts had been built, and the environment still looks somewhat neglected.

Palace of Arts (Művészetek Palotája) *IX. Komor Marcell utca 1.,* www.mupa.hu ••• Clearly a new concert hall was long overdue, but this complex which sits next to the National Theatre also houses a modern art museum and a small theatre (into which the National Dance Theatre has partially moved). The three institutions under this common roof are overseen by the general director, who is not just the building's caretaker but also an event organizer. Funding comes from the state, but ownership and operation are still in the hands of the developer and will be for a long time. The design of the building (by Zoboki, Demeter and Associates, 2001–2003) changed much along the way since the government continually modified its requirements, even as late as 2002. This was going to be a horse, but turned out to be a camel, as the old saying goes. Those who say that refer to the outside, not the inside (except for the garage, which is difficult to use, to say the least, thanks to narrow entrances and exits).

The Béla Bartók National Concert Hall is located in the heart of the building. The hall has the awe-inspiring dimensions of a Gothic cathedral: it is 25 metres-wide, 52 metres-long, and 25 metres-high (two levels higher than inner city residential

Palace of Arts

buildings). The number of seats can be varied according to the performance, but total capacity is 1,699 (including 136 standing places) and a further 190 seats can be placed on the stage. The place has phenomenal acoustics, which were designed by Russell Johnson of the American Artec consultant firm. The result is fine-tuned from production to production by the computer-operated coloured panels around the ceiling by György Jovánovics. As Music Director Zoltán Kocsis of the resident National Philharmonic put it during the first rehearsals: "here even the farts of a fly are audible" – a blessing to good orchestras, and a curse to mediocre or bad ones.

The Ludwig Museum of Contemporary Art (Lumú) www.ludwigmuseum.hu, open Tuesday to Sunday 10 a.m. to 8 p.m. (last Saturday of the month, until 10 p.m.). ••• The Lumú is located inside the Palace of Arts in the space closest to the river. This museum is based on a large gift from the Aachen-based billionaire industrialist and art patron, Peter Ludwig. It exhibits art in the making – works made since 1989. Former director Katalin Néray asked top Hungarian businesses to become co-funders of the museum, and thirteen of them did (you can read their names on a tablet at the entrance). It is a

WALK FIVE

strong collection which is occasionally funny, and sometimes even beautiful. When this building was built the museum was moved here from its much visited, but awful space in the Royal Palace.

Its pleasant, super-white interiors often present retrospective shows of great masters of the Hungarian contemporary scene – for instance of Ákos Birkás in 2006 and László Fehér in 2007 – which are all accompanied by thorough catalogues. Lumú is open until 8 p.m. since one of its sponsors supported them on that condition. They wanted to facilitate cross-visits from concert-goers and vice versa.

> Take tram 2 back to Petőfi híd. Walking back on this route won't be fun for at least another ten years, I presume.

Grand Boulevard (Nagykörút) ••• This is the city's longest thoroughfare, measuring 4,114 metres. This point was once a backwater of the Danube. By the end of the last century, the narrow streets of an unplanned suburb had developed here. Construction began in 1872 (the same time as it began on Andrássy út), and lasted 35 years. A total of 251 buildings were demolished and replaced with 253 much larger ones. The Nagykörút, which has a sewage system running underneath it, is 45 metres-wide and crosses through five districts where its sections have different names: Ferenc körút, József körút, Erzsébet körút, Teréz körút (named after Habsburg kings and queens) and Szent István körút.

The Nagykörút connected parts of the city that had previously been separate and socially distinct. The boulevard started from the suburb of Boráros tér, winded through better-off districts, and led to the ill-famed slums of the Margit híd area (which became a fashionable and well-off district when the city's balance shifted towards the Parliament buildings). So when the boulevard officially opened in 1906 it led from a poor district towards better and better-off districts – just as it does today.

The buildings along the Nagykörút are similar with their eclectic façades showing elements of various architectural styles and usually having rendered walls decorated with plaster ornaments. The designs imitate those of the buildings along Andrássy út. On the street side, there are light and spacious flats with at least two bedrooms and a bathroom. The kitchens are large and have small annexes that were once the maid's rooms. The flats at the rear of the buildings are reached from balconies in the inner courtyard.

After World War Two when the flats were nationalized, the larger front-facing flats were broken up into smaller units, often without any kind of logic. However, many flats at the rear acquired a bathroom. In the early 1980s the façades all along the Nagykörút were restored and the interiors of some buildings, such as that at Ferenc körút 5., were renovated. Rents were low compared to the cost of maintenance. All buildings have two separate staircases: the main staircase leads to the front-facing flats and the rear one was originally for tradesmen and servants. The main staircase is usually more ornate, though sometimes, as at Ferenc körút 5., it is the same as the rear one. Today everyone uses the main staircase or the lift (if one has been installed) and the rear stairs are often left un-cleaned. The courtyards were once the scene of animated social life. A reminder of those times is the wooden frame on which carpets were beaten, called the "poroló". Maids (and later housewives) took their carpets to the courtyard and beat them with a cane carpet beater, called the "prakker", which was also what children were threatened with for misbehaving. There were agreed upon times for beating carpets in the courtyard, and this started many arguments. When the ladies made peace, they gathered in the yard to chat. Sadly, the vacuum cleaner, which was in general use by the mid 1960s, brought this busy social life to an end.

Ferenc körút divides Ferencváros, the ninth district, which was named after Emperor Francis I in 1792 when he came to the throne. It remained an agricultural area until the late-19th century, by which time large mills and slaughter-houses had been established. The local population grew quickly and became working class and artisan in character. The modernisation of the district was interrupted by the Great Depression before the war.

The history of this area can be seen on a detour into Angyal utca, a street which could symbolize Ferencváros as a whole. Some buildings attempt to imitate those on the Nagykörút, but on a smaller scale. Others are single-storey buildings occupied by one family, and others are single-storey buildings arranged around courtyards and housing several families. Here, also, is the only modern block built the way the city authorities had planned. In the late 1990s two small post-modern hotels were added, which are somewhat better in quality than the neighbourhood's large-scale developments. Still, they are likely to fall prey to moral obsolescence.

Holocaust Memorial Center (Holokauszt Emlékközpont)

35G IX. *Páva utca 39.*, www.hdke.hu, open Tuesday to Sunday 10 a.m. to 6 p.m.. ••• This government-funded memorial centre opened in April 2004 in a somewhat tucked away

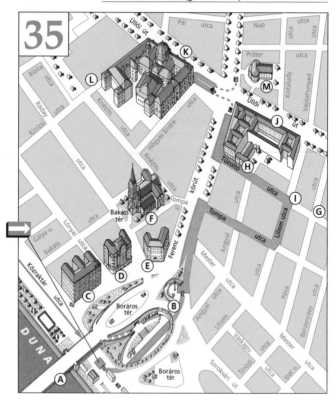

A Petőfi híd

B Memorial Column

C D E Block of flats

F Ferencváros Parish Church

G Budapest Holocaust Memorial Center

H Furniture store

I Trafó

J Former Army Barracks

K Museum of Applied Arts

L Kultiplex

M Corvin Cinema

WALK FIVE

part of Ferencváros. It's partly a museum, partly a research centre, and partly an event organizer which aims to integrate the Holocaust into the curricula of Hungarian schools. A meticulously restored classical-looking synagogue, which was built by Lipót Baumhorn in 1924, was incorporated in the newly-built complex. The synagogue, however, was last used for liturgical purposes in 1982. A new 88 square-metre prayer vault was also built. Built by the István Mányi Studio, the place is austere and elegant, and its design was feverishly attacked by some key figures in the Jewish community. They argued that the Holocaust in Hungary was not an internal Jewish affair, but was a tragedy for Hungary and for Hungarians. By building the centre here (in a non-central location), the government missed an opportunity to confront new generations with indispensable knowledge about the Holocaust. There is still a neglected and deserted synagogue near the city centre on Rumbach Sebestyén utca, which was an early work of Otto Wagner (the Vienna star architect of the fin de siècle), where the centre could have been built. Critics also said that the centre's closed character guards a

---

Auschwitz and "Operation Hoess"

The Holocaust's largest and quickest deportation began on May 15, 1944. Fifty-six days later, Hungarian authorities had deported 437,402 Jews from Hungary according to German records. With the exception of 15,000 people, all went to Auschwitz-Birkenau. In Hungary, not only the Jews were persecuted for their origin in 1944–1945. During the Holocaust thousands of Hungarian Roma were also murdered and tens of thousands were persecuted.

The largest Nazi concentration camp complex comprised the Auschwitz concentration camp, the Birkenau (Auschwitz II) extermination camp and the Monowitz (Auschwitz III) forced labor camp. During the 56 months between July 1940 and January 1945, one million Jews and roughly 100,000 non-Jews were murdered at Auschwitz. Every third victim there was a Hungarian. The Birkenau crematoriums never worked with such intensity as during the extermination of the Hungarian Jews who arrived within a period of two months during the summer of 1944. Their extermination was personally supervised by Rudolf Hoess, the most experienced of the "industrial" genocide experts and the creator of Auschwitz who served as its commander until November 1943. The 1944 murder of the Hungarian Jews was code-named "operation Hoess". *(Excerpt from the Holocaust Memorial Centre's website, 2010.)*

secret, rather than attempts to disseminate knowledge. Anyway, the complex, which cost seven million euros to build and covers 4,700 square-metres, is a high-quality memorial that successfully fulfills its mission – for those who actually go there.

"Trafó" Contemporary Arts Centre (Trafó Kortárs Művészeti Központ) 35I *IX. Liliom utca 41.*, www.trafo.hu, open weekdays 2 p.m. to 8 p.m., weekends 5 p.m. to 8 p.m. (and on performance nights, until the end of the performance). ••• "An institution, a building, a space, a medium, vibration, an intellectual adventure, risk, possibility." That's how founding director György ("Gyuri") Szabó, the workaholic-economist summarizes what Trafó is about. This arts incubator and alternative arts centre was established in a former transformer house from 1909. It opened in 1998 as an ambitious place that hosts guest performances and cultivates new productions for export. It focuses on modern dance and theatre, even innovative circus productions, but has purposely has no resident company. It hosts exhibitions, evening shows, and an exuberant club life in the evening. In the basement there are fat columns and pictures on the walls. In the first weeks after the opening there were some hundred membership cards on the wall, which were the "Young Artists' Club" id photos from the late 1970s. The club was Trafó's predecessor, and is where the author of this book found his (much) younger ego.

Former Army Barracks 35J–36A *IX. Üllői út 49–51.* ••• This large yellow building is the only one that was already here when the Nagykörút was being laid out. Built by József Hild between 1845 and 1846, during the 1956 Revolution it was one of the strongholds of the soldiers who joined the army during the 13 days of the 1956 revolution. It was heavily hit by the re-invading Soviet troops and the whole area suffered beyond imagination. Now it contains offices, warehouses and temporary housing for people whose homes are under construction.

Museum of Applied Arts (Iparművészeti Múzeum) 35K–36B *IX. Üllői út 33–37.*, www.imm.hu, open Tuesday to Sunday 10 a.m. to 6 p.m. ••• This collection was the third of its kind in Europe, after the London and Vienna institutions were established in 1872. The building, which was built by Ödön Lechner and Gyula Pártos in 1896, was one of the great achievements of the millennium celebrations. There is an immediate clash between the exterior – dominated by a colourful tile-covered dome and the main entrance's ceiling – with the stark white interior. The aula is covered with a steel-framed glass ceiling.

Elsewhere, a state-of the art steel frame is sometimes hidden under stonework and is sometimes flaunted. The interior was covered with a colourful painting by Károly Miksa Reissmann until the 1920s when the director had it covered with white paint because tastes had changed. Art nouveau was considered to be vulgar and ridiculous for some decades. The inner, glass-covered central hall is often used for receptions and award ceremonies. To the right of the main entrance is the statue of Ödön Lechner (1845–1915), one of the building's designers and the best known master of Hungarian art nouveau. The statue, by Béla Farkas and Ferenc Kende, was made in 1936 and moved here from Liszt Ferenc tér in 1948. It's a unique building that's worth internal inspection no matter which part of the rich collection is being exhibited. (A photo of the aula is on page 327.)

A Detour: Hungarian Natural Science Museum (Magyar Természettudományi Múzeum) *VIII. Ludovika tér 3.,* www.nhmus.hu, open Wednesday to Monday 10 a.m. to 6 p.m. ••• This relative newcomer on the museum scene has been a sort of new sensation in Budapest, especially for children. Like many other major museums, this one was also spun off from the National Museum in 1934. The museum is in an elegant neo-Classical building built by Mihály Pollack in 1834. It is the former riding school of the Ludoviceum, the Hungarian military college. In 1996 it was fully reconstructed from the outside by István Mányi, and given an ingeniously designed high-tech/post-modern interior. It has partly been expanded to include more and more of the entire former military college.

In front of the museum there are two dozen big lumps of stone presented by the quarry industry and arranged chronologically (note the small plaques on the rocks). Behind the main entrance, spectators are instantly confronted with the skeleton of a whale, that was brought from Vienna in 1900 (though it must have lived even farther away). The skeleton weighs more than two tons and has scars on its skull that go back to 1956 when there was a fire in the museum and it was housed elsewhere. The fights in 1956 caused terrible damage to the collection. When the National Museum was hit (it was too close to the besieged Radio building) the Africa show was fully destroyed, and parts of the mineral collection and the paleontology collection vanished. And on November 5th indiscriminate shelling from Russian tanks set parts of the National Museum on fire including the animal collection. The fire destroyed 36,000 birds, 22,000 eggs, and 200,000 flies, among others. The remaining collection has changed homes so many times that it is difficult to follow.

The museum was one of the first innovators in the somewhat backward mid-1990s Hungarian museum scene, which is still more or less dominated by professors interested in scholarly publications, rather than community outreach education or entertaining the public. It has a flavour reminiscent of American museums, and in places it even feels like Chicago's Field Museum. It has been promised that the surrounding area (called Orczy-kert) will sooner or later be added to the museum to form a new ecological park – a somewhat vague promise to speed up Hungary's rather slow change in green matters.

The museum is well-worth a detour (from the Ferenc körút station to Klinikák it is one stop on the M3 metro followed by a five minute walk, mostly through a park).

Corvin Budapest Film Palace 35M, 36C *VIII. Corvin köz,* www.corvin.hu ••• The first cinemas in Budapest were usually located on the ground floors of residential buildings. This one, built by Emil Bauer in 1923, is a rare exception. It used to have a lobby that was just about as large as its auditorium, which had 1,300 seats. Then in 1996 it was converted to a multiplex cinema with six screens. Designed by Balázs Töreky, Dezső Töreky and László Rajk, the only problem is that the entrance is too narrow – one of the few aspects of the original design that was impossible to change. Each screen is named for a legendary film director and the interior and hallways are decorated with old cinema posters. On one side there is the pleasant Casablanca café, on the other there is the Odeon art video rental shop. Along with the buildings surrounding it, the cinema, with its façade that has neo-Baroque elements, is a good example of architectural design that uses a modern structure but is conservative in its style. This was one of the headquarters of armed resistance in 1956 and was the site of some of the fiercest fighting.

Corvin/Szigony Project 35M *Práter – Szigony – Tömő – Balassa – Apáthy – Szigony – Üllői – Kisfaludy utca* ••• Over the cinema, you can see the front of an overpowering new develepoment which spans several blocks. Small apartments were razed by the hundred to make way for the offices, condominiums and shops here. It is definitely worth a detour. Completion is expected in 2016.

József körút ••• The next section of the Nagykörút is so-named because it crosses the eighth district, which was named Józsefváros in 1777 after the future Emperor Joseph II. Behind the row of buildings towards Kálvin tér, the area becomes increasingly elegant. Aristocrats had their town houses,

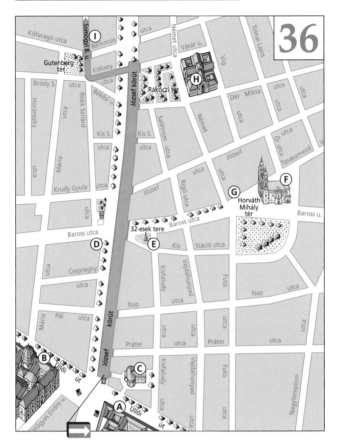

A Former Army Barracks

B Museum of Applied Arts

C Corvin Cinema

D Café Stex

E War Memorial

F Church

G Telephone Central

H Market Hall

I University of Jewish Studies

("palota" in Hungarian) built around the National Museum. To the right, however, the area is rather less grand, with many single-storey houses. Many cloak-and-dagger films have been shot around here, and there are whole streets where nothing has changed since the early 20th century, such as Futó utca,

WALK FIVE

Nagytemplom utca, and the blasphemously-named Leonardo da Vinci utca. The Corvin–Szigony real estate development project (2006–2016?) will radically change the character of the neighbourhood. Offices, apartments and shops will be erected around a new, wide avenue which will probably lure new, young, middle-class residents here, and will gentrify the area and ultimately change the connotation of "Józsefváros".

The area along the Nagykörút on the city side and as far as Baross utca was called "Cérnakorzó" (thread promenade) before the second world war. Seamstresses used to walk here after work to become acquainted with the craftsmen in the area. The ladies promenading here now are looking for less long-lasting relationships.

Café Stex (Stex Ház) 36D *VIII. József körút 55–57.*, www.stexhaz. hu, open Monday and Tuesday 8 a.m. to 2 a.m., Wednesday to Saturday 8 a.m. to 6 a.m., Sunday 9 a.m. to 1 a.m. ••• Behind the not very promising exterior, there is a huge interior which has several different rooms (including small intimate ones and private ones) and billiard tables. In Hungarian slang, stex means "money" or "cash", and the décor is organised around this theme with money and various forms of gambling presented fairly crudely, but humorously. There are photographs and documents (some fake and some real) plastered all over the walls, all with personal comments. It's as if the owner is trying to tell us about grandparents and great-grandparents who lived under the spell of gambling. There's a bronze bust of Alfréd Stex, the head of the family, on the bar. There's a variety of lottery cards available and the Józsefváros gambling locals have made themselves at home here. It's a place where you feel good, and where the food is filling. There's a non-smoking area, which is as empty as it's possible to be. There must be people who believe this tongue in cheek history of the family.

Rákóczi tér is known for its market hall and its secondary dressmakers school. But it also used to be the centre of low-prostitution in Budapest. Since 1947 all forms of prostitution have been illegal in Hungary. After years of desperately struggling in vain to end prostitution when the aim was to keep it under control, in 1999 severe anti-prostitution legislation created "zones of tolerances" to be newly outlined by local governments. But none have came into being so far. When a closed-circuit camera system was installed the girls disappeared from this square. They must be around, though.

The buildings here look the same as elsewhere in the area. The value of the flats, however, is lower because of the location's notoriety. The area beyond the Nagykörút is, if possible, an even more pathetic sight. Lights in the ground floor flats in these dark, narrow streets must be turned on even in broad daylight because natural light is so scarce.

When I lived in this area for some years, alongside the old lived many young gypsies who were settling there from the country. There were gypsy musicians with a number of kids, and dealers of second-hand goods. My flat was in a five-storey building with a shared court-yard. You reached your flat by walking down the long access balcony, passing all of the other flats that shared it. During the summer when people left their windows open, you could hear the baker's alarm clock go off at three in the morning and then, one by one, at 15 minute inter-vals, every other alarm in the building.

On this section of the Nagykörút the number of small shops increases. There's a watchmaker's shop, a pipe shop, a souvenir shop disguised as a tobacconist's, computer shops, a ballet shoe maker, an old-fashioned hairdresser, and a fountain pen shop with a long history. There is also a Totó-Lottó betting office. "Lottó" is a type of lottery, established in 1957, in which you tick off five numbers out of the 90 on your ticket. "Totó" is the Hungarian football/soccer pools where you guess the results of 13+1 matches. Now there are new forms of online lottery. If fortune wants to find you, she will find the way to do so.

Jewish Theological Seminary/University of Jewish Studies (Országos Rabbiképző – Zsidó Egyetem) 36I *VIII. Bérkocsis utca 2.*, www.or-zse.hu ••• Rabbis have been being trained in Budapest since 1877, which was the high-point of belief in the possibility of assimilation, when an increasing number of Hungarians of Jewish faith or origin thought that in a couple of decades Judaism would be no more than a faith. Currently there are about 250 students here, including about a dozen from abroad. Since the mid-1990s not only rabbis and scholars are trained here, but also teachers and social workers. This part of the institute is called the "Pedagogium". Since 1990 there has been a Jewish renaissance in Hungary, with new associations, newspapers, community centres, secondary schools, summer camps and websites being founded (see the seminary's web site for more).

Corvin Department Store: the Old and the "New" 37A ••• We approach the department store on Blaha Lujza tér from the back, which is neglected, but is still reminiscent of the original idea. The store opened in 1926, but was only com-pleted by 1929. Designed by Zoltán Reiss, the building had the first escalator in Hungary installed in 1931. Since then, it has been rebuilt a zillion times. Its appearance changed again in 1966 when a new metal-looking plastic façade was designed by

Ferenc Battka. Most people now see the building as a memorial to this wild rage of modernism. This store can no longer use its not-wildly-original slogan, which went "the largest store – the largest choice", for there are now larger department stores. Its customers mainly come from the suburbs. I can hardly wait for the plastic façade to be taken off and for the old wall underneath to be given some post-modern paint-job. It would be a perfect wall for that. The building was declared a 2nd-grade national landmark in 2004, which means that the state has the right to intervene and buy it if it is ever put up for sale. Even more importantly, it can deny permission to raze it or to change it fundamentally.

In the underpass you can buy newspapers day and night, and in the early 1960s the first automatic food dispensers were installed here. If you were tall enough, you inserted coins, but often nothing happened. You then had to bang on the machine and the person who filled it with food from behind unwillingly came out and gave you your chosen cake with his own hand (or gave your money back). Then for years the said person sat behind a window. Not any more.

Blaha Lujza tér, which bisects the Nagykörút and crosses Rákóczi út at this point, is one of the city's central squares. At one end of Rákóczi út there is Erzsébet híd, on the other you can see the great yellow mass of Keleti pályaudvar (Eastern Railway Station). The old Nemzeti (National) Theatre once stood on this square and the famous clock standing in front of it was the standard rendezvous spot for ages. "I'll meet you at seven at the Nemzeti, where the number six tram stops", went the old song. The older generation still refers to this spot as the "Nemzeti". It would have been a nice gesture to call this metro stop "Nemzeti" since it was partly due to its construction that the old theatre building had to be demolished in 1964. Architects did not consider rebuilding it since at that time the eclectic style that dominates the Nagykörút was considered worthless. Instead, we got the kind of moderni-sation that favoured angular and zig-zag lines.

Old National Theatre, as reflected on a facade 37C *VII. Rákóczi út 42.* ••• The designer of an office building on the corner of Rákóczi út and Akácfa utca erected a fine monument to the National Theatre that stood here between 1908 and 1964. If you study the façade carefully, you'll spot a negative image of the theatre repeated dozens of times. Designed by Xavier Gonzalez in 1994, the building's interior brings you to another world, which is so different from the neglected, overcrowded junction outside.

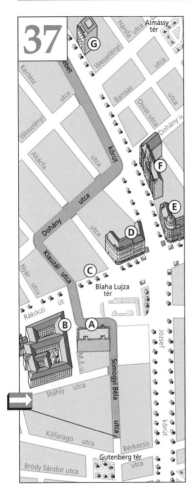

A Corvin Department Store

B Rókus Hospital

C National Theatre memorial

D Block of flats, with a supermarket on the ground floor

E New York Palace and the Café

F Madách Theatre

At midnight on New Year's Eve the carnival-like procession that fills the streets of central Budapest reaches its climax around here. Days before, vendors invade the körút selling the props; parking restrictions are set aside on this day; and even the flowerboxes are removed from the corners (where their purpose is partly to stop pedestrians from crossing).

New York Palace and Café 37F

VII. Erzsébet körút 9–11., www.newyorkpalace.hu, open daily 10 a.m. to midnight. ••• Since it is situated on the bend in the road, the New York Palace can be seen from afar and faces three streets. Built by Alajos Hauszmann between 1891 and 1895 as the headquarters for the New York Insurance Company, the building used to house Budapest's Fleet Street. The neo-Renaissance building was built of fine, long-lasting materials with a tasteful mixture of styles. It already had hints of art nouveau, especially in the tower. Boscolo hotels bought it in 2001 and has restored the café and converted the rest of the building into a luxurious five star hotel.

WALK FIVE

New York Palace

Budapest had more than 400 cafés at the turn of the 19th century, but the New York Café on the ground floor of this building was the most beautiful, the busiest and the liveliest. When the place opened, some writers were said to have thrown its key into the Danube so that it should stay open night and day. As the saying goes, at that time "every writer had his own café and every café had its own writer". The New York had many writers: virtually all of the literary men of the era were either regulars or regularly dropped in. Many came to work here from the dark, unheated rooms that they rented, and also to fill themselves up on the "writers' plate" (cold meat, cheese and bread) which they got for a discount. They also got free ink and paper. The literature-loving headwaiters knew everybody's habits and their latest works. They also allowed writers to dine on credit. Writers also sold their books here, looked for jobs, or read the latest papers. The titles of the papers that the café subscribed to were written on a notice board that read: "all the dailies and arts journals of the world" (there were 400 of them, at one time). Not only writers frequented the place, but other types of people also came, depending on the time of day. Actors, journalists and cinema staff came early in the morning. Retired actors arrived later. Groups dressed elegantly came for dinner, and card players, circus artists and waiters came to enjoy the nights. Dezső Kosztolányi, novelist and poet, immortalized the New York in a story: "It felt so good to dip ourselves in that mist, in that hot pool, not thinking of anything for a while, paying attention to how it is bubbling and wabbling, and it was a great feeling to know that all these people who are paddling here, are slowly being relaxed, being tied to each other, all will soon be melted into one single, noisy soup ... all were talking at the same time. The topics were: whether one has free will or not, what shape is the pest bacterium, how much are salaries in Britain, how far away Sirius can be, what Nietsche meant by 'eternal return', is homosexuality rightful, is Anatole

France Jewish? They wanted to get the gist of everything, in a quick and thorough manner..."

The café had its golden age in the early-1910s, and its silver age in the second-half of the 1920s and into the early-1930s. Some of the most influential Hungarian journals were edited in the gallery. Their editors were exhibited in caricatures for many decades, which were said to be lost when the café closed before the recent renovation.

In 1945, just after the siege, potatoes were sold through the windows of the shelled and burnt out café. It reopened, when during the night of January 15, 1949, a dozen people arrived to nationalize the café. The inventory is no funny reading: "69 marble tables, 7 newspaper frames, 36 coffee glasses, 11 kgs. of coffee beans, 6 liters of milk, 6 jars of artificial cane sugar." New York was seen as the symbol of the old, useless world, and so a sporting goods shop was opened there. The café reopened in 1954. It was renamed as Hungária. As long as publishing houses and newspapers operated upstairs, it was a natural meeting point. In the early 1990s they all left. The monthly 2000, a highbrow intellectual paper was edited in the gallery for some years. Its staff were given a 40 percent discount, in the memory of the Good Old Days, and Aunt Irene, the literary toilet attendant never let the editors (the author of this book included) pay if they happened to visit her institution. The New York is now listed in all the guidebooks and has become a tourist pilgrimage site. The building's meticulous restoration is universally praised, and its modern furniture and prices are mostly cursed. Expect some queuing, even if there are free tables inside.

The next section of the Nagykörút is called Erzsébet körút. It runs through district seven, which is called Erzsébetváros (named, like the bridge, after Franz Joseph's wife). It is the most densely populated part of the city with more than 50,000 people per square-kilometre. There are a number of single-storey buildings here, and along the Nagykörút there are many small shops, especially in the entrances of the buildings (and some even on the upper levels). To the left there is the Old Jewish Quarter, which by now is hardly more than a nickname. Here the disappearance of small old blocks, the unification of sites, and the low quality new apartment blocks is what threatens the very character of Budapest. Pressure groups try to prevent further damage. The problem is that the local district governments don't represent the interest of the "greater good" – that of Budapest. They say they represent their immediate voters – who are usually less educated, and don't understand the intellectuals who come here to protest against "progress".

WALK FIVE

Madách Theatre (Madách Színház) 37G, 38A *VII. Erzsébet körút 31–33.*, www.madachszinhaz.hu ••• The Madách Theatre was completed in 1961 on the site of an old cabaret (or "orpheum"). It was designed by Oszkár Kaufmann, and soon became a flagship of new trends and a stronghold of innovation and fun. The first première was Brecht's The Caucasian Chalk Circle, directed by trend-setting Ottó Ádám. When the original innovations faded, and became mainstream and tired, the original innovators retired and a new generation began to resort to musical comedies to attract larger audiences. *Cats* was the phenomenal first success in March 1983. The longest queue in living memory was on November 29, 2004 when all the tickets for the *Phantom of the Opera* performances in May 2005 were sold in two days. Budapest has more than 15 repertory theatres now, all but one of which are subsidised. Spectators pay roughly one third of the ticket prices. A thorough facelift was completed 1999 and retained most of the foyer's inner design, which was a rare good example of Central European 1950s and early 1960s style. But the extensive new mural paintings are not harmonious with the original design. They are a bit too sweet.

Grand Hotel Royal 38B *VII. Erzsébet körút 49.*, http://www.corint hia.com/budapest, www.ohb.hu/royal ••• When it opened, this hotel was one of the largest in the Austro–Hungarian Empire. Built by Rezső Ray in 1896 in French neo-Renaissance style, the Hotel Royal was originally meant for visitors to the highly successful Millennium Exhibition. By this time the Nagykörút had become Budapest's main artery and the hotel rooms had superb views of this most attractive part of Budapest. The hotel had 232 guest-rooms, 20 individual apartments in adjacent buildings, and attic rooms for the staff. Concerts were held in the Royal's celebrated ballroom. In 1909 the first Hungarian airplane was exhibited in one of the hotel's courtyards. With the growing popularity of motion pictures, the ballroom was turned into the Royal Apollo cinema. After World War Two it became the Red Star cinema, then it again became the Royal Apollo until it closed for good in 1997.

From World War Two until 1953 the building functioned as an office building. In 1953 part of the building was restored as a hotel, but three years later the roof was destroyed by fire during the 1956 revolution. A thorough renovation became inevitable and was completed between 1957 and 1961 by István Janáky. During Christmas 1959 the Red Star cinema opened with an entrance on Hársfa utca. In 1961 the building was reopened as a hotel with 367 guest rooms. The long list of celebrities who stayed here includes Max Reinhardt,

WALK FIVE

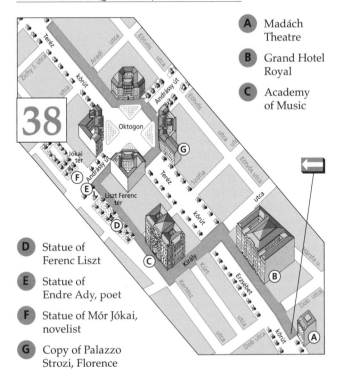

A Madách Theatre

B Grand Hotel Royal

C Academy of Music

D Statue of Ferenc Liszt

E Statue of Endre Ady, poet

F Statue of Mór Jókai, novelist

G Copy of Palazzo Strozi, Florence

Asta Nielsen, Shalapin, Professor Barnard, Anna Moffo, Renata Scotto, and Elisabeth Schwarzkopf. It was the most elegant hotel in town until the new riverfront hotels opened.

The full makeover of the Hotel Royal took place between 1999 and 2002 and cost about 100 million dollars. The Maltese Corinthia Group bought the building and commissioned Miklós Marosi, a Hungarian architect, to do the restoration. He pulled down everything except for the façade and the ballroom. He rebuilt the rest, with the idea that it would be a venue for Budapest's elite, as it had been in the grand old days. There are 414 rooms now, and an enlarged back wing facing Hársfa utca, which was previously a quasi-slum area. Now a bridge spans over it leading to the Valetta conference centre and an apartment building built around an elegant courtyard. This elegant space represents a sort of glitz that will probably age very well. The Bock Bistro – co-owned by (and named after) one of Hungary's most prestigious winemakers – opens from the street and has been an instant success, for both the wine and the food.

WALK FIVE

Liszt Academy of Music (Zeneakadémia) 38C *VI. Liszt Ferenc tér 8.,* www.lfze.hu ••• The official name of this institution, "Liszt Ferenc Zeneművészeti Főiskola", can be found inscribed between the two "geniuses" at the top of the building. Music teachers and musicians are trained here, and there are about 300 students in all. The building, which was designed by Flóris Korb and Kálmán Giergl, took three years to build and was completed in 1907. Above the main entrance the bronze statue of Ferenc Liszt by Alajos Stróbl can be seen. The Main Hall (Nagyterem) is 25 metres-long, 23 metres-wide and 16 metres-high. It has 1,200 seats, the best of which are the first from the left in the eighth row – a former director of Hungaroton, the national record company, used to get a complimentary ticket for this seat. The "best" just means that you have the best view of the stage from here, since the acoustics in the hall are extraordinarily good everywhere. You can hear everything, even from the back row of the second gallery where seats are usually taken by music students who fill the gallery with their loudly expressed opinions. If more than 1,200 people are interested in a concert, the seats behind the stage are sold. If there are even more, then some chairs are placed on stage (as happened when Maurizio Pollini last played here).

On either side of the Walcker organ there are Latin inscriptions. To the left, it says: Sursum Corda ("Lift up Your Hearts", from the Latin mass). To the right, it says: Favete Linguis ("Hold Your Tongue", or, "Be Quiet", from Horace). There are hundreds of other details to notice on the walls and the ceiling. At the bottom right corner of the organ there is a cavity the size of a person, which is where radio commentators hole themselves up to introduce the concerts. Though they may be forced out on special occasions, like at a performance of Monteverdi's Vespers, when the "Echo" tenor solo was sung from here.

The Small Hall (Kisterem), which you can reach from the first floor, seats 400 people. It, too, has good acoustics, but sometimes you can also hear sounds from the Main Hall here. This is the venue for the students' examination concerts. Decades ago I threw a bouquet of roses to my alto girlfriend after her graduation performance, not realizing that the contemporary pieces she sang towards the end were less than perfect (and were graded accordingly). Throughout the building surfaces are exceptionally lovingly shaped. This is generally true of most art nouveau buildings, but here there is a special tranquility. It's as if this art nouveau building had grown straight out of eclecticism – fire out of water. In the foyer you can spot a state-of-the-art brass "vacuum cleaner", I mean a piece of tube. In the gent's loo the graffiti that I mentioned in the first edition of the

Dohnányi Ernő utca

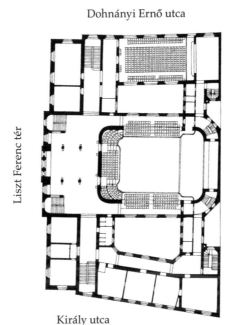

Liszt Ferenc tér

Király utca

Liszt Academy of Music – the First Floor

book – "Viva Brüggen!" – is now gone. The Dutch recorder player must have been really very good, if a concert-goer had such an urge to immortalize him that night with a felt-tip pen. The building is being renovated now, expected to reopen in 2013.

Café Paradise in Liszt Ferenc tér ●●● Since Liszt Ferenc tér was made a pedestrian zone in the early 1990s, one café after another has opened. A French businessman bought a huge dry-cleaners here, closed it, and opened it as Café Vian. In its former role, it was once visited by Allen Ginsberg as a humorous plaque memorializes (look for it over the small window between the kitchen and the café). The first trendy café to open here, Incognito, has by now been too modernized. In its early years there were pictograms at the entrance announcing what you couldn't bring into the café with you such as guns, elephants and electric drills. The signs on the toilet doors said "Zsuzsi" (Suzy) and "Rudi" (Rudy). But not any more. The most serious place in the square is a restaurant/café/beer hall called Buena Vista (www. buena-vista.hu), which serves imaginative modern Hungarian

WALK FIVE

and Mediterranean cuisine. The current most popular place at Liszt Ferenc tér is Menza (*VI. Liszt Ferenc tér 2.*, www.menza. co.hu), whose name means "cheap and smelly university canteen". The place is an exercise in retro design and brings back the Budapest of the 1970s - the one that could have existed had the Soviet Army withdrawn from Hungary in 1955 as it did from Austria.

A copy of Palazzo Strozzi 38G *VI. Teréz körút 15.* ••• This work by Alajos Hauszmann, the architect of the New York Palace, dates from 1884. The original in Florence is larger and better. Ours, which was an aristocrat's palace, now houses offices and a richly decorated wedding hall on the ground floor (perhaps the most fashionable in the city). In Hungary marriage services are conducted at district councils and central offices like this. The bride usually wears a white dress and the bridegroom a dark suit. The young couple are taken to the ceremony in cars decorated with flowers.

In the next section of Teréz körút, forget my promise that we would walk through better and better-off areas. Since all of the new shopping centres have been built in and around Budapest, the Nagykörút has been on the decline. Shops often change hands and they carry lower and lower quality stuff. The boutiques in Király utca are an exception. They somehow could also belong on Andrássy út.

Here on Teréz körút you can also find the art movie house, Művész, which is a sort of small proto-multiplex. Nearby at Teréz körút 28. there is a huge houseware store called Kátay, which was named for the shop's ex-owner. Also nearby is the Béke Hotel Radisson, which has been modernized a number of times (the last occasion was in the late-1980s). The hotel's patisserie is popular with businessmen for its good coffee, dessert and ice cream. On the façade there are two sitting lions holding a torch in their paws. Opposite the hotel, the Játékszín is a small theatre without its own company (VII. Teréz körút 48.). Rather unusually for Hungary, each production has a specially assembled cast. The theatre mostly plays commercial comedies and the tickets are heavily subsidized.

Nyugati pályaudvar (Western Railway Station) 39C *VI. Teréz körút 55.* ••• From this railway station trains set out for the north and the east, so the name is misleading. Long ago the Vienna train had to make a long detour to the north on its journey since there was no railway bridge across the Danube. The building was constructed by the Eiffel Company of Paris, and designed by August de Serres between 1874 and 1877. It was built in such a way that the old railway terminal was able to function undisturbed underneath. Over the next 100 years the

25,000 square-metre hall deteriorated and plans were made for a new building. Fortunately, the conservationists won and most of the old iron structure has been re-cast – only the paintwork has been changed to light blue, the favourite colour of post-modernism. Towards the end of the hall, on the left, there is a large closed door. Above the lintel, an inscription carved in marble reads: VIRIBUS UNITIS ("With Unity Strength"), which was the heraldic motto of Franz Joseph. This door leads to the Royal Waiting Room, which is pretty from the outside, but only used when it's rented out for receptions. The elegant glass screen of the main façade allows trains to become part of the city's traffic. In the early 1980s a train actually plowed through the glass when the brakes failed, but it stopped at the tram stop. The giant former restaurant to the right of the main entrance has been turned into a McDonald's. The interior is quite a success. Note the elegant, unobtrusive post-modern tower in the corner.

Skála Metro Department Store (Skála Áruház) 39D *VI. Nyugati tér 1–2.*, open Monday to Friday 9 a.m. to 8 p.m., Saturday 9 a.m. to 5 p.m., Sunday 10 a.m. to 4 p.m. ••• In the 1970s and 1980s Skála was perhaps the most dramatically developing Hungarian company. So declared TIME magazine in a full-page article devoted to the company with the headline "Marks and Spencer of the East". Skála's Buda shop wrested the title of "the largest store" from Corvin. This Pest location, built by György Kővári in 1984, is much smaller, occupying only the first and second floors of the building. The one-time CEO of this chain is now part of the international jet set with successful ventures after the Fall of the Wall which include major real estate development projects such as Bank Center (see Walk Two) and WestEnd City Center (see below.) There has been a real shopping mall craze in Hungary since about 1995, which has transformed the retail trade. People simply love the new malls, even if they find them expensive. The old and the new character of Nyugati tér is reflected in the two clocks. On the façade of the railway station, just below the copy of the crown, there is a traditional clock. In front of the department store, however, there is a digital clock. The times on the two clocks rarely coincide.

WestEnd City Center 39E *XIII. Váci út 1.*, www.westend.hu, open daily 10 a.m. to 8 p.m. (some shops close later, the cinema closes much later) ••• The construction of this 194,000 square-metre complex began on October 27, 1998 with an unusual "ballet" choreographed for 15 tower cranes to the music of Brahms. It announced the construction of this new "city centre" in an unused part of the Nyugati pályaudvar.

WALK FIVE

By November 12 the next year the centre was ready (except for the attached Hilton hotel and the office buildings which took another year). Bigger than anything ever seen before in Budapest, this project cost 180 million dollars. The result is gigantic, multifarious and metropolitan (in the wider sense). The place has the capacity for constant change built into it. There are more than 400 shops and a 14 screen cinema. The triangular complex opens out over the rail tracks and the interior is dissected with piazzas and throughways which are named for prominent Hungarians.

During the inauguration ceremony, which was packed with politicians, the 20 metre-high waterfall unfortunately flooded the lower part of the mall. But later it worked impeccably, just like the computer-operated fountains inside the mall. The opening ceremony was marked by wraiths of smoke since there hadn't been enough time to clear all the dust left from the construction work. József Finta, the architect, did his utmost to make this huge interior space both intimate and open. Look down from the cinema's foyer and you'll see a swarming village of toy people below. The development company has announced that it is working on plans for an express railway to the airport. It would also like to extend this complex all the way to Városliget, which would be a project ten times the size of this one. There is an interesting grassy roof garden which has too many statues, but provides an unusual panoramic view of the city.

Under Nyugati tér there is an entrance to the Nyugati pályaudvar metro station (M3). There's also another entrance from the railway station's ticket office. The underpass under Nyugati tér is a perfect introduction to Budapest's lower-classes, with dozens of low-quality shops with unattractive merchandise catering to Budapest underdogs. It's a blatant contrast to the shopping centre inside. Just outside the entrance to WestEnd there is a regular chess party (complete with clocks for all games, sometimes three or four at the same time!), with an enthusiastic following. Chess is still a popular game in all walks of Hungarian life.

The last section of the Nagykörút, called the Szent István körút, stretches from Nyugati tér to the Danube. This part of the road leads through two elegant residential districts: the 19th century Lipótváros and its extension to the north, Újlipótváros, which was built in the 1930s.

Vígszínház 40A *XIII. Szent István körút 14.*, www.vigszinhaz.hu ••• When this theatre was built in 1896, this area was so far out of town that the builder was laughed at: who on earth would walk such a long way to see a play? Soon the theatre found its audience and became known for its productions

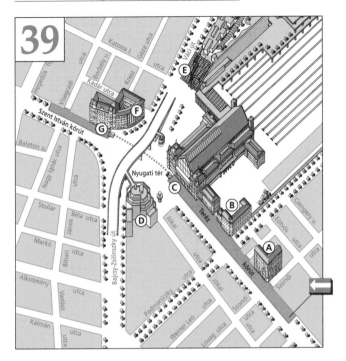

A Hotel Béke Radisson	**D** Skála Department Store
B Post Office	**E** WestEnd City Center
C Nyugati pályaudvar	**F G** Block of flats

of contemporary naturalist plays and French comedies. The theatre is one of 48 theatres built by the Austrian Fellner and the Prussian Helmer. It is where Ferenc Molnár got his start, on his way towards international recognition, before World War One. In the interwar period it was an important stop on tour maps: Max Reinhardt, Eleonora Duse, Alexander Moissi and others performed here. O'Neil and Chekhov also appeared frequently. In 1945 a bomb seriously damaged the theatre and it was reopened in 1951 with a different name: the "People's Army Theatre". This name also influenced the theatre's renovation and insignias of various parts of the armed forces were added to the plasterwork. The original name was given back to the theatre in 1960, but the ornaments were only removed during the reconstruction between 1992 and 1994, which was done in honour of its centenary. Actors at this theatre company enjoy

WALK FIVE

star status that is unrivaled anywhere else in the country. The management is trying to establish a balance between popular plays and cautious experimentation, and the theatre has also produced several musicals. When the building was constructed, theatrical scenery was much simpler and smaller. Nowadays it must be stored behind the building in a container or in the open air (as can be seen from the window of the Művész restaurant behind the building).

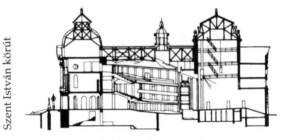

Szent István körút

Vígszínház – a Cross Section

Odeon Art Video Rental (Odeon videokölcsönző) 40C *XIII. Hollán Ernő utca 7.,* www.odeon.hu, open daily 10 a.m. to 11 p.m. ••• This unique place opened in December 1993 when the rear of the cinema was turned into this art video publisher and the chain's biggest rental shop. Since then the shop has grown, the cinema has shrunk, and a pleasant café and bookshop have been added. The shop's website tells who is on duty at every shop. It also lists the staff's favorite films. The place is a friendly, professional, and unmistakably Budapest egghead venue. Some egghead journals are for sale at the bookshop. It's owned by the municipally-owned Budapest Film Corporation.

At the end of the Nagykörút, art nouveau has left more traces such as on Szent István körút 10. and 12. Number 10 is nicknamed the "electric switch building" by children because its white, square stone decoration brings modern switches to mind (the bus stop for Bus 26 to Margitsziget is here). These buildings may look pleasant and interesting, but from the inside they are just typical narrow and dark Nagykörút buildings.

WALK FIVE

Újlipótváros ("New Leopold Town"), which is in the 13th district near the river, has quite different buildings. Dozens of Bauhaus-style modern buildings were constructed here, on the

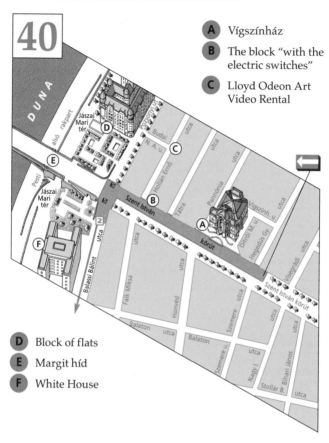

40

- **A** Vígszínház
- **B** The block "with the electric switches"
- **C** Lloyd Odeon Art Video Rental
- **D** Block of flats
- **E** Margit híd
- **F** White House

site of an old industrial district, in the 1930s and 1940s. Although they appear to be massive, closed structures from the outside, these buildings enclose large inner courtyards onto which only the windows of the kitchens and what used to be the maids' rooms open. The flats had modern, practical features included when they were built and were all centrally heated. Almost every room has a balcony and the large front windows mean that the rooms get lots of light. At the time, these were strange, unusual buildings, but they became popular with the young, forward-thinking middle-class. The area was immortalized by one of the residents, writer Antal Szerb, in his *A Guidebook to Budapest for Martians* (1935). "Nowadays you find the flattest modern palaces here. Inside the palaces young psychoanalysts are laying out each other's souls on the sofas, splendid bridge-party amazons are daydreaming in snow-white

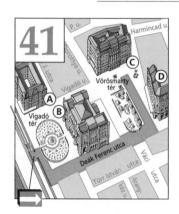

A Thonet House

B Vigadó

C Gerbeaud

D Elegant shops

bathrooms, extraordinarily intelligent clerks tune their radios to the broadcast from Moscow," he wrote. "Everything is modern, simple, objective and uniform here. The whole district is made up of two-room flats with small sitting rooms, and its residents are stubbornly, youthfully and energetically trying to conceal the only reality in their lives: that none of them have any money at all."

According the old saying "half of the people live in Buda, the other half would like to". Not so for Újlipótváros residents. They have either lived here all of their lives, or their parents or grandparents have. Or their favourite university professor, or the girl who they looked up at. The main street of Újlipótváros is Pozsonyi út, with its great bookshops, fashion and design shops, and restaurants of all kinds, where locals can meet their representative in Parliament, their doctor, the famous poet and Shakespeare translator, the male star of Vígszínház, the retired green-grocer, and even the author of this book and his grown-up daughters and grandchildren. Flats here fetch nearly the same high prices as those in Buda.

The centre of the neighbourhood is the elegant Szent István park. **Café Dunapark** (*XIII. Pozsonyi út 38.*, www.dunapark-kavehaz.hu, open 8 a.m. to midnight, at the weekend 10 a.m. to midnight) is now almost as elegant as when it originally opened in 1938. There are business people talking to each other. There are energetic, elderly, widowed ladies wearing large quantities of jewelry and celebrating birthdays, which are attended by neatly dressed older gentlemen and female family members who love their families and don't detest other joys, either. New cars abound, and so do bicycles and nice, small Parisian-style shops. The area apparently enjoys a sparkling life.

If you decide not to finish your walk in Újlipótváros or Margitsziget, just board Tram 2 at the bridge. The fifth stop is Vigadó tér, which is a short walk from our starting point.

*This was the longest walk, leading us far from Gerbeaud's fine marble tables. Although it is not as if you cannot discover anything new by sitting in the café. It was only after completing this route myself and collapsing onto a chair at Gerbeaud that I noticed that the table surfaces fall into two groups. Some are homogeneous, while others seem to have several layers, just like Gerbeaud's cakes. Surely you have noticed already that there are three different kinds of table legs: bronze, copper and curved. If you have more time to spend and wish to discover even more profound Budapest details, move on to the next chapter where you will find some distressingly non-touristy tips (even less touristy than the ones in Walk Five). To those leaving the city, I say **jó utat** (Bon voyage). I hope you come back again.*

*This neighbourhood used to be called Tabán and was
a sort of Montmartre and Grinzing combined, until it was
razed in the mid 1930s. It was too near the ruling élite.
Also, it was a health hazard. This photo was taken by
the architect/artist/photographer Iván Vydareny
(1887–1982). It was taken from the west, and the
silhouette of the original Erzsébet híd is in the
background.*

FOR SERIOUS ADDICTS

This chapter veers off the common tourist routes and is for those who have already moved past the beginner's stage in Budapest.

EIGHT BUILDINGS

Transit Art Café (and cultural centre) *XI. Bukarest utca corner (at Kosztolányi tér)*, www.tranzitcafe.hu, open daily 8 a.m. to 11 p.m.
This former long-distance bus station built by Vilmos Félix in 1964 was closed in the early 1990s and was then nicely restored by Attila Borsay in 2004 and transformed into this café and cultural centre. The evocative mosaic related to horses and transport and even the original "cashier" and "office" signs were kept. 1960s style furniture was added, as well as some low-key gardening. The place is run by Orsolya Egri, who is a spirited and

Transit Art Café in the Former Bus Terminus

known crusader for Budapest's built heritage. She has probably lost lots of money trying to realise her dream of combining reasonable prices and high-profile cultural programmes with a café with a comfortable atmosphere. There are exhibitions, lectures and all kinds of events.

Monument to the martyrs of 1956 (Új Köztemető, 301-es parcella – New Public Cemetery, Plot No. 301) *X. Kozma utca 8–10.,* open daily 7:30 a.m. to 5 p.m. year-round, and stays open longer as it darkens later (closes at 8 p.m. in May, June and July).
This monument (1992) was funded by public donations and erected after sculptor György Jovánovics had won the competition for its design. The site is in the remotest part of the cemetery and was covered by weeds until 1989. The martyrs of the revolution, among them Prime Minister Imre Nagy, were buried here face down in unmarked graves, far away from visitors. The monument is a complex work of art, relying in its symbolism on the will of one of the executed revolutionaries, István Angyal, who mentioned a "big white piece of stone" in a moving and sincere document which he wrote on death row. In the centre of the monument there is a column that is exactly 1956 millimeters high. As a former conceptual artist, Jovánovics asked the National Measurement Authority to verify that it was really 1956 millimeters in length.

Lehel Market (Lehel piac) *XIII. Lehel tér,* open Monday to Friday 6 a.m. to 6 p.m., Saturday 6. a.m. to 2 p.m., Sunday 6 a.m. to 1 p.m.

Lehel Market

This surprising market hall was built in 2002 by László Rajk on the site of a 100 year-old open-air market. Rajk, who was a liberal MP for two terms (until 1998) designed this market hall for a sleepy and ugly junction where middle class Terézváros (from over the rail tracks) and Újlipótváros meet the working class neighbourhood of Angyalföld. This building is Rajk's chef d'oeuvre, and his unmistakable attraction to theatre and film is obvious in it. He calls his style "radical eclecticism". The building's design was a shock to most neighbourhood locals and to professional critics. It's "a joke" and "the collapse of Totalitarianism, narrated in the language of the Wild East", wrote a famous, elderly architect in a long review. The more I see the building, the more I appreciate it, especially when I use it. The garage is located on the top of the building, which forces us to use the gallery space, which is often a weak and unused part of older markets.

Café Zila (Zila kávéház) *XVIII. Üllői út 452.,*
www.zilakavehaz.hu, open daily 10 a.m. to 10 p.m.
Located in Pestszentlőrinc, an eastern outskirt of Budapest, this large café was once a shooting range. It was built by a trigger happy, horse racing aristocrat named Miklós Szemere, who was immortalized in many late 19th-century stories. The place opened in 1903 and the Latin saying over the main entrance reads: Caput Gloriae Virtus (virtue is the highest glory). In 1928 shooting was banned here since it disturbed the neighbours. The building instead was used as a banquet hall for the neighbourhood, which was then a small town. From 1949 it became used as the changing room for a city bath. In 1984 permission was given to László Zila, a confectioner, to start a pastry shop. In 1998 he bought the adjacent building and began a meticulous, award-winning renovation.

The Napoleon Courtyard *VI. Hajós utca 25.*
This art nouveau building has three façades. It really should be admired from a distance, but it sits on a very narrow street. Notice the building's fine glass windows and its many small details. High above, in the middle of the façade, the figure of Napoleon looks down on the pedestrian street. No one walking there would guess that he was being watched by the emperor. By the way, "courtyard" is just a nickname – we can't actually enter the building.

VIII. Népszínház utca 16.
I had the pleasure of living in this typical building in the Józsefváros district for two years. With two inner courtyards,

the structure has had to be shored up with enough timber to make a forest. The tenants in the rear courtyard are especially dependent on each other and the moving spirit of the building is Mr. Laci, the janitor, who accepted all sorts of duties, even delivering packages in his old Volkswagen. Naturally, he also brought soda water bottles up for the tenants and let repairmen into their flats. I hope he still lives there, in good health, and is still looking after the building.

The church in VIII. Rezső tér
This Catholic church, which has a central arrangement and a dome, is situated on the main square of an eighth district residential area from the 1910s. It was built after a competition in which only neo-Classical designs were accepted. The church was finished in 1928, with ornamentation that recalls the time of the Hungarian settlement towards the end of the 9th century. The huge bulk of the building can be seen far off from Üllői út, which is the main road leading southeast (and to the airport), though only few people try to get any closer.

EIGHT STREETS AND SQUARES

VIII. Mátyás tér This square, which is in the heart of the József-város district (a sort of Budapest Harlem), is surrounded by single-storey and six-storey buildings, workshops and pubs. The unique atmosphere perhaps comes from the fact that the traditional Jewish middle-class here share the area with gypsies originally from Koszorú utca and Tavaszmező utca. There is a touching statue of a tin plate Christ on the corner of Tavaszmező utca.

VI. Városligeti fasor Formerly called Gorky Lane, this is one of Pest's most attractive streets. Leading from Lövölde tér to Városliget, it runs parallel to Andrássy út but is much quieter. The rows of horse-chestnut trees grow unmolested too. There are old and modern villas here, as well as embassies and schools. The legendary Lutheran Grammar School, where a dozen Nobel prize winning émigré scientists were educated, sits on the corner of Bajza utca. The school was closed in 1950 and reopened in 1989 but is still struggling to regain its reputation.

II. Gül Baba utca This steeply rising, cobbled street near the Buda end of Margit híd leads to the tomb of Gül Baba, a 16th century Turkish holy man. The "Father of Flowers" died in Buda in 1541 and his memorial is the northernmost Islamic holy place to be subsidised by the Turkish government. Next to the tomb there is a small look-out tower.

VIII. Baross utca This is the main street of the Józsefváros district, leading from elegant Kálvin tér, through increasingly poorer parts, and finally, to the suburbs. Many joiners and upholsterers opened workshops here and their typical products are often mocked by the name "Baross utca style". This nickname refers to richly ornamented, old-fashioned furniture which has not changed for years and is bought almost exclusively by the trades people living in the area. From Horváth Mihály tér on, the street looks like the main street of a provincial town.

XV. Drégelyvár utca This is the main street of the Újpalota housing estate which consists of ten-storey apartment blocks, and now also has a good confectioner's and a second-hand bookshop. Unfortunately, the trees are growing slowly and may never reach as high as the tenth floor. Recently hundreds of small shops opened on the ground floors. Budapest is a city of a million small entrepreneurs, and the shops change hands and characters all too often.

II. Napraforgó utca This street is in what is called the "experimental housing estate". Built by an entrepreneur in 1931 (with the city's support), architecture buffs will be interested in this place which consists of 22 cleverly arranged small buildings sitting close together. On one side, the back of the buildings overlook a small stream called Ördögárok. The names of the architects can be seen on a memorial column in the middle of the plot.

XIV. Abonyi utca This short street between Városliget and the busy Thököly út is elegant, expensive, and almost totally free of noise and dirt. The street consists of 1920s buildings built for diplomats and generals. Halfway along the street there is a landmark red brick school building which is the former Jewish Secondary School, built by Béla Lajta in 1934. Now it bears the name of Miklós Radnóti, the catholic poet who was Jewish by birth and killed by the Fascists in a forced labour camp in 1944. This is a rare school for kids from the ages of six through 18 which has an atmosphere both inspiring and funny. Some adolescents look down on their fellow students being brought by cars.

XIX. Kós Károly tér Construction on this working-class housing estate began in 1909. The estate, called the Wekerle-telep, was named for the Prime Minister who initiated the work. Over 900 houses were built here in varied formats and the centre of the estate, Kós Károly tér, can be approached through four ornamental gates built in a Transylvanian style. Altogether the impression is of a large village that has been swallowed up by the city. This square can be visited on the way to Ecseri Market *(see page 290)*.

EIGHT OLD SHOPS AND WORKSHOPS

Gallwitz Pipes And Pearls *V. Régiposta utca 7–9.*, www.gallwitz.hu
The oldest pipe seller and pipe mender in Budapest, this shop, which is situated downtown on a quiet side street, has been operating since 1880. Mr. Gallwitz, who died in 2003, was an old-fashioned person who seemed to have not realized that liberty and free business were back. He used to do business in his private first floor apartment. Check the web site to see a commercial shot in 1945 (you can also order pipes and pearls there).

Tamás T. Nagy: Cheese *V. Gerlóczy utca 3.*, www.tnagytamas.hu
This man aims to educate the Hungarian palate in terms of cheese. His small shop is in a tucked away street in a classic section of the inner city. Nagy once said that "cheese is nothing more than some milk, some time and some poetry mixed." He has commissioned artists to design posters for him, and by now he has developed into a chain specializing in affordable French cheese.

Tamás Grünberger: Chandeliers *VI. Nagymező utca 21.*
This shop seems to have been around for 100 years, and it even operated during the Communist years. The present owner is a third-generation chandelier specialist with a prima donna wife from the nearby Operetta Theatre and an active social life. This is where the biggest synagogues in Europe order replacements parts.

V & R Címfestő: Hand-Painted Signs *VI. Oktogon 4.*
This is an amazing cellar which has access from the street, which you are likely to mistake for a public lavatory. Here you can order old-fashioned hand-painted street signs and all kinds of indoor and outdoor signs.

Ági Gyümölcs Greengrocers *XIII. Tátra utca 20.*
This family greengrocer offers the freshest and best quality produce in the area. It is a small shop on the corner of Raoul Wallenberg utca with an entrance on each street. It used to be

run by the lady for whom the shop was named. In this book's first edition I wrote: "Inside, there is stern-looking Ági in her sixties (careful! do not call her Aunt Ági!), who does not pamper her customers. There are many family pictures on the walls, and children and grandchildren who have been known to work in the shop. There are also motorcycle ads and the hallmark of the shop was for many years beyond doubt a Western European poster from the 1960s which showed a small boy lifting the very short skirt of a tall young lady, and peeping upwards."

Unger Brush Products *VII. Dob utca 52.*
This amazing institution offers an incredible selection of brushes, from tiny to enormous, even the type which were used to clean barrels at the Unicum factory.

Fleisher Shirt Makers *VI. Nagymező utca 7.*
Few people still buy their shirts bespoke, but this shop (on the corners of Paulay Ede and Nagymező utcas) has remained here almost unchanged since the 1920s. The partition between the shop and the window is made from traditional engraved glass with vertical stripes.

Lajos Libál, Optician *V. Veres Pálné utca 7.*
Some of the fittings here might well be a century old, such as the small drawers. Mr. Libál is not around any more. The senior, respectable lady, who is referred to as "Aunt Libál" in the neighbourhood, is, as a matter of fact, called Brassai Józsefné.

EIGHT IMPRESSIONS

The Totalitarian Statue Theme Park *XXII. Balatoni út (corner of Szabadkai utca),* www.szoborpark.hu.
There was a debate over what to do with the Lenins, Marxes, and their local counterparts who were sculpted in marble and bronze: let them stay where they were or destroy them. It ended in a wise compromise and the statues were relocated to the outskirts of Budapest, where a park was made to house them. Most are bad art, but not all. The place became famous when it was taken to court for violating the law banning the display of totalitarian symbols. The judge in charge of the case visited the park and dismissed the charges, declaring that "the danger posed to society is negligible." The park is rarely visited – the derelict, neglected atmosphere is an unintended bonus – but it is a must for the serious Budapest addict. By car from the centre, it's about a 30 minute drive. Afterwards, have lunch or dinner at

the Communist-themed restaurant called Marxim's (*II. Kis Rókus utca 23.*, open Monday to Saturday noon to 1 a.m., Sunday 6 p.m. to 1 a.m.)

The "Ecseri" Second-Hand Market *XIX. Nagykőrösi út 156.,* open 8 a.m. to sunset, in winter until 5 p.m. (1 p.m. on Sunday.) Bus 54 or 55 will take you there in 20 minutes. Get off at Naszód utca (Használtcikk-piac).

This varied flea market has been slowly driven further and further out of town. Like an antique shop crossed with a junk store, this sprawling market puts most markets in Western cities to shame. There are silver pocket watches, Thonet chairs, folk costumes, art nouveau blankets, and re-cast copper lamps. But there are also trendy Italian jeans and the latest pop records for the price of just a few litres of milk. There are piles of clothes for 100 forints a piece, as well as all sorts of goods which may not be available in town (CDs with Communist marches, cans with "the air of liberty", and the like). Although foreigners are sometimes over-charged, they can usually find something that is in fashion again at home but is still rubbish here. Bauhaus furniture is now becoming

Statue of Lenin in the Statue Park

fashionable here, but 1950s pieces still count as trash. Since it is quite difficult to get good quality modern furniture in Budapest, some young people furnish their homes from here, fighting over a piece with set designers or Austrian antique dealers. The market is a museum of man-made shapes, where there is a mixture of old and new, poor and rich, fine and chaotic. Nobody likes being photographed here, but you can find lots of vintage pictures and postcards. Before you go to the market, consult of Budapest Bests, András Váradi – *page 69.*

The "Fuit" Stone *In Városliget (between Olof Palme sétány and Hermina út),* this simple tomb stone has one Latin word carved into it: FUIT ("he was").
A lawyer in Pest, who wished to remain unknown, left a large

amount of money to the city and asked in return to be buried here
in this manner. On All Souls Day, November 1st, many people
light candles at his stone, remembering their own loved ones.
It's located near the Museum of Transport, in the direction of
Dózsa György út. The tomb is from the early 19th century.

A38 Ship – a music venue
This ship, anchored at the Buda end of Petőfi híd near the campus
of Eötvös University, is the reincarnation of a Ukrainian stone
carrier ship. The name comes from Artemovszk 38, which is the
name of a ship prototype. Built in 1968, the ship was tugged
through international waters in 2001 to receive a complete
makeover and an infusion of new life. It offers a programme
that includes a wide range of jazz, world music, electronic music,
contemporary and rock music, and drum'n'bass. The lively place
also has a restaurant and a bar.

A38 Ship

The Lukács's Garden and the Thanksgiving Tablets
II. Frankel Leó út 25–29.
There has been a spa called Lukács (St. Luke's) on the site of
this 100 year-old building since the 16th century, which is when
the cured began placing tablets here to express their gratitude.
The tablets are mounted on an outdoor wall and praise the spa's
medicinal powers. The old-fashioned swimming-pool here used
to be an informal meeting place for aspiring young intellectuals
and writers. It was a sort of literary salon which had a dissident
flavour from the 1950s to the mid-1980s. Its complete moderniza-
tion (hated by most of the regulars) is underway.

Shoes on the Danube Promenade *On the edge of the river embankment, at the southern tip of Parliament.*
The idea to place a monument on the river embankment to the victims of the Arrow Cross terror belongs to Gyula Pauer, Hungarian sculptor and to his friend poet/filmmaker Can Togay. The monument contains of 60 pairs of iron shoes, forming a row of about 40 metres. It is a commemoration dedicated to the victims of the fascist Arrow Cross party who shot the people right into the river, sparing themselves the hard work of burials. The victims had to take their shoes off, since shoes were valuable belongings at the time. The site is symbolic, this part of the embankment was not the only one used for this purpose. The iron shoes were placed on the embankment in 2005, on 16th April. The name of the composition is Shoes on the Danube Promenade, each pair being modelled after a contemporary shoe from the 1940's. (From the website www.jewishbudapest.hu)

Duna Club of the Ministry of Interior *V. Zrínyi utca 5.*
This place used to be one of the three "casinos" in Budapest, which were actually more like clubs in the English sense of the word. The Lipótvárosi Casino was built in 1895 by the Jewish upper-middle-class industrialists and financiers who were not admitted to the two more elegant clubs. The interior is somewhat over-the-top, wherever one looks. But one couldn't look wherever one wanted to here from 1945 to 1990 when this was the Ministry of the Interior's club and entry was strictly prohibited to non-members. Mark Twain delivered a lecture here on March 29, 1899 during the six days he spent in Budapest. Since few people here spoke English then, the organisers commissioned a Hungarian-American to give his moustache a good tug whenever a laugh was required (or so the papers of the day said).

XIV. Örs vezér tere – the eastern gate of the city
The Örs vezér tere terminal of the second metro (M2) decants people by the thousand into the subway. Some are hurrying towards the housing estates, some are travelling on to neighbouring villages by the suburban train (HÉV). Three-hundred-thousand people use this subway every morning and it's where one of the funniest news vendors in the city can be found. His most famous cry is: *"Ma még van még"* ("Some more left, just today"). Real or made-up headlines make up the rest of his advertising and this popular, bearded man collects some 60 to 70 kilograms of coins every day. Another of his famous "headlines" is: "the wandering knife-grinder drank himself to death".

EIGHT STYLES

Buildings built in Budapest's most typical styles are listed here (some have already been seen in our walks). No pre-18th century styles are included here, only those which play a major role in the city's present appearance.

Baroque (especially its Austrian version) St. Anne's Church (*I. Batthyány tér*), University Church (*V. Eötvös Loránd utca 5.*), Orthodox Serbian Church (*V. Szerb utca 4.*), Franciscan Monastery and Church in Buda (*II. Margit körút 23.*), Town Hall in Buda (*I. Szentháromság utca 2.*), Endrődy palace (*I. Táncsics Mihály utca 3.*), Semmelweis House (*I. Apród utca 1–3.*), Budapest City Hall (formerly a hospital for disabled soldiers, *V. Városház utca 9–11.*), Castle in Nagytétény (*XXII. Csókási Pál utca 9–11.*).

Neo-classicism National Museum (*VIII. Múzeum körút 14–16.*), former Valero Silk Factory (*V. Honvéd utca 26–30.*), Synagogue in Óbuda (*III. Lajos utca 163.*), County Hall (*V. Városház utca 7.*), former Ludovika Academy of Military Sciences (*VIII. Ludovika tér*), Trattner House (*V. Petőfi Sándor utca 2.*), Károlyi Palace (*V. Károlyi Mihály utca 16.*), former István Főherceg Szálló (Archduke Stephen Hotel, *V. Akadémia utca 16.*).

Romantic Vigadó (*V. Vigadó tér*), Synagogue (*VII. Dohány utca 2–8.*), Unger House (*V. Múzeum körút 7.*), Pekáry House (*VII. Király utca 47.*), Kauser House (*VIII. Gyulai Pál utca 5.*), Toldy Grammar School (*I. Toldy Ferenc utca 9.*), Nyugati pályaudvar (*VI. Nyugati tér*), former House of Representatives (*VIII. Bródy Sándor utca 8.*).

Eclectic We have already seen so many examples of this style during the walks, so I list here only some fine, but lesser known, buildings. New Town Hall (*V. Váci utca 62–64.*), Palace of Alajos Károlyi (*VIII. Pollack Mihály tér*), Parish Churches in Ferencváros (*IX. Bakáts tér*) and Erzsébetváros (*VII. Rózsák tere*), Ádám House (*VIII. Bródy Sándor utca 4.*).

Art Nouveau Museum of Applied Arts (*IX. Üllői út 33–37.*), Parish Church in Kőbánya (*X. Szent László tér*), Apartment Building (*V. Honvéd utca 3.*), Gresham Palace (*V. Roosevelt tér 5.*), Geological Institute (*XIV. Stefánia út 14.*), Academy of Music (*VI. Liszt Ferenc tér 8.*), Post Office Savings Bank (*V. Hold utca 4.*), Gellért Hotel and Baths (*XI. Szent Gellért tér*).

Neo-neo-baroque Corvin Cinema (*VIII. Kisfaludy köz*), Kaffka Margit Grammar School (*XI. Villányi út 5–7.*), Cistercian Grammar School (*XI. Villányi út 27.*), Apartment Building Built for a Mining Company (*V. Kossuth Lajos tér 13–15.*), Former Cyclop Garage (*VII. Kertész utca 24.*), the newer (yellow) part of the Széchenyi Baths (*XIV. Állatkerti körút*), Original Façade of the Corvin Department Store (*VIII. Blaha Lujza tér*).

Bauhaus Row of Apartment Buildings (*XIII. Szent István park*), Atrium Houses and Cinema (*II. Margit körút 55.*), Apartment Building (*V. Régi posta utca 13.*), Airport in Budaörs (*1112 Budapest, Kőérberki út 36.*, bus 87 from Kosztolányi Dezső tér), Bell Tower of the Catholic Church in Városmajor (*XII. Csaba utca 7.*), Apartment Building (*VII. Rákóczi út 4.*), Post Office Headquarters (*VII. Hársfa utca 47.*), Calvinist Church and Office Buildings (*V. Szabadság tér 2.*), Housing Estate (*II. Napraforgó utca*).

The style of the 1950s Second District Council House (*II. Mechwart tér*), Dubbing Film Studio (*II. Hűvösvölgyi út 68.*), College of Applied Arts (*II. Zugligeti út 9–25.*), Residential Building Complex (*XIV. Pákozdi tér area*), Party Headquarters in Óbuda (*III. Flórián tér*), Student Hostel (*XI. Bercsényi utca 28–30.*), MOM Cultural Centre (*XII. Csörsz utca 18.*).

Millenáris Park – Jövő Háza Complex

A CITY TO ENJOY

FOR INDEPENDENT VISITORS

Governor Miklós Horthy gives a dinner in honour of
Cardinal Pacelli (later Pope Pius XII) in May 1938,
in the Royal Palace. The governor is giving his speech,
on the left. It is a pity that the palace was not restored
in its earlier form. Despite the serious damage, it would
have been possible. The photographer is unknown.

EATING WELL AND NOT TOO MUCH

Those with long memories speak nostalgically of Budapest's restaurants during the years between the wars. In what was the most peaceful, easygoing and least expensive city in Europe, an enormous number of restaurants competed for the discerning customer. Then came World War Two and the lean years that followed. In a dictionary published in the 1950s, the entry for banana is an illustration with a minimal attempt at explaining this phenomenon which was so outside of the ordinary experience. Like many other children of the 1960s, I felt that things were getting better, improving all the time. The exception, however, was eating out. My childhood memories are of rows of waiters and of food left barely touched on the plates. I later came to understand that all restaurants had the dead rigid hand of large catering companies on them. The hotels built in the 1970s brought new standards with them, and they attracted the talented and the ambitious. Eventually, in the early 1980s a contract leasing system whereby restaurants were let out on three to five year leases to the highest (sealed) bid, came into being. This led to a proliferation of privately-run restaurants, which were often in impossible locations (like on a street known only for its courtrooms and rows of ambulances parked on standby). During the last ten years of the totalitarian system, establishments ranging from those serving hamburgers to those using fine silverware have joined together to provide good home-cooking for their delighted neighbours. Who remembers that now, just after the restaurant revolution? Since 1990 there has been a constant, ongoing revolution, first in the side streets, then in the major sites. At least three things have fundamentally changed in Budapest:

– The clientele is not based on tourists, but on Hungarian middle-class people (who remember last week, last month, last year).

– Modern sophistication appeared in the décor, and in the menus. There are now fewer (and sometimes no) misprints in the foreign menus.

– The fame of new places spreads not only by hearsay, but through printed media, the Internet, and in columns written by food writers.

All in all, higher-end eating has become a reality. No wonder that Costes in 2010, Onyx in 2011 was awarded with long-awaited first Michelin stars.

HUNGARIAN COOKING

The predominant influence on Hungarian cooking has long been Austrian and thus, indirectly, French. The French chefs who were employed by the aristocracy "liberated" Hungarian cooking from the Austrian yoke. Just as French cuisine had turned to peasant and traditional dishes for inspiration, these chefs looked to Hungarian peasant cooking and brought it into mainstream European taste.

The basis of Hungarian peasant cooking is a heavy roux (rántás) made from flour and pork lard. Naturally, it requires rich flavors, which it gets from the addition of paprika. Ground paprika is a genuine Hungarian innovation, but although paprika is thought of as a defining feature of Hungarian cooking, its use only dates from the second half of the 18th century. Eating the fiery pepper slowly became a Hungarian virtue, and a saying goes: "a real Magyar can handle his strong paprika well". But you should not think that all paprika is hot. Hungarian cuisine, in general, is not hot. Another feature of Hungarian cooking is the use of sour cream for flavouring. Soups figure strongly, and so does pasta because of the excellence of our strong flour. Our traditional cooking was only "Europeanized" at the end of the 19th century, the period when foreign influence was willingly accepted and blended with traditionally Hungarian flavours. It first happened in the great and luxurious hotels on the Pest riverfront, and it then trickled down to chefs in the better restaurants.

The heyday of Hungarian restaurants was that commonly-evoked European golden-age – the two decades before the outbreak of World War One. In Hungary, this golden-age had its own chronicler: the novelist and short story writer Gyula Krúdy (1878–1933), whose statue can be seen on Szentlélek tér in the third district. His work, still as popular as ever in Hungary, abounds in sensuous evocations and celebrations of food and eating. His name has been bequeathed to more than 100 dishes, all of which are worth trying. It would be only a slight exaggeration to say that today's Hungarian cooking is his interpretation of the peasant cooking during his time.

For many of us, Krúdy's name evokes a marrowbone. Let me explain. Zoltán Huszárik's 1971 film Szindbád was based on Krúdy's stories of the same name (*see "Going Out", page 329 for more*). It contains a scene in which the eponymous hero – and the camera – gaze lovingly at a golden bowl of soup. Szindbád expertly cracks the marrowbone and the camera closes in on the marrow as it shimmers on the surface of a crispy slice of toast. Audiences involuntarily and inevitably gasped with pleasure. The scene has passed into the nation's subjective consciousness, and it may well have contributed to the revival and rejuvenation of traditional dishes.

The following restaurants are some of Budapest's finest. It is a select list in a fast changing scene. The best updated list can be found in Time Out Budapest and in Budapest Funzine – both have excellent websites. Also see www.budapest-criticalguide.hu for the author's updated list of favourites.

THREE ELEGANT RESTAURANTS IN WHICH TO ALLOW YOURSELF TO BE INVITED

Fausto's *VI. Székely Mihály utca 2.*, www.fausto.hu, open Monday to Saturday noon to 3 p.m. and 7 p.m. to 11 p.m.
Fausto's is an outstanding, unpretentious place, where it is almost impossible to park. It is named for the owner, Fausto di Vora, who is from Udine. It is reputed to have the best Italian food in Central Europe, which is no small feat considering the supplies available. The wine list offers about 130 varieties of Hungarian wine from Villány, Eger and Tokaj and Italian wine from Tuscany, Puglia and Sicily. The restaurant moved to this location in 2007. The old location is now an Osteria, an informal, more moderately priced place at VII. Dohány utca 5.

Cyrano *V. Kristóf tér 7–8.*, www.cyranorestaurant.fw.hu, open daily 11 a.m. to midnight.
Cyrano opened in 1993 and its central location ensured that it become trendy overnight. The name of the place goes back to a big chandelier that was a stage prop during the shooting of the Cyrano film (the Dépardieu version). But don't look for it: the

restaurant has gotten five facelifts since those early days. Cosmo used to be a separate restaurant, but now is just a private room upstairs. Try escargots Provençal as a starter, then move on to the pheasant breast with kumquat sauce or one of the substantial salads. There are great desserts. Service is also great, but a bit more continuity in the décor, please. The small balcony has pleasant tables.

Gundel See Walk Four, *page 232–233.*

THREE TRADITIONAL, "SHIRTSLEEVE" RESTAURANTS WHITH A MIXED CLIENTELE, AND GOOD VALUE

Rosenstein *VIII. Mosonyi utca 3.,* www.rosenstein.hu, open Monday to Saturday noon to 11 p.m., closed in August.
This restaurant is a favourite among Budapest's gourmets, and is between a railway station and a police barracks. Located far from any of the city's other good restaurants, its location is an improbable one. It is favoured by media people and the Budapest gourmands who hate salads and love rich, traditional Hungarian dishes in big portions. The latter smile at the faux elegance of the place. The menu is reliable and chef/owner Tibor Rosenstein is a master of Hungarian and Jewish specialties. His family serves the food.

Kisbudagyöngye *III. Kenyeres utca 34.,* www.remiz.hu, open Monday to Saturday noon to midnight.
The "Small Pearl of Buda" opened in 1990 and is the successor of a well-known place that was shabby, but charming. The décor is a cross between post-modern and fin-de-siècle. It seems as if the designer ransacked low-quality antique shops and the Ecseri flea market in order to panel the walls with cupboard sides and doors, pieces of drawers, and hardwood of all kinds, tints and patterns. The mixture adds up to an elegant, intimate atmosphere. The menu, which pleasingly has few misprints, features Hungarian and international dishes. Booking is essential.

Marquis de Salade *VI. Hajós utca 43.,* ww.marquisdesalade.hu, open daily 11 a.m. to midnight.
Originally, this place was just a salad bar that opened after the Changes of 1989-1990. Later it was transformed into one of the city's more adventurous restaurants. East meets West in the menu here, or rather, Paris meets the Caucasus. The extensive menu is also in Russian (and the place has not been ruined by

the uneducated among the Russian expat community). It is worth sitting at one of the tables in the cellar, preferably at one of the inner ones where you feel as if you are being served in a comfortable cave, away from the troubles of the world. The restaurant is run by an immigrant lady from Azerbaijan, who speaks excellent Hungarian by now (but still with a charming accent).

MODERN, ATYPICAL BUDAPEST PLACES, WHERE WE WILL NOT NECESSARILY GAIN 10 POUNDS IN 4 DAYS

Café Kör *V. Sas utca 17.,* www.cafekor.hu, open Monday to Saturday 10 a.m. to 10 p.m.

This intimate place is now a Budapest classic. Kör means "circle", but it is no coincidence that it also hints at the French word coeur, which means "heart". It looks and feels like a French bistro, one that has been here for a century (a compliment that is hard to give in present-day Budapest). Located on a small side street near the Basilica, the daily specials are written on a blackboard. Avoid the place at early-lunch-time, when it is full of mostly junior diplomats from the nearby American Embassy. Real insiders – like professors from the Central European University with their egghead friends or guests from abroad – come later. Café Kör is one of my all-time favourites. I always order fish here.

Arcade *XII. Kiss János altábornagy utca 38.,* www.arcadebistro.hu, open Tuesday to Sunday 11 a.m. to 11 p.m.

According to the otherwise ultra-picky Wittman Boys (who used to be the restaurant reviewers for Hungary's biggest daily newspaper, *Népszabadság*), this restaurant is "overwhelming happiness, a continuous state of agitation, constantly reproduced creative energies..." This compliment is no small feat. The place is a singularly high-quality, reasonably priced restaurant with a style of its own, pretty much the only one in Buda. It serves adventurous, international, modern cuisine and is a favourite of the art world. It was established in January 2001 and is a younger sister of Café Kör in Pest.

MEET THE RULING ELITE, IN THEIR NATURAL HABITAT

Kárpátia *V. Ferenciek tere 7–8.,* www.karpatia.hu, open daily
11 a.m. to 11 p.m.
Kárpátia is a high-quality traditional Hungarian establishment,
(with a fitting clientele) which has been open continuously since
1877. It regained its former prestige when the restaurateur Ákos
Niklai managed to buy it and re-introduce high standards to the
place, ones that he learned from acting as a luxury hotel director.
The interior looks as if it could have been one of the fancy halls
of a medieval castle in the times of the legendary king Matthias.
It is an especially appropriate place to impress relatives from
the provinces. There is a separate pub, a main dining room, four
private rooms and a terrace.

Remíz *II. Budakeszi út 5.,* www.remiz.hu, open daily 9 a.m. to
midnight.
This place's old-fashioned name refers to the big tram depot that
sits 200 metres from the door. Another visible landmark is the
front of a yellow interwar tram made of brick. You'll find pretty
much everybody here from the inner-Buda new middle-class
to artists, and business people to junior diplomats from nearby
embassies. It's not a very touristy place, and it has a nice garden
with a playful fountain featuring the "self-portrait of the artist as
an acrobat" (designed by Vladimir Péter, blacksmith and professor at the nearby Academy of Applied Arts). Parking is difficult,
and booking is essential.

Biarritz Restaurant and Café *V. Kossuth Lajos tér 18.,*
www.biarritz.hu, open Monday to Friday 9 a.m. to 11 p.m.,
Saturday and Sunday 10 a.m. to 11 p.m.
This small, cosy neighbourhood establishment is located on the
only residential block on this part of the riverfront. Members of
Parliament are often seen here. The original restaurant with the
same name was opened here in 1938, though it was much bigger
and probably less friendly.

THREE RESTAURANTS WITH HUNGARIAN FOOD AT ITS BEST

Bagolyvár (Owl Castle) *XIV. Állatkerti körút 3.*,
www.gundel.hu, open daily noon to midnight.
After Gundel opened, the adjacent building was left empty for
a year and was then turned into a restaurant devoted to the
theme of "grandma's home cooking". It is an all-female operation, with a limited menu that changes daily and specials written
on a blackboard. The place is decorated with tables and chairs
of various styles. It has some of the most beautiful waitresses in
town (with some of the nicest, non-sexy smiles) who flaunt the
proverbial dignity of the Hungarian peasant girl. It's an equally
nice place for a business dinner or a Sunday lunch with the kids.
Lions roaring can often be heard in the restaurant, and during
the summer, families with children tend to gravitate towards
the zoo after their meal. Guests of Bagolyvár are invited for free
tours of the zoo (perhaps the restaurant gives its leftovers to the
lions in return). Reservation are advisable.

Kéhli vendéglő (Mrs. Kéhli's Place) *III. Mókus utca 22.*,
www.kehli.hu, open daily noon to midnight.
Kéhli is perhaps the only more or less genuine place left of the
many that were once patronized by the gourmet writer, Gyula
Krúdy. There is a plaque here commemorating his table, and his
spirit is everywhere from the menu and the décor to the witty
inscriptions on the walls. Kéhli used to be much smaller, dirtier
and cheaper. To incorporate the cobble-stoned gate area was a
good idea, to flaunt the Gösser beer signs was not. The menu is a
delight in itself. To re-live the famous scene in the film Szindbád
order "forró fazék velőscsonttal" (hot pot with marrow bone),
which is served in the type of cosy red pot used by impoverished
old ladies. Other favourites (which the menu fully explains) are:
"Szindbád margitszigeti Étke" (What Szindbád liked to eat on
Margaret Island) and "Fidó Apó magyarkúti medvetalpa" (The
Bear Sole of Uncle Fidó). There is live accordion music as well as
miscellaneous music from a cheap stereo, which is a less than
perfect sight here.

Náncsi néni *II. Ördögárok út 80.*, www.nancsineni.hu, open
daily noon to 11 p.m.
This restaurant was one of the early birds in the culinary revolution of the 1980s. It was established in 1980, quite far out in the
Buda hills, and the name refers to an idiom that expresses incre-
dulity (something like "tell it to the marines"). It is one of the
most popular summer dinner retreats for Budapest's traditional

middle classes. Apart from its large portions of food, it puts a real emphasis on attentive service. The last time I was there I had forgotten my glasses. The server noticed my problem right away and there turned out to be a whole collection of extra glasses. There is a nice garden open during the summer. Its website is almost an animated film which reveals the character of the place through amusing drawings and sounds. The birds on the trees drop what they sometimes do, and you can select music or simple garden noises or silence.

RESTAURANTS EVERYONE CAN AFFORD, WHERE WE CAN SPOT ORDINARY HUNGARIANS

Some of the following restaurants can be very modest to the discerning eye of the independent traveller, which you certainly are if you have bought this book.

Kerék *III. Bécsi út 103.,* www.kerekvendeglo.hu, open daily noon to midnight.
The name of this restaurant means "wheel" (i.e. the wheel of a cart, as a sign of simplicity). Kerék is a symbol of the traditional, convivial, neighbourhood restaurant, where hungry craftspeople are supposed to have dinners on weekdays, and where families go to have Sunday lunches between the river and the hills of Northern Buda. It is a nostalgic destination for connoisseurs who remember it from when it was a rare reliable oasis in the culinary desert of 1970s and early-1980s Budapest. The city has improved so much in terms of its restaurant offerings that it is sometimes dangerous to come here, to this place where time seems to have come to a standstill. It's especially charming in the garden during the summer.

Kisbojtár *XIII. Dagály utca 17.,* www.kisbojtar.hu, open Monday to Saturday noon to 11 p.m.
"Small Shepherd Boy" is a museum piece of a restaurant that preserves the genuine cosiness of the late 1950s and early 1060s. A small shepherd boy can be seen on an incredibly kitschy oil painting and on the iron railings and windows. There are several rooms, each with unforgettable design subtleties. It's a camp experience proper (to use the term as it was elaborated by Susan Sontag). Food here is delicious and represents Hungarian home cooking traditions. The restaurant has been in the same hands since 1972.

Tüköry söröző (Tüköry Beer Hall) *V. Hold utca 15.,* www.tukory.hu, open Monday to Friday 10 a.m. to midnight (closed on all public holidays except August 20).
In the centre of Lipótváros (Walk Two), this place can get almost unbearably hot during the summer, even on the enclosed terrace. Inside there are booths and a long central table. The place serves Hungarian Dreher draught beer. At noon it is full of clerks from the nearby banks, and later in the afternoon it is often still full. One has the feeling that customers here always talk business. The décor is unbelievably shabby and includes paper reproductions of modern Hungarian paintings glued to the wall. The food is plain Hungarian village cooking at its best.

SALAD BARS, WITH PROMISING BEGINNINGS

Falafel Faloda *VI. Paulay Ede utca 53., corner of Nagymező utca*
A vegetarian salad bar, with falafel and crowded seating upstairs. Students of the nearby Conservatory like this place, sometimes professors as well, including one of the greatest cellists of our times.

Napos oldal *VI. Jókai utca 8.,* www.naposoldal.com
The name means "sunny side" – and, indeed, it is situated on the sunnier side. It is possibly the most original health food shop and cafeteria in town, with nice music and delicious-smelling food. There are sandwiches and sweets, and no hurry! Sit down and eat, and pay after you have finished.

Roosevelt Self-Service *V. Roosevelt tér 7–8.*
This reasonably-priced self-service place is friendly and international in style. It is located near the riverfront with Lánchíd views. They will ask if you are paying with cash. Cash is 10 percent cheaper. But the other option is not credit, but food voucher. It serves healthy food for the very well-dressed crowd.

Csirke Csibész *VI. Nagymező utca 35., between Andrássy and Bajcsy-Zsilinszky*
Probably the best fried chicken in town, plus a limited choice of salads, can be had here. There is no seating, but the place seems to be a favourite eatery of motorcycle policeman. It is slowly developing into a chain, but the other branches are not so great.

Főzelék Faló *VI. Nagymező utca 22.*
This very small shop has hardly any space to stand, and there is
a constant queue in lunchtime. The speciality here is főzelék, a
vegetable dish with roux. It is located in the heart of Budapest's
"Broadway", the theatre district. Actors and theatre folks are
here until quite late.

Millennium Court Salad *Millennium Court, V. Váci utca between
Régiposta utca, Galamb utca and Pesti Barnabás utca*
This is probably the best modern place in town, with one queue
for salad and another for sandwiches, though you can head
directly to the refrigerated sandwiches and drinks. There is even
a modest pre-packed sushi supply and free Internet access. There
is great seating in the courtyard, and it's a favourite of the expat
community.

Hold utca Market *V. Hold utca 13.*
This traditional market has a great choice of all kinds of quick
bites. The clientele is bank ladies of all ages, mixed with tourists
and construction workers. The good fish vendor should not to
be overlooked.

WHY SHOULD I BUY WINE IN BUDAPEST? AND WHERE?

All of Hungary is a wine-growing zone. This fact, along with the
special soil and climatic qualities of various regions, explains
how such a small country can boast 22 strictly delimited quality
wine districts. Indeed, one of the most amazing facts about
Hungarian wines is their great variety: Hungary belongs to the
few wine-growing countries in the world to produce the entire
range of classic wine styles including whites, rosés, reds, sparkling wines, and naturally sweet wines (botrytis whites). These
different wines are made from an impressive range of grape varieties characterized by a certain equilibrium between international and local varieties. Hungary is often considered a white
wine country – though red wines are getting better and better.
Since 1990 amazing development has taken place on the wine
scene, and at a fast pace. Wine culture here is still in the process
of being re-established to its pre-war glory.

PROBABLY THE BEST WINE SHOPS IN TOWN

Bortársaság (Budapest Wine Society) *I. Batthyány utca 59.,*
www.bortarsasag.hu, open Monday to Friday
10 a.m. to 8 p.m., Saturday 10 a.m. to 6 p.m.
Attila Tálos and his colleagues will guide you through the
stunning complexity of Hungarian wine regions and grape
varieties and the growing number of quality-conscious wine
producers at this tastefully furnished cellar-shop. There's a
good choice of wine from all of Hungary's interesting regions
sold at reasonable prices. The shop is a five-minute walk from
Moszkva tér (on the way up to Castle Hill), and be sure to
mind the steps when you're leaving. While you're here, don't
miss the habos mákos, a delicious cake with poppy seeds and
meringue at the Bécsi kapu confectioner's shop around the
corner on Ostrom utca. Bortársaság has several other shops
around the city including one at IX. Ráday utca 7. and V. Szent
István tér 3.

La Boutique des Vins *V. József Attila utca 12.,*
www.malatinszky.hu, open Monday to Friday 10 a.m. to 8 p.m.,
Saturday 10 a.m. to 3 p.m.
Owner Csaba Malatinszky, who is an ex-Gundel sommelier as
well as a winemaker, will be glad to share his knowledge if you
find him in the shop. The staff here is competent and there is a
good range of Hungarian wine from many wine regions, but it
is difficult to see what is actually on the shelves. The shop is a
two-minute walk from Vörösmarty tér.

Bock Bisztró and wine shop *VII. Erzsébet körút 43–47.,*
www.bock.hu, open Monday to Saturday noon to midnight.
This is an informal restaurant with great food (mentioned in the
Michelin restaurant guide in 2007 and 2008, no stars, though,
of course.) It is the joint venture of a wine producer (József Bock
from the Villány region) and of a chef. One wall of the restaurant
holds a substantial collection of select bottles.

Első Pesti Borház (First Wine House in Pest)
V. Bajcsy-Zsilinszky út 18., www.borbazilika.com, open Monday
to Friday 10 a.m. to 6 p.m.
This very large store is partly underground.

Debunking Five Myths about Hungarian Wines

András Egyedi, *wine expert, adopted son of the Tokaj Region*

1. Hungarian wine, at its best, is a cheaper and lower-quality substitute for Australian, New Zealand, South African, and other foreign wines.
This view is generally held by foreigners who are unaware of recent developments in Hungary. It is also, unfortunately, reiterated in many wine guides, encyclopedias, and other writings. It can partly be explained by the disastrous marketing efforts of Hungarian wine producers and the Hungarian state, which fails to emphasize that Hungarian winemaking traditions are in the same league as those of France, Italy, Germany, Spain or Portugal, and that very promising efforts have been made by many small winemakers, and a few larger-scale wineries, since 1991.

2. Hungarian wine is the best in the world.
Full stop. This is the intimate conviction of most of my compatriots. This, along with some similar statements concerning various other domains of life, is the logical counterpart to Hungarian defeatism.

3. Egri Bikavér (Bull's Blood) is the best Hungarian wine.
Thanks to its captivating name, this red blend from the Eger and Szekszárd regions has acquired a certain reputation in the United States, Britain, and Canada as a cheap table wine sold on the bottom shelves of supermarkets. One of the most important grapes in the traditional blend, a variety called kadarka, has practically disappeared from the Eger wine region. Some winemakers are now considering replanting it in order to return the spicy aroma to their Bikavér, which is what once distinguished it. There are some attractive Bikavérs being produced in the Eger region, such as those from Vilmos Thummerer, Tibor Gál and Béla Vincze. In the Szekszárd region, Ferenc Vesztergombi's Bikavér stands out. But for the time being, most wine makers tend to make other wines, typically single varietals such as cabernet sauvignon, their flagship products.

4. There is so little real Tokaj wine produced in the Tokaj region that it is no use buying it: you are doomed to buy a fake bottle.

This old myth has caused a lot of harm to this unique (and not so small) wine region. The region consists of more than 5,000 hectares (12,350 acres) and its most famous product is Tokaji Aszú, which is what Louis XIV of France called "the wine of kings, the king of wines". Because of its extraordinary quality and its legendary reputation, Tokaj's name has been borrowed by different wines around the world. The most famous among these is probably Tokay d'Alsace, which is actually pinot gris. This French variety is also widely cultivated in Hungary under the name szürkebarát and it yields some very pleasant wines north of Lake Balaton. The Italian white varietal, Tocai, is another well-known wine which has borrowed the name. Neither of these two wines has anything to do with Hungarian Tokaj and their confusing names will soon disappear from wine labels. They should not be considered to be fake Tokaj, however, since they are different wines, made from different varietals, with different vinification methods.

5. Tokaj wines are for women because they are too sweet.

No comment.

WINE FOR THE SOCIAL EXPERIENCE

For the social experience, rather than for the oenological merit, visit a borozó. These wine bars, however, are unlike their counterparts in London or New York. They are neither overpriced nor pretentious, and most have stand-up tables where customers take their wine at leisure, occasionally helping it down with slices of zsíros kenyér (bread with pork dripping, paprika, and often onion slices). Many of these places are supplied by wine growers' co-operatives, but most of the wines offered in these places are almost undrinkable. There is another type of place called the talponálló, which is a simple wine-counter and is generally filthy and full of drunks. In Hungary it is common to add soda to your wine. Our word for the spritzer is fröccs, and there are five common varieties:

Name of mix	Wine	Soda water	Meaning
kisfröccs	10 cl	10 cl	small spritzer
nagyfröccs	20 cl	10 cl	large spritzer
hosszúlépés	10 cl	20 cl	long step
házmester	30 cl	20 cl	janitor
viceházmester	20 cl	30 cl	under-janitor

A NOTE ON SOME HUNGARIAN SPIRITS

Pálinka is Hungarian fruit brandy and the best known variety is barackpálinka, apricot brandy. It is often perversely drunk as an aperitif, thus well and truly numbing the taste buds. Another variation is óbarack, old apricot, which has been aged. Other types include cseresznye (cherry), szilva (plum), and körte (pear). A worthwhile type of pear pálinka is called Vilmos Körte. The best Cognac-type drink distilled here is Tokaji Borpárlat.

All cafés and coffee houses serve spirits in measures of 5 cl or, increasingly, of 4 cl (which are called féldeci or feles, which means a half-decilitre). Waiters tend to turn up their nose if asked for a kis (small) measure of spirits, this being only 3 cl. It is advisable to ask for a kis szóda or a kísérő, which will get you a glass of soda water. Mixers and ice are generally unknown in Hungary. If you ask for a vodka and tonic, you will most often get a glass of vodka and a separate glass of tonic.

"Das ist ein Unicum", Kaiser Joseph II said when he first tasted the drink created by Dr. Zwack, the royal physician, in 1790. Though the king died the same year, this Hungarian bitter remains popular and is still called Unicum. It is a dark brown liquor containing more than 40 herbs and has a passing resemblance to Underberg and Fernet Branca. The authors of *Time Out Budapest* call Unicum "the Hungarian National Accelerator." They say "it looks like an old-style anarchist's bomb, and smells like a hospital corridor. It's vaguely sweet and minty, and bitter as a winter's night". It made me wonder why I like it, but I do. The pre-war placards for Unicum are much sought after for their fantastic design. In 1990 Péter Zwack, who had fled the country when he was young and lived in the United States and Italy, returned to Hungary and bought back the family factory on Soroksári út, where there is now also an interesting Unicum museum.

(*IX. Soroksári út 26.*, www.zwack.hu, open Monday to Saturday 10 a.m. to 6 p.m.)

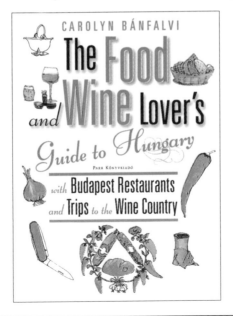

Also by Park Publishing

CAROLYN BÁNFALVI

The Food and Wine Lover's

Guide to Hungary

PARK KÖNYVKIADÓ

with Budapest Restaurants and Trips to the Wine Country

When a bank building was renovated in Szabadság tér,
the designers persuaded the owner to recreate the wooden
entrance of the one-time "Budapest Workshop", a designer
furniture shop from 1913. When the bank was later
merged with another Italian bank, the then owners seem to
have tired of the homeless problem, and commisioned this
primitive (but affordable) metal barrier.

ART TO SEE, ART TO BUY

PROLIFERATION OF CONTEMPORARY ART IN VÁRFOK UTCA

Károly Szalóky (who can be recognized by his spectacularly-oversized moustache) was the workaholic manager and later director of a major cultural centre in Buda. He opened his first contemporary gallery on sloping Várfok utca (between busy Moszkva tér and Castle Hill) in 1990, and it instantly changed Budapest's gallery scene. The gallery, which is named for the street, offers serious programmes dedicated to artists known all over Europe. It also keeps a keen watch for talented academy students. He travels to Paris, to the art fairs called FNAC, and to other international markets. He has been successful, and his efforts have certainly been noticed (even by the newspaper *Le Monde*).

As the economic revival of the late 1990s began, an increasing number of young fast-lane business people have been decorating their offices with contemporary art. Szalóky's galleries are often contacted to assist with pictures and ideas for these offices. The crowded New Year's Eve reception at Várfok Gallery (between 11 a.m. and 2 p.m.) is now an annual event which can be visited without an invitation. But it is really only fun if you are with a friend who can fill you in on the gossip about the art celebrities in attendance. The gallerist never misses an opportunity to lose some money, which is why he opened Café Alkoholos Filc (Felt-tip Pen Café) down the street at Várfok utca 15/b. The walls here are covered with the works of artists represented by the gallery.

(Várfok and Spiritusz Galleries:
I. Várfok utca 11. and 14., www.varfok-galeria.hu, open Tuesday to Saturday 11 a.m. to 6 p.m.)

ENTERS GLITZ

"*THE ONLY GOOD ARTIST IS A DEAD ARTIST*" goes the age-old Budapest art dealers' witticism. Although it seemed to have lost some of its validity in the spring of 1995 when the first glitzy New York-style gallery opened in downtown Budapest, between the river and the touristy part of Váci utca. The openings at this new gallery were as popular with the more elderly Hungarian yuppies as with egghead society (what little of it remains from the good old days). The gallery's artists tend to paint huge, colourful, sensuous canvases. The couple who opened the gallery must have know all too well that their investment was unlikely to show much of a return in the next century. One of the owners, Katalin Délceg, was an exceptionally elegant lady in her thirties when the gallery opened. She was the one who actually ran the gallery, until she suddenly died in 2010. Her husband, the other owner, is a successful real-estate dealer who is always present at the evening openings (perhaps they always take place so late so he can make them). He shows up flaunting his unorthodox dress code, which on some days makes him look like a cross between a futures trader and a rock opera set-designer. With the opening of this gallery, contemporary Hungarian art inevitably began its long march towards becoming chic. It definitely happened by 2005.

(**Dovin Gallery** *V. Galamb utca 6.*, www.dovingaleria.hu, open Tuesday to Friday noon to 6 p.m., Saturday 11 a.m. to 2 p.m.)

BY FAR THE BEST IN SZENTENDRE

Szentendre is the classic Budapest day trip for tourists as well as for serious travellers. The latter, however, avoid the museum devoted to sculptor/potter Margit Kovács (1902–1977), who was an innovator in the 1930s and later became an over-decorated grand dame of kitsch. Instead, they go to the Erdész Galéria where they will find lots of great art by artists hitherto unknown to them. Erdész has enlarged his gallery several times, and it is located in one of Szentendre's finest courtyards. It is a revelation both for those who have always admired early 20th century Hungarian painting, as well as those who haven't heard about it. Sándor Bortnyik and Lajos Vajda are the two stars of the gallery, amongst about a dozen other names. Here you can closely and intimately admire them in this unusual atmosphere.

(**Erdész Galéria** *Szentendre, Bercsényi utca 4.*, www.gallery erdesz.hu, open Tuesday to Sunday 10 a.m. to 4 p.m.)

THE STATE AS SANTA CLAUS

In terms of literature and art, the arrival of liberty in Hungary favoured the very good and the very bad writers and artists. The mass in the middle, which was the vast majority, found themselves frustrated, poor and with their careers somewhat in question. Beginning in the early-1980s a new generation emerged which was much more market-oriented, familiar with modern European museums (and sometimes even with American museums), and able to speak foreign languages (even if not brilliantly). A little later they capitalized on a somewhat artificial, politically-oriented interest in Hungarian art, during the wonderful second half of the 1980s. But thousands had to learn that they were on their way to becoming Sunday painters. Now they are art teachers, civil servants, paste-up artists at illustrated papers, and graphic designers during the week. The once all-powerful Fine Arts Fund, which bought pictures from hundreds of artists weekly, had in the meantime lost its monopoly and most of its marketable assets. But it was not relieved of its obligation to pay pensions to old artists, and it now had to do this with insufficient income. It was turned into a quasi-independent foundation, which the state has to put money into every year. It still has some of its galleries, selling a very mixed, commercial range of art. One of the surviving Communist-era commercial galleries is at VI. Teréz körút 11.

A FORMERLY REALLY FAVOURED ARTIST

Few contemporary Hungarian artists can hope to live to see a museum solely devoted to their work. Imre Varga, the maverick octogenarian sculptor is one of the few. But the road was a long one for this artist, who has been so liked by the general public and so sneered at by many of his fellow artists. For a decade or so, in the 1950s and early-1960s, he was treated like a pariah. He came from a land-owning family, and as a young man during the war, he had been a fighter pilot in the Hungarian air force. Later, during the first political "thaw", he let himself be lured into the role of being a conspicuously non-party-member favoured artist, hoping that fate and good luck would allow him to influence things for the better. He was even "elected" to be a MP in that parody of a Parliament which had four sessions a year: one per season and each a maximum of three days long.

There was a year when Varga was said to have used about 75 percent of the capacity of the only bronze statue foundry in Hungary. He slowly began to fit into the cookie-cutter mould of a great Hungarian artist. He became known all over Europe, was able to blend tradition with modernity, and was often on television. He has had about 300 of his works erected, which is a rare feat. Undoubtedly, his masterpiece is the Wallenberg monument (II. Szilágyi Erzsébet fasor, corner of Nagyajtai utca). It is located in a tucked-away part of Buda because even in 1986 it took considerable bravery to commemorate the Swedish diplomat who saved tens of thousands of Jews before finally vanishing into the Soviet gulag.

With the arrival of democracy, Varga again became a sort of pariah who was accused of having been some kind of collaborator. He mainly works for German commissions now, but he recently had a Bartók statue erected in Brussels. He spends his time in the museum devoted to his work, and he is a wise old man who still has an imposing presence (he is more than six feet-tall with ultra-short silver hair, like a retired four-star general in the U.S. Air Force). He speaks German and French well, though not (as far as I know) English.

(**Imre Varga Collection** *III. Laktanya utca 7.*, www.budapest-galeria.hu, open Tuesday to Sunday 10 a.m. to 6 p.m.)

ARTIST-WATCHING, BUDAPEST

Artists live everywhere in Hungary. To spot them in Budapest, you can go to two purpose-built artists' colonies. The bigger one, called the Százados út Artists' Colony, is in outer József-város (100 metres from the Stadionok underground station). Built before World War One, it consists of about three dozen various sized homes, each with a studio (some of which are very big). A communal garden surrounds the houses and there is a fence around the colony with an iron gate that is never locked. The style is sometimes loosely called National Romanticism. It consists of a lot of woodwork, complicated latticed roofs, and undressed stone on the outside (especially near the bottom). The colony is still a lovely place, even after some major alterations were made that were not done with the necessary expertise. The right to live here was theoretically granted to artists and not to their widows or their offspring. But few of the families ever left. There are unfinished statues all around, and even some finished works of totalitarian "art" by the dreaded former dean of the Academy of Fine Arts. It is definitely worth taking a walk here, and anybody can freely walk in.

(**Százados út Artists' Colony** *VIII. Százados út 3–13.*)

The other colony is a nice art nouveau apartment building with studios, which was built in 1903. It is located 100 metres up the hill from the elegant Gellért Hotel (see Walk Three). The typical tenants here are couples, both painters, who have launched successful graphic design careers. They work a lot, participating in the rat race, so they leave early and get home late. The husband gets away for three weeks once or twice a year, to a summer colony for artists in Kecskemét (about 100 kilometres south of Budapest). During that time he does not want to hear about business. He even switches off his cell phone.

(Apartment Building with Studios *XI. Kelenhegyi út 12–14.*)

ARTIST-WATCHING, NORTHWEST HUNGARY

Lake Balaton, the "Hungarian Sea", is a naff place on the whole. But not the relatively untouched villages north of it which sit roughly between Veszprém and Tapolca. It is one of the most attractive parts of Hungary, and is known for its volcanic hills. The fashion for buying summer homes and studios here started in the early 1980s, as more and more villagers abandoned their houses. The craze spread from a village called Kapolcs, where the composer/theatre director István Márta and his friends organize the annual "Valley of Arts" festival (http://www.muveszetekvolgye.hu), which has a fringe of hundreds of smaller events between mid-July and mid-August. By now, several dozen better-known painters have studios here, and writers and actors are also crowding in. Writer György Konrád has a wonderful house in a village called Hegymagas. The traditionalist painter/semi-professional hussar Győző Somogyi moved permanently to a village called Salföld and gathered quite a herd of different animals. His house is a frequent destination of pilgrimage for dewy-eyed egghead students dreaming of the simple life. The last outpost is a shore resort called Szigliget, where there is a writers' "Creative Centre" (which is a relic of the past, even the name). It's a big, yellow, dilapidated complex on a large estate that once belonged to an aristocratic family. One of their scions, the cult figure/writer Péter Esterházy traditionally spends three weeks there at the beginning of August, always with the same bunch of friends (writers, musicians and artists). It is no small privilege to be invited, even for the day.

(Szigligeti Alkotóház *Szigliget Creative Centre, Szigliget, Veszprém County.*)

BUYING ARTWORK

During the last two or three decades most art of any quality has been sold straight by the artists, directly from their studios to friends and collectors. Collectors should first go to galleries and look around. Ask the gallery owners to organize visits to artists who catch your eye. It will be worth paying the gallery's mark-up since you will also be able to leaf through catalogues and colour transparencies and you will be helped with formalities like the necessary permit for taking works of art out of the EU (which might prevent embarrassing moments at the border). The gallery world is still a small one in Hungary: friendliness, jealousy and pickiness are all features. It is worth visiting some artists through their galleries to see the rather old-world, unspoiled way of life they lead. They are artists, daydreamers, social critics and craftspeople at the same time – so different from the stars of the Western hemisphere. A good prelude to purchasing Hungarian art might be a visit to Lumú (the Ludwig Museum of Contemporary Art). You can visit any of the artists exhibited there through practically any of the galleries mentioned above. (See Walk Five).

NAME-DROPPING: ART TO LIVE WITH

I know many artists, and I will try to avoid offending them by emphasizing that the following list is not about their artistic greatness, but about friendliness and decorative value. This list of my favourites is a highly subjective one. There are others, who are great for museums or for real collectors (who will hardly rely on my advanced-amateur advice concerning what to buy).

In my home there are two paintings by Gábor Karátson, the writer, painter, eco-advocate and Oriental thinker. He is a living legend, a maverick with long silver hair, who practically never sells his art. He would rather face difficulties paying his electricity bill. I especially like his oil paintings from the 1970s with picturesque titles (like the one that hangs in my living room: Borg hits the ball during serving in the 1974 Monte Carlo Open Tournament) and his illustrations to Goethe's Faust. Obviously, he is not represented by galleries, but any of them can contact him.

Károly Kelemen paints large, sensual canvases, full of bright colours. Since the mid 1980s they always include some teddy bears. He loves to paraphrase some of Picasso's classics. He is a large man with a permanent smile. Like a giant teddy bear, he is very easygoing and he rarely says no to one more glass.

László Fehér is a rare artist who is universally acclaimed by the man in the street, the Hungarian art critic guru, and the international gallery world. They all agree on his importance as an artist. Fehér has intense, usually large canvases. They often have a white, outlined little boy against black backdrops. His other favourite colour is yellow. You probably will not have enough cash with you to buy one of his paintings, and only certain kinds of American Express cards allow withdrawals that large. He has a large studio in a village called Tác, which is between Budapest and Lake Balaton. If you visit, don't eat for three days. He insists on entertaining guests at his dinner table in a manner worthy of 2nd and 3rd century Roman emperors.

Being his godfather, I have long been biased towards the art of István Orosz, at least since I suggested he take a Greek pseudonym OUTIS ("ooh-tis"), which means Nobody in Greek. Odysseus pretended to be called this when Cyclops, the one-eyed giant, asked him his name. (So when he had been blinded and was howling in agony and his fellow giants asked who had hurt him, he thundered: "Nobody hurt me! Nobody hurt me".) István is a self-confessed disciple of M. C. Escher, the Dutch graphic artist, and much more. He resurrected the ancient medieval genre of "anamorphosis". He has been an animated film director, and he is also a highly successful poster-designer. In my flat I have some of his brilliant, illusionist etchings that express his constant homage to classical antiquity and to Piranesi. He isn't represented by galleries (as far as I know). He lives in Budakeszi, a suburb about 20 kilometres west of Budapest.

I mentioned Győző Somogyi, the Salföld hermit, above. For many years he only made bitter black-and-white prints that provided a sort of X-ray of an impoverished Hungary sinking into intellectual mediocrity and torpor. Then he decided to switch to painting colourful, large canvases of historical scenes. He became obsessed with military heroism. He is also active as an illustrator of books on the history of hussars. You might come across some of his original drawings made for these books.

I also own some works by my friend and co-author of this book, painter/illustrator András Felvidéki. He has considerably helped to open my eyes to the subtleties of Budapest's architecture and urban fabric. The works of his that I have are etchings of Budapest details and of imaginary, symbolic scenes that are unmistakably Budapest. Over the last couple of years he has begun to paint city scenes, trolley bus interiors, lit-up telephone booths at night, and couples kissing on a bench in the old underground. He is a solitary figure who taught art students for many years.

Another six names I would buy, if I ever sold an unexpectedly high number of copies of this book: Imre Bak, Ákos Birkás, István Nádler, Tamás Soós, Erzsébet Vojnich and Zsuzsi Csiszér.

SOME CONTEMPORARY GALLERIES

Acb Gallery *VI. Király utca 76.*, www.acbgaleria.hu
Arte Galéria *V. Ferenczy István utca 14.*
Deák Erika Galéria *VI. Mozsár utca 1.*,
www.deakgaleria.t-online.hu
Dovin *V. Galamb utca 6.*, www.dovingaleria.hu
Erdész Galéria *Szentendre, Bercsényi utca 4.*,
www.galleryerdesz.hu
Godot Galéria *XI. Bartók Béla út 11.*, www.godot.hu
K. Bazovsky Ház *VIII. Horánszky utca 13.*, www.bazovsky.hu
Knoll *VI. Liszt Ferenc tér 10. First Floor*, www.knollgalerie.at
Pintér Sonja Galéria *V. Falk Miksa utca 10.*
Stúdió Galéria *VII. Rottenbiller utca 35.*,
http://studio.c3.hu/studio_galeria
Kisterem Galéria *V. Képíró u. 5.*, www.kisterem.hu
Várfok *I. Várfok utca 11. and 14.*, www.varfok-galeria.hu
Vintage Gallery (photography) *V. Magyar utca 26.*,
www.vintage.hu

The Museum of Applied Arts (1896) was the third purpose-built museum of this kind in the world. Nowadays it skillfully balances its efforts between traditional crafts and modern design. This photo was taken by the author while his youngest daughter was discovering the site-specific work of art in the organic architecture exhibition in 2008.

GOING OUT

BUDAPEST AS A MUSEUM

Much of Budapest is still like a big open-air museum. So going for a walk, in whatever direction, can be most enjoyable if you are open for adventure.

There is a curious old-fashioned quality to most of the streets outside of the tourist areas. Budapest remains a largely un-segregated city, so you still can't tell what kind of people live behind the façades. If you bought this book back home (in the Tattered Cover in Denver, or Powell's in Portland, or Kramerbooks in Washington DC, or the Triangle Bookshop in London, or the Athenaeum Boekhandel in Amsterdam) and have read the "Crash Course" in your own armchair, then you will already have your pair of binoculars. If not, you can still buy a cheap pair at one of the flea markets. Then you can start your field-work in what I call "applied people watching". Take a close look at Budapest's balconies. Most people who store stuff there are oblivious of the fact that their stuff is not hidden. A family's balcony is as much of a telltale sign of its values and tastes as its rubbish is, but the balcony is easier to see. The very rich have already left Budapest, but in the urban jungle of quickly gentrifying Pest there are tens of thousands of middle class people who like it here – especially since locals can park for free (thanks to the parking revolution). That is the situation in Pest, the big open-air museum where I have lived all of my life. After all, "nothing ever happens in Buda". That is to say, theatres, cafés and most of the cinemas are in Pest. Buda is mostly residential, except for the museums in the Castle.

THE SMALL MUSEUM EXPERIENCE

In all of Budapest's museums, big and small, elderly ladies work as underpaid attendants. But in the small ones, one often finds a pleasantly peculiar small-town quality. Budapest's small museums are characterized by their attendants who have a sort of personal pride and go out of their way to show visitors the collections. They very sweetly try to explain everything in Hungarian, even to guests who obviously don't speak the language. Travellers might recognise this characteristic from museums in other cities, like London's Sir John Soane Museum, for example. While the big museum means that the attendant (who perhaps has job insecurity) is alienated from the visitors, small museum attendants are indispensable, like family. For visitors this is an extra bonus. The Stamp Museum, for example, is one of Budapest's most interesting small museums:

Stamp Museum *VII. Hársfa utca 47.*, www.belyegmuzeum.hu, open April 1 to October 31, 10 a.m. to 6 p.m., rest of the year 10 a.m. to 4 p.m.

This small museum is really a big one, one of the biggest of its kind in the world. It is housed in a classic late 1930s modern building. It is a huge ministry building in a small, impoverished side-street which is lined up with "the least finished avenue" in Budapest. District seven's Madách Imre út (beginning at Madách tér) was planned from the 1920s to the 1940s, but was never realised except for a big arch and the first 100 metres. The museum's permanent exhibition of about 11 million stamps is displayed in quite an ingenious way (something had to be done, otherwise it would have taken up the whole building) on 3,200 pull-out metal frames, uniting the requirements of storage and exhibition.

An Oversize Small Museum: Thermae Maiores –
The Big Bath *III. Flórián tér 3–5.*,
www.aquincum.hu, www.btm.hu/furdo/furdo.htm,
open from spring to autumn by appointment.

Most Budapesters do not know about the Big Bath, they simply drive over it on the overpass on the M11 leading towards Szentendre and the Danube Bend. The Bath, a small piece of which was unearthed in 1778, is to many of us Budapest freaks, the symbol of a changed attitude towards the city. During its heyday in the first part of the 3rd century, the Roman settlement in northern Buda (called Aquincum) was a sizeable town with at least 10,000, and perhaps 12,000, inhabitants. There has been a museum here since 1892 featuring the extensive remains of the centre of the civilian town, "the municipium". The area was the one-time Roman military settlement, and the immediate surrounding neighbourhood of Óbuda was bulldozed in the mid- and late-1970s. The most awful ten-storey pre-fab buildings were erected by the dozens. In 1981, when the pillars of the overpass were being dug, workers hit a section of the Big Bath exactly in the place where experts had predicted. It became impossible to continue with the construction and bury the ruins forever, as some construction lobbyists quite possibly wanted. Instead, the pillars were redesigned almost overnight, the site was excavated, and a unique underground passageway was built that criss-crosses around the open-air museum. In the underground passage there are dozens of replica statues and tablets and big glass-covered panels explaining the bath's history. The glass seems to be a problem with the younger generation. The more liberal society became in the early 1980s, the more glass was broken here. The authorities should experiment with enameled, graffiti-resistant signs.

ELEVEN OTHER GREAT SMALL MUSEUMS

György Ráth Museum Chinese art downstairs, Japanese upstairs. *VI. Városligeti fasor 12.*

Pál Molnár C. Collection The charming family establishment of an artist much influenced by art deco with many stylish prints from the 1930s. *XI. Ménesi út 65.*

Telefónia Museum The old, mechanical switchboard of the Castle District. *I. Úri utca 49.*

"Golden Eagle" Pharmacy Museum An authentic museum interior, from the end of the 18th century. *I. Tárnok utca 18.*

Lutheran Museum Sándor Petőfi, the great poet, was a slightly problematic student at this former school. Now you are shown around by retired ministers. *V. Deák tér 4.*

Music History Museum A great 18th-century palazzo, now partly a museum of instruments and a research center (with a great riverfront view). It is part of the Hungarian Academy of Sciences and Letters. *I. Táncsics Mihály utca 7.*

Jewish Museum adjacent to the Great Synagogue A history a Hungarian Jewry, and also a room for changing art exhibitions. *VII. Dohány utca 2.*

The Imre Varga Collection The representative sculptor of the 1970s, Varga is still often around. *III. Laktanya utca 7.*

Vasarely Museum For those who fancy the op-art master. *III. Szentlélek tér 1.*

Museum of Electrotechnology Located in a massive, elegant art-deco building in the heart of the former Jewish District. *VII. Kazinczy utca 21.*

Gizi Bajor Actors' Museum Great for émigré eggheads, who usually remember childhood performances better than anyone. *XII. Stromfeld Aurél út 16.*

INFORMATION ON GOING OUT – NOT TO MUSEUMS

Below I have recommended eleven obvious places to go out and nine more adventurous ones. Being invited to a Hungarian home would probably be the best way to spend an evening, but I can't produce enough invitations for that. I can't invite everyone to my own home, although there were times when I attempted to. When my family moved to Leopold Town, we quite incidentally found ourselves on the route of Walk Two. I often met readers clutching this book and scrutinizing the rooftop ornaments of the immortal Post Office Savings Bank. I had to discontinue the practice of inviting them up due to the more than symbolic pressure from my wife. If you are invited to a Hungarian home, here is some advice.

Going to a Hungarian Home It would beat most of my other ideas for going out. It is relatively easy to be invited to a Hungarian home. The best way to secure an invitation is to always forewarn the friends of the friends of the friends of your close friends, whose phone number was reluctantly given to you. Call them in advance and let them know you're coming, better yet, write in advance. Most Budapest professionals (not only egg-heads) tend to have at least one extra job and busy social lives. So it might not be easy for them to devote time to you while you are in Budapest. For a guaranteed non-invitation, give them very short notice by calling only after you have arrived.

On the day you arrive, offer to take them out to some luxury/ moderately-priced chic restaurant *(see "Eating Well", page 301).* When you talk to them on the phone, give them five or six ideas, remarking that they were reported to be a well-known gourmet couple/person in town. They will be flattered, and your invitation to their home will be an inch closer. You might offer to expand the invitation to some of their friends for that first meeting. That might make it easier for them, as they could include some people with whom a meeting was long overdue. Your local contacts will be grateful and will unlikely expect you to pay their friends' bill. If the invitation finally materialises, you can mention again that you would be delighted to meet some other friends of theirs.

Inside a Hungarian Home Once you are invited, you can relax and be as inquisitive as you wish. "You don't mind if I look around, do you?" is considered an entirely natural question, but is rarely heard since the hosts will almost certainly show you around. You will probably see many more books in the homes of Hungarian professionals than in the homes of their European or American counterparts. And it can be embarrassing how in

Hungary a high IQ and a fine wit are not necessarily accompanied by good taste. You will see incredibly low-quality, naff furniture (especially lamps). Neglected, broken parts are commonly seen in intellectually exuberant and vibrant homes. The naffest part of a home (if you like that kind of inverted, camp enjoyment) is often the balcony. It is rarely shown, unless you ask, as I often do when I look around homes on my first (and sometimes my last) invitation: "Can I enjoy the panorama for a moment?" And I can't withhold a reluctant warning: in some elite, intellectual homes you might be confronted with toilets you do not regularly see, except on movie screens, if you know what I mean.

NINE ADVENTUROUS EVENINGS OUT

Trafó Contemporary Arts Center: Going to see practically anything here *(See page 258.)*

Menza Restaurant: People watching along with your dinner *(See page 272.)*

Reading Paul Street Boys by Ferenc Molnár: If you can't find it in a bookshop, read it at the National Library (closing time: 9 p.m.) *(See page 116.)*

Municipal Circus: Dividing your attention between the show and the spectators *(See page 234 map.)*

Capella Café: Going to see a gay cabaret *(See page 342.)*

Collegium Budapest: Attending an evening lecture on some scholarly subject; have a pre-lecture nap in the afternoon, the lectures can be heavy and long *(See page 108.)*

Wichmann's Pub: Brooding over the meaning of life
VII. Kazinczy utca 55.

Kétballábas Pub: Watching an international soccer event with Hungarian fans (definitely not for the faint-hearted)
VI. Teréz körút 66.

Dancing on top of Corvin Department store: At a bar called Corvintető, only during spring to autumn
VIII. Blaha Lujza tér 1.

ELEVEN OBVIOUS PLACES TO GO OUT IN BUDAPEST

Music Academy: A major concert in the Great Hall (when renovation will be over) *(See page 270.)*

Music Academy: A graduation concert in the Small Hall (bring a bouquet of roses)

National Concert Hall (Palace of Arts): Zoltán Kocsis
conducting the National Philharmonic *(See page 252.)*
Műcsarnok: An exhibition opening *(See page 241.)*
Opera House: Cosí Fan Tutte, followed by dinner at Bel Canto
(See page 216.)
Opera House: A classical ballet
Open-air Concert: At Vajdahunyad (in Városliget) or
Martonvásár (on the M1 motorway), which is devoted
exclusively to Beethoven
National Dance Theatre (Palace of Arts): A genuine folk
dancing evening *(See page 112, 252.)*
Budapest Operetta Theatre: A genuine operetta, like the
Csárdás Princess
Matthias Church: A Bach or Liszt organ concert by the Notre
Dame organist or a rising Hungarian star *(See page 107.)*
A38 Ship: A world music concert

ELEVEN HUNGARIAN FILMS NOT TO MISS

During the summer months some cinemas and clubs show recent
Hungarian films with English subtitles. They can also be rented
from Odeon/Lloyd Video Rental *(see page 276)*. The following are
not to be missed (their Hungarian titles are in parentheses):

Miklós Jancsó: Confrontation (Fényes szelek, 1969) A historical
parable telling the story of some "revolutionary guardists" in the
late-1940s who attempt to disrupt the ancien régime with gusto
until they are pushed out of the scene. (The original Hungarian
title means "shining winds".)

Péter Bacsó: The Witness (A tanú, 1969) A hilarious comedy
about the Hungary of the early-1950s, when the authorities even
experimented with growing cotton and oranges. It premiered
only in 1979. "A satirical comedy worthy to rank with Schweik",
wrote *The Times* in London in February 1982.

Zoltán Huszárik: Szindbád (Szindbád, 1971) A sensuous, poetic
film portraying the last days of an ageing hedonist. It is based
on the writings of Gyula Krúdy, the chronicler of small town
fin de siècle and is an exceptionally successful collaboration
between director, cameraman, composer and actor. "A striking
tour de force of visual technique and metaphysical imagery,"
declared Films and Filming in December 1981. See "Eating Well",
page 301.

Gyula Gazdag: The Whistling Cobblestone (A sípoló macskakő, 1972) A philosophical satire on the perspectives of the post-1968 generation. Set in a summer student work camp, this black and white feature film was made using documentary techniques and an amateur cast. It's a "high-spirited and sly satire of government incompetence," raved the *Village Voice* in October 1979.

Pál Sándor: Football of the Good Old Days (Régi idők focija, 1973) A very funny and moderately sentimental film about an impoverished laundry owner who persists in sponsoring a football team in 1920s Budapest, which was the first low ebb of Hungarian football, because "the team must go on!". The great comedian Dezső Garas stars in the film.

András Jeles: Little Valentino (A kis Valentino, 1979) A young man runs away with some 10,000 forints and loiters around some of the most depressing Budapest neighbourhoods. It's a malicious, black, but delightful film about human values in the late-1970s and it explains a lot about this city. It was filmed in black and white with an amateur cast.

István Szabó: Mephisto (1981) A two-part, well-made, spectacular film about the life of an actor in Germany during the first half of the 20th century. It explores the limits of cooperation between the gifted and the powerful. Starring Klaus Maria Brandauer, the Oscar-winning film was based on the novel by Klaus Mann.

János Szász: Woyzeck (1992) A black-and-white film rendering of the Büchner classic, transferred to an unspecified time in the 20th-century. There is excellent, breathtaking acting and a dense, tense apocalyptic atmosphere. The photography in this world famous film is highly original.

Nimród Antal: Kontroll (2004) A film shot in the Budapest metro network, from beginning to end. It's an absurd comedy with a great plot and a group of ticket controllers as its main characters. It portrays a strong atmosphere, and was made by a very promising new director.

Áron Gauder: The District (Nyócker, 2004) "Nyócker" refers to district eight, which is an impoverished neighbourhood inside and outside of the Nagykörút (see Walks Three and Five). This is a unique animated film, with a social and political agenda, about a group of kids and their parents. It portrays gang warfare and ethnic and social differences and features great music (and strong language). The co-author of the script is László Jakab Orsós, an iconoclast journalist and crusader for sincere speech. (Only for over 16s).

György Pálfi: Taxidermia (2006) Three generations of men – from the last war, the 1960s Communist sports scene, and the arts scene of today's Vienna – feature in an inconceivable narrative of comic and tragic events, based on the stories of Lajos Parti Nagy. It is a serious adventure even for experienced film buffs.

A NOTE ON THE DANCE HOUSE MOVEMENT

A large number of people moved to the capital from the countryside at the end of the 19th century. They cherished their folk songs for a while, but rarely passed them on the next generation. The middle class favoured (as they still do) a type of folk-like romantic songs, called magyar nota ("Hungarian song"), which are the equivalent of Loch Lomond in its connection to real Scottish folk-music. Around 1970, quite out of the blue, two young musicians, Ferenc Sebő and Béla Halmos, brought the real folk music back into fashion overnight. This music is

Molnár Gál Péter (a.k.a. MGP),
wit, theatre critic, the wickedest pen

Cafés once bloomed on every corner of Szabadság tér. People who worked at the stock exchange, the banks and the ministries once sipped their coffees and read their newspapers at these many cafés. Later, people only visited this square to lay wreaths on the monuments. Cafés disappeared or changed functions. In some cafés, dentures were even manufactured. Cafés have certainly benefited from the re-emergence of bank life in this neighbourhood. They are opening among the flowerbeds one after another on the square. Café Liberty is a peaceful island in the square called Liberty. This café brings back the peaceful coffee-sipping, fierce gossiping, and politicking without muzzles from the days of Franz Joseph. The aroma of the coffee has a beneficial effect on free thinking. The owners provide a family atmosphere on top of the coffee and mineral water. On the corner of Zoltán utca and Szabadság tér, Café Farger opened in 2004 and was immensely popular less than half a year later. One owner is named Edit Farsang. Her husband, born in Vancouver and raised in Virginia, is John (or János Gerencsér, in the Hungarian still alive around the village of Szék in Transylvania (in the part of Romania which used to belong to Hungary). It was not only folk music that became trendy at that time, but traditional dancing also captured the imagination of the young. They gathered in "dance houses" (*táncház*) week after week to dance to live Transylvanian music, to learn new dances, and to enjoy the melodies. Anyone could join at any time and newcomers were taught the steps that had been mastered by earlier converts. Soon dance houses for children appeared. Dance houses have unique atmospheres and the devotees regard each other as extended family members. This rising interest in folk music has also been reflected in a number of records. Attending dance house events is not only lots of fun, but is also rewarding. You just might fall in love with both the music and the dancing after experiencing one. Check www.tanchaz.hu for dance houses around the country.

Fonó Music Hall This privately-owned folk and world music centre in Buda holds regular dance house events and also has a fantastic music and bookshop. The name fonó refers to a social custom in traditional Hungarian village life, and it also means spinning or spinning room. It's a magical place, which hosts some of Budapest's best and liveliest dance house events. Its

---

way). Don't try to pronounce the café's name in the French or the British way. The first syllable of each of the owners names is embedded in the name. Far-Ger (faahr-gher). The lady's name is at the front, in order not to sound indecent in Hungarian. The place is crowded from seven in the morning. There are sandwiches, salads, cookies, excellent coffee (long, short, espresso, cappuccino, white and with whipped cream), and fresh cookies. Everybody has breakfast here, until the afternoon. The place starts to empty around four o'clock when business in the neighbourhood finishes and office workers go home. Half an hour later, Farger fills up again with neighbourhood locals. Youngsters with laptops immerse themselves in their work. As if there was an intellectual census in effect here, this is a favorite place for eggheads to congregate. Dogs are allowed, and my spaniel leaves his order in the kitchen, on his own. Fresh water is always ready: a thirsty dog can arrive any minute. In Café Farger people somehow like each other better than usual. It is not far from Parliament, and to tell you the truth, I expect more from Farger than from the Parliament.

slogan "surprise and diversity" sums up its varied schedule of performances. Fonó also has a struggling, but great, record label with a programme called "24th Hour". It has brought authentic bands from Transylvania, made digital recordings in the studio, and then presented them live in Fonó. Support Fonó's efforts by going there, listening to some music, and buying some recordings. You will not regret it. (*XI. Sztregova utca 3., off Fehérvári út,* www.fono.hu.)

A NOTE ON GYPSY MUSIC

Gypsy music is a highly problematic genre. My generation, which was brought up with genuine folk music from an early age, unanimously sneers at it and it is confused with Hungarian folk music all over Europe. Even Franz Liszt confused the two. The Gypsy bands play *magyar nóta* (see above), which are sugary, quasi-folkloristic songs which were originally written for the hundreds of thousands who migrated to Budapest from the countryside. Later *magyar nóta* was also adopted by the upper classes. Nowadays it is rapidly losing its audience, even in the countryside. Twenty years ago there were about 20,000 professional Gypsy musicians in Hungary, today there are just 2,000, and they live largely off tourists. The classic Gypsy ensemble originally consisted of no fewer than eight musicians: the prímás (violin), the kontrás (second violin), the bass, the cimbalon player, the clarinetist, the second kontrás, the cellist and the second prímás. Now they are rarely seen in ensembles of more than four or five. A number of outstanding Hungarian jazzmen have also come from Gypsy musician families, such as the Lakatos dynasty. If you are interested in genuine Gypsy folk music, check out the CDs from a group called Parno Graszt (Black Flame).

This photo, taken by the author at the metro terminus at Örs vezér tér, attempts to illustrate the wise words of a gay friend: "No, gays are not exactly like the straight – but they should be entitled to the same rights." In 2009 a giant step was taken by the Hungarian legal system. Gays and lesbians were granted the right to establish "permanent lifelong companionship", in front of a public official in the framework of a public ceremony.

GAY AND LESBIAN BUDAPEST

As a big city which attracts people from far beyond its borders, Budapest has always had a significant gay component. But it is mostly invisible, and gays and lesbians still tend to keep low profiles. Things here are somewhat Victorian: a lot is implied, but little is said. There is an annual Gay Pride Parade in early-July, which includes a march along the main streets with police assistance. But the number of participants has never exceeded 2,000. Practically no public figures, such as actors, politicians, writers or TV celebrities, have ever declared themselves to be gay, even if most people know that they are. (The first two politicians who broke the tradition of secrecy were a former liberal MP who openly talked about being a lesbian. Then in 2007 a state secretary in office came out openly at the Gay Pride Parade's official opening.) There is hardly any harassment, but it is widely understood that gays will keep a low-profile and exercise self-restraint. But among themselves, as anywhere else in the western hemisphere, there is a colourful and lively scene. Since January 1, 2010 couples of the same sex have the right to sign a "registered partnership", very similar to marriage, except for three things: they can't use each other's names, they can't adopt children and they can't undergo artificial insemination. But the couples are entitled to use the official marriage parlours ("házasságkötő terem"), which has a great emotional impact for them. Just after the vote in Parliament, a 2009 poll conducted by Szonda Ipsos showed that 58 per cent of the Hungarian public supported that new institution.

Written by a friend of the author, Miklós Graff, who was kind enough to tap the Budapest gay community.

GAY BARS

Action *V. Magyar utca 42.*, www.action.gay.hu, open daily
9 p.m. to 4 a.m.
The toughest, cruisiest bar in town is in a rustic cellar with
video screens, go-go dancers and a darkroom. It's practically
men only. There are live sex shows on Fridays which attract big
crowds.

Capella Café *V. Belgrád rakpart 23.*, capella.uw.hu, open
Wednesday to Saturday 9 p.m. to dawn.
This huge labyrinth of a place is frequented by many non-gays
(often amounting to 70 percent of the crowd), yet it has a dis-
tinctly gay atmosphere. While once an elite venue, it is still
going, but has lost its sparkle. Wednesday nights are popular,
though.

Coxx *VII. Dohány utca 38.*, www.coxx.hu, open Sunday to
Thursday 9 p.m. to 4 a.m., Friday and Saturday 9 p.m. to 5 a.m.
In this pub-like cellar bar there is a dance floor and a huge new
"play area". The ground floor Internet café is open Monday to
Friday from noon. Perfect. Dead mid-week, but lively at the
weekends.

The Funny Carrot *V. Szép utca 1.*, open daily 7 p.m. to 4 a.m.
This small and cosy place is used mainly for cruising, and for
occasional encounters. It is intimate and friendly.

Habroló Bisztró *V. Szép utca 1/b.*, open daily 7 p.m. to 5 a.m.
Neighbourhood bar with occasional karaoke nights.

Mylord Café *V. Belgrád rakpart 3.*, open Monday to Friday
10 p.m. to 4 a.m., Saturday and Sunday 3 p.m. to 4 a.m.
Situated on the Danube bank, this place has a mixed clientele
during the day which gets gayer and gayer as night falls. It has
a pleasant, relaxed atmosphere.

Le Café M *V. Nagysándor József utca 3.*, www.mysterybar.hu,
open daily 4 p.m. to 4 a.m.
This mid-sized café is friendly, offers Internet access, and is
good for information and orientation help.

Alterego Bar & Lounge *VI. Dessewffy utca 33.*, open Fridays
and Saturdays 10 p.m. to 5 a.m.
This very popular club is now the top dance and night club.

LESBIAN PARTIES

Living Room *V. Kossuth Lajos utca 17.*, www.livingroom.hu.
There are lesbian parties here on the last Saturday of each month.

Eklektika *VI. Nagymező utca 30.*, www.eklektika.hu, open daily
noon to midnight.
This ordinary, low-profile café is especially lesbian friendly.
There's lesbian night from 10 p.m. on the second Saturday of
every month.

A GAY-FRIENDLY CAFÉ

Amstel River *V. Párizsi utca 6.*, www.miwo.hu/amstelcafe,
open daily 11 a.m. to midnight.
This small Dutch style café/pub/restaurant has handsome
waiters. There's a street terrace during the summer. Theo, the
friendly Dutch owner, recommends his favourite pasta on the
menu, which is worth trying.

GAY SAUNAS

Magnum Sauna *VIII. Csepreghy utca 2.*,
www.magnumszauna.hu, open daily 1 p.m. to 1 a.m., Saturday
from 1 p.m. and then non-stop all weekend.
This Western-style modern gay sauna is for men only.

Szauna 69 *IX. Angyal utca 2.*, www.szauna69.hu, open Sunday
to Thursday 1 p.m. to 1 a.m., Friday 1 p.m. to
2 a.m. Saturday 1 p.m. to 6 a.m.
The crowd here is younger than the Magnum.

BATHS OF GAY INTEREST

Király fürdő *See page 160* for contact information.
This bath is almost exclusively frequented by gays, who tend
to behave very openly. Swimsuits are needed here, unlike in
the saunas of the Rudas and the Gellért (where locals consider
them to be a touch of bad taste). Regulars sport neat little aprons
which are distributed at the entrance. Open for men on Tuesday,
Thursday and Saturday, and for women on Monday, Wednesday
and Friday. There was an RTL Klub (a local television news
program) "sting" when they secretly filmed there. Though the

place is apparently still quite gay, there is an ERÉNYŐR ("guardian of virtue") who shouts at any guests who get too frisky in public!

Rudas fürdő *I. Döbrentei tér 9.,* www.rudasfurdo.hu.
This bath house has a swimming pool, rooftop sunbathing terrace, and a 400 year-old Turkish steam bath. There is a mixed crowd, including gays, but there are also non-gay sportsmen who get easily offended. Maximum discretion is required, this is no longer a par excellence gay establishment.

Gellért fürdő and Széchenyi fürdő *See page 181 and page 236* for contact information.
These non-gay establishments have outdoor swimming pools and steam baths, the latter are popular with gays. Many tourists still believe they can make gay acquaintances there, but probably not true.

Palatinus *XIII. 1138 Margitsziget,* open May 1 to end of August.
The Palatinus open-air swimming pool has a nudist sun terrace which is frequented almost only by gays.

CRUISING AREAS

Dunakorzó The Pest side of the Danube embankment between the Marriott Hotel and the Erzsébet híd is frequented by many hustlers, some from the neighbouring countries, who send their earnings home to support their wives and children.

Park on the riverside This park on the Buda side of Margit híd is unsafe at night, but it is quite busy after dusk until midnight in good weather.

OTHER USEFUL INFORMATION

Gay help-line (Háttér) T: 329-3380 (daily 6 p.m. to 11 p.m.), www.hatter.hu.
This help-line offers information on gay rights, health and general counseling.

Toucan Tourist *XIII. Radnóti Miklós utca 15/b.,* T: 329-7481, www.toucantourist.hu

Gay Budapest, Quarter to Seven

The Post Office Clerk is looking at his non-quartz-driven watch: another 15 long minutes until they close. The Scholar is struggling with an electric drill: is there a reinforced concrete pillar behind this bathroom wall? The Wickedest Pen in Town is browsing an iconoclastic theatre quarterly, edited by one of his protégés. The Doctor is reviewing the photo-CD of his holiday – a medium he is overwhelmed with. The Actor is putting a substantial amount of makeup on his face: tonight he has to double his actual age. The Civil Servant is preparing some leftover dinner for his three unbecoming daughters, his almost only consolation in life. The Newsletter Publisher has just read the proofs of the obituary of William Burroughs. The Music Teacher is pouring some beer into a glass of "secondary cleanliness" in his 8th storey prefab flat in the outskirts of working-class Pest.

They are all expecting important phone calls – from close friends. And they are all intrigued: to march or not to march at the first ever Gay Pride Parade.

Twilight is slowly falling on a big town, somewhat satiated with the summer.

Connection Guesthouse *VII. Király utca 41.,* T: 267-7104, www.connectionguesthouse.com

Sex shop *VII. Dob utca 11.,* open Monday to Saturday 10 a.m. to 10 p.m., Sunday noon to 8 p.m.

Lesbians www.labrisz.hu.

Christian gays www.otkenyer.hu.

General information www.pride.hu

General information www.gay.hu

This photo by András Bánkuti (1958–) was taken during the First National Meeting of a new party that was formed in 1989 and went on to win the elections next year. Their meeting was held in the foyer of the Budapest University of Economics, previously called Marx University. As the university did not want to remove the statue (it is still there, the name is now Corvinus), they covered it.

READING:
ON THE SPOT AND
TAKE AWAY

LIBRARIES

Libraries had a special significance in keeping free thought alive in Hungary during the Communist era. They were a link to the past, and also to the free world. Big libraries regularly ordered basic social science works, and they were accessible to all university students. That was an intrinsic characteristic of the mild totalitarianism of the régime in Hungary: expertise was more or less allowed to develop – it just wasn't used (or very little of it was). In Russia, undesirable books had a special catalogue which was accessible only to reliable comrades. In Hungary, that would have been unthinkable. There were two telltale letters stamped on the catalogue cards of a few hundred openly anti-communist books which were in English or published by émigré Hungarian presses. Z.A. meant restricted, or literally, "closed material". But they were not really that restricted. Professors could sign requests for students, and the books became available. On the other hand, the library of the Academy was the cradle of the dissident movement. It helped everyone with inter-library loans. First it tried the Uppsala University Library, and if the book wasn't there, it contacted an American library. As far as I was concerned, Uppsala had everything.

National "Széchényi" Library (Országos Széchényi Könyvtár) *I. Royal Castle, Wing F,* www.oszk.hu, open Monday 1 p.m. to 9 p.m., Tuesday to Saturday 9 a.m. to 9 p.m.
This library is huge and pompous, without being elegant. But the main reading room has nice natural, overhead light. Small electric trains come and go between the glass roof and the false ceiling, making me feel like a railway man with defective hearing when I am here. Still, it's a singularly appropriate place to spend a whole day sinking into your work. It is located in the

huge part of the Castle overlooking Buda. The easiest way in is by the special lift from Dózsa György tér.

Library of the Hungarian Academy of Sciences and Letters (MTA Könyvtár) *V. Arany János utca 1.*, www.mtak.hu, open Monday to Friday 9 a.m. to 8 p.m., Saturday 9 a.m. to 5 p.m.
Until its renovation in the mid-1980s this library was housed in the adjacent historically protected building (to the left of the main entrance on the ground floor). The building was built between 1862 and 1865 and the reading room had not changed since the 1860s, with oil paintings of benefactors, famous scholars and writers on the walls. There were only 38 seats, of which four were reserved for the academicians who hardly ever came. It only slowly dawned on me that this library, where I once religiously spent every day, was the hub of the dissident movement. These days the quietest seats in the new library are near the smoking area. The lower the number, the better the seat. It's a modern library with hundreds of seats and tailor-made furniture that is mildly posh. Now you don't have to wait two days for some of the books you want, the floor doesn't creak, and there are computers. Yet… you know what I mean.

Parliament Library (Országgyűlési Könyvtár)

V. Kossuth tér 1–3., www.ogyk.hu, open Monday to Thursday 9 a.m. to 7:45 p.m., Friday 9 a.m. to 2 p.m., Saturday 9 a.m. to 6 p.m.
As a student I sometimes went to this library inside the celebrated Parliament building. I discovered that the beautiful leather-bound volumes around the gigantic reading room were the Unites States congressional papers. But when I wanted to use them, they turned out to be entirely un-catalogued. I was given a ladder to look at them, and I eventually found what I needed. The library is still beautiful, but still makes one sleepy. There is still no catalogue for the United States congressional papers, but there are some new computerized services. The other major change is in the actual building, which is being used for its original purpose again. A visit to this library will save the tourist a trek around the rest of the building.

Budapest Public Library (Központi Szabó Ervin Könyvtár)

VIII. Szabó Ervin tér 1., www.fszek.hu, open Monday to Friday 10 a.m. to 8 p.m., Saturday 10 a.m. to 4 p.m.
Before the great reconstruction of 1998 to 2002, there was a lovely sign in the cloakroom which was a citation from the great 19th century poet, János Arany:

"Oh, what a burdensome life / Dressing and undressing every morning and evening."
("Ah, kínos élet: reggel, estve / Öltözni és vetkezni kell!")
The new library is incredibly superior, except for this missing sign. The entrance is on Reviczky utca, just off of Kálvin tér. See Walk Three, *page 188–189.*

University Library (Egyetemi Könyvtár) *V. Ferenciek tere 6.,* www.konyvtar.elte.hu, open Monday to Friday 10 a.m. to 6 p.m. Established in 1561, this library was transferred to the Buda Castle in 1777. It has been at this location in Pest since this building was completed in 1876. It was seriously damaged when the metro was built under it in the 1970s, and has just been renovated. The main reading room on the first floor was traditionally the place where medical students spent their lives. It has an awesome, cathedral-like quality. Sitting here, students feel like they will never be able to remember everything on exam day. Among the valuable treasures housed here are 171 codices, including 11 of the famous Corvinas from the legendary library of 15th century King Matthias Corvinus. They also have a Greek gospel from the 11th century.

Central Foreign Language Library (Idegennyelvű Könyvtár) *V. Molnár utca 11.,* www.oik.hu, open Monday to Friday 10 a.m. to 8 p.m. (on Wednesdays only from noon).
This building was a YMCA before the war, but the only reminder is a word under the front door mat: SALVE. After "the changes" (the previous ones) it became a Russian language library, but from the early 1960s it began to collect literature in a dozen or so other languages. It is still, however, popularly called "the gorky". The reading room on the first floor has been redecorated three or four times since the 1980s, but except for the name change and the removal of Gorky's bust, hardly anything else is different. The new music collection, however, is a fine improvement.

TWELVE BOOKS NOT TO MISS

My friends from Western Europe remark with surprise on the number of books in the homes of Budapesters. Because of a high level of state subsidies, books were cheap compared to many other forms of entertainment in the 1970s and early 1980s. In 1989 the monopoly held by several state publishers disappeared and some 400 small publishers sprang up. Anyone can publish a book in Hungary. Books are sold everywhere from the streets and the pedestrian underpasses to the supermarkets, which is also quite a recent development. By 2000, the number of publishers sank to about 100, which is still a large number for a country of 10 million people (plus about another two million native speakers abroad). The following books are great reads, and would also make nice gifts.

István Bart: Hungary and the Hungarians (the Keywords): A Concise Dictionary of Facts and Beliefs, Customs, Usage and Myths (Translated by Judy Sollosy) (Corvina, 1999) A very funny and wise book which reveals everything you have always wanted to know about us. It is a relative of the present guide in scope and approach, written by a writer, translator and editor.

Budapest, the Pearl of the Danube: The Hungarian Capital Between the Two World Wars (Pictures chosen and captions by Katalin Jalsovszky and Emőke Tomsics, preface by Gyula Zeke) (Helikon, 2001) A great compendium of everyday life experience, from the collection of the Historical Photo Archive of the National Museum.

Budapest, anno... (Corvina, 1996) A selection of the work of György Klösz, court photographer and a major 19th-century photographer. His work depicts many scenes that have hardly changed, as well as contemporary advertisements. Klösz worked with glass plates, hence the fantastic detail. Some of his great pictures, covered with graffiti, are reproduced in the underpass near Erzsébet híd.

Budapest: Architectural Guide: Architecture in Budapest from the Turn-of-the-Century to the Present (Authors: András Ferkai, János Gerle, Zsuzsa Lőrinczi and Mihály Vargha) (6Bt, 1997) This is a finely produced, definitive guide, with superb and reliable data.

Encounters – a Hungarian Quarterly Reader (ed. Zsófia Zachár) (The Hungarian Quarterly Society with Balassi kiadó, 1999) The best of The Hungarian Quarterly offers a cross section of Hungarian literature and scholarship.

History Written in Light: A Photo Chronicle of Hungary: 1845–2000 (eds. Katalin Jalsovszky and Ilona Balog Stemler) (Helikon, 2001) From the National Museum's scholars, this is a history of Budapest and Hungary with long, well-written captions.

Jewish Budapest: Pictures of Present and Past (Photography by László Lugosi-Lugo, Postscript by Tamás Raj) (Vince, 2002) A beautifully-produced book by the chronicler of vanishing Budapest. (Meet him in "Running Amok", *page 361*).

Milorad Krstic: Budapest (Magyar Könyvklub, 2003) A previously never-before-seen photographic portrait of the city by a Serbian immigrant visual artist. He is also a stage set designer, a cartoon film director and a painter. He fell in love with a digital camera with a 10× optical zoom.

Lukács, John: Budapest 1900: A Historical Portrait of a City and Its Culture (Weidenfeld and Nicolson, New York, 1988). An intimate and engaging look at an astonishing story: how Budapest experienced a remarkable "exfoliation" during the last third of the 19th century. This is a scholarly, but readable book by a Budapest-born American historian.

Ferenc Molnár: The Paul Street Boys (Corvina, 1998) A children's classic, which is a funny and moving story, for kids and grown-ups alike. Everyone in Italy and Poland (and other countries) knows it, but this is the first English reprint since 1927.

István Örkény: One Minute Stories (Translated by Judy Sollosy) (Corvina, 1997) A selection from a cult book, by the master of Hungarian grotesque. The hilarious miniature stories give a deep insight into the Hungarian psyche, and draw a funny and sorry picture full of irony, cynicism and occasional self-hatred. It makes a good gift, and is read by all Hungarian students.

György Dragomán: The White King (Translated by Paul Olchavary, Doubleday, 2007). A dark and funny story from totalitarian Romania, told by an 11-year old boy, a modern Huckleberry Finn. It is an amazing success, and has been translated to 29 languages by now.

TEN GOOD BOOKSHOPS NOT SPOTTED WHILE WALKING

Bookshops are generally open between 10 a.m. and 6 p.m. on weekdays, and from 9 a.m. to 1 p.m on Saturdays. Times are only given in the following list when they differ from these. During Book Week at the end of May or beginning of June, the book stalls that sprout up everywhere are open on Sundays too. The following list is a mix of stores selling new books, old and rare books, and used books. As we saw on Walk Three, the Mecca of old, rare and used books is the inner (odd) side of Múzeum körút. None of the dozen or so shops located there are listed here.

Alexandra *V. Nyugati tér 3.*, open daily 10 a.m. to midnight. This mega-store opened in early 2005.

It is Barnes and Noble, Budapest style. It has an awkward design, interesting lectures, and a superb view from the top-floor window, especially when the sun is going down. *(See Alexandra's other mega store in Walk Three, page 198–199.)*

BUDAPEST BESTS

Péter Lengyel novelist, short story writer*

My city is such a city. She is always found among the men and women in my books. Her visitors had better walk and walk and walk. We natives have no better way to get close to her, intimately close, if that's what we want to do. Sacrifice your entire day. Avoid Tárnok utca and Szentháromság tér in the Castle. Those are places to meet other visitors and pseudo-peasants, who are possibly computer technicians by night. Avoid the things that were created just to impress you – they are unreal, never genuine. If you crave bustle, take the metro to the Keleti pályaudvar and tread the streets around Garay tér. Visit Mátyás tér in district eight, and see the city that is never boasted about to foreigners. Slip into her subways, and feast on the bazaars of seven nations. At Nyugati tér, Astoria, and Batthyány tér put your money in the most secure of your secure pockets. If you do not happen to have any, madam, sew one somewhere inside, right away. The pickpockets' favourite hunting grounds are Váci utca, Petőfi Sándor utca, and the trams running along the Nagykörút. Beware of those who offer their services, whether their bodies or their bank rates, you'll find fault with them all in the end. Take tram 17 from the Buda side of Margit híd all the way to Óbuda. Get off at Szépvölgyi út. Have a look at the enclosure of the small car park, and try to imagine that on the few inches of concrete there used to be a market. It was complete with vegetables, fruit, food, some rows of stalls, a well, a street, and a narrow alleyway. It was a sort of chaotic urban Eden, steaming with perspiration and heavy secrets. From Lajos utca, cross Evező utca, turn into Uszály utca, and stroll among the Bauhaus-style

*His celebrated book, Macskakő (Cobblestone) was published in English, from Readers International, London.

Corvina *V. Kossuth Lajos utca 6.*

There is a fair selection of Hungarian books in foreign languages to the left of the entrance, and sheet music and records are to the right. The shop is in an unbearably busy thoroughfare, where it's impossible to park.

Erkel *VII. Erzsébet körút 52.*

Opposite the Grand Hotel Royal, the three showrooms here also offer a large selection of sheet music and CDs. The latter are on the first floor.

---

buildings amid the three-storey high trees. From Dereglye utca, head to the Danube bank. Sit quietly on a bench in the small park under the tallest of the hollow willow trees and try to see the Uszály utca of the 1950s. The trees are not yet taller than a man. Street kids like me played foot tennis at the top of the street. "Autó!" they shouted, no more than three times a day, so the game could stop until the approaching car passed. Three cars a day. Not a bad life, to be a street kid in that time, in that place. At the northern side of the park, turn back towards the city. To the right there is, within a few steps, the Military Amphitheatre of ancient Roman times. We are on the eastern frontier, the limes of the Roman Empire, just as at other times we were on the western limes of other empires, like the Ottoman and Soviet. Old Buda alone has two amphitheatres: the other one, farther away, was the one for civilians. We went there on breaks between classes from the nearby Árpád Grammar School. Our gym classes were held there by Master Iglóy, the trainer of the national athletic team, whose disciples then held every single world record for middle- and long-distance events. Then, after this heavy work of imagination, rest in any of a half dozen tiny cafés on a street parallel to the Danube: the bumpy, once wholly cobble-stoned Bokor utca. Order a soft drink. The lady owner might know everything you should ever know about popular medicine. If you're lucky, from your table you will have an unobstructed view of the site where a small building was recently pulled down. That was the house where a hero in one of my books, Rókus Láncz, the famous fencer of stolen goods, committed and re-committed his crimes. And lo, now life has hurried to imitate fiction. A small company operates in the new building on the same site, and it bears the name of the heroine of the same novel*: "Bóra BT". Remember: Hungarians do read books – every now and then.
(2001)

Fókusz *VII. Rákóczi út 14.*
Occupying two large floors, this is one of the country's biggest bookshops. Maps, music and Hungarian books in translation are all available. Remaindered books are on the first floor if they haven't rearranged the stock, which they often do.

Kódex *V. Honvéd utca 5.*
Not far from the Parliament (on Walk Two), this large, well-designed bookshop has two floors. The upper floor stocks books in many foreign languages.

Láng Téka *XIII. Pozsonyi út 9.*
This shop offers a nice supply of Judaica and Jewish-related books. "Books should be respected," said owner Éva Rédei in an interview. "Books are not potatoes." It stays open until 8 p.m. on weekdays.

Litea *I. Hess András tér 4.*
In the courtyard opposite the Hilton, the name of this place combines the words literature and tea and offers a choice selection of both. It's a pleasant place with a full range of Hungarian books in translation. It also ships books abroad, with free postage for purchases above a certain amount. There's iced tea, Irish coffee, grog and Portuguese tea.

Mammut Libri *II. Margit körút 87–89.*, open Monday to Thursday 10 a.m. to 9 p.m., Friday and Saturday 10 a.m. to 10 p.m., Sunday 10 a.m. to 8 p.m.
Inside the Mammut II shopping mall, this two-storey bookshop is another attempt at Barnes and Noble, Hungarian style.

Font *VI. Andrássy út 56.*
Near Oktogon, this small old and rare book shop has a Left Bank Parisian atmosphere. Run by two bearded friends, it is strong in old art books and eccentric postcards. Be sure to go upstairs. The complete Köchel catalogue has been longing for a new owner. Are you the one? The place is also strong in old maps and prints, and is a traditional winter gathering place for Buda families after Sunday lunch.

Árkád *VIII. Üllői út 40.*, open Monday to Friday 10 a.m. to 7 p.m.
Near the Corvin cinema, this is one of the most pleasant second-hand book shops in town, with singularly friendly service.

Óbuda *III. Lajos utca 49/b.*

This is a neighbourhood used book shop, and a very good one. It's located in Óbuda, opposite Kolosy tér, and is run by a known great book maniac.

Budapest Egghead society is diverse – they are a hyperactive lot, each with several jobs and interests. They never lost sight of the "final questions": that of society. That is why I inserted this photo here: "Boy with a Scooter", by the sculptor called Boldi. It is a nice piece of public art – of the contemporary kind which makes us think every time we bump into it.
(Corner of V. Duna utca and Váci utca.)

RUNNING AMOK IN BUDAPEST EGGHEAD SOCIETY

An Imaginary Hour by Hour Journey Through the City

7 a.m. A swim with Júlia Király, honorary egghead, in the Gellért Baths. For those of you who aren't lucky enough to have friends willing to share their big downtown apartments with you, I wouldn't stay anywhere else but the Gellért Hotel. At this hour there is hardly anyone in the bath. Júlia is pretty much the only one of who can be persuaded to go for a swim with you this early at the Gellért. Budapest eggheads tend to be late risers. She is the daughter of a legendary professor of literature, descendent of Protestant preachers and known Communist subversive elements. Despite being deputy governor of the National Bank, Júlia will most probably arrive here on her bicycle. She is very much a Pest person, an omnivorous reader, and an alternative theatre freak. She spends a lot of money on good causes, mainly in the field of culture. She is divorced, but is never lonely – not even after her grown son moved out. Ask her about anything but the rates and the possible date of Hungary's joining the euro zone. She is a very funny and very intensive talker. Be prepared to cut into her words, if you want to speak too. (*XI. Kelenhegyi út 4.*) See Walk Three.

9 a.m. Café Művész, a coffee with László Lugosi-Lugo Lugo, photographer. He is a chronicler of vanishing Budapest, a former graduate of Hungarian and English studies programs. He has had an unusual and varied career in Budapest demi-monde and intellectual salons. In his student days he looked like Apollo at his best with golden locks and ideal proportions, but he was not really successful with or interested in girls. He has never had a nine-to-five job, of course. Rather, he supported himself for ages by giving English classes, and then spent his remaining time having more or less private classes from some of the greatest names in Hungarian photography. Then he found his real subject: the old and the new in the city. He is a born perfectionist and is constantly changing to bigger film formats, bigger digital resolutions. In 2000 he published a book of Budapest photographs with each photograph taken from the same angle as those by György Klösz, the classic fin de siècle photographer. It was such a success that he was asked to do the same for Athens and Salzburg. He has already published a dozen books. Try to grill him about new, positive developments in Budapest, and whether four by five inches is big enough for him, and does he want, one day, to change to large glass plates. *(VI. Andrássy út 27.)* See Walk Four.

11 a.m. Lukács Baths, with Gergely Bikácsy This recently modernised, open-air bath is set amidst century old trees and hundreds of small ex-votos. It used to be the hotbed of free-thought, a kind of witty intellectual salon, even in the darkest days of the 1950s. The last of the Mohicans, who could hardly have seen the

Judit N. Kósa, journalist, local historian, the better ego of Hungarian museums

I fell in love with those two balconies right away. It was a foggy, rainy evening in the early spring and I couldn't see anything but the lustreless glistening of the rooftops all around. I could look down on inner Erzsébetváros, nearby Klauzál tér, and the narrow, meandering Dob utca. As I discovered the sights, one after the other, I suddenly felt tout *Budapest at arm's length. I especially appreciated the towers and spires. To the left, there are the two slender spires of the Erzsébetváros Parish Church on Rózsák tere. Then there was the New York Palace. From here, I could witness the rebirth of both of them, formerly smoke-grey, now transparent and white as lace. A bit nearer to us there are the Romanesque chimneys of the Kertész utca school, and directly in front of us is a strange, almost vertical, roof that reaches out for the sky. That one belongs to the residential building that hides the Klauzál tér market hall. The latter now holds a crowded grocery chain store, a few other shops, a sausage bar, a junk shop and a Turkish mobile phone dealer. It is hard to imagine that once so many market women applied for stalls that an extra space in the cellar had to be added. From our balcony one can spot even the National Theatre's orphaned water tower. Every now and then there is light in the windows: is there a reception or an endless meeting in the place of the water tank, one wonders. Then there are the two onion-shaped towers of the Dohány utca Synagogue. At* place at its peak back then, spends almost all of his days between the spring and the autumn here. He is the eccentric film critic, short story writer and porn-epic writer, Gergely Bikácsy, a.k.a. Tamás Glauziusz. He is a bald, white-bearded, muttering French egghead, a theoretician of the French Nouvelle Vague, and a lover of Paris and Rome. He would like to be in all the three places at the same time, all of the time. It's no use asking him about gloom, since he is the gloomiest of all Budapest eggheads. "Have you found a publisher for your porn-epic yet?" could be a good question to rattle his cage with. The epic follows the legend of the Holy Grail: the most indecent, most parodistic work of travesty since Apollinaire and Bataille. The name Tamás Glauziusz refers to a character in a play and the film based on it: Uncle Glauziusz, who was a good-hearted accountant in the good old days, who didn't understand the intrigues of these cruel, new times, but served his new masters nevertheless. Bikácsy has typically Budapest egghead manners. *(II. Frankel Leó út 25–29.)* *See page 291.*

---

the end of Dob utca, there is Gellérthegy with the Statue of Liberty. To its right is a vulgar office tower called the Madách Centre. One wonders if, in 1939 when our building (and this balcony) was completed, it was possible to see the arched beginning of Madách tér. Possibly, since our building was placed on the imaginary line of the planned avenue which was never actually built because of the war. The shady strings of long "rental barracks" with their iron gangways never disappeared from inner Erzsébetváros, and for quite a long time nothing else was built but the wall of the ghetto in 1944. From the kitchen balcony it must have been possible to see the thick wooden fence as it was being built. Now, this area encourages one into peaceful contemplation. Our balcony is ideal to watch the fireworks launched from Castle Hill. Beyond the adjacent building, the line of houses seems to discontinue from up here. It does not. As a matter of fact, there is a tiny two-storey building, with the proverbial iron gangways around the courtyard. During the summer a pleasant courtyard pub operates there, and the uninhabited walls give forth a pleasant chill. They were left by their tenants years ago, to be destroyed and replaced by some new buildings. Now, as far as one can see, practically every building has been listed as a historic landmark. When looking down on the neighbourhood in the evenings, I try to guess what this small building will be converted to. A club, an office, a local history museum? Anything would fit. It might even have tenants again, as it once did.

1 p.m. Café KINO, a sandwich with Ádám Nádasdy Ádám, the arch-egghead of Budapest, often comes here, since it is not far from his home in Újlipótváros. He is a scholar, a poet, a wit, an iconoclastic university lecturer in English linguistics, an innovative university administrator, and the translator of A Midsummer Night's Dream, Hamlet and other Shakespeare plays, and openly gay grandfather of three grandchildren. He is often seen here giving advice to some younger poet, scholar or foreign visitor. He is best enjoyed during one of his lectures, on stage or at his home. To see his home is really a privilege, and almost impossible except if you are invited to one of his parties (which used to happen once every season). His natural habitat is a mixture of high-class art, thousands of books, and low-tech, naff home electronics. Ask about his gloom, about how he tried to reform his university and about the government changes. You can talk to him in English, German, Italian or French. He is much less eloquent in Russian, Polish and Persian. He's not tall and has a round face with short white hair and a beard. He's generally a bit stockier than he'd like to be. He is currently translating Dante's Divina Commedia, with as many footnotes as possible. He still thinks it was a mistake to change from WordPerfect (DOS-version) to MS Word. (*V. Szent István körút 7–9.*)

3 p.m. Café Centrál, with Dr. András Polgár, the egghead philanthropist. András is an economist with a scholarly vein who wanted to reform "existing socialism", but he was born too late for that. He wandered into privatization and the real estate business, where he proved to be phenomenally successful, consequently, filthy rich. At the age of 50 he decided to give something back to society. He contacted the author of this book, (who was three years his senior in grammar school) for advice, then set up a foundation for Roma education programmes and an ongoing subsidy package for theatre innovation. András is a big, balding, self-ironic personality, a very educated, sophisticated guy, with a keen eye for detail. Not only a generous philanthropist, he is also a reformer of the sector. He demands every cent to be spent properly. He hates summer and the beaches and the usual attractions for rich people. Ask him about good governance, his sons, what theatre performance to attend, but not about the solution of the Roma problem. Then he can get very gloomy. (*V. Károlyi Mihály utca 16.*) See pages 177 and 372.

5 p.m. The Courtyard of "the nest", with Miklós Vajda Vajda is the "last literary gentleman". He was the literary editor, and later the editor of *The Hungarian Quarterly*, a high-quality journal published in English, which is indispensable for serious eggheads anywhere in the world who are interested in Hungary. He is the translator of possibly 100 plays from English. He looks and behaves like a gentleman, has read everything (old and new), and has lived a remarkably colourful life. Born into a wealthy upper-middle class family, he had his cake and ate it too in terms of mothers. His father's first wife was the greatest actress on the Hungarian stage, and lavished adoration on him. He published his first book at the age of 78, entitled "Mother, in an American Frame" – a concise and beautiful memoir-chronicle of the second part of the 20th century. He has singularly unbiased opinions about life and literature today. Of course, ask him about gloom, and about Hungarian literature in English. Try to get out of him the name of one (just one) Hungarian novel in English that is a must-read for visiting eggheads. The "Nest" (Fészek) is an artists' club established in 1903 which has always retained some form of self-government, but has become increasingly naff in the eyes of the younger generation, perhaps because the leadership is padded with "favoured" artists. (*VII. Kertész utca 36.*) *See page 372.*

7 p.m. Spinoza House, with the Budapest Round Table Budapest-connoisseur-eggheads are an interesting sub-species. You can spot a higher than average concentration of them on the first Tuesdays of the month at the Spinoza House, a Dutch/Jewish/Hungarian café/theatre/club/cabaret which opened in 2003. The Round Table was established in May 2002 and originally met in the Café Centrál, but wanted to find a more intimate place, a real café, in accordance with the classic café definition: "when you are not at home, but you still don't have to be outdoors, in the fresh air". The origin of this quip is a nice "apple of Eris" at the table, and quite a few versions could emerge in five minutes. The real centres of conversation are Mihály Ráday (landmark specialist and former television crusader), Noémi Saly (café historian and eccentric French philologist), Péter Buza (local historian/author/journalist/gentleman, which is a rare concoction in post-1990 Budapest) and myself. There are also others, as the roster changes monthly. An hour earlier, at 6 p.m., a few of them gather as the editorial board of the illustrated monthly *Budapest*. (*VII. Dob utca 15.*) *See page 201.*

9 p.m. Winston's, with Ferenc Takács for a beer or two Takács is perhaps the most curious fruit of the intellectual orchard that was Budapest over the last 20 years. Gargantuan, rebellious, scholarly, and without ambition (though he married for the second time in the 1990s), he is a storyteller champion and the Joyce and Eliot lecturer at Budapest University. His English is phenomenal, and is rich in idioms. He even translated Péter Esterházy's The Transporters into English. Written by the paradigmatic contemporary writer, it is short, but impossibly difficult and metaphoric. Cynical to the utmost (or so he pretends), he does his best to camouflage his larger-than-life vanity by flaunting his ego. A brilliant mind and a fine stylist, he published an allusion-rich first chapter of a gargantuan novel. Since 2000 he seems to have begun to long for power and fame. Be careful what you say: he will always contradict any statement you make. So just ask questions. "Was life in the Kádár era really sweet?" could be a good start. Though he seems to pay attention only to himself, he is a very attentive listener. (*VI. Jókai tér 4.*)

11 p.m. Mosselen, with András Barabás Barabás is one of the funniest and most entertaining in today's Budapest egghead scene. He lives next door, in the "Phönix Block" (in the square where Pannonia, Katona, Tátra and Wallenberg utcas meet). Fun is his natural vernacular, no doubt. His favourite subject is himself, his awkward personality and his alleged physical clumsiness. He is the editor of a music monthly, an expert conjurer of English and Hungarian, and a translator of Wodehouse, Lodge, Durrell, Carver and Frank McCourt. Barabás is nicknamed "Bari" (which is partly an abbreviated form of his surname, and partly an epithet referring to his sheepish hair). For him, the lengthy process of adaptation to grown-up life has not ended. His discourse is rich (almost overburdened) with metaphors, allusions, references and camouflaged quotations. Above all, he is interested in the opposite sex. Him and his wife have agreed to tell each other everything after having turned 60. He could easily agree, he says, since he finds it fantastic to live to that age. You don't have to ask him about gloom. He throbs with it without being asked. (*XIII. Pannónia utca 14.*)

After midnight, possibly alone on the Szabadság híd I bet you will not ponder the answers to questions of a theoretical kind at this hour. The only exception might be: "Hey, civic boosterism, so widespread in Budapest in the last couple of years, is scarcer nowadays. But it's not all gone. Not yet, anyway." Watch the night lights of the city. Try to gather the stamina needed to crawl to your bed. Try harder, you'll get there. Some day.

"Newspaper Vendor in Apponyi tér" – this photo, taken in 1935, survived in the collection of the National Museum. Today the square is called Ferenciek tere. The blatant social difference between the seller and the buyer tells a lot about the inter-war Hungarian society, which was rich in extremes. The scholar Gyula Szekfü dubbed it "Neobaroque Society".

A HELPING HAND FOR HOSTS WITH SPECIAL GUESTS

7 NEGATIVE BITS OF OPINION, OFTEN EXPRESSED BY BUDAPESTERS, NOT ALWAYS SHARED BY FOREIGNERS

"Public transport is lousy in Budapest"
This is basically not true. This statement tends to be voiced by people who don't travel much. Budapest's public transport is still very good. Changes last year further improved it. (One number is now allotted to either a tram or a bus, and some very long lines were created.) There are 253 bus lines, 35 tram lines, 4 commuter rail train lines, three metro lines, two ship lines, a cogwheel railway, a funicular railway and a chair-lift. Quite nice for a town of 1.7 million people. Cleanliness and general condition of the vehicles is another thing.

"Budapest has dwindled its lead in the region, one that was so obvious in 1990"
No doubt, it is true for Hungary, and a sentence like that can't be denied with regards to Budapest. The traffic situation, the virulence of the homeless situation, the emergence of 23 semi-independent districts with elected mayors – they all slowed down promising developments. But despite of that, it is still a very pleasant place to live, or to visit!

"Budapest is dirty as hell".
A common woe of Budapesters, not substantiated by facts. There are efforts in pressing the dog owners to make them remove the waste of their pets. In Terézváros recently, pretty enamel plaques were erected saying: "Even Theresa Town dogs can't clean up after themselves!"

"It is a culinary desert. One Michelin star does not bring the spring!"
That is a ridiculous opinion, in the light of the improvements of the last ten years. There are two dozen remarkable places worth visiting, in every price category. The problem is, rather, consistency: a serious one, no doubt. The gourmet public opinion especially singles out the following restaurants, any of which could earn a star or two in the coming years: Fausto's, Csalogány26, Bock and Olimpia.

"Corruption is up to our chin".
Unfortunately, this can't be denied. Analysts say that it is a very serious problem that robs the Hungarian economy of some of its dynamism, and nurtures anti-democratic sentiments and extremism. They add that while there is corruption everywhere, here both the quantity and the quality is different. Particularly the latter is remarkably damaging: in most European countries the corruption serves to get the commission, but the companies do a complete job afterwards. The nastiest character of corruption in Hungary is that here the highest bidder can get the job, irrespective of capabilities, then the lousy work brings additional costs for the public purse.

"There seems to be more homelessness in the centre of Budapest than in any major city of Europe".
It is difficult to deny that this phenomenon is relatively new and very annoying for residents and tourists alike. There are not just beggars, but a high number of homeless people sleeping in public spaces day and night. It is a kind of hypocrisy mixed with human rights extremism that prevents action. Maybe the extra support for specialised foundations and more shelters would be the first step. Legal barriers can only come afterwards.

"Budapest is not on the cultural trail."
That is not true, not any more. For many years the Budapest Spring Festival was the period when world stars of higher-end culture came to Budapest. But since 2004, when the Palace of Arts opened, there is a sort of continuous festival here. The appointment of the present directors at the Museum of Fine Arts, Kunsthalle/Műcsarnok and Ludwig Museum have also made a marked change.

7 PLACES FOR AN AFFLUENT CANADA-BASED UNCLE, WHO WANTS TO IMPRESS HIS ADOLESCENT SWEETHEART AFTER 50 YEARS, IN ONE SINGLE DAY

Hotel Gresham Palace Four Seasons – The Café In a building named after the founder of the London Exchange (see his portrait in gold on the middle of the façade), the café has a phenomenal riverfront view. It is possibly the glitziest hotel between Vienna and San Francisco.
(*V. Roosevelt tér 5.*, www.greshampalace.com)

The Balcony of the József Pécsi Photography Library The fanciest building on the "Broadway of Pest" was built by a photographer in 1894. You can only enter the third floor balconies if you visit the library (closed weekends). Look for the fantastic paintings that represent the six fictitious Muses of Photography.
(*VI. Nagymező utca 20.*, www.mainamo.hu)

Uránia Cinema This cinema is partly Venetian Gothic and partly Oriental Moorish, and it was most likely completed in 1894.
(*VIII. Rákóczi út 21.*, www.urania-nf.hu)

The Tower of the Elephant House As part of an exotic diplomatic story, the tower of the Elephant House was pulled down in 1917 because Turkey saw it as a parody of a minaret and protested. In the late-1990s the Hungarian Landmark authority had it rebuilt.
(*XIV. Állatkerti körút 6.*, www.zoobudapest.com)

Tom-George A trendy and expensive Italian place, to see and to be seen, it's a perfect place for applied people watching. You will see early-career business people, and artsy folks with some of the most beautiful women in town.
(*V. Budapest, Október 6. utca 8.*, www.tomgeorge.hu)

Box of the General Director, State Opera House His large box, for eight people, is to the right of the stage on the stage level. Opposite, there is a similar one, which is at the disposal of the Minister of Culture. This is one of the greatest opera houses in Europe.
(*VI. Andrássy út 22.*, www.opera.hu)

Restaurant Gundel Be sure to look at the paintings decorating the walls. You could mention that your favourite is the Rippl-Rónai (to find out which it is, consult the last page of the menu). (*XIV. Állatkerti út 3.*, www.gundel.hu)

7 RETRO SPACES (FAKE OR AUTHENTIC) IN BUDAPEST

Bambi Café (1961: authentic) Named for the little animal from the woods, this place has miraculously survived successive modernisation waves. It still has its regulars, and it is a highly authentic place. *(See page 158.)*
(*II. Frankel Leó út 2–4.*)

Café Centrál (1887–1949, 2000: fake) The quintessential old literary café: re-created. Re-vamped in 2010, the bar counter that blocks the entrance is controversial. *(See page 177.)*
(*V. Károlyi Mihály utca 16.*, www.centralkavehaz.hu)

Fészek Restaurant in Winter (1903: authentic) The "Nest" (Fészek) is an artists' club which has always retained some form or other of self-government. The interior of the restaurant is closed during the summer. The pleasant garden is nice, but is hardly retro.
(*VII. Kertész utca 36.*)

Kádár étkezde (1960s: authentic) This charming, legendary neighbourhood eatery is in the main square of the former Jewish quarter. It is only open for lunch, and you should share a table. Closed sunday and monday.
(*VII. Klauzál tér 9.*)

Kisbojtár (1950s: authentic) The "Small Shepherd Boy" is a museum piece of a restaurant which preserves the genuine cosiness of the late-1950s and early-1960s. The small shepherd boy can be seen on an incredibly kitschy oil painting and on the iron railings on the windows. *(See page 308.)*
(*XIII. Dagály utca 17.*, www.kisbojtar.hu)

Menza Café & Restaurant. (2004: 100% fake) The word "menza" refers to the cheap students' cafeteria, a curse word which emanates aluminum trays and cutlery, a heavy greasy smell, and a crowded cheap environment. This place, the trendiest-of-trendy retro spaces, does not. *(See page 272.)*
(*VI. Liszt Ferenc tér 2.*, www.menza.co.hu)

Tisza Cipő (2003: fake) A yuppie businessman revived this 1971 totalitarian shoe brand. It has even been noticed by some trend-setter international magazines like Face and ID.
(*VII. Károly körút 1.*, www.tiszacipo.com)

7 STATUES WITH STORIES BEHIND THEM

The Very First Kossuth Statue The émigré freedom fighter and statesman Lajos Kossuth (1802–1894) could not have a statue of him erected in a public space until his great opponent, Emperor Franz Joseph I, was no longer around. So one was erected in a private space, in 1908, in the tympanum of Inter-Európa Bank.
(*V. Szabadság tér 15.*)

A Column in Museum Gardens To the left of the National Museum, there is a slender column which is now encircled by bushes. This was the surprising gift from Italian dictator Benito Mussolini, who visited Hungarian regent Miklós Horthy. The column is from the Forum Romanum. There were so many there, nobody must have missed that single, inconspicuous one.
(See page 193.)
(*VIII. Múzeumkert*)

The Knight and His Page In 1974 in the Castle between the palace and the residential part, near the wall on the Buda-facing side, archaeologists found two dozen fragmented statues of 14th-century dignitaries. It was the celebrated "Gothic Statue Find", and they have been on display ever since in the nearby Budapest Historical Museum. This is how they could have looked when they were new. Not easy to find, near the entrance to the House of Royal Wines.

Maria Theresa, Empress of Austria, Queen of Hungary Located in the foyer of Museum of Fine Arts, this statue was originally in the colonnade on Heroes' Square. It was removed along with the other four Habsburgs in 1918, put back in 1920, removed again in 1945, and then found in a warehouse and re-erected in 2002.

Baron Podmaniczky and the Stolen Lance of Pallas Athene The eccentric 19th-century campaigner for new urban projects is portrayed in a statue on Podmaniczky tér holding a statue of Pallas Athene which has become the symbol of the conserva-tionists. Traditionally she has a lance in her hand. But not in this one. It is a complicated hint at the subtitle of a monthly television programme: "The Lance Is Sometimes Stolen From the Hand of Pallas Athene, City Defender".

General Bandholtz This statue sits in Szabadság tér, near the US Embassy. As the commander of the tiny American peace-keeping force in Budapest in 1919, he defended the treasures of the National Museum when the Romanian army wanted to "loot" it. He "sealed" the museum's main gate with the only seal that was at his disposal: "United States Customs Office" stickers. Luckily, the Romanian officers did not speak English then.

Raoul Wallenberg, Swedish Diplomat He saved the lives of thousands of Jews in 1944/45, and was then kidnapped and killed by the Soviets in 1948 (or later). This is his second monument, the first (in Pest) was stolen by unknown agents during the night before it was going to be unveiled in 1947.
(*II. Szilágyi Erzsébet fasor, corner of Küküllő utca*)

7 PLACES TO MEET A LADY OF YOUR DREAMS, IF YOU DON'T NECESSARILY WANT TO TELL IT TO THE WORLD

Ráth György Museum One of the nicest and least-visited small museums in Budapest's rich museum scene. The name refers to the original owner of the villa (1828–1905). He was the one-time director of the Museum of Applied Arts, who left this villa and his Oriental collection to the public. Closed Monday.
(*VI. Városligeti fasor 12.*)

Burger King, Oktogon, second floor This is a busy place, but mainly on the ground floor. Few visitors go upstairs unless they have a reason. Apart from meeting someone, you can also enjoy the view of the Nagykörút. If you sit at the right table, you can spot a familiar building – you are right, it is an exact copy of Florence's Palazzo Strozzi.
(*VI. Oktogon tér 3.*)

Budapest Public Library, at the building's model In a deserted corner of the ground-floor section of the newly built spiral staircase (near the lift), there is a white plaster model of the new complex sitting under glass. It consists of three parts: the original neo-Baroque palace, the former residential block, and the recently added wing. (*See page 188.*)
(*VIII. Szabó Ervin tér 1.*)

Millennium Court Café This little-visited, almost secret place in the heart of Pest, has shops which often change owners and character. The New York-style deli which was located here did not close, it just moved 100 metres south. (The latter is far too busy for a secret mission.)
(V. Váci utca between Régiposta utca, Galamb utca and Pesti Barnabás utca.)

The giant underground section of Pintér Antik With a small entrance and just one window, it is easy to miss this labyrinth, a universe full of artwork and all kinds of furniture. A meeting point inside, worthy of spy movies, is the luxury bathtub covered with lacquered wood panels. It costs 10,000 euros.
(See page 153.)
(V. Falk Miksa utca 10.)

Odeon Art Video Rental Shop, the upstairs, catalogue part At this much loved Pest institution, bigger and bigger parts of a 1930s cinema are being converted into the video rental space. It is the venue of many unplanned incidental meetings.
(See page 276.)
(XIII. Hollán Ernő utca 7., www.odeon.hu)

The Internet counter of the bookshop in the upper part of the Batthyány tér market This bookshop has probably the nicest and least known view of the river and the Parliament building. It is the same view (but much cheaper) as at the otherwise pleasant café in the upstairs middle part of the market.
(I. Battyhány tér 5.)

7 RESIDENTIAL BLOCKS IN PEST TO CONSIDER BUYING A HOME IN CASE OF A SUBSTANTIAL LOTTERY WINNING

The author is very much biased towards Pest. He thinks nothing ever happens in Buda and only goes there to look down on Pest; to enjoy the view.

Though there are dozens of types of lottery now, the real lottery is still considered the "5-type lottery", in which you have to find out five numbers out of 90. The mathematical chance is 1:43.949.268. The record so far was close to three billion forints. The average is close to a billion – but a "substantial winning" needed to buy the home of your dreams in Pest is about 100 million forints.

V. Honvéd utca 3. This is the celebrated Bedő House, off Szabadság tér, recently restored. Now there is a small private museum of art nouveau and a café downstairs. You can even follow the fireworks on August 20th from the balconies. Main strengths: elegance and silence.

V. Vörösmarty tér 1. This is at least the fourth building on this site: a theatre, an office block, the "House of Musical Arts", and this block of shops, offices and condominiums upstairs. The latter are split-level large spaces with balconies. Strengths: central location and a garage.

V. Kossuth Lajos tér 18. The only private residence on the riverfront between Parliament and Margit híd, a Bauhaus gem. If you can, choose a home on the south-western wing: you can have a view of Parliament and of the river: Strengths: river view, good public transport.

VI. Városligeti fasor Almost any villa between Bajza utca and Dózsa György út. these are very pretty villa estates, parallel with Andrássy út, but much quieter, built between 1900 and World War One. Strengths: gardens despite the central location and good public transport.

VI. Nagymező utca 3. This is a very fancy red-brick building, unusual in that part of Budapest, the former headquarters of a German language newspaper. Preferably, choose the top floor. Strengths: nice view, good inner spaces, proximity to theatres and the Music Academy.

VI. Andrássy út 89. This is the "crescent" section, the corner of Felsőerdősor utca, which is presently being given a facelift. This is where Zoltán Kodály, the great 20th century composer lived most of his life. His home was converted to a museum. But how about the newly built loft space just over it? Strengths: A combination of old elegance and modern fittings, as well as great public transport.

XIII. Pozsonyi út 49. This well-designed Bauhaus block in Szent István park is in the heart of Újlipótváros, the busy and friendly quarter north of the Margit híd (just opposite the Dunapark Café). The best apartment on the block is no doubt the top one, redesigned by the celebrated architect and interior decorator Attila F. Kovács. It has balconies to three different directions of the compass, one of them so large that his daughter learned to ride her bicycle on it. Stengths: great river view, an interior with Moroccan hints, and specially-designed baths.

7 MOST-TALKED ABOUT SUBJECTS IN BUDAPEST (2010 / 2011)

The long-awaited Michelin Star in Budapest When the first Michelin star in Hungary was awarded to a Budapest restaurant called Costes, in the spring of 2010, the debate instantly began: was it well deserved? Can it be true that it is still losing money? Has it put Budapest on the map? How unjust of Providence, that the Portuguese chef who launched the place and who earned the star had already left (don't panic, by the autumn of 2010 Miguel Vieira had already returned).

Is Budapest Lagging Behind Prague and Bratislava? This subject has been on the agenda since 1989/90, when Budapest was so much ahead – since it was so much ahead in free business and in free press. Some think that Budapest has lost the lead gradually, others think the loss was dramatic and sudden, just after 2000. The reasons seem to be clear for many: political strife and compartmentalization of the city (which is 23 fiefdoms, rather than a unified city.) There is a tiny minority (where the author belongs) who think Budapest is special – it has not collapsed under the sudden influx of the hordes of tourists, its development was gradual, it has preserved its character, and it is still a very much liveable city. It is "the hottest cool spot" if not of all Europe, but of the region, anyway.

Graffiti vs. Dog-Shit With the advent of liberty, graffiti was considesed by many to be a consequence, then the proliferation followed. By about 2000 it had grown to be unbearable. At about this time on a Buda riverbank gallery a sign appeared: "Dear graffiti artists! Don't smear our façade! You are welcome to visit inside!" The city hall launched a coordinated campaign in September 2008 with posters and a public, televised removal. The penal code also might be adjusted soon. Graffiti might take the role of Public Evil No. 1 away from dog-shit (the latter public campaigns have helped this). The little blue notices, for instance, in Terézváros, state: "Even Theresa Town dogs are not intelligent enough to remove their own waste. Please do it yourself."

The Scandal of Metro Line 4 How is it possible that the costs keep on growing and the deadline for completion grows further? Is it because of corruption or is it the combination of various factors?

Did the ultra-expensive stations lit by natural light (praised by world design papers) amount to wasting public money? Should the rest of the line from Baross tér to Bosnyák tér be built at all? Or should we build state-of-the-art tram lines instead?

Should Skyscrapers be Allowed? The current maximum building height is 55 meters, and there is business pressure to lift the ban on skyscrapers – at least in some restricted areas (such as in the northern tip of Csepel Island and at the crossroads of the outer körút and Váci út, near the Pest end of Árpád híd). Those for it argue that tall buildings belong to most serious metropolises, and that they could add a flavour to Budapest. Those against it want to preserve the traditional character of the city (and they say that there is so much unused space in the city anyway). Nevertheless, one of the largest European banks has reportedly filed permission for a tower. Opponents hold their breaths, waiting to see what is next.

The Shopping Malls – A Blessing or a Curse? Most people love them, but at the same time lament that they have ruined the inner city. More and more shopping malls have popped up, and they are bigger and bigger each time (they seem to kill each other). On the other hand, there are good signs in the inner city. The shopping street development has created a sort of Bond Street or P. C. Hoofstraat (in Amsterdam.) And Andrássy út has become a heaven of luxury brands. Though, after Octogon square there is hardly any life.

Restructuring Budapest: How to Do It? "Everybody" agrees that Budapest cannot continue to be governed this way – instead of one metropolis, it is 23 semi-independent fiefdoms called districts, all with elected mayors and city councils. But how to change it? Should we go back to 1949, or unite the city, within the Outer Boulevard as one entity, with three larder districts in Buda, and give back the traditional Pest suburbs their former independence?

7 GREAT CHRISTMAS GIFT IDEAS

If you are confronted with the recurring problem of giving a Christmas present to you expat friends, don't commit the terrible mistake of giving him/her bottles of Unicum or Tokaj wine, or extra hot red paprika in a cloth bag. Everyone else will do that. The following ideas will put you ahead of the pack:

The White King, **a phenomenal novel by the young Hungarian writer György Dragomán** This novel is a dark and funny tour de force from a child's perspective, set in the Hungarian community of the Transylvania of the Ceausescu regime. Every chapter could be a short story in itself, with the fun, unpredictability and originality of Huckleberry Finn (no kidding). As it was translated into about 30 languages, it is likely that you can buy it in the native language of your expat friend, other than English, if needed.
(Bestsellers, *V. Október 6. utca 11.,* www.bestsellers.hu)

Modern print of a 1930's photograph Several of the world's most renowned photographers came from Hungary. Kertesz, Brassaï, Munkacsi, Capa, and others. But whilst they were making their names abroad, their lesser known contemporaries stayed behind. Now, beautiful modern prints of some of their photographs are available at very reasonable prices from the Mai Manó Ház bookshop, and are great for home decoration.
(*VI. Nagymező utca 20.,* www.maimano.hu).
If your friend is a collector of art, and you are willing to spend some hundred euros, you can find great vintage copies in Vintage Gallery
(*V. Magyar utca 26.,* www.vintage.hu)

A Subscription for the *Hungarian Quarterly* This is a serious title edited in Budapest, with a lot of fun reading – from poems and short stories to reviews of the cultural scene and essays on history and the contemporary social scene. It is well-designed and a great feeling comes from leafing through it, even if one doesn't read it from cover to cover. This is an English language entrance to a "culturally over-developed country". Don't deterred by the fact that the paper can now be accessed through the Internet. It is not the real thing – in this case.
(www.hungarianquarterly.com)

Three Hungarian Films, Your Personal Selection Young (or early-career) Hungarian filmmakers have produced some great movies in the last ten years. To buy three of them on DVD with English subtitles (and to put them in a fancy box with a tailor-made cover) is fun. If I were you, I would certainly include "Kontroll" (a hilarious and original comedy on the daily life of metro controllers, shot entirely underground), "White Palms" (the Bildungsroman of a talented gymnast in the late totalitarian Hungary) and Taxidermia (a complex, poetic and funny history of three generations in Hungary, loosely connected, a very

memorable film indeed.) Odeon art video rental will most prob-ably have them, if not, they will order them for you, or will give you even better ideas.
(*XIII. Hollán Ernő utca 7.*, www.odeon.hu)

Any CD from the Bartók New Series Probably the greatest artistic effort in this part of the hemisphere, this is a fresh and new series of recordings of Bela Bartók (1881–1945) based on the genius of Zoltán Kocsis (pianist and conductor, music direc-tor of the National Philharmonic). It was initiated by a private donor, financed by the National Cultural Fund, and overseen by a group of experts (who also constitute the Board of a founda-tion created for the project). So far 15 CDs have been released, many of them winning prestigious awards. The series is half completed now.
(www.bartoknewseries.hu)

A Gift Card to Europe's Smallest Cinema The Cirko-Gejzir cinema is a 15 year old, two-hall, highly original place. It is an importer of some of the most original European movies (includ-ing Danish pieces like After the Wedding or Adam's Apple). It is situated on the Pest riverfront, between Parliament and White House. The gift card costs some 70 euros, and you can visit the cinema any number of times. You can even get a tax receipt, since formally it is a donation for the foundation.
(*V. Balassi Bálint u. 15–17.*, www.cirkofilm.hu).

And Best of All: A Personal Tour of Budapest Expats are prob-ably well-aware of the usual sights, which they have probably shown around to their own visiting friends. They are likely to know the "hidden treasures", like "The Small Museum Tour", and the like. Instead, give them a choice of itineraries based on your personal life:
– neighbourhoods I have lived in,
– neighbourhoods I dreamed to live in,
– neighbourhoods where girls/women who I dated lived,
With a little planning you can put together a great tour, with some insight into your personal life.

7 IDEAS FOR AN EVENING OUT IF YOU ARE OVER 50 YEARS OLD, AND PLAN TO START YOUR LIFE ALL OVER AGAIN WITH A LADY JUST A LITTLE YOUNGER

KogArt House, for the opening of an exhibition followed by a drink in the elegant restaurant This fine, imposing arts exhibition centre opened in 2004. Its highly-polished exhibitions are geared for those in the business elite with tastes on the conservative side. There is an exclusive ground floor restaurant with old pictures on the walls. Here you can demonstrate that you are knowledgeable in both the art and the wine worlds. *(See page 328.)*
(VI. Andrássy út 112., www.kogart.hu)

Menza Retro Restaurant Though the Hungarian name of this fashionable restaurant means "canteen", it is in reality anything but. It is a real work of art. If only this sort of thing could have been allowed in 1975, Budapest would have been as exciting as London. You can tell the story of your young years, when you did have your lunches in actual menzas. *(See page 272.)*
(VI. Liszt Ferenc tér 2., www.menza.co.hu)

Café Zila This large, beautifully restored coffee house has rooms upstairs, as well as on the ground floor. It is situated in the centre of a Pest suburb in a building which, long ago, was used as a gentlemen's shooting range. Here you can demonstrate that you are a connoisseur of great places off the beaten path. *(See page 285.)*
(XVIII. Üllői út 452., www.zilakavehaz.hu).

Concert in the Great Hall of the Music Academy This is one of Europe's most attractive art nouveau concert halls, and it has excellent acoustics. The experience of the place is more important than who is actually playing and what is on the programme. Though visitors know it primarily for its concerts, its main function is actually as a music conservatory, which was founded in the 19th century by Hungarian composer Franz Liszt. Here you can quip: "What really fires me up is music written before 1800." *(See page 270.)*
(VI. Liszt Ferenc tér 2., www.lfze.hu)

Dinner in the garden of the Fészek Club The Fészek Club is just a three minute walk from the concert hall. The building dates from 1903, but its garden reminds one of the inner courtyard of a private mansion during the Renaissance. It is a special feature in the cultural life of Budapest, frequented by many older artists and upstanding members of the community who like to move in those circles. Here you can flaunt familiarity with octogenarian painters and actors, and even call them by their first names.

(*VII. Kertész utca 36.*)

Budapest Operetta Theatre Budapest was once regarded as third in importance, after Paris and Vienna, in the world of operetta. Nowadays there are confident signs of a resurgence as operetta and musicals are once again enjoying huge popularity in the part of the city which is sometimes dubbed "Budapest's Broadway".

(*VI. Nagymező utca 17.*, www.operettszinhaz.hu)

Late-night movie at the WestEnd City Center, followed by a walk under the stars in the roof-top garden The WestEnd City Center was designed by one of Hungary's leading architects, József Finta, and opened in 2000. It is one of modern Budapest's most renowned buildings – a colossus containing shops, offices, a hotel and a multi-screen cinema. Here, the last film starts later than at other cinemas, well after dinner in fact. Afterwards, have a walk in the roof-top garden and take in the view towards the slumbering city centre. The first building you will see is the imposing Nyugati pályaudvar, designed by the office responsible for the Eiffel Tower. Here you will feel like Gulliver as a giant when peeping downwards on the tiny shoppers.

(*VI. and XIII. between Nyugati tér and Lehel tér, numerous entrances*)

7 WINDOWS WITH A VIEW

Many Budapesters pay exorbitant sums to live in apartments with views, mostly in the "little boxes on the hillside", as Pete Seeger, the folk singer once sang. The list below includes different views, most of which are accessible to ordinary people.

National Gallery, historical paintings exhibition, second floor This large Castle Hill museum, inside of the former Royal Palace, includes four of the five riverfront wings. On the second floor there is a show of large sombre canvases, focusing on the highlights of the ups-and-downs of the country's history, full of names a visitor needs an encyclopedia to decode. On the riverfront there are large windows covered with semi-transparent linen curtains. They convert views into quasi-paintings, which is a great comfort for tired eyes.

WestEnd roof garden Windows usually offer views on the outside world. Not in this case. If one walks to the top of this giant complex, it is a singular feeling to peep into the maelstrom of consumerism, where thousands come and go like ants directed by supply and demand - especially in the evening, when teenage couples flood the benches outside, and the inside is illuminated.

Burger King, Oktogon Oktogon is an eight-sided, pretty intersection of Andrássy út and the Nagykörút, where there is a large, three-level fast food restaurant. It flaunts its food, though it also offers something exquisite: a view only known (so far) to the initiated. On the second floor there are tables which offer excellent views of the Nagykörút, the section towards Király utca. Teréz körút 13. is the sight to look for. It is an exact copy of Florence's Palazzo Strozzi. It was the rendering of a great Hungarian architect for a Battyhány count.

Institut Français, bibliothèque This Buda riverfront building is a rare exception: a high-quality contemporary design, erected just after the fall of the wall (George Maurios, 1992). It has a great café, bookshop and auditorium, but the view to enjoy is really from the Mediatheque on the 4th floor. It is a singular view of the Parliament, Lánchíd and everything else (from 10 a.m. to 7 p.m. daily, and until 1 p.m. on Saturday). There is another view, from the first floor lounge, towards the inside of the adjacent block where you can glimpse the postman bringing Mrs. Kovács's pension.
(*I. Fő utca 17.*)

The pool at the Four Seasons Hotel Gresham Palace All riverfront rooms in this 100 year-old building offer great views, but none as great as the one from the attic-level pool through those relatively small circular windows under the roof structure.
(*V. Roosevelt tér 5–6.*)

The cafeteria of AEGON Insurance When this large Kálvin tér bank palace was renovated at the end of the 1990s, and a large window in the loft space was added, everyone in Budapest thought it was meant to be a luxury board room for the few. On the contrary. It is the staff cafeteria, which has a great and unexpected view of inner Pest and University Church.
(*VIII. Üllői út 1.*)

The American Ambassador's window (formerly Cardinal Mindszenty's) Szabadság tér was miraculously renewed in

recent years, which benefited the American Embassy. The embassy overlooks the former stock exchange, which is now the headquarters of the public television. Richard Baltimore III, an American diplomat, looked out of his window in the 1990s and said: "it looks like the cross of a Greek Temple and Angkor Vat". The ambassador works in the third floor corner office, where Cardinal Mindszenty lived from 1956 to 1971 after taking refuge there at the end of the 1956 revolution.
(*VI. Szabadság tér 12.*)

7 STREET NAMES WITH STORIES BEHIND THEM

V. Vörösmarty tér This central square was once called Spazieren Platz (Walking Square), and then Theatre Platz (for the German theatre here). In 1874 a rich merchant of Greek origin, who had a large house on the square, offered a large sum for the square to be named after his family. The city council hesitated, and chose the name "Gizella" for the newborn daughter of the king. Since 1926 the square has been named for the great Romantic poet (1800–1855).

V. Falk Miksa This street lined with antique shops is named after a sort of child prodigy of modest origin (1828–1908). He started his journalism career at the age of 15. He was an influential editor and a MP during the 1870s and 1880s. His name was taken off the street twice: from 1943 to 1945, and later from 1953 to 1990.

V. Miatyánk utca The tiny street between the hotels Le Méridien and Kempinski has a nice name: "Lord's Prayer Street". It is named that because it is so short that it offers just enough time to say a prayer, one missed during the week. During Communist times this street name was never officially changed. There was no need to, since no address contained the name. The street signs were simply taken off, and were put back in 1990.

V. Váci utca This downtown shopping street was once simply called main street. Then it became Leopold street (Lipót utca), after the Habsburg king who liberated the city from Turkish rule (around 1695). The northern part was renamed Váci utca at the end of the 18th century, when the so-called Vác Gate was pulled down. A century later the merchants of the southern part, still called Leopold street, sent a request to city hall: they want to be called Váci utca as well. They were listened to.

VIII. Karácsony Sándor utca This street, which is in a not very pretty part of Józsefváros, is now named after a trade union leader and resistance hero who was murdered by Hungarian fascists in 1944. Earlier it was called Karpfenstein utca, after the family that owned the land nearby. That's the clue to the widely known anecdote. One day some time near the end of the 19th century and the beginning of the 20th century a horse collapsed and died in this street. A policemen arrived to write the memo – but he was unable to spell the difficult name. Then he asked the onlookers: "Well guys, help me to drag this poor animal to Magdolna utca, round the corner..." And so they did. For many years Budapesters referred to Karpfenstein utca in the following way: "In the street where the horse kicked the bucket".

VII. Barát utca This is a short side street, running parallel with Rákóczi út, between Szövetség and Hársfa utcas. The buildings are all from the 1930s, constructed in the so-called Bauhaus modernist style. Most of the apartments are very small here. Since "barát" in Hungarian means "friend", the popular belief in the neighbourhood is that it is called like that since most of the apartments were originally bought by rich industrialists as presents for some young(er) ladies, as tokens of their admiration.

II. Gül baba utca This steep, romantic, cobbled street leads to a small, but nice memorial of a Dervish, or Turkish monk, who died in 1541, a couple of weeks after the Turkish army conquered Buda. His name means "father of Roses", and the hill was named after him as well. The neighbourhood is still called Rózsadomb ("rose hill"), and today it is a chic residential area.

7 IDEAS FOR ENTERTAINING A VISITING CEO FROM PORTLAND, OREGON

River Ride amphibious tour in Budapest
A funny looking luxury bus that is registered in Malta can take you partly on land and in water. As it did not get permission to splash in the river downtown, it will take you to some of the real Budapest... The narration was written by the author of this book, but it is related every time by a live guide who adds his personality.
(*Leaves from Roosevelt tér*, www.riverride.com)

Budapest Public Library between 6 p.m. and 8 p.m.
At this Revival Baroque baronial palace, with modern extensions, it is quite an adventure to take a look around the café (that was once

a stable). There are students packing their bags, every conceivable type of newspaper and periodical, hundreds of computers, dozens of clever faces and beautiful Hungarian girls.
(*VIII. Szabó Ervin tér 1.*) *(See page 188.)*

The Wekerle Housing Estate in Kispest by bicycle This 99 year-old neighbourhood was meant to provide healthier homes for working class families, and was designed after the British model. Now it is fast gentrifying, and doctors, professors and business people move here. The initiator, Sándor Wekerle, was the first Hungarian Prime Minister who was not of noble origin.
(*District XIX. Határ út – Ady Endre út – Rákóczi út – Nagykőrösi út*)

The Poor People's Flea Market at Petőfi Hall, Városliget Every Saturday and Sunday morning (until about 2 p.m.) this place is a cross of a garage sale and a social safari. There is everything from remote controls from every conceivable type of television to postcards of old Budapest, and from shoes in reasonable condition to DVDs. There are also coins and old books, as well as tools you have always wanted to acquire, but your wife did not let you, so far.

A Beer in Kuplung, a "Ruin Pub" In the early 2000s, particularly in the seventh district, "ruin pubs" started to appear. They are generally open-air beer halls located in the inner courtyards of temporarily unused buildings which are open for a single season. One of the last Mohicans is this place, in a former garage. It is a great authentic student hangout, and is open year-round. The name translates as "clutch".
(*VII. Király utca 46.*)

Opera Visit Touring the Opera House has the reputation of being a waste of time, but it is not. The old ladies disappeared and the young ones speak great English and enjoy their work. They share all of the building's secrets (1877–1884) as well as the habits of the then royal couple. They will even help you learn to make out the gods on the ceiling.

Dinner on the A38 Ship, a Music Venue This ship, anchored at the Buda end of Petőfi híd, near the campus of Eötvös University, is the reincarnation of a Ukrainian stone carrier ship. The name comes from Artemovsk 38, which is the name of a ship prototype. Built in 1968, the ship was tugged through international waters to receive a complete makeover and an infusion of new life and the A38 opened in 2002. *(See page 291.)*

THE INGREDIENTS

INDEX

An Index to Budapest – a Good Read in Itself

BIBLIOGRAPHY

„OUR BUDAPEST" SERIES

Urban history booklets of Budapest City Hall, general editor: Gyöngyvér **Török** (1992–2010)

Adamkó, Péter – **Dénes**, György – **Leél-Őssy**, Szabolcs: *The Caves Of Buda,* 1992

Bodor, Ferenc: *Coffee Houses,* 1992

Boros, Géza: *Statue Park,* 2002

Buza, Péter: *Bridges Of The Danube,* 1992

Buza, Péter: *Springs And Fountains,* 1994

Buza, Péter – **Gadányi**, György: *Towering Aspiration,* 1998

Csernus-Lukács, Lajos – **Triff**, Viktor – **Zsigmond**, János: *The Cemeteries Of Budapest,* 1999

Dent, Bob: *Budapest For Children,* 1992

Faurest, Kristin: *Ten Spaces,* 2010

Ferkai, András: *Housing Estates,* 2005

Ferkai, András: *Modern Buildings,* 2009

Ferkai, András: *Shopfronts,* 1996

Földes, Mária: *Ornamentation,* 1993

Gábor, Eszter: *Andrássy Avenue,* 2002

Gábor, Eszter: *Villas In Budapest,* 1997

Gál, Éva: *Margaret Island,* 2002

Gerle, János: *Palaces Of Money,* 1994

Gerle, János: *The Turn Of The Century,* 1992

Hajós, György: *Heroes' Square,* 2001

Holló, Szilvia Andrea: *Budapest's Public Works,* 2010

Juhász, Gyula – **Szántó**, András: *Hotels,* 1999

Kiss, Katalin: *Industrial Monuments,* 1993

Kocsis, Irma: [penname of **Lábass**, Endre] *A Tour Of Our Locals,* 1993

Korniss, Péter – **Erdős**, Virág: *Courtyards*, 1993

Matits, Ferenc: *Protestant Churches*, 2003

Meskó, Csaba: *Thermal Baths*, 1998

Molnár, József–Szilas, Péter: *Night Lights*, 1993

N. Kósa, Judit–Szablyár, Péter: *Underground Buda*, 2002

N. Kósa, Judit–Szablyár, Péter: *Underground Pest*, 2002

Nemes, János: *Healing Budapest*,1993

Pongrácz, Erzsébet: *The Cinemas Of Budapest*,1998

Prakfalvi, Endre: *Roman Catholic Churches*, 2003

Prakfalvi, Endre: *Architecture Of Dictatorship*, 1999

Prohászka, László: *The Danube Promenade*, 1998

Prohászka, László: *Polish Monuments*, 2001

Prohászka, László: *Equestrian Statues*, 1997

Radó, Dezső: *Parks And Forests*, 1993

Szablyár, Péter: *Step By Step*, 2010

Szablyár, Péter: *Sky-High*, 2007

Szatmári, Gizella: *Walks In The Castle District*, 2001

Szatmári, Gizella: *Signs Of Remembrance*, 2005

Szegő, Dóra–**Szegő**, György: *Synagogues*, 2004

Tóth, Vilmos: *Funereal Art*, 2006

Várnagy, Zoltán: *Urban Transportation*, 1994

Vujicsics, Sztoján: *Serbs In Pest-Buda*, 1997

Zádor, Anna: *Neoclassical Pest*, 1993

Zeidler, Miklós: *Sporting Spaces*, 2000

NON-FICTION

Augustin, Andreas: *Grand Hotel Royal Budapest*. The Friends of the Most Famous Hotels in the World, 2007.

Balázs, Géza: *The Story of Hungarian* – A Guide to the Language. Corvina, Budapest, 2001.

[Bart, István ed.:] *Budapest krónikája*. Corvina, 2007.

Bart, István: *Hungary & the Hungarians. The keywords. A Concise Dictionary of Facts and Beliefs, Customs, Usage and Myths*. Corvina Books, Budapest, 1999.

Buzinkay, Géza: *The Illustrated History of Hungary*. Corvina, Budapest, 1988.

Culinaria Hungary. (**Gergely**, Anikó: Photographs by Christoph Büschel, Ruprecht Stempell.) Könemann, Köln, 1999.

Dent, Bob: *Every Statue tells a Story*. Európa Publishers, 2010.

Dent, Bob: *Budapest 1956, Locations of a Drama*. Európa Publishers, 2006.

Frojimovics, Kinga – **Komoróczy**, Géza – **Pusztai**, Viktória – **Strbik**, Andrea: *Jewish Budapest*. CEU Press Budapest, 1999.

[ed. **Gáll**, Imre — **Holló**, Szilvia Andrea]: *The Széchenyi Chain Bridge and Adam Clark*. Budapest City Hall, 1999.

Gerő, András: *Heroes' Square, Budapest: Hungary's History in Stone and Bronze*. Corvina, Budapest, 1990.

Gundel *Hungarian Cookbook*, Corvina, Budapest, 1997.

Jacobs, Michael: *Budapest: A Cultural Guide*. Oxford University Press, 1998.

(**Kemény**, Mária – **Farbaky**, Péter ed.:) *Nikolaus Ybl Architekt*. Hild–Ybl Alapítvány, Budapest, 1991. (Catalogue to accompany an exhibition in Budapest History Museum.)

Kósa, László: *A Cultural History of Hungary*. Corvina, Budapest, 2001.

Lang, George: *The Cuisine of Hungary*. Bonanza Books, New York, 1971.

Lang, George: *Nobody Knows The Truffles I've Seen*. Alfred A. Knopf, New York, 1998.

Lehne, Andreas – **Pintér**, Tamás: *Jugendstil in Wien and Budapest*. J & V Edition, Wien, 1990.

Lukács, John: *Budapest 1900. A Historical Portrait of a City and Its Culture*. Weidenfeld and Nicholson, London, 1988.

Magyar, Elek: *The Gourmet Cook Book: Hungarian Cuisine*. (Translated by Bodóczky, Caroline; Elliott, Judit and Kemenes, Inez.) Corvina, Budapest, 1989.

Nádasdy, Ádám: *"Ungarisch - ein goldener Kaefig?"* Die Zeit, 14. Oktober 1999. (An Essay on Hungarian language.)

Perczel, Anna: *Unprotected heritage / Védtelen örökség*, Budapest City Hall, 2007 (With photos by Endre Lábass)

Sárközi, Mátyás: *Budapest*. (World Bibliography Series 198.) Clio Press, Oxford, 1997.

Szerb, Antal: *A Martian's Guide to Budapest*, translated by Len Rix, The Hungarian Quarterly, No. 180, Winter 2005.

(**Zachár**, Zsófia, ed.:) *Encounters*. (A Hungarian Quarterly Reader.) The Hungarian Quarterly Society, Balassi Kiadó, Budapest, 1999.

ART, ARCHITECTURE AND PICTURE BOOKS

Bachman, Gábor – **Rajk**, László – **Peternák**, Miklós: *Ravatal – Catafalque.* Na-ne Galéria, Budapest, 1989.

(Baróti, Judit ed.:) *Belváros – Inner Town.* (Belvárosi Photographiák series.) Századvég Kiadó, Budapest, 1993.

Benkő, Imre: *Grey lights.* Budapest 1970–1999. Photo Essay. 9S Műhely, Budapest, 2000.

Budapest anno. (The Photograph of György Klösz). Corvina, 1996.

Ferkai, András – **Gerle**, János – **Lőrinczi**, Zsuzsa – **Vargha**, Mihály: *Budapest: A 20th century Architectural Guide. (283 buildings.)* 6BT Publishers, Budapest, 1997.

(Gábor, Eszter – **Verő**, Mária ed.:) *Schickedanz, Albert 1846–1915. (Millennial Monuments for the Past and the Future.)* Exhibition Catalogue for the Museum of Fine Arts, Budapest, 1996.

Gerő, András – **Jalsovszky**, Katalin – **Tomsics**, Emőke: *Once Upon a Time in Hungary. (the World of the Late 19th and Early 20th Century.)* Hungarian National Museum, 1996.

Hajdú, József: *Ipari táj ("Industrial Landscape.")* Városháza, Budapest, 1998.

Inkey, Tibor: *Memoirs of a Photographer.* Pelikán Kiadó, Budapest (with the Hungarian Association of Photographers), 1993.

Krasznai-Korcz, János – **Zsigmond**, Gábor: *Magyarok '94.* Más Kép Más Kft., Budapest, 1994.

(Lőrinczi, Zsuzsa, ed.:) *Budapest in Detail.* 6Bt Publishers, Budapest, 1999. (Wrought Iron – Cast Iron – Carved Wood – Architectural Ceramics – Window Design – Decorative Glass.) Photographs by **Hajdú**, József; **Budai**, Enikő; **Gerle**, János; **Gyarmathy**, László; **Mattyasovszky Zsolnay**, Tamás; **Mester**, Éva; **Stumpf**, Róbert; **Szilágyi**, Edit.

(Németh, Lajos ed.:) *Csontváry.* Corvina, Budapest, 2001.

Rózsa, György: *The Finest Views of Budapest.* HG & Társa Kiadó, Budapest, 1997.

Saly, Noémi: *Törzskávéházamból zenés kávéházba.* Séta a budapesti körutakon. Osiris, 2005.

Tímár, Péter: *Budapest Plein Air.* (Intera, Budapest, 1998.)

(Vargha Mihály ed.:) *Architektur in Ungarn* 1989–1999. Gyorsjelentés Kiadó, Budapest, 1999.

FICTION

Csáth, Géza: *Opium and Other Stories*. Corvina, Budapest, 2001.

Esterházy, Péter: *A Little Hungarian Pornography*. (Translated by Judith Sollosy.) Corvina, Budapest, 1995.

Gyula, Illyés: *29 Poems*. (From the Hungarian by István Tótfalusi.) Maecenas, Budapest, 1996.

Kosztolányi, Dezső: *Darker Muses (Nero)* Corvina, Budapest, 1990.

Lengyel, Péter: *Cobblestone. "A Detective Sory"*. Readers International,London, 1992.

Mándy, Iván: *Fabulya's Wives and Other Stories*. (Translated by John Bátki.) Corvina, Budapest, 1999.

Molnár, Ferenc: *The Paul Street Boys*. (Translated by Louis Rittenberg, Revised by George Szirtes.) Corvina, Budapest, 1994.

Örkény, István: *One Minute Stories*. (Translated by Judith Sollosy.) Corvina, Budapest, 1997.

Petőfi, Sándor: *János vitéz – John the Valiant*. Bilingual Edition. (Translated into English by John Ridland. Illustrated by Peter Meller. Foreword by George Szirtes.) Corvina, Budapest, 1999.

(**Upor**, László ed.:) *Hungarian plays*. (New Drama from Hungary, by **Nagy**, András. Nick Hern Books, London, 1996.

(**Szakolczay**, Lajos ed.:) *Give or Take a Day*. (Contemporary Hungarian Short Stories.) Corvina, Budapest, 1997.

URBAN STUDIES

Benevolo, Leonardo: *The city in the history of Europe*. (A város Európa történetében, Atlantisz, 1993.)

Jacobs, Jane: *The Death and Life of Great American Cities*, Random House, 1961.

Mumford, Lewis: *Cities in History*. (A város a történelemben. Létrejötte, változásai és jövőjének kilátásai, Gondolat, 1985.)

Olsen, Donald J.: *The City as a Work of Art* (London, Paris, Vienna). Yale University Press, 1986.

Ouden, Bernard: *In Defence of the City*. (A város védelmében, Corvina, 1972.)

Peters, Paulhans: *A város az emberért. Védőbeszéd a városi élet mellett*. Corvina, 1979.

Schneider, Wolf: *Cities, from Ur to Utopia* (Városok Urtól Utópiáig, Gondolat, 1973.)

[Vidor Ferenc ed.:] *Urbanisztika*. Gondolat, 1979.

Whyte, William H.: *City. Rediscovering the Center*. Doubleday, New York, 1988.

PHOTO CREDITS

p. 7.: Peasant Girl at Eastern Railway Station, 1930,
Gyula Eötvös, MNMTFT

p. 11.: Villagers Following St. Stephen's Day in the Castle,
István Kerny, BTM Kiscell, reproduction was made by
Judit F. Szalatnyay with the permission of Hungart ©

p. 19.: Café Muskátli, a golden youth, 1967, György Lőrinczy,
MFM, reproduced with the permission of Hungart ©

p. 37.: Façade of former Hungaria Bath, now part of
Continental Zara hotel, 2010, archive of the author

p. 41: Two Street Signs, 2010, archive of the author

p. 55.: The Walk of Iván Mándy, the author, 1969, János
Reismann, MFM, reproduced with the permission of
Mrs. Garai György (Garai Györgyné)

p. 65.: The Flag with a Hole, 1956, Ferenc Berendi, MFM,
reproduced with the permission of Hungart ©

p. 85.: Full House at the Dunacorso, 1930, Vadas Ernő, FSzEK
BGy, reproduced with the permission of Hungart ©

p. 91.: The original Mathias Church, 1874, BTM Kiscell,
reproduction was made by Judit F. Szalatnyay

p. 129.: István Bethlen, Prime Minister, arrives to Parliament,
1925, Martin Munkacsi, MNMTFT

p. 171.: Tram No. 6, some time in the 1950s, unknown
photographer, www.fortepan.hu, reproduced with the
permission of Fortepan

p. 209.: Király utca Scene, 1929, Imre Kinszki, FSzEK BGy,
reproduced with the permission of Judit Kinszki

p. 247.: The National Theatre with Cows, 1947, Tibor Bass,
MNMTFT, reproduced with the permission of
Gábor Bass, Katalin Bass and Ágnes Bass

p. 281.: Tabán quarter in rain, Before 1933, Iván Vydareny,
MFM, reproduced with the permission of
Katalin Vydareny

p. 299.: Governor Miklós Horthy gives a dinner in honour
of Cardinal Pacelli, 1938, unknown photographer,
MNMTFT

p. 317.: An entrance blocked (Budapesti Műhely), 2010,
András Török

p. 327.: The Museum of Applied Arts, 2009, András Török

p. 339.: Stones at the metro terminus at Örs vezér tér, 2010,
András Török

p. 347.: Statue of Karl Marx, covered, 1989, András Bánkuti,
MNMTFT, reproduced with the permission of
András Bánkuti

p. 359.: Boy with a Scooter, 2010, archive of the author

p. 367.: Newspaper Vendor in Apponyi tér, 1935, unknown
photographer, MNMTFT

LIST OF ABBREVIATIONS

MNMTFT: Magyar Nemzeti Múzeum Történeti Fényképtár
(Hungarian National Museum Historical Photo Archive)
BTM Kiscell: Budapesti Történeti Múzeum Kiscelli Múzeum
(Budapest Historical Museum, Kiscell Museum)
A reprodukciókat F. Szalatnyay Judit készítette
FSzEK BGy: Fővárosi Szabó Ervin Könyvtár Budapest
Gyűjtemény (Municipal Szabó Ervin Library, Budapest
Collection)
MFM: Magyar Fotográfiai Múzeum (Hungarian Museum of
Photography)

ACKNOWLEDGE-MENTS

SPECIAL THANKS TO

JUDIT N. KÓSA and GÉZA BUZINKAY who helped to drag some of the far-fetched conclusions closer to the world of facts

CAROLYN BÁNFALVI, who improved the present English text and gave me dozens of great ideas, not related to her mother tongue

THE AUTHOR AND THE ILLUSTRATOR ARE ALSO INDEBTED TO

Márta Aczél, Judit Ambrus, Mária Andrássy†, Iván Bächer, János Balázs, Csaba Bán, András Barabás, Pál Baross, István Bart, Judit Béres, Ákos Birkás, Éva Blaschtik, Ferenc Bodor†, Alexander Brody, Endre Bojtár, Mária Borbás, Péter Buza, Allan Ceen, László Ceiner, Peter Czipott, Emese Danks, László Darvas, Anne Dauvergne, Júlia Debreczeni, Katalin Délceg†, Imre Del Medico, Peter Doherty†, Klára D. Major, Győző Duró, András Elekes, Ágnes Eperjesi, Edit Erki†, Zoltán Erő, Péter Esterházy, Katalin Farkas†, András Ferkai, József Finta, Ádám Fischer, Doris Fischer, Tibor Frank, András Fűrész, George and Julie Gábor, Zsuzsa Gáspár, Péter Gauder, Éva Gedeon, János Gerle, Tamás Glaser, Zsuzsanna Gyenge, Miklós Haraszti, József Hegedüs, Robert Hetzron, Iván Horváth, Zsuzsa Hunyadi, Péter Inkei, Éva Jeles, Csaba Károlyi, György Kassai, Mária Kemény, János Kenedi, Géza Kerényi, Károly Kincses, László Kis Papp, Gábor Klaniczay, Tibor Kollet, Magdolna Koltai†, János Mátyás Kovács, Zulejka Kuha, László Kúnos, Pál Kövi†, Endre Lábass, George Lang, Tony Lang, Alain Lombard, László Lugosi Lugo, Geert Mak, István Margócsy, Miklós Molnár, Prof. John Molony, Ákos Nagy, Ádám Nádasdy, Vilma Nádasdy, Dr. Péter Nádori,

CONTACT
THE AUTHOR

DEAR READER,

I am sincerely interested in your opinion – about the book itself, and your experiences in Budapest.
You can e-mail me at andraas.torok@gmail.com

Your Invisible Host:

Dear András,

I found your book:
I missed the following:
I found the following things inaccurate:
I can add from my experience:
My name:
My sex and age:
My address (optional):
My e-mail address:
Date of my visit:

György Németh, András Nyergest, Ágnes Padányi,
Walter Peruzzi, Vera Pécsi, Klára Pétert, Attila Pogány,
András Polgár, Péter Polgár, Gábor Preisicht, Mihály Ráday,
Balázs Rendes, István Rév, András Rochlitz, Vera Rochlitz,
Dr. András Romántt, Noémi Saly,Tibor Sándor, Róbert Sarlós,
János Schulek, Jean-Luc Soulé, Erzsébet Szabados,
György Tibor Szántó, Anna Szemere, Dr. János Sziklai,
Ákos Szilágyi, Tamás T. Nagy, Miklós Tamási, István Teplán,
Lionel Tiger, Lionel Tiger, Gergely Tolnai, Ágnes Tompa,
Iván Tosics, István Tótfalusi, Gyöngyvér Török, Mihály
Varghat, András Váradi, Júlia Váradi, Benedek Várkonyi,
Anna Veress, Tibor Vidos, Miklós Vincze, Júlia Váradi,
Péter Virágvölgyit, Katalin Vörös, Richard Saul Wurman,
Zsófia Zachár, Gyula Zeke

and all the members of the "Nagy Budapest Törzsasztal"
(a loose, informal gathering of Budapest lovers and experts),
not mentioned above.